Bibliography of
Place-Name Literature

United States and
Canada

Second Edition

How
CAWKER CITY
Got Its Name

The idea of founding a town at this point was conceived by

E. H. CAWKER

R. G. F. KSHINKA } of MILWAUKEE, WISC.

J. P. RICE

JOHN J. HUCKLE } of TOWANDA, PA.

● They filed on their section of land at the Junction City Land Office 1870 and started buildiing in spring of 1871. Each of the four town proprietors interest was confined to his respective quarter section of land.

● The naming the new town was settled by a poker game, with E. Harrison Cawker holding the winning hand, hence CAWKER CITY.

● It might have been
Huckletown - Riceville - Kshinkaburg

● Streets bisecting the city, Pennsylvania Avenue and Wisconsin Ave., got their names honoring the states from which these gentlemen came.

Cawker City
The Biggest Little Town in Kansas

The Kansas State Historical Society, Topeka

Bibliography of
Place-Name Literature

United States and
Canada

by RICHARD B. SEALOCK
Kansas City, Missouri, Public Library

and PAULINE A. SEELY
Denver Public Library

Second Edition

American Library Association
Chicago, 1967

FOREWORD

In European countries the investigation into the origin and meaning of names is a recognized and assiduously studied branch of philology. The study of geographical terms has proved an invaluable help in the delineation of primeval periods of history for which no recorded documents are available. The names of rivers, lakes, mountains, and other features are often the only records of the onetime presence of a people whose language and culture have completely disappeared. For later periods, place-names show not only the migrations and the shifting of linguistic boundaries of the various sections of Europe, but also the presence or absence of plants, animals, natural resources, and cultural manifestations. The chief purpose of European place-name research is, therefore, the etymology and evolution of geographical terms. The editions of the English Place Name Society and similar, less voluminous publications in Germany, France, Scandinavia, and other countries have for many years disseminated the results of such studies.

Place-name research in the United States presents a different aspect. With the exception of the great number of native Indian names, and some smaller groups like the Aztec terms in the Southwest, names in this country present few problems to the etymologist. This does not mean that they are less interesting or less important. They are an intrinsic part of everyday life, and in them are reflected all phases of the nature of the country and the history and culture of the people. Interest in American geographical names goes back to the very beginning of the settlement of North and South America, and interpretations of certain names have not been lacking. But a systematic effort to put name research on a scholarly basis was not undertaken until the present generation.

A number of monographs and articles on regional nomenclature, especially on Indian names, had been published before then. Even a brave, though unsatisfactory, attempt to cover the place-names of the United States had been made by Henry Gannett, which appeared as a *Bulletin* of the U.S. Geological Survey in 1902. In the 1920's and 1930's a number of state surveys were published—for Arizona, Minnesota, Nebraska, Oklahoma, Oregon, Pennsylvania, South Dakota,

v

and Washington—some of which were comprehensive and adequate. But it was the publication of Henry L. Mencken's *The American Language* in 1929, and its various supplements, that gave a dynamic impulse to the science, for the sage of Baltimore discussed the importance of names in his stimulating and provocative fashion.

A solid foundation for American name research was established in the decade following World War II. In 1945, George R. Stewart's *Names on the Land* appeared, representing the first attempt to treat geographical names in a scholarly and objective, yet sprightly and entertaining, manner. Three years later the American Library Association issued *The Bibliography of Place Name Literature* by Richard B. Sealock and Pauline A. Seely—an indispensable tool for all future work in North American toponymy. In 1951, the American Name Society was founded in Detroit, and the first issue of *Names,* the official publication of this Society, appeared in March, 1953.

Since then the importance of and interest in the study of names have been growing steadily, and this branch of philology has begun to take root in the fertile soil of American culture. The new edition of Sealock and Seely's *Bibliography* is another important step in the right direction.

Erwin G. Gudde
Emeritus Associate Professor
University of California, Berkeley

PREFACE

The present *Bibliography of Place-Name Literature — United States and Canada*
is a second edition of the authors' *Bibliography of Place Name Literature — United
States, Canada, Alaska and Newfoundland,* published by the American Library
Association in 1948. Like the first edition, it has been prepared to assist the
librarian, the researcher, the historian, and the general interested reader in the
location of information about place-names—local, state, provincial, or regional—
in the United States and Canada. The Second Edition lists many new items published since 1946 and shows an important and gratifying increase in scholarly
studies in the field of place-name literature. Alaska, listed as a territory in the
first edition, is now included among the states. Hawaii, appearing for the first
time, is also included among the states. Newfoundland is now to be found among
the provinces of Canada.

The Second Edition includes the available published material in place-name
literature, both books and periodical articles, and some manuscript compilations
to be found in libraries, arranged in two main sections: by states under the United
States and by provinces under Canada. Since there is still no adequate dictionary
of place-names for the United States or Canada, and very few of the states or
provinces have comprehensive historical guides to the origin and meaning of their
place-names, the authors have found it necessary to include many articles from
little-known or ephemeral publications to record the place-names in use and to
explain the origin and meaning of local names. The publications listed can be
consulted at libraries or historical societies. Gazetteers have been included because of their usefulness in establishing the basic list of place-names for a given
area and the dates when the names were used. They also list variant forms and
names no longer in use. No attempt has been made to include sections of county
histories or other books limited to a specific region since these publications
seemed obvious sources of reference for such names or areas.

For the convenience of the reader two indexes have been supplied: an author
index and a subject index. The detailed subject index directs the reader to specific place-names, broad categories of names (such as rivers, mountains, etc.),

foreign-language names (such as Celtic names, French names, etc.), and types of names (such as Indian). It does not attempt to include all the many individual place-names given in the titles of articles or in the annotations.

A large part of the new material in the Second Edition has appeared as a regular bibliographical feature in *Names*, the quarterly magazine of the American Name Society. The authors wish to express their appreciation to the editors of the magazine for their kind permission to reprint this material. The first editor of the magazine, Erwin G. Gudde, not only requested the series but supported the project as well, and has written a Foreword to this Second Edition, for which the authors are extremely grateful.

The authors also wish to express their gratitude to Miss Mamie Meredith of Nebraska University, and Mr. Gerald D. McDonald of the American History Division, New York Public Library, who have continually supplied them with references to be found in obscure publications. Frequent contributions have also been received from Mr. Virgil J. Vogel, of Bowen High School, Chicago.

The *Selected Bibliography of Canadian Toponymy*, published in 1964 by the Geographical Branch of the Canadian Department of Mines and Technical Surveys, made possible a review of the Canadian sections and the addition therein of several important references.

Richard B. Sealock
Kansas City, Missouri, Public Library

Pauline A. Seely
Denver Public Library

CONTENTS

UNITED STATES

UNITED STATES—GENERAL

1. Abbott, N. C. Lincoln; name and place. Nebraska State Historical Society. Publications 21:8-133. 1930.

Traces the origin of the name Lincoln to Celtic-Latin. Includes biographies of various Lincolns for whom towns have been named. Has notes on all communities in the United States, with special emphasis on those in Nebraska, using the name Lincoln alone or in composition.

2. Aboriginal etymology. *Olden time* 1:325-29, July 1846.

"The derivation and significance of some Indian place-names, such as Allegheny, Winnipee, and Ohio, as interpreted by the Reverend Timothy Alden in the *Allegheny magazine,* are quoted here in this article."—Price.

3. Aboriginal names. *Southern literary messenger* 7:477-78, July 1841. Signed: G. S. M'k.

Emphasis on Indian names of rivers in the Middle West. Both the discarded name and the one in popular use in 1841 are noted.

4. Adkinson, Burton W. Some research problems on geographical names. Association of American Geographers. Annals 33:220-21, Dec. 1943.

Abstract of paper presented at annual meeting Sept. 1943, describing the routine of research on cases submitted to the United States Board on Geographical Names. Lists twelve types of geographical name problems which must be considered in planning a research program.

5. Alexander, Gerard L. Nicknames of American cities, towns, and villages, past and present. New York, Special Libraries Assoc., 1951. 74p.

Arranged by state, with an alphabetical index by place-name. Nicknames are

given without explanation or history.
    Review: by Albert Keiser, *Names* 2:68-69, March 1954.

6. Alexander, Henry. The new advance in place name study. *Queen's quarterly* 33:194-201, Oct.-Dec. 1925.
    First part is a discussion of a publication of the English Place Name Society, Introduction to the study of place names. The author then discusses the peculiarity of American place-names, citing examples, and suggests that there is room for much investigation along this line.

7. Alleghany—what is the meaning of this word. *Historical magazine* 4:184, June 1860.
    The derivation and meaning of this word as applied to the river is "Cold water."

8. Allen, E. L. The devil's property in the United States. *Outlook* 126:246-47, Oct. 6, 1920.
    The use of the word devil in place-names.

9. Allen, Harold B. Distribution patterns of place-name pronunciations. *Names* 6:74-79, June 1958.
    The effect of native speech and the prestige factor on the pronunciation of local place-names. Examples drawn from The linguistic atlas project of the upper Midwest.
    Comment on this article and the pronunciation of some of the place-names mentioned in it (Iowa, Omaha, Missouri, Chicago, Illinois) appeared in *Omaha world-herald* Nov. 3, 1958, p. 8, col. 2, taken from *Chicago tribune*.

10. Allen, Mary Moore. Origin of names of army and air corps posts, camps and stations in World War II in United States. Goldsboro, N.C., The Author, n.d. 352p.
    Originally published in separate parts for each state.

11. American ghost towns. *American notes and queries* 3:152, 187-88, Jan., March 1944; 4:14, 63, April, July 1944.

12. America's Christmas postmarks. *Good housekeeping* 145:60, Dec. 1957.
    A list of town names related to Christmas, such as Santa Claus, Ind.

13. America's inept place-names. *Literary digest* 53:790-91, Sept. 23, 1916.
    An unimportant article about some of the place-names of the western states.

14. Another view of town nomenclature. *Nation* 8:147-48, Feb. 25, 1869.
    "Mentions some of the disagreeable place names in this country but suggests that association with men will dignify and endear what primarily is trivial or low."—Price.

15. Ashley, James M. The naming of Montana. *Montana magazine of history* 2:65-66, July 1952.
    Reprinted, with comments, in *Names* 4:176-77, Sept. 1956.
    A letter to Judge William H. Hunt, dated April 28, 1892. James M. Ashley explained his choice of names for western territories while serving as chairman of the Committee on Territories (1863-69) in the House of Representatives. Those included are Montana, Arizona, and Wyoming in addition to others not named.

16. Ashton, J. W. Some folk etymologies for place names. *Journal of American folklore* 57:139-40, April-June 1944.

17. Ashton, William E. Names of counties and county seats. *Names* 2:14-20, March 1954.
Relationships between some of our counties and the seats thereof.

18. —— Presidential place-name covers. *Weekly philatelic gossip* 53:590-91, 622-23, 642, 654-55, 671, 822-23, 829, Jan. 12, 19, 26, March 1, 1952; 54:42-43, 52, 78-79, 94, 170-71, 202-03, 330-31, 374-75, 382, 490-92, 757-58, 761, 810-11, 825, March 15, 22, April 12, 19, May 17, 24, June 21, Aug. 16, 30, 1952; 55:42-45, 106-07, 338-40, 526-27, 622, 692-93, 782, Sept. 13, 27, Nov. 15, Dec. 27, 1952, Jan. 17, 31, Feb. 21, 1953; 56:18-19, 181, 337-40, 500-01, 684-87, March 7, April 11, May 16, June 20, Aug. 1, 1953; 57:45-46, 430-31, 688-91, Sept. 12, Dec. 5, 1953, Jan. 30, 1954; 58:300-02, 461, 678, May 8, June 12, July 31, 1954; 59:464-65, 818-19, Dec. 11, 1954, Feb. 26, 1955; 60:182-83, 326-27, 522-23, April 9, May 14, June 25, 1955.
Author decided to collect covers with presidential stamps canceled at post offices named for the president. Includes origin of name of places with the name of a president.

19. Austin, Mary. Geographical terms from the Spanish. *American speech* 8:7-10, Oct. 1933.
In the Southwest.

20. Bailey, John. Hysterical history—state names. *Saturday evening post* 226:38, April 3, 1954; 226:40, May 1, 1954; 226:44, June 12, 1954; 227:38, Aug. 21, 1954; 227:46, Sept. 11, 1954; 227:44, Oct. 16, 1954; 227:38, Nov. 6, 1954; 227:40, Dec. 4, 1954; 227:38, Jan. 29, 1955; 227:40, Feb. 26, 1955; 227:38, April 2, 1955; 227:40, April 30, 1955; 227:40, May 28, 1955; 228:38, July 23, 1955; 228:38, Aug. 20, 1955; 228:42, Sept. 17, 1955.
Nov. 6, 1954 issue has title How the states got their names.
Satire (on Post Scripts page).

21. Bakal, Carl. Town namer. *Cosmopolitan* 139:79, Sept. 1955.
Brief statement on the work of Meredith F. Burrill, Director of the Office of Geography.

22. Barbour, Philip L. Toponymy in the service of biography. *Names* 12:108-18, June 1964.
The place-names given by Captain John Smith, as seen on his maps, contribute to his biography and have effectively altered the entire picture of his later life. The study illustrates how place-names can prove to be an extremely valuable adjunct to biographical research.

23. Bayer, Henry G. French names in our geography. *Romanic review* 21:195-203, July-Sept. 1930.
"Names selected from Part I of his forthcoming work entitled French names in the geography of the United States, containing 5,000 names."
"Part II to contain 600 French names in the ethnology of the American Indian."
Names arranged under headings: explorers, missionaries, etc.
A newspaper article on this proposed publication appeared in *New York times* Sept. 14, 1930, sec. 2, p. 1, col. 4.

24. —— French place names in America. *Légion d'honneur* 3:115-20, Oct. 1932.

25. Beeler, Madison S. On etymologizing Indian place-names. *Names* 5:236-40, Dec. 1957.

26. Beer, William. The "Dixie bill." *Magazine of history* 20:1-3, Jan. 1915.
    Presents arguments for one of the possible origins of the word Dixie as applied to the extreme Southern states.

27. Bell, Laura. Some geographical names and their significance. Geographical Society of Philadelphia. Bulletin 18:31-34, Jan.-April 1920.
    Discusses in a general way the assignment of names to places.

28. Benét, Stephen Vincent. American names. *Life* 16:48-57, Jan. 31, 1944.
    Poem, accompanied by editorial comment; pictures of places with unusual names; and a list, U.S. is full of odd and wonderful names.

29. Bentley, Harold Woodmansee. A dictionary of Spanish terms in English; with special reference to the American Southwest. New York, Columbia Univ. Press, 1932. 243p. (Columbia University studies in English and comparative literature)
    An alphabetical list of Spanish place-names in the United States arranged under each state, p. 221-36. A discussion of place-names, p. 16-18.

30. —— & M. Robert Snyder. Place names in the United States, a tentative bibliography. n.p., 1938. 8, 5p.
    A mimeographed list containing 195 items, which was distributed at the Dec. 1938 meeting of the Modern Language Association.

31. Best, Katharine & Katherine Hillyer. Very funny name, Peculiar; history and whimsy go into the naming of our home towns, and the results are sometimes pretty weird. *Coronet* 37:75-78, Jan. 1955.

32. Birss, John Howard. Nicknames of the states; a note on Walt Whitman. *American speech* 7:389, June 1932.
    Nicknames for the inhabitants of the various states.

33. Blakeslee, Alton L. How to find your friend's house—in 10 easy lessons. *Chicago sun-times* March 11, 1956, p. 40.
    Description of a numbering system devised by Ambrose Ryder and set forth in a booklet Where is where.

34. Bonnell, Jesse W. Etymological derivation of the names of states and territories. *Journal of education* (Boston) 47:378, June 16, 1898.

35. Booth, George D. Indian names for towns. *New York times* Aug. 17, 1930, sec. 3, p. 2, col. 5.

36. Boyd, Stephen Gill. Indian local names, with their interpretation. York, Pa., The Author, 1885. 70p.
    "Names of places in a number of Indian languages, among them the Abnaki, Delaware, Minsy, Algonkin, Powhatan, Lenape, Shawnee, and Chippewa."—Pilling.

37. Bradsher, Earl L. Some aspects of American place names. *South Atlantic quarterly* 13:174-88, April 1914.

The great varieties of names from "European and native white sources, and their interest as a study in the history, the geography, the social customs, and the psychology of the people of our country."—Griffin.

38. Brainerd, Ezra. The significance of some familiar names of persons and places. *Education* 19:140-51, Nov. 1898.

Discussion of the factors involved in the forming of names.

39. Brant-Sero, J. Ojijateckha. Indian place names in Mohawk, collected by J. O. Brant-Sero and Chief Alexander Hill. Toronto. Ontario Provincial Museum. Annual archaeological report 1898:171-72.

A list of Canadian and American names with their Indian equivalents and meanings.

40. British towns greet American namesakes. *New York times* Feb. 6, 1938, sec. 4, p. 6, col. 8.

More than 50 British towns maintain contact in various ways with more than 600 of their namesake towns in the United States.

41. Brower, Jacob Vradenberg. The Missouri River and its utmost source; curtailed narration of geologic, primitive and geographic distinctions descriptive of the evolution and discovery of the river and its headwaters. [2d ed.] St. Paul, Minn., [The Pioneer Press], 1897. 206p.

Montana, Iowa, Nebraska, and Kansas; historical letters defining the true meaning and derivation of the names of several western states: p. 178-81.

42. Brown, Dee. Looking behind America's colorful place names. *Sun*, Baltimore, Sept. 11, 1938.

43. Brown, Fredric. Cardinal street names. *American printer* 119:48, Aug. 1944.

44. Buchanan, Milton Alexander. Notes on Portuguese place-names in northeastern America; *In* Estudios hispánicos, homenaje a Archer M. Huntington. Wellesley, Mass., 1952. p. 99-104.

Principally Newfoundland; also Labrador, Nova Scotia, New England coast.

45. Burrill, Meredith F. The Board on Geographic Names. *Military engineer* no. 348, p. 2, July-Aug. 1960.

Written by Meredith F. Burrill, Director of the Board, though not credited to him in the issue.

46. —— Generic terms in United States watercourse names. International Congress of Onomastic Sciences. 6th, Munich, 1958. v. 2, Report of Congress and section meetings. 1961. p. 175-80.

47. —— Localized toponymic generics. Association of American Geographers. Annals 47:156, June 1957.

Abstract of paper presented at 53d annual meeting April 1-4, 1957. Copy of the full paper is in the office of the U.S. Board on Geographic Names.

48. —— Official standardization of geographic names in the United States.

International Congress of Toponymy and Anthroponymy. 3d, Brussels, 1949.
v. 2, Proceedings and transactions. 1951. p. 394-99.

49. Burrill, Meredith F. Principles underlying domestic place name decisions
in the United States. *Revue internationale d'onomastique* 1:197-212, Sept. 1949.
   Abstract in Association of American Geographers. Annals 37:16, March 1947.

50. —— The reorganization of the United States Board on Geographical
Names. Association of American Geographers. Annals 33:222-23, Dec. 1943.
   Abstract of paper presented at annual meeting Sept. 1943, describing the program of the Board and its reorganization to handle increased work due to the
war.

51. —— The reorganization of the United States Board on Geographical
Names. *Geographical review* 35:647-52, Oct. 1945.
   By the director of the Division of Geography of the U.S. Board.

52. —— Stream terms in U.S. geographic names. Association of American
Geographers. Annals 45:173, June 1955.
   Abstract.

53. —— Toponymic generics. *Names* 4:129-37, 226-40, Sept., Dec. 1956.
   A fundamental essay on generic names used in the geography of the United
States.
   "Gat and gut," comment by A. R. Dunlap on derivation of these generics as
given in Burrill's article, *ibid.* 5:248, Dec. 1957.

54. —— & Edwin Bonsack, Jr. Use and preparation of specialized glossaries;
In Conference on Lexicography, Indiana University, 1960. Problems in lexicography; report. Ed. by Fred W. Householder and Sol Saporta. Bloomington, 1962.
p. 183-99. (Publications of the Indiana University Research Center in Anthropology, Folklore, and Linguistics, 21) (International journal of American linguistics, v. 28, no. 2, pt. 4, April 1962)

55. Burton, W. E. Derivation of names affixed to various places upon the
American continent. *Burton's gentleman's magazine* 4:37-38, Jan. 1839.

56. Bye, John O. Why these names for rivers, creeks, buttes and mines; *In his*
Back trailing in the heart of the short-grass country. Everett, Wash., Alexander
Print Co., 1956. p. 367-68.

57. Byington, Steven T. On European and American river-names. *American
speech* 2:425-28, July 1927.
   The use and omission of the substantive river in connection with the names of
rivers. Shows how the word river, although it duplicates the foreign term for
the word, has gradually become widely used on maps and in speech.

58. Calkins, Ernest Elmo. Punxsutawney and points west. *Good housekeeping*
120:42, 105-08, Feb. 1945.
   United States place-names.

59. Carlton, W. R. Podunk. *American speech* 13:174, Oct. 1938; 14:73-76,
Feb. 1939.
   In origin, an Algonquin Indian place-name or location.

60. Chamber of Commerce of the United States of America. Civic Development Dept. Origin and changes of names of American cities. n.p., 1925. 17p.
Comp. by Dorsey W. Hyde, Chief, National Civics Bureau.
Bibliography: p. 15-17.

61. Childears, Lucille. An analysis of Indian place names in four Rocky Mountain states. Denver, 1949. 186p.
Thesis (M.A.) Univ. of Denver.

62. Chisholm, George Goudie. Note on the spelling of place-names with special reference to the United States; *In* American Geographical Society of New York. Memorial volume of the Transcontinental excursion of 1912 of the American Geographical Society of New York. New York, 1915. p. 47-48.

63. Chrisman, Lewis H. The romance of American place names. *Education* 50:173-78, Nov. 1929.

64. ―――― What's in a name? National Education Association. Journal 21:276, Nov. 1932.
"On the value of the study of place-names."—*American speech.*

65. Clark, Ellery H., Jr. United States place names honoring the Navy. Annapolis, U.S. Naval Institute, 1948. 452-455p.
Reprinted from the United States Naval Institute. Proceedings v. 74, no. 4, April 1948.

66. Clarke, James Freeman. On giving names to towns and streets. *Christian examiner* 86:19-29, Jan. 1869.

67. ―――― On giving names to towns and streets. Boston, Lockwood, Brooks & Co., 1880. 19p.
Proposes historic names.

68. Coard, Robert L. The possessive apostrophe in names. *American speech* 33:176-79, Oct. 1958.
Includes place-names.

69. Colby, Frank. Romance in American place names. *Omaha world-herald* Nov. 4, 1945, p. 19-C.
One of a series of syndicated daily articles on language, entitled "Take my word for it."

70. Counts, Dorothy Ayers. Naming the western states. *Frontier times* 37 (n.s. no. 24):47, 70-72, June–July 1963.
The names of 17 western states fall into four categories.

71. Coxe, A. Cleveland. American geographical names. *Forum* 4:67-77, Sept. 1887.
Urges use of historical and, if possible, aboriginal names in the United States.

72. Crane, William Ward. Our street-names. *Lippincott's monthly magazine* 60:264-66, Aug. 1897.

73. Cray, Ed. Ethnic and place names as derisive adjectives. *Western folklore* 21:27-34, Jan. 1962.

74. Cross, Marion Hood. Happy birthday, U.S.A.; a rhymed account of the origin of the names of the fifty states and of their year of entry into the Union. New York, Comet Press Books, 1960. 56p.

75. Crouch, Kenneth Elwood. Bedford and its namesakes; *In* Bedford County bicentennial, official program. 1954. p. 107.
   Bedford, Va., and other Bedfords, with origin of the name for each.

76. —— Bedford and its namesakes. *Annals of Wyoming* 29:38-40, April 1957.
   Discussion of the various places in the United States named Bedford. Traces migration of name.

77. —— "Kenneth Elwood Crouch." n.p., 1959. [9]p.
   Places with the same names as the author's: Kenneth, Elwood, and Crouch.

78. —— Names of county postoffices are popular throughout United States. *Altavista (Va.) journal* July 30, 1959, p. 7.
   The 12 post offices in Campbell County, Va., and the county itself have namesakes in 32 states of the United States.

79. —— Places named Bridgewater in the United States. U.S. Congress. Congressional record 106:A3462, April 21, 1960.
   Reprinted in *Bridgewater (Mass.) keynote* May 19, 1960, p. 1, 6.
   Extension of remarks of Hon. A. Willis Robertson in regard to the 125th anniversary of Bridgewater, Va.

80. —— Thurman named for 19th century Ohio senator. *Sidney (Iowa) argus-herald* June 11, 1959, p. 7, col. 1-3.
   Places in Iowa, Ohio, New York, and Idaho named Thurman, and in West Virginia and South Carolina named Thurmond, for members of the Thurman family of Virginia.

81. Cushman, Horatio Bardwell. North American Indian names; *In his* History of the Choctaw, Chickasaw and Natchez Indians. Greenville, Tex., Headlight Print House, 1899. p. 592-607.

82. —— —— *In his* History of the Choctaw, Chickasaw and Natchez Indians. Ed. and with a foreword by Angie Debo. Stillwater, Okla., Redlands Press, 1962. p. 477-94.
   Choctaw and Chickasaw ancient names of places, towns, villages, rivers, creeks, lakes, mounds, bluffs, etc. in the now states of Mississippi, Alabama, Georgia, Florida, Louisiana, and others, with the derivations, corruptions, originals, orthography, and significations.

83. Cutler, H. G. Romance of the map of the United States, how California was named. *Magazine of American history* 23:288-96, April 1890.
   "Gives the origin and meaning of the place-name, California, p. 290, besides other names which were applied to it. In addition, historical data on the Southwest is included."—Price.

84. Daly, Reginald A. The nomenclature of the North American cordillera between the 47th and 53d parallels of latitude. *Geographical journal* 27:586-606, June 1906.
   Bibliography: p. 604-06.
   A systematic nomenclature is needed for this vast mountain system so that the geology may be more adequately described. Various definitions used for the mountain ranges, systems, etc. are included.

85. A Defiant little town. *Literary digest* 54:648-49, March 10, 1917.
   An amusing article which deals with the request of Oakland, Calif., that Oakland, Kan., change its name to avoid confusion; also Salem, Ore., and Salem, Mass.

86. De Ford, Miriam Allen. Two-state towns and cities. *American notes and queries* 4:64, July 1944; 5:112, Oct. 1945.

87. Derrickson, Lloyd. Wayoutsville, U.S.A. *American mercury* 91:134-36, Nov. 1960.
   Brief comment on variety of names.

88. Desert place names. *Desert magazine* v. 1-5, Feb. 1938-April 1942.
   A regular monthly department. Earlier numbers compiled by Tracy M. Scott. Gives origin of names in Arizona, California, New Mexico, Nevada, and Utah.

89. De Voto, Bernard. The Indian all round us. *Reader's digest* 62:61-64, April 1953.
   Includes place-names of Indian origin.

90. Dillon, Richard H. Name indexes in American libraries. *Library journal* 81:56, 58-60, Jan. 1, 1956.
   Brings up to date the status of card files of place-names in libraries throughout the United States as originally (1947) listed in Ireland, Norma Olin. Local indexes in American libraries.

91. Dobie, James Frank. The mustangs. Boston, Little, Brown, 1952. 376p.
   American places named for wild horses: p. 330.

92. Donovan, Frank P., Jr. Named for railroad presidents. *Railroad magazine* Feb. 1965, p. 24-27.
   Communities in the United States and Canada that were named for railroad presidents.

93. Duckert, Audrey R. Cottage Grove from coast to coast: the genealogy of a place name. *Names* 6:180-83, Sept. 1958.
   The author finds no ties between the 11 towns with this name in all parts of the United States.

94. ――― Gutter: its rise and fall. *Names* 4:146-54, Sept. 1956.
   A proposal to change the name of Grassy Gutter Road, a street in Longmeadow, Mass., touched off this study of the use of the term Gutter in geographic terminology.

95. Dunlap, Arthur Ray. Corner Ketch. *Names* 11:71-73, March 1963.

Speculation on the origin of this place-name in Delaware, Maryland, and Pennsylvania.

96. Dunlap, Arthur Ray. English and American place-name studies; a contrast. *American speech* 31:119-21, May 1956.
     In reviewing Simeon Potter's article on Cheshire names and David Lindsey's Ohio's Western Reserve, author indicates means of broadening American studies.

97. ———— & E. J. Moyne. The Finnish language on the Delaware. *American speech* 27:81-90, May 1952.
     Place-names: p. 88-90.

98. Eastern names in the western world. *Aramco world* 5:6-7, Aug. 1954.
     139 communities in the United States have names taken from the Middle East.

99. Eastman, Elaine Goodale. Indian names for country places. *Country life in America* 24:72, Oct. 1913.
     The article merely lists Sioux words with their meanings.

100. Eberle, William. Humor zigzags through American town names. *Plymouth traveler* July-Aug. 1960, p. 20-21.

101. Editorial on origin of French and Indian names in the United States. *New York times* May 17, 1939, p. 22, col. 4.

102. Ellis, Erl H. That word "Idaho." Denver, Univ. of Denver Press, 1951. 35p. (Denver. University. Publications. Studies in humanities, no. 2, *i.e.*, 3)
     A shortened version appeared in *Western folklore* 10:317-19, Oct. 1951, with title Idaho.
     Bibliography: p. 33-35.
     Traces the use of the word in various places in the West: the state; Idaho Springs, Colo., proposed for Colorado Territory, etc.

103. Emrich, Duncan. It's an old wild west custom. New York, Vanguard Press, 1949. 313p.
     To name the land: p. 27-36; ... And the mines: p. 37-42.

104. Eno, Joel Nelson. Picture-like American geographical names. *Journal of education* (Boston) 82:73-74, 101-02, Aug. 5-12, 1915.
     North and South American place-names, language from which derived, and the meaning of the names.

105. Fairclough, G. Thomas. Notes on some unusual street names in Nebraska City. *American speech* 34:70-71, Feb. 1959.
     Use of Corsos in this city of Nebraska. Half the article lists unusual terms for streets found in the United States and requests information on their current use.

106. ———— An onomastic miscellany. *American speech* 34:226-27, Oct. 1959.
     Addendum to his article The style of street names, and the articles mentioned under it (see no. 107).
     The form which street names take in common speech; unique thoroughfare terms; city segments whose names are points of the compass.

107. Fairclough, G. Thomas. The style of street names. *American speech* 33:299-300, Dec. 1958.

A note in reply to Allan F. Hubbell, *ibid.* 32:233-34, Oct. 1957, and Jerome Rhodes, *ibid.* 33:116-17, May 1958.

108. ―――― A variant of "downtown." *American speech* 37:158, May 1962.

109. Faris, Rush C. American town names. *Chautauquan* 19:723-26, Sept. 1894.

On the repetition of names in America and some of the causes.

110. Farnham, Amos W. The origin of some geographic names. *Journal of geography* 9:9-15, Sept. 1910.

The origin and meaning of topographic features in place-names.

111. Farquhar, Francis Peloubet. Naming America's mountains—the Cascades. *American alpine journal* 12:49-65. 1960.

Eight peaks selected because they are the dominant ones and the circumstances of their naming have historical significance: Adams, Baker, Hood, Jefferson, Olympus, Rainier, St. Helens, Shasta.

112. Fay, Charles E. Our geographical nomenclature. *Appalachia* 3:1-13, June 1882.

Suggests certain principles to follow in naming places.

Review: *Nation* 34:523, June 22, 1882.

113. Feipel, Louis Nicholas. American place-names. *American speech* 1:78-91, Nov. 1925.

Also reprinted as a separate.

Offers "a few prolegomena to the study" of United States place-names. Divided into types, as Indian; historical; from other languages; corrupted; from persons; religious; literary and patriotic; prosaic and artificial; and other arbitrary names.

114. ―――― More place-name words. *American speech* 1:395, April 1926.

Names for articles derived from American place-names.

115. Ferguson, De Lancey. Two queries about American place-names. *American speech* 18:309-10, Dec. 1943.

"What are the limits, in time and geography, of the Virginian practice of omitting the word 'county' in county names?" and the question of local pronunciation of imported names.

See the article by George Rippey Stewart, Some American place-name problems, no. 417.

116. Field, David Dudley. On the nomenclature of cities and towns in the United States. American Geographical Society. Bulletin 17:1-16. 1885.

Also published as a separate, New York, M. B. Brown, 1885. 15p.

An appeal for the use of Indian names.

117. ―――― Pleasant names for pleasant places. Address before the American Geographical Society. 1884; *In his* Speeches, arguments and miscellaneous papers. New York, Appleton, 1890. 3:352-62.

Suggests Indian names.

118. Finnie, W. Bruce. Ohio Valley localisms: topographical terms, 1750–
1800. *American speech* 38:178-87, Oct. 1963.
    Includes a long list of terms, with source where used.

119. First-aid towns, U.S.A. *Good housekeeping* 146:111, Jan. 1958.
    A list of names such as Pillow, Pa.; Hygiene, Colo.

120. Flanagan, John T. An early discussion of place names. *American speech*
14:157-59, April 1939.
    Mentions interest of James Hall in place-names as demonstrated by material
in his Letters from the West. 1828 (see no. 154).

121. Florin, Lambert. Ghost town album. Maps and drawings by David C.
Mason. Seattle, Superior Pub. Co., 1962. 184p.

122. ——— Ghost town trails. Maps and drawings by David C. Mason. Seattle,
Superior Pub. Co., 1963. 192p.
    Bibliography: p. 190.
    A roster of known ghost towns: p. 191-92.
    Includes western states and British Columbia.

123. ——— Western ghost towns. Maps and drawings by David C. Mason.
Seattle, Superior Pub. Co., 1961. 174p.

124. Ford, Zillah. The pronunciation of Spanish place names in the southwestern United States.
    Thesis (M.S.) Univ. of Oklahoma, 1947.

125. Franciscans, Saint Michaels, Ariz. An ethnologic dictionary of the Navaho
language. Saint Michaels, Ariz., The Franciscan Fathers, 1910. 536p.
    Names of places, p. 130-37.

126. ——— A vocabulary of the Navaho language. Saint Michaels, Ariz., 1912.
2v. in 1.
    v. 1. English-Navaho. v.2. Navaho-English.
    Geographical names: 1:226-28; 2:202-06.
    Limited to the states adjacent to the Navaho Reservation, *i.e.*, Arizona, New
Mexico, Colorado, and Utah.

127. French on the map. *Chicago daily tribune* May 11, 1961, pt. 1, p. 16.
    Pronunciation of some French place-names in the United States.

128. Freudenberger, Ruby W. Celtic elements in place names. *Country life in
America* 29:80-82, April 1916.
    "No element could be better suited as basic material for picturesque combina-
tions than the Celtic as exemplified by this alphabetical list of such name elements with their meanings."—Price.

129. Froman, R. Who puts the names on maps? *Science digest* 27:77-80, April
1950.
    Condensed from the *Elks magazine* Jan. 1950.
    Concerning the work of the Board on Geographic Names.

130. Frugality, Pa. dropped; New Deal on postal map. *New York times* July 7,

1935, p 3, col. 6.
Changes in Postal guide. New Deal, Mont., etc.

131. Furnas, J. C. The names we go by. *Saturday evening post* 230:36-37, 71, Dec. 28, 1957.
Popular article on personal and place-names, including towns, city streets, and "developments."

132. Gannett, Henry. American names, a guide to the origin of place names in the United States. Washington, Public Affairs Press, 1947. 334p.
A reprint of the 2d ed. of the author's The origin of certain place names in the United States. 1905.

133. —— The origin of certain place names in the United States. 2d ed. Washington, Govt. Print. Off., 1905. 334p. (U.S. Geological Survey. Bulletin no. 258)
1st ed. issued in 1902 as Bulletin no. 197.
Authorities: p. 10-14.
"Unfortunately it was chiefly the work of subordinates, and notable mainly for its inaccuracies."—George Rippey Stewart.

134. —— The work of the United States Board on Geographic Names. *National geographic magazine* 7:221-27, July 1896.

135. Gemmill, William Nelson. Romantic America. Chicago, Jordan Pub. Co., 1926. 143p.
Short lists of Spanish, French, English, and Indian names; also state names, Illinois counties, and Chicago street names.

136. Geographic Board wars on place names like Uz. *New York times* Jan. 23, 1937, p. 19, col. 2; editorial Jan. 26, 1937, p. 20, col. 4.
Changes made in freak names.

137. Geographic posers settled by Board. Nearly 1,000 queries answered during the past year. *New York times* Feb. 14, 1937, sec. 4, p. 12, col. 6-7.

138. Gerard, William R. The adopted Indian word "Poquosin." *American anthropologist* n.s. 1:586-87, July 1899.
A different interpretation of the derivation and meaning of the term Poquosin from that presented by W. W. Tooker in the Jan. and Oct. numbers of this same volume.

139. Githens, Harry W. Animal towns. *Nature magazine* 47:463, Nov. 1954.
Towns with animal names.

140. —— Bird towns. *Nature magazine* 48:132, March 1955.
Towns with bird names.

141. —— Tree towns. *Nature magazine* 47:516, Dec. 1954.
A list of towns named for trees, as Birch, N.C., etc.

142. Goforth, Elena. What's in a state name. *American mercury* 79:125-28, Aug. 1954.
Meaning of the state names.

143. Gregg, Jacob Ray. What's in a name?; *In his* Pioneer days in Malheur County. Los Angeles, Priv. print. by L. L. Morrison, 1950. p. 11-20.
Naming of some of the great rivers and smaller streams of the West.

144. Gregory, Herbert Ernest. Geographic terms, with table of geographic names in the Navajo country; *In his* The Navajo country, a geographic and hydrographic reconnaissance of parts of Arizona, New Mexico, and Utah. Washington, Govt. Print. Off., 1916. (U.S. Geological Survey. Water-supply paper 380) p. 189-97. Also in his Geology of the Navajo country, a reconnaissance of parts of Arizona, New Mexico, and Utah. Washington, Govt. Print. Off., 1917. (U.S. Geological Survey. Professional paper 93) p. 149-55.

145. Grinnell, George Bird. Cheyenne stream names. *American anthropologist* n.s. 8:15-22, Jan.-March 1906.
A list of place-names alphabetically arranged—with pronunciation, derivation, and meaning—which were given by Cheyenne Indians to some of the rivers in the country over which they roamed.

146. —— Some Indian stream names. *American anthropologist* n.s. 15:327-31, April-June 1913.
The names bestowed on rivers by two Indian tribes: the Gros Ventres of the Prairie, and the Pawnees. Attention is also paid to pronunciation, source, and meaning.

147. Gudde, Erwin Gustav. Frémont-Preuss and western names. *Names* 5:169-81, Sept. 1957.
A study of the place-names assigned and recorded on maps by John Charles Frémont and Charles Preuss on Frémont's expeditions between the Mississippi and the Pacific Ocean.

148. —— Mohave and Mojave. *Western folklore* 7:169-71, April 1948.
Arizona and California.

149. —— Sugarloaf. *Names* 4:241-43, Dec. 1956.
A strange generic topographical term.

150. Hafen, LeRoy Reuben. Armijo's journal. *Huntington Library quarterly* 11:87-101, Nov. 1947.
Antonio Armijo, on Old Spanish trail, 1829. Hafen's excellent place-name footnotes make this extremely valuable.

151. Haines, Elijah Middlebrook. The American Indian (Uh-nish-in-na-ba). Chicago, Mas-sin-na-gan Co., 1888. 821p.
Indian geographical names, p. 704-806; Indian names by which localities here given were formerly known, p. 807-21.

152. Hale, Edward Everett, Jr. French place-names in the Far West. *French review* 2:500-10, May 1929.

153. —— Geographical terms in the Far West. *Dialect notes* 6:217-34, July 1932.

154. Hall, James. Letters from the West; containing sketches of scenery, manners, and customs; and anecdotes connected with the first settlements of the

western sections of the United States. London, Henry Colburn, 1828. 385p.
Names of places: p. 103 214.

155. Hannant, Owen. Indian place-names, a beautiful heritage. *Central States archaeological journal* 2:15, July 1955.

156. Harper, Roland M. Pronunciation of certain place names. *Journal of geography* 16:255-58, March 1918.
Names of Indian origin, principally in southern United States.

157. Harrington, John Peabody. American Indian place-names; abstract. *Nature* 142:960, Nov. 26, 1938.

158. —— The origin of our state names. Washington Academy of Sciences. Journal 34:255-59, Aug. 15, 1944.
Based on lengthy study of state and territory names—a preliminary, brief version of the ethnological and historical origin of the names.

159. —— Our state names. Smithsonian Institution. Annual report 1954:373-88.
Reprinted as: Smithsonian Institution. Publication 4205. 1955.
Includes Canadian names of Indian origin: p. 387-88.

160. Harris, Clement Antrobus. The devil in place-names. *Chambers's journal* 7th ser. 13:84-87, Jan. 6, 1923.
"There are good reasons why some places should be associated in people's minds with the devil. Citing some examples in the United States and abroad, the author traces the connection between the term and the location."—Price.

161. Harrisse, Henry. The discovery of North America; a critical, documentary, and historic investigation, with an essay on the early cartography of the New World, including descriptions of two hundred and fifty maps or globes existing or lost, constructed before the year 1536; to which are added a chronology of one hundred voyages westward, projected, attempted, or accomplished between 1431 and 1504; biographical accounts of the three hundred pilots who first crossed the Atlantic; and a copious list of the original names of American regions, caciqueships, mountains, islands, capes, gulfs, rivers, towns, and harbours. London, H. Stevens and Son; Paris, H. Welter, 1892. 802p.
Reprinted Amsterdam, N. Israel, 1961. 802p.
Geographical index, p. 751-84.

162. Harshberger, John W. Geographic names and terms of significance in plant geography and ecology. Geographical Society of Philadelphia. Bulletin 18:100-07, Oct. 1920; 19:14-22, 45-50. 1921; 20:32-46. 1922.
A compilation of geographic names and terms—physiographic, phytogeographic, and ecologic—with significations. The vegetation of a place combined with physiographical features is very often responsible for its name. The author interprets the meaning of many such terms in general use.

163. Hartesveldt, Richard J. & Jane Hartesveldt. The campsite finder. Cartoons by Marian Smith. San Martin, Calif., Naturegraph Co., 1957. 2v.

164. Haugen, Einar Ingvald. The Norwegian language in America; a study in bilingual behavior. Philadelphia, Univ. of Pennsylvania Press, 1953. 2v.

v. 1, Chap. 9, "Names in a new world," p. 222-32, concludes with an analysis of place-names in Norwegian communities in America.

165. Heck, Henry J. State border place-names. *American speech* 3:186-90, Feb. 1928.
Examples from 26 states.

166. Heck, Lewis. Geographic names in the U.S. Coast and Geodetic Survey. *Names* 1:103-11, June 1953.
By the chief of the Geographic Name Section, Chart Division, of the Survey.

167. Heier, Edmund. Russo-German place-names in Russia and in North America. *Names* 9:260-68, Dec. 1961.
Names resulting from the Russo-German immigration are discussed on p. 266-68.

168. Helfer, Harold. Ever been to Mugfuzzle Flat? *American mercury* 81:12-14, Oct. 1955.
A popular article on odd town names.

169. Hello! His hobby is "meatography." *Saturday evening post* 224:48, Oct. 6, 1951.
An advertisement of the American Meat Institute giving place-names that remind one of aspects of the meat business.

170. Hewes, Gordon W. American Japanese place names. *American speech* 21:100-05, April 1946.
Methods of treatment of American place-names which have passed into American-Japanese literary usage, with a table of Japanese equivalents for certain American place-names.

171. Hill, Robert T. Corruption of American geographic names. *Science* 10:143, Sept. 16, 1887.
Reasons for the origin of some place-names which are misnomers. Also considers factors that corrupt the original name.

172. Himes, George Henry. Nomenclature of Northwest mountains. *Mazama* 4:1-5, Oct. 1912.
Principal peaks in the Coast, Cascade, and Blue Mountain ranges.

173. Hitchman, Robert. Onalaska, Washington. *Western folklore* 8:368-69, Oct. 1949.
Connection with towns of same name in Wisconsin, Arkansas, and Texas.

174. Hixon, Jerome C. Place names. *Words* 2:8-9, 13, 20-22, Sept. 1936; 2:14-15, Oct. 1936; 2:8-9, 20, Nov. 1936.
Readable, lengthy account of place-names of cities, towns, and states in the United States.

175. Hockett, Charles F. Reactions to Indian place names. *American speech* 25:118-21, May 1950.

176. Hodge, F. W. The name of Canadian River. *Masterkey* (Southwest Museum, Los Angeles) 23:91, May 1949.

177. Hoge, Thomas A. Streets of America. *Service* (Cities Service Company) July 1960, p. 12-15.

178. Hollis, C. Carroll. Names in Leaves of grass. *Names* 5:129-56, Sept. 1957.
Conclusions from an investigation of new manuscript evidence of Walt Whitman's concern with names, particularly place-names, presented with the explanation of his theory and practice.

179. Holmer, Nils Magnus. Indian place names in North America. Cambridge, Harvard Univ. Press, 1948. 44p. (American Institute in the University of Upsala. Essays and studies on American language and literature)

180. Holt, Alfred Hubbard. American place names. New York, Crowell, 1938. 222p.
Bibliography: p. 221-22.
A collection of general names giving pronunciation only.
Review: *American speech* 14:134, April 1939.

181. Homburg, Frederick. Names of cities. *Journal of geography* 15:17-23, Sept. 1916.
A study of the principles of forming place-names by combining prefixes or suffixes to indicate location with proper or scenic names.

182. Honest creeks, their names reflect rare quality of accuracy. *Life* 29:108, Aug. 21, 1950.
Letters to the editors, Sept. 11, 1950, p. 12, 16, contain readers' additions.

183. Horgan, Paul. The names of the Rio Grande; *In his* Great river: the Rio Grande in North American history. New York, Rinehart, 1954. 2:981.

184. How cities chose their names. *American city* 73:173, Aug. 1958.
Different factors that influence the choice of name, also names from famous places and famous persons.

185. How oil fields get their names. *Sunray news* Feb. 1954, p. 10-11.
The naming of new oil fields is usually casual, although the names must be approved in most states by the commission which administers oil and gas matters.

186. How to study place-names. *Badger folklore* 1:23-24, April 1948.

187. Hubbell, Allan F. Form of street addresses. *American speech* 32:233-34, Oct. 1957.
Variation in American usage regarding use or omission of street, avenue, road, and boulevard. For further information see article by Jerome Rhodes, *ibid*. 33:116-17, May 1958, and reply by G. Thomas Fairclough, *ibid*. 33:299-300, Dec. 1958.

188. Hyde, John. The National geographic magazine and the U.S. Board on Geographic Names. *National geographic magazine* 10:517-19, Nov. 1899.

189. In the driftway. *Nation* 124:421-22, April 20, 1927.
Some peculiar place-names that are to be found in the United States—particularly Long Island, N.Y.—and abroad are mentioned in this article.

17

190.   Indian cuss words. Associated Press dispatch, Washington, D.C., Dec. 5, 1936.
Printed in many newspapers.
"G. C. Martin of the U.S. Board on Geographical Names reveals that Indian expressions of irritation, misunderstood as place-names, were often preserved as such in America."—*American speech.*

191.   Indian cuss words responsible for many strange place names. *Cumberland (Md.) evening times* Dec. 4, 1936.

192.   Indian geographical names—Chillakothe. *Magazine of American history* 3:512, Aug. 1879.
Indicates the probable origin and application of the place-name Chillakothe found in several states.

193.   Indian names of American states. *Chambers's journal* 4th ser. 15:663-64, Oct. 19, 1878.
Considers the source of aboriginal appellations of states.

194.   The Indians said it first. *Aramco world* 11:13-15, Dec. 1960.
25 states bear Indian names. Origin of these and other state names.

195.   Interesting post office names. *Hobbies* 63:99, Oct. 1958.
Examples of many different categories of post-office names.

196.   Interpretation of Indian names. *Historical magazine* 9:90-91, March 1865.
The derivation and meaning of a short list.

197.   Interstate towns. *School science and mathematics* 21:24, Jan. 1921.
The names of towns which indicate that they lie partly in one state and partly in another, for example, Texarkana.

198.   Iroquois names of places. *Historical magazine* 8:373, Nov. 1864.
Several Indian names with derivation and meaning are listed.

199.   Irving, Washington. National nomenclature, by Geoffrey Crayon. *Knicker-bocker* 14:158-62, 203, Aug. 1839.
Reprinted in his Biographies and miscellanies, ed. by Pierre M. Irving. New York, Putnam, 1866. p. 522-30.

200.   Isaacs, A. S. Towns with strange names. *Harpers weekly* 54:33, Oct. 1, 1910.
A general article about some of the unusual names in the United States.

201.   Jacobs, Jane. Nombres de lugares de Estados Unidos. *Revista geografica americana* 35:257-66, junio 1953.
Popular article in Spanish on place-names in the United States.

202.   Jaeger, Edmund C. Names of desert things and places. *Desert magazine* 22:22-23, March 1959.
On borrowed desert names, such as vada, barranca, mesa.

203.   Jenks, Albert Ernest. Influence of wild rice on geographic nomenclature;

In his The wild rice gatherers of the upper lakes. U.S. Bureau of American Ethnology. Annual report v. 19, pt. 2, p. 1115-26 1897-98.

204. Jennings, Gary. Naming names—and backgrounds. *Denver post* Oct. 29, 1961, Roundup, p. 31.
Condensed in *Reader's digest* 79:114-16, Dec. 1961 under title Why did they call it that?
General article on names in the United States.

205. Jensen, Andrew. Origin of western geographic names, associated with the history of the "Mormon" people. *Utah genealogical and historical magazine* 10:1-16, 81-85, 120-28, 181-90, Jan.-Oct. 1919; 11:34-40, 82-91, 141-44, 170-77, Jan.-Oct. 1920; 12:41-48, 125-30, 188-92, Jan., July, Oct. 1921; 13:38-43, Jan. 1922.
A list of place-names in Utah, Idaho, Montana, Oregon, Nevada, California, Wyoming, Colorado, New Mexico, and Arizona—also Alberta, Can., and Mexico—that have had Mormon settlements.

206. Johnson, Amandus. Indian geographical names; *In* Lindeström, Peter Martensson. Geographia Americae. Philadelphia, Swedish Colonial Society, 1925. p. 299-408.
Sources for the location, meaning and derivation of the words: p. 291-98.
Includes names in the Delaware Basin.

207. Johnson, E. Gustav. The study of American place-names of Swedish origin. Chicago, 1946. 16p.
Reprinted from *Covenant quarterly* Nov. 1946.

208. Jones, Nathan W. A brief account of Chinese voyages to the north-west coast of America, and the interpretation of 200 Indian names. New York, C. A. Alvord, 1869. 26p. (Indian bulletin, no. 2, 1868)

209. Kane, Joseph Nathan. The American counties; a record of the origin of the names of the 3,072 counties, dates of creation and organization, area, 1960 population, historical data, etc., of the fifty states. Rev. ed. New York, Scarecrow Press, 1962. 540p.
1st ed. 1960. 500p.
Includes a summary chapter on derivation of names of counties; an alphabetical list of all counties in the United States giving origin of name; a list of counties with changed names, giving earlier names; an alphabetical list of county seats; a list of persons for whom counties have been named.

210. Katz, Sol. Rainbow hued streets. *American city* 61:115, April 1946.
Suggests scheme for using names of colors in street nomenclature.

211. Kellogg, David Sherwood. Early mention of some events and places in the valley of Lake Champlain. A paper read before the Vermont Historical Society, in the hall of the House of Representatives, Oct. 30, 1902. Vermont Historical Society. Proceedings 1901-02:51-64.

212. Kelly, Francis J. Towns on state borders go by interesting names. *Austin (Tex.) Statesman* Aug. 27, 1953, p. B-12.
A.P. story, also in *Omaha world-herald* Aug. 16, 1953.

213. Kelton, Dwight H. Annals of Fort Mackinac. Ruggles edition. Detroit, Detroit Free Press Print. Co., 1888. 144p.
 Earlier edition: Island edition. Detroit, 1884. 158p.
 Ancient names of rivers, lakes, etc.: p. 117-21; Indian and French geographical names: p. 145-58.

214. —— Indian names of places near the Great Lakes. Detroit, Mich., Detroit Free Press, 1888. 55p.
 Most of the names are derived from the Ojibway, Cree, and Delaware languages.
 Review: by A. S. Gatschet, *Journal of American folk-lore* 2:69, Jan.-March 1889; by D. G. Brinton, *American antiquarian* 11:68, Jan. 1889.

215. Ker, Edmund Thomas. River and lake names in the United States. New York, Woodstock Pub. Co., 1911. 47p.

216. Kilpatrick, Jack Frederick. An etymological note on the tribal name of the Cherokees and certain place and proper names derived from Cherokee. *Journal of the Graduate Research Center* 30:37-41, April 1962.

217. King, Edith Morgan. No namee. *New Yorker* 20:55-57, Aug. 26, 1944.
 A modest research in the field of house and estate names.

218. Kinneman, John A. Nationalism in names of counties. *Education* 51:483-90, April 1931.
 "A comparative study of states to determine which national names are oftenest used for county names."—*American speech*.

219. Krahn, Cornelius. Mennonite names of persons and places. *Mennonite life* 15:36-38, Jan. 1960.
 In North and South America.
 For a complete list of Mennonite villages, see article Villages in v.4 of Mennonite encyclopedia. 1959.

220. Kramer, Fritz L. Andover moves West. *Names* 1:188-91, Sept. 1953.
 Traces the name Andover across the Atlantic and westward through the United States.

221. —— More on "Idaho." *Western folklore* 12:208-10, July 1953.
 Mentions items that are missing or treated only insufficiently in Erl H. Ellis, That word "Idaho" (see no. 102).

222. Krapp, George Philip. The English language in America. New York, Century, for the Modern Language Assoc. of America, 1925. 2v.
 The chapter on Proper names treats of place-names in the United States, 1:169-200.

223. Krueger, John R. A pronunciation standard for place names of the Pacific Northwest. *American speech* 37:74, Feb. 1962.
 Local pronunciations of some tribal names and place-names.
 Further comments by C. F. Voegelin, *ibid.* 37:75, Feb. 1962.

224. Kuehne, Oswald Robert. Place names in the United States as an incentive to foreign language study. *Modern language journal* 25:91-107, Nov. 1940.

Classification of European-language place-names by languages and by parts of speech or their combinations within languages.

225. Kuethe, J. Louis. Pocosin. *Modern language notes* 52:210-11, March 1937.
Meaning marsh or swamp, the term is now used in southern states, but appears in Rent rolls of Baltimore County, Md. in 1700.

226. Lanos, J. M. What's in a name? *Queen's quarterly* 17:44-57, July-Sept. 1909.
A plea for regeneration in the practice of name-giving in the United States and Canada. Article deals largely with place-names in western Europe, showing how beautiful and appropriate is the terminology used by the Anglo-Saxons, Northmen, and Celts.

227. Laurent, Joseph. Etymology of Indian names by which are designated certain tribes, towns, rivers, lakes, etc.; *In his* New familiar Abenakis and English dialogues. Quebec, Printed by L. Brousseau, 1884. p. 205-22.

228. Lawrence, Frederick W. The origin of American state names. *National geographic magazine* 38:105-43, Aug. 1920.

229. Leigh, Rufus Wood. Naming of the Green, Sevier, and Virgin Rivers. *Utah historical quarterly* 29:137-47, April 1961.
Adapted from his full-length book manuscript, Indian, Spanish, and government survey place names of the Great Basin and Colorado plateaus.

230. Longstreth, Joseph & John Ludwig. 48 plus 1: Washington, and the District of Columbia; the story of how the forty-eight states and their capital cities got their names. New York, Abelard-Schuman, 1957. 176p.

231. Loomis, C. Grant. Names in American limericks. *Names* 2:229-33, Dec. 1954.
The rhymes used in limericks give some indication of early pronunciation of some place-names.

232. Ludwig, John Warner. City names, our forgotten memorials. *American city* 70:242-45, March 1955.

233. Lyman, William D. Indian myths of the Northwest. American Antiquarian Society. Proceedings n.s. 25:377-79, Oct. 1915.
Aboriginal names of rivers, mountains, etc. used in the northwestern part of the United States are mentioned in connection with myths.

234. McAdoo, William Gibbs. American geographical nomenclature. Address to the associated alumni of East-Tennessee University, at Knoxville, Tenn. June 20th, 1871. Milledgeville, Ga., Federal Union Book and Job Office, 1871. 24p.

235. McClelland, M. K. Towns with a sense of humor (I hope). *American Motors news illustrated* 3:4, Feb. 1960.
Places the author would like to visit because of their intriguing names.

236. McConnell, Raymond. Where is the "Middle West"? *Lincoln (Neb.) evening journal* April 30, 1956.
Part of the column More or less personal.

237. McCutcheon, John T., Jr. A line o' type or two. Why is "street" in disfavor? *Chicago tribune* May 11, 1954, p. 20; May 12, p. 24; May 13, p. 18.
"The term 'street' in names of streets is being supplanted by other terms, for which etymologies are given."—*American speech.*

238. McDavid, Raven I., Jr. Linguistic geography and toponymic research. *Names* 6:65-73, June 1958.
The relationship between these two disciplines and a plea for cooperation among the students of the two fields.

239. McDermott, John Francis. Madame Chouteau's grandchildren. *Names* 9:108-11, June 1961.
Place-names derived from the family, illustrating the spread of the family's activities.

240. McDonald, Gerald Doan. Doane place names. Doane Family Association of America. Report of proceedings. Reunion 1953, p. 3-11.
Published 1955.

241. McMillan, James B. A further note on place-name grammar. *American speech* 27:196-98, Oct. 1952.
A rejoinder to George R. Stewart in *American speech* 25:197-202; supplements the author's article in *American speech* 24:241-48.

242. —— Observations on American place-name grammar. *American speech* 24:241-48, Dec. 1949.

243. McMullen, Edwin Wallace. The term prairie in the United States. *Names* 5:27-46, March 1957.
True and false generics. The result of a preliminary study of names containing the word prairie on 773 topographical maps.

244. Mahr, August C. Aus praktischen Gründen gebildete Fluss- und Ortsnamen der algonkischen Indianer in Nordamerika. *Rheinisches Jahrbuch für Volkskunde* 11:212-32. 1960.

245. Mallery, Richard D. Place names in America; *In his* Our American language. Garden City, N.Y., Halcyon House, 1947. p. 91-122.

246. Marckwardt, Albert Henry. American English. New York, Oxford Univ. Press, 1958. 194p.
The names thereof: p. 151-66.
"A summary statement. Treatment is sound, although he is able to include little that will be of interest to the specialist in onomastics."—Review, by David W. Reed, *Names* 6:246, Dec. 1958.

247. Marshall, James Leslie. Santa Fe town names; *In his* Santa Fe, the railroad that built an empire. New York, Random House, 1945. p. 351-59.
Names on the Santa Fe lines, from Illinois to California. Lists of Indian and Spanish names with meaning, and places named for officials and employees of the railroad.

248. Marshall, Orsamus Holmes. The historical writings of the late Orsamus H. Marshall relating to the early history of the West; with an introduction by

William L. Stone, Albany, J. Munsell's Sons, 1887. 500p. (Munsell's historical series, no. 15)

Besides Indian material, this book contains his Niagara frontier, p. 275-320, and a valuable Index rerum, p. 343-468, which includes many references to place-names in various early works and maps, the most important and accessible of which is the Jesuit relations.

249. —— The Niagara frontier, embracing sketches of its early history, and Indian, French and English local names. Read before the Buffalo Historical Club, February 27th, 1865. Buffalo, N.Y., J. Warren & Co., 1865. 46p.

Also published in Buffalo Historical Society. Publications 2:395-429. 1880. Also reprinted from the Publications of the Society, Buffalo, 1881. 37p. Also in his Historical writings. Albany, Munsell, 1887. p. 275-320.

The history of the region with the signification of many place-names. An appendix contains lists of Seneca names with their meanings and locations, and Early names applied to the Great Lakes and rivers, and to some of the prominent localities on their borders.

250. Martin, Lawrence. The dates of naming places and things for George Washington; *In* U.S. George Washington Bicentennial Commission. History of the George Washington bicentennial celebration. Literature series. Washington, 1932. 3:308-12.

251. Matthews, Brander. On the poetry of place names. *Scribner's magazine* 20:22-28, July 1896.

Also in his Parts of speech. New York, Scribner, 1901. p. 271-91.

252. Maurer, David W. Underworld place-names. *American speech* 15:340-42, Oct. 1940; 17:75-76, Feb. 1942.

A list of place-names used by criminals for cities of the United States.

253. Meanings of state names often lost. *Sun,* Baltimore, July 31, 1937.

254. Mencken, Henry Louis. The American language; an inquiry into the development of English in the United States. 4th ed., cor., enl., and rewritten. New York, Knopf, 1936. 769p.

1st ed. 1919; 2d ed. 1921; 3d ed. 1923.

Place-names: p. 525-54.

Indicates the variety of the names found in the United States and includes street names, appellations applied to the residents of a particular place, and the joke towns, such as Podunk.

255. —— The American language; an inquiry into the development of English in the United States. Supplement II. New York, Knopf, 1948. 890p.

Place-names: p. 525-75; State nicknames: p. 596-642.

256. —— The American language; an inquiry into the development of English in the United States. The 4th ed. and the two supplements, abridged, with annotations and new material, by Raven I. McDavid, Jr., with the assistance of David W. Maurer. New York, Knopf, 1963. 777p.

Place names: p. 642-701.

The material from the 4th ed. and Supplement II abridged, reorganized, and

considerably rewritten.
Review: by Audrey R. Duckert, *Names* 12:123-26, June 1964.

257. —— American street names. *American speech* 23:81-88, April 1948.

258. —— Names for Americans. *American speech* 22:241-56, Dec. 1947.
Names for residents of the United States and of the states.

259. —— Postscripts to the American language: the Podunk mystery. *New Yorker* 24:75-81, Sept. 25, 1948.
Additional note, unsigned, Oct. 16, p. 26-27, on Podunk River, tributary of Connecticut River.

260. —— Some opprobrious nicknames. *American speech* 24:25-30, Feb. 1949.
For residents of states and cities.

261. —— What the people of American towns call themselves. *American speech* 23:161-84, Oct. 1948.

262. Meredith, Mamie. "Chicagonese," "Buffalonians," "Manhattaniten," "Omahogs," and other name lore. *American speech* 14:77-80, Feb. 1939.
Form of city name given to its residents.

263. —— A crack in the track. *American speech* 10:236, Oct. 1935.
A variant for Podunk.

264. —— Indian place-names as viewed by a Scotch noblewoman. *American speech* 4:364-67, June 1929.
Notes taken from Amelia M. Murray, Letters from the United States, Cuba and Canada. New York, G. P. Putnam, 1856.

265. —— Language mixture in American place names. *American speech* 5:224-27, Feb. 1930.
"The author mentions some examples of combinations of geographic names when they become Anglicized and traces the changes which words undergo as they are interpreted in turn by the Indians, the French and the English."—Price.

266. —— Local discolor. *American speech* 6:260-63, April 1931.
American Indian names.

267. —— "Mail box," "Flag-station," "Hell on wheels," and other synonyms for "Podunk." *American speech* 12:320-21, Dec. 1937.

268. —— "Miracle miles" in the U.S.A. *American speech* 31:230-31, Oct. 1956.
"A new name for an out-of-city shopping center," first noted in Lincoln, Neb.
See additional article by Homer Aschmann, Miracle mile, *ibid.* 32:156-58, May 1957.

269. —— Picturesque town names in America. *American speech* 6:429-32, Aug. 1931.
"In different eras towns are named according to the popularity of some particular vogue at the time."—Price.

270. Mickelsen, John. Origin of the names of towns on the Northern Pacific Railway.
"The author states in a letter that he has endeavored to compile a record of the origin of the names of all towns on this railroad line. There are about 1520 towns on the system. This work is not yet in a published form as the author is still working on it."—Price.
Author is in Engineering Dept. and has typewritten list of all cities, towns, and villages on the system, still unpublished.

271. Minkel, Clarence W. Names in the mapping of original vegetation. *Names* 5:157-61, Sept. 1957.
Analyzes and evaluates the place-name method of reconstruction of the original vegetation patterns in areas where the original plant cover has been greatly altered. Uses Minnesota as a testing ground.

272. Missouri Pacific Railroad Company. The empire that Missouri Pacific serves. St. Louis, Von Hoffmann Press, 1956? 352p.
Origins of the names of most of the communities served by the Missouri Pacific Lines.

273. Momsen, Richard. Similarities in settlement names of Brasil and the United States. Coimbra. Universidade. Centro do Estudos Geograficos. Boletim v. 3, no. 19, p. 41-55. 1962.
Résumés in Portuguese and French, p. 55.
Some general parallels in the derivations of the names of their settlements, arranged as Descriptive, Proper, Mining, Pseudo-classical, etc.

274. Mooney, James. The Siouan tribes of the East. Washington, Govt. Print. Off., 1894. 101p. (U.S. Bureau of American Ethnology. Bulletin no. 22)
Local names from Siouan tribal names in Virginia and Carolina: p. 87-88; Some notes on names, p. 46-47.

275. Moore, M. V. Did the Romans colonize America? *Magazine of American history* 12:113-25, 354-64, Aug., Oct. 1884.
Correlations between American place-names and Latin words; such as, Tennessee and Tenassy, Mississippi and Messisapa.

276. ———— North and South American aboriginal names. *Popular science monthly* 44:81-84, Nov. 1893.
Many names of natural features in North América have their counterparts in South America, indicating that the languages of the people of the two continents had similar words and meanings.

277. ———— Southern rivers. *Names* 3:38-43, March 1955.
A poem on the colorful names of the rivers of the South, which first appeared in *Harper's new monthly magazine* of Feb. 1883.

278. Moyer, Armond & Winifred Moyer. The origins of unusual place-names. Emmaus, Pa., Keystone Pub. Assoc., 1958. 144p.
Review: by A. R. Duckert, *Names* 7:265-67, Dec. 1959.

279. Mussey, June Barrows. Tied for first in the hearts of his countrymen. New York Public Library. Bulletin 54:55-60, Feb. 1950.

A summary of place-names found in J. D. B. De Bow's Statistical view of the United States...being a compendium of the seventh census.

280.   The Name game. All aboard for Big Shanty. *Denver post* Nov. 24, 1963, Roundup, p. 9.
Unusual town names in the United States.

281.   The Name of your town. *Ladies home journal* 30:3, Sept. 1913.
The origin of the names of some of the places in the East explained by historical legends.

282.   Names and places. *Western folklore* (formerly *California folklore quarterly)* v. 4- . 1945- .
A department containing articles and brief notes on place-names and inquiries about them.

283.   Names in brief; News, comments, queries.
Regular sections in *Names*.

284.   Names of American towns run the gamut of variety; many Washingtons and Lincolns may be found but Zipp and Author are not repeated. *New York times* Feb. 23, 1930, sec. 8, p. 17, col. 2-3.
Zipp and Author in Indiana.

285.   Names of places in the United States. *Chambers's Edinburgh journal* n.s. 4:217-18, 254-56, Oct. 4, 18, 1845.
Names used in the United States include many from ancient times, from Europe, and from literature.

286.   Names of topographic features in the United States. American Geographical Society. Bulletin 39:103-06, Feb. 1907.
Authoritative decisions handed down by the U.S. Geographic Board as to the extent of the region to which certain names of mountains apply.

287.   Names of towns in the United States. *Knickerbocker* 9:19-25, Jan. 1837.
Signed: A. B. C.

288.   National Geographic Society. U.S. town-city names spell enchantment, surprises too. Washington, D.C., 1955. 6p.

289.   Nature names in America. *Journal of geography* 5:476-80, Dec. 1906.
A general article on the meanings of the words creek, freshet, swamp, etc. which now have different meanings in England and the United States.

290.   Naughton, William A. What's in a name? *Américas* 16:27-31, Dec. 1964.
Names given during the exploration, conquest, and settlement of the Western Hemisphere. Mostly in Spanish America, but includes some in the United States.

291.   Nestler, Harold. Poughkeepsie, as a place name. Dutchess County Historical Society. Year book 35:64-66. 1950.
In New York, Indiana, Arkansas, and Colorado.

292.   New names for old streets. *New York times magazine* Oct. 28, 1930, p. 24.
Based on Pittsburgh's newest roadway called KDKA Blvd.

293. Nichols, Maynard. Berlin, U.S.A. *New York times magazine* Oct. 22, 1944, p. 36.

An article on odd names in the United States inspired by attempts to secure change of one of the cities named Berlin to Distomo, a Nazi-destroyed Greek city.

cf. Letters to the editor, *ibid.* Nov. 12, p. 51; Nov. 26, p. 50.

294. Nicknames of the states. *Current literature* 24:41, July 1898.

Reprinted from the *Philadelphia evening bulletin.*

295. Nicknaming the states. *Mentor* 14:64, Jan. 1927.

A popular article which gives the significance of the nicknames attached to the states.

296. Numbers as street names. *Notes and queries* 178:12, 174-75, 286, Jan. 6, March 9, April 20, 1940.

The practice of using numbers and letters for street names in America.

297. O'Callaghan, Edmund Bailey. Indian names of localities and their derivations. *Historical magazine* 3:84-85, 189-90, 278, 367, March-Dec. 1859.

A list of Algonquin and other Indian place-names in the East giving the origin and meaning.

298. —— Indian names of places with definitions. *Historical magazine* 6:30, 133, Jan., April 1862.

"This list of Indian place-names which belong to the Algonquin family gives the possible origin and meaning."—Price.

299. Och, Joseph Tarcisius. Der deutschamerikanische Farmer; sein Anteil an der Eroberung und Kolonisation der Bundesdomane der Ver. Staaten, besonders in den Nord Centralstaaten; nebst Wurdigung der kulturellen Bedeutung des deutschen Farmers, und Wertung der deutschen Auswanderung und deutschen Kolonisationsarbeit in Amerika vom amerikanischen und deutschen national-politischen Standpunkt. Eine statistische und volkswirtschaftliche Untersuchung. Columbus, Ohio, Heer Print. Co., 1913. 248p.

Verzeichnis deutscher Staedte- und Ortsnamen in den Ver. Staaten: p. 228-35.

300. Odd names adorn American cities and towns. *Geographic news bulletin* Nov. 11, 1932, p. 1-3.

Prepared as a news release by the National Geographic Society.

301. Oddities in postmarks, such as Odd, W.Va., fill Massachusetts collector with glee. *New York times* Oct. 3, 1937, sec. 2, p. 8, col. 2-3.

Fred G. Richardson claims to have oddest collection of postmarks in the country.

302. Ogden, Herbert G.; Gustave Herrle; Marcus Baker, & A. H. Thompson. Geographic nomenclature. *National geographic magazine* 2:261-78. 1890.

Need for standardization of names by the newly formed Board on Geographic Names.

303. Olson, James C. "Trace" and "trail." *American speech* 26:137, May 1951.

Question regarding use.

304. On the streets where we live. *Aramco world* 9:6-7, Sept. 1958.
Systems of forming addresses in many countries including the United States.

305. Origin of names of projects and project features in reclamation territory.
Reclamation era 30:63-65, 144-48, 179-81, 241-42, 253-57, 294-99, March-June,
Aug.-Oct. 1940.
Deals with states in the West.

306. Orth, Donald J. Domestic geographic names activity in federal mapping.
Surveying and mapping 24:603-06, Dec. 1964.
Presented at the 23d annual meeting of the American Congress on Surveying
and Mapping, Washington, D.C., March 26-29, 1963, by a member of the Geographic Names staff, U.S. Geological Survey.

307. Our classical belt. *Nation* 85:203-04, Sept. 5, 1907.
Some of the classical names in the United States.

308. Our Indian names. *New York times* July 28, 1937, p. 18, col. 3-4.
Meaning of Indian names of states as set forth by the Smithsonian Institution.

309. Our station names—their family trees. *Louisville and Nashville magazine*
25:18-19, May; 18-19, June; 20-21, July; 14, Aug.; 14-16, Sept.; 14-15, Oct.;
14-16, Nov.; 16-17, Dec. 1949; 26:16-17, Jan.; 34-35, March; 23, July 1950.

310. Our town nomenclature. *Nation* 7:499-500, Dec. 17, 1868.
The author regrets that, in this country, place-names have not had time to grow
up. The people of this country have been compelled "to invent place names and
impose them, without regard to appropriateness, upon places."

311. P.O. nomenclators. *New York times* Feb. 28, 1938, p. 14, col. 2; letter
March 13, sec. 4, p. 9, col. 7.
Changes in Feb. supplement of U.S. postal guide.

312. Pace, G. B. Linguistic geography and names ending in <i>. *American
speech* 35:175-87, Oct. 1960.
Focuses attention on pronunciation of Missouri and Cincinnati.

313. Palmer, C. B. O death! O misery! *New York times* Jan. 30, 1955,
Magazine, p. 69.
Place-names in the United States and other countries taken from disasters.

314. Parry, Albert. Russian names for American towns. *Russian review*
3:30-43, Spring 1944.

315. Pearce, Thomas M. Animal place names in the West. *Western folklore*
13:203-05, July 1954.

316. —— Chicarica, Chico Rico, Sugarite: a puzzle in place naming. *Western
folklore* 14:124-25, April 1955.

317. —— The lighter side of place naming. *Western folklore* 11:118-21,
April 1952.

318. —— Names and places. *Western folklore* 8:157, April 1949.

The writer succeeded E. G. Gudde as editor of this regular column, and reviews situation in the West.

319. —— Place-name pronunciation guides for western states. *Western folklore* 10:72-73, Jan 1951.
Project of National Association of Radio News Directors.

320. —— Spanish place name patterns in the Southwest. *Names* 3:201-09, Dec. 1955.

321. —— Three Rocky Mountain terms: Park, Sugan, and Plaza. *American speech* 33:99-107, May 1958.

322. —— Western place name sketches. *Names* 2:272-74, Dec. 1954.
The status of work on place-names in the western states and the work of the Western Place Name Committee.

323. Pence, Monroe Conger. A history of Pence place names and early Pences in America, with genealogies. Mountain View, Calif., 1961. 31p.
Pence family place-names arranged geographically.

324. Pennsylvania Railroad Company. Alphabetical and geographical list of bituminous and anthracite coal mines on the Pennsylvania Railroad and lateral lines with names and post office address of operators. Philadelphia, 1956. 68p.

325. Perkins, Franklin. Geographical names. *Journal of education* (Boston) 45:367, 403. 1897.
Prefixes and suffixes used in compounding place-names.

326. Perrin, Noel. Rod-Island is real, but I'll never believe in Wisconsin. *New Yorker* 38:48-51, Nov. 24, 1962.
Place-names that foreigners change into their own language (e.g., Filadelfia on a Spanish map) illustrate the First Law of Geographical Reality, which is: The places in any country that seem authentic to the people of any other country may be determined by observing which place-names the other country changes.

327. Phelps, Dawson A. & Edward Hunter Ross. Place-names along the Natchez Trace. *Journal of Mississippi history* 14:217-56, Oct. 1952.

328. Pierce, Phillip. Ghost town directory of the West. Cheyenne, Wyo., Pierce Pub. Co.. 1964. 36p.

329. Pioneers got place names often mixed. *Cumberland (Md.) evening times* Nov. 13, 1935.
A summary of a National Geographic Society bulletin.

330. The Place Name Committee. *American speech* 14:136-38, 212-14, April, Oct. 1939.
The appointment of a committee by the Present-day English Section of the Modern Language Association to further the study of place-names in the United States. Mentions distribution of tentative list by Harold Woodmansee Bentley and M. Robert Snyder (see no. 30). Oct. issue includes comment by Prof. Max. Förster.

331. Place name study aids in the classroom; educator says hobby provides adventure for history and geography students. *New York times* Nov. 9, 1932, p. 23, col. 7.
An interview with Lewis H. Chrisman.

332. Place-name study in the United States. *Geographical review* 24:659-60, Oct. 1934.

333. Place-names masquerade in strange disguises. *Geographic news bulletin* Nov. 13, 1935, p. 1-3.
A news release of the National Geographic Society.

334. Plank, Robert. Projection in topographic names. *Names* 6:80-87, June 1958.
A study of the psychological principle of "projection" in descriptive place-names.

335. Poast, Florence Maude. Indian names, facts and games for Camp Fire girls. Washington, James William Bryan Press, 1916. 78p.
Contains list of Indian names, with pronunciation and meaning, suitable for camps, country homes or bungalows, and boats.

336. Podunk was Indian name. *Pennsylvania archaeologist* 5:71, Oct. 1935.

337. Popular names of the states. *Magazine of history* 23:27-30, July 1916.
This alphabetical list contains most of the states with their nicknames and reasons for such terms. There is also a list of popular names applied to the inhabitants of some states.

338. Porter, P. W. Thanks to readers, Polecat Hollow is in the same orbit as Mars. *Cleveland plain dealer* May 5, 1958.
An additional article, April 24.
Odd place-names.

339. Porter, Philip. Porter on odd names. *Cleveland plain dealer* Sept. 13, 1958.
An editor of this paper lists odd place-names sent in by readers of his column. Similar lists appeared in the April 24 and May 5 issues.

340. Pound, Louise. "Gag" towns. *American speech* 26:137, May 1951.
Kalamazoo, Peoria, etc.

341. ——— The locus of Podunk. *American speech* 9:80, Feb. 1934.

342. A Pretty idea at least. *New York times* July 20, 1923, p. 12, col. 5.
Editorial on abbreviations for state names, citing plan of *Richmond-times dispatch* to write out Virginia.

343. Preuss, Charles. Exploring with Frémont; the private diaries of Charles Preuss, cartographer for John C. Frémont on his first, second and fourth expeditions to the Far West; trans. and ed. by Erwin G. and Elisabeth K. Gudde. Norman, Univ. of Oklahoma Press, 1958. 162p. (The American exploration and travel series, no. 26)
The editors pay special attention to place-names and comment on them in

numerous footnotes.

Review: by Fritz L. Kramer, *Names* 6:187-88, Sept. 1958.

344. Price, Edward T. A geography of color. *Geographical review* 54:590-92, Oct. 1964.

Includes chromotoponyms, names in which a color is used, giving evidence of the importance of color to observers.

345. Price, Esther Frances. Guide to material on place-names in the United States and Canada. Urbana, Ill., 1934. 250p.

Thesis (M.A.) Univ. of Illinois, 1934. On file in the University Library.

346. Prucha, Francis Paul. A guide to the military posts of the United States, 1789-1895. Madison, State Historical Society of Wisconsin, 1964. 178p.

Includes an alphabetical catalog of more than 475 military posts of every description: forts, camps, barracks, and cantonments.

347. Quigg, Doc. American towns pose problem for writer. *Austin (Tex.) Statesman* Oct. 4, 1957, p. 14.

Humorous names of American towns.

348. Raup, Hallock Floy. Center vs. Centre. *Names* 1:259-61, Dec. 1953.

Are the variations in spelling due to fads in naming places?

349. Read, Allen Walker. The basis of correctness in the pronunciation of place-names. *American speech* 8:42-46, Feb. 1933.

Fails to find a basis for correctness in legislative action, in etymology, in spelling, or in the so-called authorities.

350. —— Derivative forms from place-names; the contrast between England and America.

Paper read before the 1941 meeting of the American Dialect Society.

351. —— The pronunciation of place names on the frontier, 1829-1830. *American speech* 13:263-67, Dec. 1938.

Information from the correspondence of Joseph Emerson Worcester.

352. —— The rationale of "Podunk." *American speech* 14:99-108, April 1939.

Adopted by the early settlers from the Indians for places in Connecticut, Massachusetts, and New York and then used in a series of humorous letters of 1846.

353. Read, William Alexander. A few American place-names. *Journal of English and Germanic philology* 22:242-44. 1923.

Study of the pronunciation of a few chosen names.

354. —— Research in American place names, 1920-1926. *Zeitschrift für Ortsnamenforschung* 4:185-91. 1928.

"Bibliographical account of recent publications relating to American place names, which the writer divides into 3 classes—investigations of the geographic and historical significance of place names, articles and books of a popular character, and scientific studies of Indian names."—Griffin.

355. —— Research in American place-names since 1928. *Zeitschrift für Ortsnamenforschung* 10:222-42. 1934.

356. Reade, John. The testimony of names of places. *Rose-Belford's Canadian monthly* 1:602-04, Nov. 1878.
The source of some of the names in North America.

357. Remington, Frank L. How it got that name. *Think* (International Business Machines Corporation) 17:14-15, Oct. 1951.
Some unusual American place-names.

358. ——— Please write in ink. *Surveying and mapping* 13:185-87, April-June 1953.
Reprinted through the courtesy of *Pen*, March 1953.
Stories concerning the choice of unusual names for places in the United States.

359. Rice, Charlie. Fireman, name my street! *This week magazine* Jan. 26, 1963, p. 14.
Street names in developments.

360. Richardson, Charles F. The pronunciation of American names. *Critic* n.s. 2:73-74, Aug. 16, 1884.

361. Richthofen, E. von. The Spanish toponyms of the British Columbia coast, with sideglances at those in the states of Washington, Oregon and Alaska. Winnipeg, Ukrainian Free Academy of Sciences, 1963. 22p. (Ukrainian Free Academy of Sciences. Series: Onomastica, no. 26)

362. Robertson, Robert S. Long Island Indians. *Magazine of American history* 2:370-71, 501, June, Aug. 1878.
The interpretation and derivation of some Indian place-names.

363. Roe, Frank Gilbert. Buffalo place-names; *In his* The North American buffalo. Toronto, Univ. of Toronto Press, 1951. p. 817-28.
Also miscellaneous references in index: Place-names.

364. Rogers, P. Burwell. Inland ports. *American speech* 35:203-05, Oct. 1960.
Influence of inland streams and canals on use of ports, harbors, and havens in town names.

365. Romero, B. A. Origin of state names. *New York times* Sept. 19, 1937, sec. 4, p. 9, col. 6.
Believes many names of states and places could be traced back to Spanish words.

366. Rostlund, Erhard. The geographic range of the historic bison in the Southeast. Association of American Geographers. Annals 50:394-407, Dec. 1960.
Place names: p. 403-05.

367. Rothsteiner, John M. On the study of place-names. *Mid-America* 12:58-62, July 1929.
Discusses the relation of place-names to history.

368. Rouillard, Eugène. À propos de Jolliet. Société de Géographie de Québec. Bulletin 11:354-55, nov. 1917.
Concerns the orthography of the name. The State of Wisconsin officially decided on Jolliet.

369. Rupert, William W. The significance and importance of geographical names. American Bureau of Geography. Bulletin 1:316-27, Dec. 1900.
Treats of names in the United States, some that were given by explorers, others which came into being in colonial times.

370. Russ, William A., Jr. The export of Pennsylvania place names. *Pennsylvania history* 15:194-214, July 1948.
On the transplanting of Pennsylvania names to the South and West, as a result of the Delaware migration (*ca.* 1765).

371. Russell, Israel C. The names of the larger geographical features of North America. Geographical Society of Philadelphia. Bulletin 2:55-69, Nov. 1899.
A discussion of topographical terms with a suggested nomenclature for the larger geographical features.

372. Ryan, Jack. What's in a name? *Family weekly magazine* Sept. 16, 1956, p. 2.
"Humorous names of American towns."—*American speech.*

373. Sage, Evan T. Classical place-names in America. *American speech* 4:261-71. April 1929.
From the standpoint of their linguistic interest, regardless of any sociological or historical inferences that might be based upon them.

374. Salmon, Lucy Maynard. Place-names and personal names as records of history. *American speech* 2:228-32, Feb. 1927.
A collection and arrangement of common nouns, adjectives, and verbs derived from proper nouns. Emphasis is placed on words derived from the names of persons and places of every nationality that have been identified with inventions, discoveries, and manufactures. Their significance is shown in geographic nomenclature.

375. Sandham, William R. Patrick Henry, orator, statesman and patriot for whom Henry County, Ill. was named. Illinois State Historical Society. Journal 18:1039-48, Oct. 1925.
Biographical account of Patrick Henry, prefaced and concluded by a few paragraphs on number of counties and towns named for him.

376. Schele De Vere, Maximilian. Americanisms; the English of the New World. New York, Scribner, 1872. 685p.
Sections of the chapters The Indian, and Immigrants from abroad, treat of Indian and foreign influence in place-names. In the chapter New words and nicknames is a list of nicknames of states and cities.

377. Schoolcraft, Henry Rowe. Mohegan language and geographical names. *Knickerbocker, or New York monthly magazine* 10:214-16, Sept. 1837.
Emphasis on names in New York.

378. The "Science" of street names. *American city* 75:7, Nov. 1960.
Editorial on systems of naming streets.

379. Sealock, Richard Burl. Place names in genealogy. *Indiana historical bulletin* 23:69-75, Jan. 1946.

380. Settlers imprint left on town names. Wisconsin geographer points out how American places reflect characteristics. *New York times* Aug. 18, 1929, sec. 2, p. 23, col. 5.
R. H. Whitbeck, the geographer.

381. Shankle, George Earlie. American nicknames: their origin and significance. 2d ed. New York, H. W. Wilson Co., 1955. 524p.
1st ed. 1937. 599p.
Includes places.

382. —— State names, flags, seals, songs, birds, flowers and other symbols; a study based on historical documents giving the origin and significance of the state names, nicknames, mottoes, seals, flags, flowers, birds, songs, and descriptive comments on the capitol buildings and on some of the leading state histories, with facsimiles of the state flags and seals. Rev. ed. New York, H. W. Wilson Co., 1941. 524p.
1st ed. 1934. 512p.; rev. ed. 1938. 522p.

383. Shea, John G. Indian names. *Historical magazine* 10:58, Feb. 1866.
A list of several Mohawk aboriginal place-names with their meanings.

384. Shelton, William E. Town and station names on the Illinois Central. *Illinois Central magazine* 44:21, Nov. 1955.
Groups of Bible, presidential, feminine, masculine, and curious names.

385. Sherwin, Reider Thorbjorn. The Viking and the red man: the Old Norse origin of the Algonquin language. New York, Funk & Wagnalls, 1940-48. 5v.
Algonquin place names: 1:254-310; 2:162-78; 3:155-61; 4:172-208; 5:170-99.
Bibliography of principal sources of Algonquin place names: 1:331; 2:191.

386. Short names for long ones. *New York times* Nov. 4, 1928, sec. 3, p. 4, col. 6.
Editorial on protest in San Francisco on shortening of Spanish names, and mentions Filly and K. C. Another editorial against nicknames for cities appeared June 8, sec. 3, p. 6, col. 6.

387. Short (Va.) Story (Ark.), U.S.A. *Good housekeeping* 146:143, Feb. 1958.
A list of unusual town names.

388. Shulman, David. Nicknames of the states and their inhabitants. *American speech* 27:183-85, Oct. 1952.

389. Smelser, Marshall. Poets and place names. *Names* 1:15-19, March 1953.
Some comments on the English poet Robert Southey's concern over place-naming in America as evidenced in his review in the *Quarterly review* 12:317-68, Jan. 1815, of Lewis and Clark's Travels to the source of the Missouri River.

390. Smith, Elsdon Coles. Bibliographia onomastica. United States. 1951- . *Onoma* v. 3- . 1952- .
An annual bibliography of place-name literature.

391. The Soul of places. *New York times* Oct. 23, 1934, p. 18, col. 4.
Editorial on strange names.

392. Soulas, Jean. Toponymie nort-américaine. *Annales de géographie* 50:22-36, janv.-mars 1941.

An attempt by a French geographer to rationalize the seeming vagaries and incongruities of the pattern of North American place-names by a system of classification. Certain inaccuracies in this study illustrate some of the pitfalls for the unwary interpreter of place-names.

393. Spain. Ejército. Servicio Geográfico. Cartografía de ultramar. Carpeta II. Estados Unidos y Canadá. Toponimia de los mapas que la integran relaciones de ultramar. Madrid, Imprenta del Servicio Geográfico del Ejército, 1953. 598p.

A list of maps of the United States and Canada of the 17th and 18th centuries, with lists of place-names on the maps.

394. Speaking of pictures; tourist visits Europe's big cities without leaving U.S. *Life* 26:10-11, Jan. 10, 1949.

A trip through cities with foreign names in New York and Pennsylvania, with pictures showing some connection with each city's namesake.

395. Spelling of geographical names. American Geographical Society. Bulletin 34:155. 1902.

Maintains that certain rules should be followed in assigning new names to places.

396. Spiegelman, Julia. Map of America is dotted with names from Holy Land and Bible. *Kansas City times* Dec. 31, 1962, p. 24.

397. Spofford, Ainsworth Rand. American historical nomenclature. American Historical Association. Annual report 1893:33-42.

The composition of American place-names, the use many times over of imported names, and a summary of the types of names which might be used in the future.

398. Sprague, Marshall. Many "President" towns. *New York times* Oct. 10, 1937, sec. 12, p. 2, col. 2.

Towns named for presidents.

399. Springer, O. Ortsnamen in der Neuen Welt. *Germanisch-Romanische Monatsschrift* 21:125-46, March-April 1933.

"Concerning American Indian place-names."—*American speech.*

400. Stanford, Annabella. The names of the states. *American antiquarian and oriental journal* 29:305-08, Sept.-Oct. 1907.

"The author's discourse is confined to the source and meaning of early names that were suggested or applied to the states and their reasons for being applied and why they were not retained."—Price.

401. Staples, Hamilton Barclay. Origin of the names of the states of the Union. American Antiquarian Society. Proceedings n.s. 1:366-83, Oct. 1881.

Also issued separately, Worcester, C. Hamilton, 1882. 25p.

402. State names and origins. *Louis Allis messenger* Jan.-Feb. 1953, p. [28-29].

403. States have Indian names; original designations range from Alibamu to Massawadschuasch. *New York times* Jan. 12, 1930, sec. 11, p. 6, col. 2.

404. States perpetuate Indian words. *Kansas City star* Sept. 29, 1960, p. 11.

405. Steel, William Gladstone. Place names. *Steel points, junior* v. 1, no. 4, Jan. 1928. 23p.
Includes short biography of Henry Gannett, upon whose work this is probably based.

406. Stegner, Wallace. C. E. Dutton—explorer, geologist, nature writer. *Scientific monthly* 45:82-83, July 1937.
Refers to his use of architectural names, particularly oriental, in national parks of the Southwest.

407. ——— Powell and the names on the plateau. *Western humanities review* 7:105-10, Spring 1953.
Later published as a section in his book Beyond the hundredth meridian. Boston, Houghton Mifflin, 1954. p. 191-98, Notes p. 395-96.
The relationship of Major John Wesley Powell to some place-names in Utah, Wyoming, Colorado, and Arizona.

408. Stevenson, Andrew. Many towns named in honor of Santa Fe men. *Santa Fe magazine* 22:55-56, Aug. 1928.
From Illinois to California, but greatest number are in Kansas.

409. Stewart, George Rippey. A classification of place names. *Names* 2:1-13, March 1954.
Postulates nine classes of names.

410. ——— Further observations on place name grammar. *American speech* 25:197-202, Oct. 1950.

411. ——— Leah, woods, and deforestation as an influence on place-names. *Names* 10:11-20, March 1962.

412. ——— The names; *In his* U.S. 40, cross section of the United States of America. Boston, Houghton Mifflin, 1953. p. 303-09.

413. ——— Names of wild animals for natural features in the United States and Canada. *Revue internationale d'onomastique* 12:282-92, déc. 1960.
Estimated about 40,000 natural features in the United States bear the names of wild animals; in Canada, about 10,000.

414. ——— Names on the land: a historical account of place-naming in the United States. Rev. and enl. ed. with illustrations. Boston, Houghton Mifflin, 1958. 511p.
1st ed. New York, Random House, 1945. 418p.
Rev. ed. contains a few minor changes in the plates, plus new chapters on Alaska, Hawaii, and current affairs, 1944-1958, and a valuable section of Notes and references (p. 442-82).
The process of place-naming is treated chronologically with definite trends and fashions noted: the unselfconscious names given by the early settlers, the influence of various national groups, the use of Indian names, and the names resulting from important historical events.
Review of 1st ed.: by Harold W. Bentley, *American speech* 20:285-88, Dec.

1945; by Raye R. Platt, *Geographical review* 35:659-64, Oct. 1945; by H. L. Mencken, *New York herald tribune weekly book review* April 22, 1945, p. 5.
Review of rev. ed.: by D. J. Georgacas, *Names* 8:89-94, June 1960.

415. —— "Names on the land," Virginia, Susquehanna, Chicago, Roanoke, Massachusetts, Des Moines, Red Dog, the Bronx; American names come from hills and streams, Indians, and white men, history and whimsy. *Life* 19:47-57, July 2, 1945.

416. —— Place name patterns. *Names* 4:119-21, June 1956.
A further discussion of the classification of place-names, in answer to Thomas M. Pearce, Spanish place name patterns in the Southwest, *ibid.* 3:201-09, Dec. 1955.

417. —— Some American place-name problems: a letter from Professor Stewart. *American speech* 19:289-92, Dec. 1944.
Discussion of practice of omitting County in county name, and local pronunciations of imported names, questions raised in article by De Lancey Ferguson, Two queries about American place-names, *ibid.* 18:309-10, Dec. 1943.

418. —— What is named?—towns, islands, mountains, rivers, capes. California. University. Publications in English 14:223-32. 1943.
An essay on the principles of naming places, with illustrations drawn chiefly from the naming of the territory of the United States.

419. Still, James A. Place names in the Cumberland Mountains. *American speech* 5:113, Dec. 1929.
Names found in the vicinity of Cumberland Gap.

420. Straubenmuller, Gustave. Meaning of geographical names. *Journal of school geography* 3:332-37. 1899.
"The author has written in a popular style an interesting article about the definitions of topographical words."—Price.

421. Straw, H. Thompson. Geographical gazetteers and the Board on Geographic Names. *Geographical review* 46:274-75, April 1956.
A statement on the work of the Board, especially the series of gazetteers which eventually will achieve world-wide coverage.

422. Survivances françaises en Amérique du Nord: carte des villes et lieux géographiques qui ont conservé des noms français. *Illustration* 196:389, avril 10, 1937.

423. Swanton, John Reed. Early history of the Creek Indians and their neighbors. Washington, Govt. Print. Off., 1922. 492p. (Smithsonian Institution. Bureau of American Ethnology. Bulletin no. 73)
The author contributes accurate information about many place-names.

424. —— Indian names in historical documents. Mississippi Valley Historical Association. Proceedings 3:341-46. 1909-10.

425. Swartz, George. The Tennessee River's name. A letter to Mrs. Howard Jones from Capt. George Swartz. *Arrow points* 15:12, Aug. 1929.

426. Tanner, Henry Schenck. An alphabetical index to the four sheet map of the United States. Philadelphia, Rackliff and Jones, 1836. 99p.

427. —— Memoir on the recent surveys, observations, and internal improvements, in the United States, with brief notices of the new counties, towns, villages, canals, and rail roads, never before delineated. Intended to accompany his New map of the United States. Philadelphia, The Author, 1829. 108p.
Lists of new counties and of new towns for each state and territory included.

428. Taylor, Allan. Communique from C. A. P. N. *New York times* Nov. 6, 1955, Magazine, p. 34, 36.
A member of the Connoisseurs of American Place Names warns that changes in our native nomenclature can go too far.
Reply: by Robert Sonkin, *ibid.* Nov. 20, 1955, p. 5.

429. Taylor, Isaac. Words and places; or, Etymological illustrations of history, ethnology, and geography. 4th ed. rev. and compressed. London, Macmillan, 1873. 375p.
The chapter Names of recent origin deals with American place-names. Also part of the chapter Onomatology, or, The principles of name giving.

430. Territory of Lanniwa. U.S. Congress. Congressional globe, 37th Congress, 2d session, 1861-62, p. 1678, 2495, 2912; 37th Congress, 3d session, 1862-63, p. 25, 915.
A bill to organize the Territory of Lanniwa, a territorial government in the Indian Territory, was tabled.

431. Territory of Shoshone. U.S. Congress. Congressional globe, 37th Congress, 3d session, 1862-63, p. 403.
James M. Ashley's efforts on behalf of a bill to provide a temporary government for the Territory of Shoshone apparently failed.

432. Thomas, George Francis. Legends of the land of lakes; or, History, traditions and mysteries, gleaned from years of experience among the pioneers, voyageurs and Indians; with descriptive accounts of the many natural curiosities met with from Lake Huron to the Columbia River; and the meaning and derivation of names of rivers, lakes, towns, etc. of the Northwest, by George Francis [pseud.]. Chicago, G. F. Thomas, 1884.
pt. 1. Lake Superior and surroundings. pt. 2. Wisconsin.

433. Titular tour. *Atlantic monthly* 154:639-40, Nov. 1934.
Curious American place-names.

434. Tolchin, Martin. More changes in place names urged as Kennedy memorials. *New York times* Nov. 30, 1963, p. 13.

435. Tooker, William Wallace. The adopted Algonquian term "Poquosin." *American anthropologist* n.s. 1:162-70, 790-91, Jan., Oct. 1899.
The writer discusses the derivation and meaning of the word Poquosin, low land or swamp, and its effect on place-names.

436. —— Algonquian names of some mountains and hills. *Journal of American folk-lore* 17:171-79, July-Sept. 1904.

437. —— The Algonquian terms Patawomeke (Potomac) and Massawomeke, with historical and ethnological notes. New York, F. P. Harper, 1901. 02p. (The Algonquian series, VIII)
From the *American anthropologist* 7:174-85, April 1894.

438. —— The name Susquehanna; its origin and signification. *American antiquarian and oriental journal* 15:286-91, Sept. 1893.

439. —— The names Susquehanna and Chesapeake, with historical and ethnological notes. New York, F. P. Harper, 1901. 63p. (The Algonquian series, no. 3)
First printed in the *Virginia magazine of history and biography* 3:86-88, July 1895.

440. Toomey, Thomas Noxon. Proper names from the Muskhogean languages. St. Louis, Hervas Laboratories, 1917. 31p. (Hervas Laboratories of American Linguistics. Bulletin 3)
Literature: p. 31.
Based on a systematic survey of all present-day names of Indian origin in the territory south of Tennessee and South Carolina and east of Texas. Includes a section on personal names.

441. Town names show settlers' whims, map reveals that religious and patriotic instincts were invoked by them. *New York times* Aug. 3, 1930, sec. 8, p. 11, col. 2-4.

442. Towns protest U.S. changes in place names. Citizens petition Board on Geographic Names in long, stubborn fights. *New York herald tribune* Feb. 27, 1949.

443. A Treatise on the art of naming places. *Southern literary messenger* 4:257-61, April 1838.
"In this article some unknown writer shows the prevailing practice in assigning names to places in America. He points out the disadvantages and proposes a better method."—Price.

444. Trumbull, James Hammond. The composition of Indian geographical names, illustrated from the Algonkin languages. Connecticut Historical Society. Collections 2:1-50. 1870.
Also issued separately, Hartford, Case, Lockwood & Brainard, 1870. 51p.
A basic essay on place-name study. This work marks the beginning of sound scholarship in place-name study.

445. —— Pembina. *Magazine of American history* 1:47-48, Jan. 1877.
Proposed name of a new territory in the Northwest. Name is a corruption of the Cree name Nipiminan.

446. U.S. Army. Corps of Engineers. Report of an examination of the Upper Columbia River and the territory in its vicinity in September and October, 1881, to determine its navigability, and adaptability to steamboat transportation. Made by direction of the commanding general of the Department of the Columbia, by Lieut. Thomas W. Symons. Washington, Govt. Print. Off., 1882. 135p. (U.S. 47th Congress, 1st session. Senate. Ex. doc. no. 186)
The geographical nomenclature of the Columbia River region: p. 125-33.

447. U.S. Board on Geographic Names.
History of the Board is as follows:

U.S. Board on Geographic Names.
Established by Executive order Sept. 4, 1890.

U.S. Geographic Board.
Change of name, Aug. 10, 1906.
Abolished by Executive order April 17, 1934 and functions transferred to Dept. of the Interior.

U.S. Board on Geographical Names.
Created by Departmental order no. 1010 of the Dept. of the Interior Dec. 10, 1935.
Abolished by the law of July 25, 1947.

U.S. Board on Geographic Names.
Established by law in the Dept. of the Interior July 25, 1947. Congressional action leading to the establishment of the present Board will be found in U.S. Congress. Congressional record v. 93, 80th Congress, 1st session, 1947 as follows:

H. R. 1555:
p. 711, Jan. 30—Introduced by Mr. Welch and referred to the Committee on Public Lands.
p. 5227, May 13—Committee report submitted; with amendments. Report no. 366. (See no. 453).
p. 9554-55, July 21—Laid on the table. S. 1262 passed in lieu of it. Copy of the bill included.

S. 1262:
p. 4847, May 9—Introduced by Mr. Cordon and referred to the Committee on Public Lands.
p. 5779, May 26—Committee report submitted; without amendment. Report no. 205. (See no. 455).
p. 7008, June 16—Passed the Senate.
p. 9554-55, July 21—Passed the House (in lieu of H. R. 1555). Copies of both H. R. 1555 and S. 1262 are included.
p. 9926, July 24—Examined and signed by President pro-tempore of the Senate.
p. 9982, July 24—Presented to the President of the U.S.
p. 10290, July 26—President of the U.S. approved and signed on July 25. It became Public Law no. 242. (See no. 456).

448. —— Decisions. no. 4301- . July 1943- . Washington, Dept. of the Interior.
Frequency varies: the earlier issues were mostly monthly or quarterly; July 1950-Dec. 1958, cumulative; 1959- , three issues a year, each covering the quarter period.
Following the series of annual pamphlets which ended with June 30, 1943, the Board has published a series of numbered pamphlets containing miscellaneous lists of decisions.
Title varies slightly. Contents vary: 1943-55, most of the issues included, or consisted entirely of, foreign names; 1957- , limited to U.S., with some issues including Puerto Rico and/or the Virgin Islands.
Many issues contain lists of changes from earlier decisions.
The following numbers contain material on names in the United States (for

those which also contain material on Alaska and Canada, see entries under
Alaska and Canada): 4301-4303 (July-Dec. 1943); 4401-4403, 4405, 4408 (Jan.
March, May, Aug. 1944); 4501-4512 (1945); 4601-4609 (Jan.-Sept. 1946); 4701-
4709 (Jan.-Sept. 1947); 4801-4812 (1948); 4903, 4905-4912 (March, May-Dec.
1949); 5003, 5006 (Jan.-March, April-June 1950); 5401 (July 1950-May 1954);
5701 (May 1954-March 1957); 5901 (April 1957-Dec. 1958); 5902-5904 (1959);
6001-6003 (1960); 6101-6103 (1961);6201-6203 (1962); 6301-6303 (1963); 6401-
(1964-).

449. —— Sixth report. 1890 to 1932. Washington, Govt. Print. Off., 1933.
834p.
Supersedes all previous reports. Earlier reports published 1892, 1901, 1906,
1916, 1921, and Index and supp. 1924.
Many of the earlier decisions were published in *National geographic magazine*
v. 11-18, 1900-07.
The Sixth report is supplemented by Decisions, no. 19-41, May 4, 1932—May 2,
1934; and annual issues 1934-35 to 1941-43. In July 1943 a new series of Deci-
sions was started, numbered 4301- (see preceding entry).
A brief administrative report of the Board has appeared in U.S. Dept. of the
Interior. Annual report, 1934-date.
Reviews of the earlier work of the Board are in American Geographical Soci-
ety. Bulletin 22:531-32, 651-56. 1890; 24:162-64, 267-69. 1892; 30:156-57. 1898;
Journal of education (Boston) 67:697-98, June 18, 1908.
Review of 1933 ed.: *New York times* Feb. 19, 1934, p. 15, col. 3-4; *Geographi-
cal review* 25:150-51, Jan. 1935.

450. —— Special decision list no. 1. Commemorative domestic names approved between Sept. 1950 and Feb. 1951. Washington, 1951. 2p.

451. U.S. Bureau of American Ethnology. Circular of information regarding
Indian popular names. Washington, Govt. Print. Off., 1915. 8p.
Camp names: p. 5-6.

452. U.S. Bureau of the Census. Geographic identification code scheme; United
States censuses of population and housing, 1960. Washington, Govt. Print. Off.,
1961. v. p.
"United States P H C (2)-1."
A system of codes to identify all the political and statistical subdivisions for
which data are tabulated. Each state divided into two sections: the Geographic
identification code scheme, which lists all the areas within the state, in alphabetic sequence by county, minor civil division, and place; and an Alphabetical
list of place names, which lists all the places within the state, in alphabetic sequence.

453. U.S. Congress. House. Committee on Public Lands. Promoting uniformity
of geographic nomenclature in the federal government. May 13, 1947... Report
to accompany H. R. 1555. 13p. (U.S. 80th Congress, 1st session. House. Report
no. 366)

454. U.S. Congress. House. Committee on Public Works. Subcommittee on
Flood Control. Flood control projects, authorizing name changes. No. 87-24.
Hearing on H. J. Res. 417, H. R. 9243, H. R. 9320, May 9 and 10, 1962. Wash-
ington, Govt. Print. Off., 1962. 8p.
To designate the lake formed by Terminus Dam on the Kaweah River in

California as Lake Kaweah; to designate the reservoir created by the John H. Kerr Dam (Virginia and North Carolina) as Buggs Island Lake; change in name of the Beardstown, Ill., Flood Control Project, to the Sid Simpson-Beardstown Flood Control Project.

455. U.S. Congress. Senate. Committee on Public Lands. Providing a central authority for standardizing names for the purpose of eliminating duplication in standardizing such names among the Federal departments. May 26 (legislative day, April 21), 1947... Report to accompany S. 1262. 4p. (U.S. 80th Congress, 1st session. Senate. Report no. 205)

456. U.S. Laws, statutes, etc. An act to provide a central authority for standardizing geographic names for the purpose of eliminating duplication in standardizing such names among the Federal departments, and for other purposes. Public law 242. (United States statutes at large. 80th Congress, 1st session. 1947. v. 61, pt. 1, p. 456-57, Chapter 330)
   Establishes Board on Geographic Names and abolishes Board on Geographical Names in the Dept. of the Interior created by Departmental order. Membership of the new Board includes one representative from each of the Depts. of State, War, Navy, Post Office, Interior, Agriculture, and Commerce; from the Government Printing Office; and from the Library of Congress.

457. U.S. Map Information Office. Named peaks of the continental U.S. including Alaska in order of altitude above sea level of 14,000 feet or over. Rev. ed. Washington, 1955. 3 l.

458. U.S. town-city names spell enchantment and surprise. *Omaha world-herald* April 17, 1955, p. 18-G, 19-G.
   Based on the release by the National Geographic Society (see no. 288).

459. U.S. town urged to take the name of Distomo, destroyed by Nazis with 1,100 residents. *New York times* Aug. 31, 1944, p. 19, col. 5.

460. Utley, Francis Lee. The linguistic component of onomastics. *Names* 11:145-76, Sept. 1963.
   This paper was read in much abridged form at Cambridge in Aug. 1962. See the abstract in Preprints of papers for the Ninth International Congress of Linguists (Cambridge, Mass., 1962), p. 105.
   "Onomastics has many components; the question at issue is whether certain of these, like history, logic and etymology, have tended to obscure and overwhelm the potential linguistic component." "American onomastics needs much more linguistic rigor than it has yet acquired." The author makes a plea for a planned national project on place-names for the whole United States, similar to that of the British Isles.

461. Utter, Gus. She finds fun on the map. *Cleveland plain dealer* April 29, 1962.
   Mrs. Anne Celene Solomon has made a hobby of collecting United States names.

462. Vogel, Virgil J. The origin and meaning of "Missouri." Missouri Historical Society. Bulletin 16:213-22, April 1960.
   An examination of the early sources on the name of the Indians and the river.

463. Wagner, Henry Raup. The cartography of the northwest coast of America to the year 1800. Berkeley, Univ. of California Press, 1937. 2v.

List of maps: 2:273-364.
Place names still in use: 2:371-422.
Obsolete place names: 2:423-525.
Bibliography: 2:527-43.

464. —— Quivira, a mythical California city. *California Historical Society quarterly* 3:262-67, Oct. 1924.
Traces the appearance of the name Quivira in various locations on early maps of the northwestern part of America, far from the actual location—northeast of New Mexico—of the city Coronado called Quivira.

465. Wagner, Leopold. More about names. London, Unwin, 1893. 287p.
Popular definitions of Nicknames of American states and people, p. 23-37, and Pet names of American cities, p. 243-47.

466. Wagner, Rudolph F. & Marney H. Wagner. Stories about place names. Portland, Me., J. W. Walch, 1963. 80p.
Bibliography: p. 73.

467. Wallis, Richard P. Names on the lakes. *Inland seas* 14:15-25, Spring 1958. Supplement, by Janet Coe Sanborn, *ibid.* 14:150-51, Summer 1958.
Great Lakes region.

468. Walsh, W. H. No passport needed. *Service* (Cities Service Company). April 1949, p. 14-15, 18.
Names of places in the United States that suggest foreign cities.

469. Walton, Ivan H. Origin of names on the Great Lakes. *Names* 3:239-46, Dec. 1955.
Names of the lakes and their connecting waterways, with some mention of surrounding territory.

470. Watkins, Arthur Vivian. Western place names from Virginia sources; extension of remarks of Hon. Arthur V. Watkins of Utah in the Senate of the United States. U.S. Congress. Congressional record 103:A5009-11, June 24, 1957.
Includes reprint of articles, Bedford-born Mormon bishop gave names to Idaho towns from the *Bedford (Va.) Democrat* of April 18, 1957, and Settlement of Bedford 80 years ago told in bicentennial feature by Kenneth E. Crouch, from the *Star Valley Independent,* Afton, Wyo., of March 22, 1957.
Bedford, Va., and other Bedfords, and the naming of places in the intermountain area.

471. Weidhaas, Walther E. German religious influences on American place names. *American German review* 23:32-34, Aug.-Sept. 1957.

472. Welty, Eudora. Place-names and our history. *New York times book review* May 8, 1945, p. 1.

473. West, Robert C. The term "bayou" in the United States; a study in the geography of place names. Association of American Geographers. Annals 44:63-74, March 1954.
Abstract in its Annals 43:197-98, June 1953.

474. What's in a name? *American magazine* 144:82, Nov. 1947; 144:80, Dec. 1947; 145:130, Jan. 1948; 145:132, Feb. 1948; 145:128, March 1948; 145:65, April 1948.

475. What's in a name? *Bermudian* 33:19, Nov. 1962.
Popular article on meaning of names of the states.

476. What's in a name? *Omaha world-herald* Nov. 3, 1958, p. 8, col. 4.
Quotes Joe Creason in *Louisville courier-journal.*
Lists a few names of places that make interesting combinations when followed by their state abbreviations: High, Mass.; Bless, Me.; Pigs, Penn.

477. What's in a name? *Nation* 108:315, March 1, 1919.
A popular article about some of the freakish names in the United States.

478. What's in a name? Some doubt as U.S. changes 436 for maps. *New York times* July 10, 1960, p. 44.
Brief report on the standardization of 436 place-names throughout the country by the Dept. of the Interior.

479. What's in a name? Worry! *Outlook* 134:449, July 25, 1923.
A brief article on the troubles of the post office with the duplication of place-names.

480. Whitbeck, Ray Hughes. Geographic names in the United States and the stories they tell. *National geographic magazine* 16:100-04, March 1905.

481. —— The meaning of the names of places. *Independent* 72:444-46, Feb. 29, 1912.
Historical effects on place-names in the United States.

482. —— Regional peculiarities in place names. American Geographical Society. Bulletin 43:273-81, April 1911.
"A study of the place-names of New England, New York, New Jersey, Pennsylvania, Virginia and the mountains of Kentucky and Tennessee and their significance, historical, etc."—Griffin.

483. White, Eliot. Sonorous names of states destroyed by abbreviations; our habit of saving time often takes beauty and romance from historical titles. *New York times* Aug. 24, 1930, sec. 3, p. 2., col. 3-4.

484. White, William. Walt Whitman, "Western nicknames": an unpublished note. *American speech* 36:296-98, Dec. 1961.
Names for people of a state, as Buckeye.

485. Whitney, Josiah Dwight. Names and places; studies in geographical and topographical nomenclature. Cambridge, Mass., Univ. Press, 1888. 239p.
Contents: Appalachian and Cordilleran. Oregon and Pend' Oreilles. Topographical nomenclature.

486. Why map makers go mad. *Antiquarian bookman* 20:1343, Oct. 28, 1957.
Name changes and some origins.

487. Wilkins, Ernest Hatch. Arcadia in America. American Philosophical

Society. Proceedings 101:4-30, Feb. 15, 1957.

A well-documented study tracing the use of the name Arcadia and all its various spellings from earliest maps and journals to place-names in the United States, Canada, and South America today. All derive from the name of a novel Arcadia by Jacopo Sannazzaro, written *ca.* 1485.

For further information on the process by which Arcadie became Acadie see the author's article Ar Cadie, no. 3200.

488. Wilson, Herbert M. A dictionary of topographic forms. American Geographic Society of New York. Bulletin 32:32-41, July 1900.

A list of definitions intended to include all those terms employed popularly or technically in the United States to designate the component parts of the surface of the earth.

489. Wilson, P. W. Far-gathered names of our cities; the world's geography and history have contributed to the stories they tell. *New York times magazine* April 9, 1933, p. 18.

490. Wolle, Muriel Vincent Sibell. The bonanza trail, ghost towns and mining camps of the West. Bloomington, Indiana Univ. Press, 1953. 510p.

491. —— From "Sailors' Diggings" to "Miners' Delight." (How mining towns are named) *Western folklore* 13:40-46, Jan. 1954.

492. Wraight, A. J. Field work in the U.S. C. and G. S. *Names* 2:153-62, Sept. 1954.

How the U.S. Coast and Geodetic Survey carries out its field work on geographic names.

493. Wrenn, C. L. The name Bristol. *Names* 5:65-70, June 1957.

A study of the English origin of the name.

494. Wright, John Kirtland. The study of place names, recent work and some possibilities. *Geographical review* 19:140-44, Jan. 1929.

Most American studies have been of the accumulative or collective type rather than the ecological in which "investigation is made into the nature of the geographical nomenclature in the large and more especially in its relation to the environment, past and present, physical and human."

495. The Wrong state. *New York times* Jan. 13, 1940, p. 14, col. 4; Jan. 17, p. 20, col. 4.

Arkansas City, Kan., and other state names used for cities.

496. You name it! *Home life* Jan. 1955, p. 12-13.

Popular article on names in the United States.

497. Yount, W. H. Origin of the name Ozark Mountains. *Missouri historical review* 20:587-88, July 1926.

A brief article which also appeared in the *Barnard bulletin* March 18, 1926, on the derivation of the name.

498. Zelinsky, Wilbur. Generic terms in the place-names of the northeastern United States: an approach to the demarcation of culture areas. Association of

American Geographers. Annals 44:288-89, Sept. 1954.
Abstract.

499. ——— Some problems in the distribution of generic terms in the place-names of the northeastern United States. Association of American Geographers. Annals 45:319-49, Dec. 1955.

UNITED STATES—GAZETTEERS

500. Alcedo, Antonio de. Diccionario geográfico-histórico de las Indias Occidentales ó América: es á saber: de los reynos del Perú, Nueva España, Tierra Firme, Chile, y Nuevo reyno de Granada. Madrid, En la impr. de B. Cano, 1786-89. 5v.

501. ——— The geographical and historical dictionary of America and the West Indies. Containing an entire translation of the Spanish work of Colonel Don Antonio de Alcedo, with large additions and compilations from modern voyages and travels, and from original and authentic information. By G. A. Thompson. London, Printed for J. Carpenter, 1812-15. 5v.

Atlas to Thompson's Alcedo. London, Printed by G. Smeeton, 1816.
Descriptions of Jamaica, Newtown, and Flushing, N.Y., and others are strangely reminiscent of Jedidiah Morse, The American gazetteer (see no. 522).

502. Allen, William Frederick. Gazetteer of railway stations in the United States and the Dominion of Canada. Designating telegraph, express, post, and money-order offices, with the population. Also, a list of the counties and county towns of the several states, with the date at which the several courts are held, together with much other valuable statistical information. Comp. from information obtained from official sources. Philadelphia, National Railway Publication Co., 1874. 412p.

503. The American gazetteer. Containing a distinct account of all the parts of the New World: their situation, climate, soil, produce, former and present condition; commodities, manufactures, and commerce. Together with an accurate account of the cities, towns, ports, bays, rivers, lakes, mountains, passes and fortifications. London, Printed for A. Millar, 1762. 3v.

Translation published: Il Gazzettiere americano. Livorno, M. Coltellini, 1763. 3v.

504. Baldwin, Thomas & J. Thomas. A new and complete gazetteer of the United States; giving a full and comprehensive review of the present condition, industry, and resources of the American confederacy. Philadelphia, Lippincott, Grambo & Co., 1854. 1364p.

505. Bradstreet, J. M. & Son. Gazetteer of the manufactures and manufacturing towns of the United States, containing a full and comprehensive review of the extent and condition of the manufacturing interests and resources of the United States, including a large amount of valuable geographical, geological, topographical, historical and statistical information, carefully comp. from recent reliable and original sources to the present date. New York, J. M. Bradstreet & Son, 1866. 172p.

506. Chapin, William. A complete reference gazetteer of the United States of North America; containing a general view of the United States, and of each state and territory, and a notice of the various canals, railroads and internal improvements. New York, T. & E. H. Ensign, 1843. 371p.
Earlier editions published 1838, 1839, 1840, 1841.

507. Colange, Leo de. The national gazetteer; a geographical dictionary of the United States, comp. from the latest official authorities and original sources. Cincinnati, J. C. Yorston & Co.; Philadelphia, G. Barrie, 1884. 1125p.
Also published London, Hamilton, Adams & Co., 1884.

508. Darby, William & Theodore Dwight. A new gazetteer of the United States of America, including geographical, historical, political, and statistical information; with the population of 1830. 2d ed. rev. Hartford, E. Hopkins, 1834. 608p.
1st ed. 1833. 630p. The 2d ed. reprinted 1835.

509. Davenport, Bishop. A history and new gazetteer, or geographical dictionary, of North America and the West Indies. Comp. from the most recent and authentic sources. A new and much improved ed. New York, S. W. Benedict & Co., 1842. 592p.
Earlier editions published in Baltimore, Philadelphia, and Providence, 1832, 1833, 1835, 1836, 1838 under title A new gazetteer.

510. ―――― A pocket gazetteer, or Traveller's guide through North America and the West Indies; containing a description of all the states, territories, counties, cities, towns, villages, seas, bays, harbors, islands, capes, railroads, canals, &c. connected with North America, and the West Indies, to which is added a large amount of statistical information, relating to the population, revenue, debt, and various institutions of the United States. Comp. from the most recent and authentic sources. Baltimore, Plaskitt & Co., 1833. 468p.
Also published in Trenton, N.J.
Other editions published 1834, 1838.

511. Fanning's illustrated gazetteer of the United States, with the population and other statistics from the census of 1850. Illus. with seals and thirty-one state maps in counties and fourteen maps of cities. New York, Phelps, Fanning & Co., 1853. 400p.

512. Fisher, Richard Swainson. A new and complete statistical gazetteer of the United States of America, founded on and comp. from official federal and state returns, and the census of 1850. New York, J. H. Colton and Co., 1855. 960p.
Also published 1852, 1853.

513. Gannett, Henry. A dictionary of altitudes in the United States. 4th ed. Washington, Govt. Print. Off., 1906. 1072p. (U.S. Geological Survey. Bulletin no. 274) (Subject series F, Geography, 47)
Issued also as House doc. no. 207, 59th Cong., 1st sess.
1st ed. 1884. 325p. (Bulletin no. 5); 2d ed. 1891. 393p. (Bulletin no. 76); 3d ed. 1899. 775p. (Bulletin no. 160)
Arranged by states, except 2d ed. which is in a single alphabetic arrangement.
Included for its gazetteer value.

514. ―――― The mountains of the United States. Washington, Map Information Office, Board of Surveys and Maps, 1928?. 37p.

515. Haskel, Daniel & J. Calvin Smith. A complete descriptive and statistical gazetteer of the United States of America with an abstract of the census and statistics for 1840, exhibiting a complete view of the agricultural, commercial, manufacturing, and literary condition and resources of the country. New York, Sherman & Smith, 1850. 770p.
Also published 1843, 1844, 1845.

516. —— Vollständiges Orts-Lexikon der Vereinigten Staaten von Nordamerika. Nach amtlichen und zuverlässigen Quellen. Hildburghausen, Druck und Verlag des Bibliographischen Instituts in Hildburghausen, 1852. 1108p.
"Based on the 1845 ed. of the above, with new material added to bring the work down to the year 1850."—L. C. card.

517. Hayward, John. A gazetteer of the United States of America to which are added valuable statistical tables, and a map of the United States. Hartford, Case, Tiffany, and Co., 1853. 861p.

518. Heck, Lewis. The problem of a national gazetteer. *Names* 1:233-38, Dec. 1953.

519. Logan's post-office, census, express, telegraph, railroad and river directory of the entire West & South, containing the names of all post-offices with a supplement complete to June, 1875. St. Louis, N. Orleans, Logan Pub. Co., 1875. 100, 30p.

520. Mitchell, Samuel Augustus. An accompaniment to Mitchell's reference and distance map of the United States: containing an index of the various counties, districts, parishes, townships, towns, etc., and an index of the rivers; together with a geographical description of every state and territory in the Union; also an accurate synopsis of the population in the year 1840, according to the sixth census, and a synopsis of the new postage law. Philadelphia, S. A. Mitchell, 1845. 302, 208p.
Also published 1834, 1835, 1836, 1839, 1840.

521. Morse, Jedidiah. An abridgement of the American gazetteer. Exhibiting, in alphabetical order, a compendious account of the states, provinces, counties, cities, rivers, bays, harbours on the American continent, and its appendant islands; particularly the West Indies. To which is annexed an accurate table of all the post-offices in the United States. Pub. according to act of Congress. Printed at Boston, by Thomas & Andrews. Sold by them, by E. Larkin, and other booksellers, in Boston; by I. Thomas, Worcester; by Thomas, Andrews & Penniman, Albany; and by Thomas, Andrews & Butler, Baltimore. June 1798. 388p.
Also published in London, 1798.

522. —— The American gazetteer, exhibiting a full account of the civil divisions, rivers, harbors, Indian tribes, &c. of the American continent: also of the West-India and other appendant islands: with a particular description of Louisiana. Comp. from the best authorities. Illus. with maps, and accompanied by a new and elegant general atlas of the world. 3d ed. rev. and cor. Boston, Thomas & Andrews, 1810. 600p.
1st ed. Boston, 1797; 2d ed. Boston, 1798, London, 1798, Charleston, 1804.
The decision to compile and publish this was reached in 1786 while Morse was traveling for the purpose of collecting material for his American geography. The gazetteer was delayed by the work of revising the geography. Capt. Thomas

Hutchins, Geographer General of the United States, had started a similar project, but upon learning of Morse's intention turned over to him all of his material. Morse said also, "After all it is but proper here to observe, that a very considerable part of the matter of this volume has been selected and alphabetically arranged, under the proper heads, from The American universal geography."
cf. Preface, London ed. 1798, dated Charleston, June 1, 1797.
  cf. also note under Joseph Scott, The United States gazetteer, no. 528.

523. ——— & Richard C. Morse. The traveller's guide; or, Pocket gazetteer of the United States; extracted from the latest ed. of Morse's Universal gazetteer. With an appendix. 2d ed. enl., rev., and cor. New Haven, S. Wadsworth, 1826. 336p.
  1st ed. New Haven, N. Whiting, 1823. 323p.
  Review: *United States literary gazette* 4:305-06, July 1826.

524. The North-American and the West-Indian gazetteer. Containing an authentic description of the colonies and islands in that part of the globe, shewing their situation, soil, produce, and trade; with their former and present condition. Also an exact account of the cities, towns, harbours, ports, bays, rivers, lakes, mountains, number of inhabitants, &c. Illus. with maps. 2d ed. London, G. Robinson, 1778. 218p.
  1st ed. London, G. Robinson, 1776. 220p.

525. Rand McNally geographical handbook. Chicago, Rand, McNally, 1942. 128p.
  On cover: A keyed index of the United States. All counties, all cities and towns of over 100 population.
  Also published 1932.

526. Rowell, George P. & Co. Geo. P. Rowell & Co's gazetteer, containing a statement of the industries, characteristics, population and location of all towns in the United States and British America, in which newspapers are published. New York, G. P. Rowell & Co., 1873. 243p.

527. Scott, Joseph. A geographical dictionary; of the United States of North America. Containing a general description of each state. With a succinct account of Indiana, Michigan, and upper and lower Louisiana territories. Philadelphia, Printed by Archibald Bartram, for Jacob Johnson, and Co., 1805. 584p.

528. ——— The United States gazetteer: containing an authentic description of the several states. Their situation, extent, boundaries, soil, produce, climate, population, trade and manufactures. Together with the extent, boundaries and population of their respective counties. Illus. with nineteen maps. Philadelphia, Printed by F. and R. Bailey, 1795. 292p.
  Although said to be the first gazetteer of the United States, Jedidiah Morse, in the Preface to his The American gazetteer, dated Charleston, June 1, 1797, says, "From this work [The American universal geography, by Morse], Mr. Scott, author of the Gazetteer of the United States, derived no small part of the information contained in his book, though he has not been candid enough to acknowledge it in his preface."—p. v, London ed. 1798.

529. Steinwehr, Adolph Wilhelm August Friedrich von. The centennial gazetteer of the United States. A geographical and statistical encyclopaedia of the states, territories, counties, townships etc. in the American union. Philadelphia,

Cincinnati, Ziegler & McCurdy, 1873. 1016p.
Reprinted 1874.

530. U.S. Map Information Office. Principal lakes in the United States. Preliminary ed. 1929. Washington, 1929. 4p.

531. U.S. Post Office Dept. Directory of post offices. Washington, 1955- .
Replaces U.S. official postal guide, Part 1, Domestic.
1955-56 kept up to date by loose-leaf pages; 1957- , revised annually, kept up to date by changes in the Postal bulletin, which is published weekly.
Includes military installations with post offices. Lists post offices discontinued and names changed.

532. ——— Post offices by counties. Washington, 1955-56. 2v.
Replaces the county list formerly contained in the U.S. official postal guide, Part 1. Was to have been revised and reissued annually as of July 1, but only two issues were published.

533. ——— Street directory of the principal cities of the United States, embracing letter carrier offices established to April 30, 1908. Rev. in the Division of Dead Letters under the direction of P. V. De Graw, Fourth Assistant Postmaster-General. 5th ed. Washington, Govt. Print. Off., 1908. 904p.
1st ed. 1881; 2d ed. 1884; 3d ed. 1891; 4th ed. 1894.

534. ——— United States official postal guide. Washington, U.S. Govt. Print. Off., 1874- .
Various official and unofficial editions were published, 1800-1873.
Includes list of post offices, and shows changes in names made by the Department over the years.

535. Upham, Warren. Altitudes between Lake Superior and Rocky Mountains. Washington, Govt. Print. Off., 1891. 229p. (U.S. Geological Survey. Bulletin no. 72)
By places along railway lines, including supplementary lists, With indexes for Hills and mountains; Lakes; and Towns and stations.

536. Worcester, Joseph Emerson. A gazetteer of the United States, abstracted from the Universal gazetteer of the author; with enlargement of the principal articles. Andover, Mass., Printed for the author by Flagg and Gould, 1818. 358p.

UNITED STATES—ITS NAME

537. American names. *Democratic review* 11:475-81, Nov. 1842.
Primarily concerned with the name United States, which should be changed because of its ambiguous nature.

538. Barnes, Homer Francis. Charles Fenno Hoffman. New York, Columbia Univ. Press, 1930. 361p. (Columbia University studies in English and comparative literature)
p. 160-65 describes the controversy over the name Alleghania proposed by a committee of the New York Historical Society, of which Hoffman was a member.

539.   Boggs, Ralph Steele. The baffling designation "American." *American speech* 24:312-13, Dec. 1949.
Use for residents of the United States.

540.   Burnett, Edmund C. The name "United States of America." *American historical review* 31:79-81, Oct. 1925.
"Some early instances of the use of the name, showing how it gradually became the official name."—*American speech.*

541.   Douglass, C. H. J. Our national name—what does it mean? *New Englander* 40:629-34, Sept. 1881.
History and meaning of the name United States of America.

542.   Dunlap, Leslie Whittaker. American historical societies, 1790-1860. Madison, Wis., Privately printed, 1944. 238p.
On p. 117-19 he tells of the proposal made in 1845 by the New York Historical Society to change the national name of the country from America to Allegania.

543.   Fitzpatrick, John C. The "United States of America" and the "U.S.A." *Daughters of the American Revolution magazine* 54:17-20, Jan. 1920.
Also in his The spirit of the Revolution. Boston, Houghton Mifflin, 1924. p. 228-36.
Congress decided that kegs of gunpowder be inspected and marked U.S.A. if acceptable, 1776.

544.   Irving, Washington. National nomenclature, by Geoffrey Crayon [pseud.]. *Knickerbocker* 14:158-62, 203, Aug. 1839.
Reprinted in his Biographies and miscellanies, ed. by Pierre M. Irving. New York, Putnam, 1866. p. 522-30.
Includes remarks on a national name for the United States.

545.   Jones, Joseph. Hail Fredonia! *American speech* 9:12-17, Feb. 1934; 11:187, April 1936.
The lack of a suitable name for the United States and the attempt to introduce Fredonia about 1804-12. Takes Samuel Latham Mitchill's article Generic names . . . , which is reprinted here in full, too seriously.

546.   Maclellan, W. E. America. *Dalhousie review* 7:523-24, Jan. 1928.
Application of the title Americans to the people of the United States justified.

547.   Mitchill, Samuel Latham. An address to the Fredes, or people of the United States on the 28th anniversary of their Independence. New York, G. & R. Waite, 1804. 8p.
Poem in which author asserts "that Fredonia is a cant phrase which certain 'small scribblers or prosaic poets' would have the nation adopt."—Courtney Robert Hall, A scientist in the early republic. New York, Columbia Univ. Press, 1934. p. 116.

548.   —— Generic names for the country and people of the United States. *Monthly anthology* 1:342-45, June 1804.
Originally published in the *New York daily advertiser.*
Reprinted in *Monthly magazine, or British register* 23:242-44, April 1807. Submitted by John Coakley Lettsom.
Reprinted also in article by Joseph Jones, Hail Fredonia. *American speech*

9:12-17, Feb. 1934.
Suggests the use of Fredonia; perhaps an attempt at humor in the eyes of the editor of the *Monthly anthology*.

549. Moore, George H. The name "Columbia." Massachusetts Historical Society. Proceedings 2d ser. 2:159-65, Dec. 1885.
Traces the use of the name Columbia for America, both in England and in the United States.

550. New York Historical Society. Report of the Committee on a National Name; *In its* Proceedings 1845:18-22, 115-24, 209-29.
Also published separately and sent to historical societies and prominent individuals.
Includes resolution calling for the selection of a specific name, and that Allegania be recommended as the best. The society voted in the negative. The committee included David Dudley Field, Henry Rowe Schoolcraft, and Charles Fenno Hoffman.
Massachusetts Historical Society. Proceedings 2:310-11, 315-17, April-May 1845, notes receipt of the New York report, with reply that there is no reason for discarding United States of America.

551. Nörrenberg, Constantin. Aussprache über America—U.S. America. *Petermanns Mitteilungen aus Justus Perthes' geographischer Anstalt* 63:306-09, Oct. 1917.

552. Proposal of a general name for the United States. *Monthly anthology* 1:217-18, March 1804.
Signed: "A National man."
Discussion of Jedidiah Morse's suggestion (in The American gazetteer) that the name be Fredonia.

553. Stovall, Benjamin F. Now we U-S-ians. *Literary digest* 124:2, Nov. 13, 1937.
"Suggests 'Uessian' (U-S-ian) instead of 'American' since 'American' rightly belongs to any person in North or South America."—*American speech*.

554. Tudor, William. Concerning a name for the United States. *Monthly anthology* 1:293-97, May 1804.
Letter to editor conveying Tudor's article was signed "Aconteus." Article dated Dec. 1799.
Proposes use of Columbia.

555. Tyler, Moses Coit. The historic name of our country. American Historical Association. Papers 3:176-78. 1889.
Abstract.
America should be the name, not the United States of America.

556. Willson, Beckles. Must we be Americans. *University magazine* 13:59-67, Feb. 1914.
Since the terms America and American have been appropriated by the United States, they should be restricted to that nation and not applied in a broader sense to include Canadians and South Americans.

557. Zabriskie, George A. Why we are called Americans. New York Historical

Society. Quarterly bulletin 27:79-86, Oct. 1943.
Includes also a note on a national name, as Republic of Washington, Columbia, or Allegania.

ALABAMA

558. Adams, John D. Coosa County; present day place names showing aboriginal influence. *Arrow points* 2:73-75, April 1921.

559. Alabama county names. *Magazine of history* 25:54-59, Aug. 1917.

560. Bibb, J. Porter. Montgomery County; present day place names showing aboriginal influence. *Arrow points* 2:14-17, Jan. 1921.

561. Bonner, Jessie Lee. Where Oak Hill got its name. *Arrow points* 12:23, March 1926.
Legendary account of the place-name.

562. Brame, J. Y. Lowndes County; present day place names showing aboriginal influence. *Arrow points* 2:55-56, March 1921.

563. Brannon, Peter A. Aboriginal towns in Alabama; showing locations by present county boundary lines. *Arrow points* 4:26-28, Feb. 1922.

564. ——— Alabama postoffice and stream names, 1922; a study of the etymology of the names of the state's present postoffices and streams. *Arrow points* 6:3-7, Jan. 1923.
Detailed account of locations having aboriginal significance followed by a list giving the modern post offices in their present spellings and a parallel list giving their aboriginal nationalities. Further list gives rivers and 25 of the largest streams still called by their native names.

565. ——— Barbour County. *Arrow points* 5:32-37, Aug. 1922.
Present day place-names showing aboriginal influence.

566. ——— Certain place names in Choctaw County. *Arrow points* 11:8-12, July 1925.

567. ——— Clay County; present day place names showing aboriginal influence. *Arrow points* 3:56-58, Oct. 1921; 4:96-98, May 1922.

568. ——— County names in Alabama history. *Arrow points* 6:33-34, Jan. 1923.

569. ——— Elmore County; present day place names suggesting aboriginal influence. *Arrow points* 4:46-51, March 1922.

570. ——— Jackson County place-names; a study of the names, suggesting the aboriginal history of the county. *Arrow points* 13:9-11, Sept. 1928.

571. ——— Macon County; present day place names suggesting aboriginal influence. *Arrow points* 5:5-9, July 1922.

572. ——— Monroe County; some sketches of its places. *Arrow points* 8:39-42, March 1924.

573. ——— The name "Alabama." *Arrow points* 10:19-21, Jan. 1925.
   Thorough etymological and historical analysis of the state name, discrediting the traditional and poetic translation, "Here we rest."

574. ——— Name places affected by the Indian war of 1813-14. *Alabama historical quarterly* 13:132-35. 1951.

575. ——— Pike County; present day place names suggesting aboriginal influence. *Arrow points* 3:18-19, Aug. 1921.

576. ——— Place names in Clarke County. *Arrow points* 6:103-07, June 1923.

577. ——— Russell County place names; present day names perpetuating aboriginal and early historic points in the county. *Alabama historical quarterly* 21:96-103. 1959.
   Embodies in a measure a paper very similar and published in *Arrow points* v. 1, Oct. 5, 1920. Apparently a reprint of the article as published in *Arrow points* 8:5-12, Jan. 1924.

   On p. 104 of *Alabama historical quarterly* v. 21, 1959: Origin of county name. This is about Gilbert Christian Russell, reprinted from Heitman, Historical register, U.S. Army, v. 1, p. 853.

578. ——— Tallapoosa County; present day place names suggesting aboriginal influence. *Arrow points* 3:46-49, Sept. 1921; 5:104-08, Dec. 1922.

579. Brown, Virginia Pounds & Jane Porter Nabers. The origin of certain place names in Jefferson County, Alabama. *Alabama review* 5:177-202, July 1952.

580. Chase, Carroll & Richard McP. Cabeen. The first hundred years of United States territorial postmarks, 1787-1887. Alabama Territory. *American philatelist* 55:78-82, Nov. 1941.
   Includes list of post offices, 1817-19, with notes on origin of some names.

581. ——— The first hundred years of United States territorial postmarks, 1787-1887. Mississippi Territory. *American philatelist* 55:220-26, Jan. 1942.
   Includes list of post offices, 1803-17, with notes on some names.

582. Danton, Emily Miller. Alabama place names, a selection. *Alabama review* 9:68-69, Jan. 1956.
   Includes towns and communities, rivers and creeks. Omits Indian names.

583. Edwards, Thomas H. Lee County; present day place names showing aboriginal influence. *Arrow points* 2:112-14, June 1921.

584. Elmore, Frank H. Baldwin County; present day place names showing aboriginal influence. *Arrow points* 4:13-15, Jan. 1922.

585. Foscue, Virginia Oden. Sumter County place-names: a selection. *Alabama review* 13:52-67, Jan. 1960.
   Abstracted from M.A. thesis, Univ. of Alabama, Dept. of English, Aug. 1959.

586. Gatschet, Albert Samuel. Towns and villages of the Creek Confederacy in the XVIII. and XIX. centuries. Alabama History Commission. Report 1:386-415. 1900.
Reprinted separately.
Rev. and largely supplemented from the list in his A Creek migration legend. Philadelphia, 1884. 1:120-50.

587. Halbert, Henry Sale. Choctaw Indian names in Alabama and Mississippi. Alabama Historical Society. Transactions 3:64-77. 1898-99.

588. Hoppen, Harry E. Randolph County; present day place names showing aboriginal influence. *Arrow points* 2:86-87, May 1921.

589. Jenkins, William H. Some Alabama "dead" towns. *Alabama review* 12:281-85, Oct. 1959.

590. McNeel, Allen. Escamba County; present day place names showing aboriginal influence. *Arrow points* 2:32-35, Feb. 1921.

591. Maxwell, Thomas. Tuskaloosa, the origin of its name, its history, etc. A paper read before the Alabama Historical Society, July 1, 1876. Tuskaloosa, Office of the Tuskaloosa gazette, 1876. 86p.

592. Meaning of the Creek Indian name Eufaula. *Chronicles of Oklahoma* 40:310-11, Autumn 1962.
A city in Alabama and Oklahoma.

593. Names in Alabama. *New York times* March 16, 1929, p. 18, col. 5.
Notes beauty in Alabama river names.

594. Nelson, Mildred N. Folk etymology of Alabama place-names. *Southern folklore quarterly* 14:193-214, Dec. 1950.

595. Owen, Thomas McAdory. Alabama: state name, boundaries, capitol, executive mansion, seal, flag, holidays, song and flower. Montgomery, Brown Print. Co., 1915. 11p. (Alabama. Archives and History Dept. O. S. R. separate no. 1)
Reprinted from Alabama. Dept. of Archives and History. Alabama official and statistical register 1915:7-15.

596. ——— Jefferson County; present day place names showing aboriginal influence. *Arrow points* 3:10-11, July 1921.

597. Read, William Alexander. Indian place-names in Alabama. Baton Rouge, Louisiana State Univ. Press, 1937. 84p. (Louisiana State University studies, no. 29)
Bibliography: p. 80-84.
Supplemented in *American speech* 13:79-80, Feb. 1938.
"Deals with the origin and meaning of Indian geographical names in Alabama. It does not include a detailed history either of aboriginal place-names in Alabama or of the tribes that inhabited the state. Its primary aim is linguistic."—Review by J. R. Swanton, *American speech* 12:212-15, Oct. 1937.

598. ——— Ten Alabama place names. *American speech* 13:79-80, Feb. 1938.

599. Robertson, Ann Eliza Worcester. Some Choctaw names. *Arrow points* 19:15-16, Aug. 1931.

600. Scaife, Walter Bell. Was the Rio del Espiritu Santo of the Spanish geographers the Mississippi? *In his* America: its geographical history, 1492-1892. Baltimore, Johns Hopkins Press, 1892. p. 139-72.
    An examination of maps and early writings convinced the author that "the Mississippi was not discovered by Pinedo, and that the early Spaniards did not know that river under the name Espiritu Santo; but... they applied this name, generally, if not exclusively, to the stream which now bears, in its different parts, the names Coosa, Alibama, and Mobile."

601. Street, O. D. Cherokee towns and villages in Alabama. Alabama History Commission. Report 1:416-21. 1900.

602. U.S. 88th Congress, 1st session. House. A bill to designate the lake formed by the Walter F. George Lock and Dam, Alabama and Georgia, as "Lake Chattahoochee." H. R. 2127. Jan. 17, 1963. Washington, 1963. 1p.
    Introduced by Mr. Forrester and referred to the Committee on Public Works.

603. U.S. 88th Congress, 1st session. Senate. A bill to designate the lake formed by the Walter F. George Lock and Dam, Alabama and Georgia, as Lake Eufaula. S. 454. Jan. 23 (legislative day, Jan. 15), 1963. Washington, 1963. 1p.
    Introduced by Mr. Hill and Mr. Sparkman and referred to the Committee on Public Works.
    An identical bill was introduced in the House as follows:

    U.S. 88th Congress, 1st session. House. A bill to designate the lake formed by the Walter F. George Lock and Dam, Alabama and Georgia, as Lake Eufaula. H. R. 3163. Jan. 31, 1963. Washington, 1963. 1p.
    Introduced by Mr. Andrews and referred to the Committee on Public Works.

ALASKA

604. Alaska. Office of the Governor. Community gazetteer of Alaska, including geographic coordinates and latest population figures, issued jointly by Office of the Governor, Department of Health & Welfare, Department of Labor, Alaska Legislative Council. Juneau, Alaska, 1964. [69]p.

605. Alaska town's name changed by colonists. *New York times* May 20, 1935, p. 17, col. 2.
    Palmer, Alaska, changed informally to Valley City, by a group of Minnesota colonists.

606. Alaskan and Canadian nomenclature. American Geographical Society. Bulletin 29:439-40. 1897.
    The U.S. Board on Geographical Names has imposed artificial spelling on points in the Upper Yukon region in case of Indian names.

607. Baker, Marcus. Alaskan geographic names. U.S. Geological Survey. Annual report 21:487-509. 1899-1900.
    Also published separately.

608. —— Geographic dictionary of Alaska. 2d ed. Prepared by James Mc-
Cormick. Washington, Govt. Print. Off., 1906. 690p. (U.S. Geological Survey.
Bulletin no. 299)
   Issued also as House doc. no. 938. 59th Cong., 1st sess.
   1st ed. 1902. Bulletin no. 187.
   Includes obsolete and current names.

609. Chase, Carroll & Richard McP. Cabeen. The first hundred years of United
States territorial postmarks, 1787-1887. Alaska Territory. *American philatelist*
55:82-85, Nov. 1941.
   Includes list of post offices, 1867-87.

610. Clark, John Drury & L. Sprague De Camp. Some Alaskan place names.
American speech 15:60-61, Feb. 1940.

611. Coolidge settled dispute, decided lakes and peaks called after explorers in
Alaska should stand. *New York times* Jan. 22, 1928, p. 19, col. 1-3.
   Decision two years earlier in regard to names in Valley of Ten Thousand
Smokes which overruled U.S. Geographic Board in favor of National Geographic
Society.
   Editorial *ibid.* sec. 3, p. 4, col. 5 outlines U.S. Board's rule against naming
places for living persons.

612. Davidson, George. Origin of the name "Cape Nome." *National geographic
magazine* 12:398, Nov. 1901.
   Illustrates the manner in which a permanent place-name will result from a
series of mistakes due to misinterpretations.

613. DeArmond, R. N. Some names around Juneau. Sitka, Sitka Print. Co.,
1957. 48p.
   An alphabetical list of 123 names for 142 places or geographic features in
Juneau and its immediate vicinity, plus some 70 obsolete or seldom-used names
mentioned in the text. Locates the place and gives origin of the name.

614. Farquhar, Francis Peloubet. Naming Alaska's mountains, with some accounts of their ascents. *American alpine journal* v. 11, no. 2, p. 211-32. 1959.

615. Forbes, H. A. Gazetteer of northern Canada and parts of Alaska and
Greenland. Ottawa, Geographical Bureau, 1948. 75 l.

616. Jacobin, Louis. Guide to Alaska and the Yukon. 11th ed. Los Angeles,
Guide to Alaska Co., 1957.
   The towns and villages—how they got their names: p. 51.
   This same list, with slight variations, has appeared in each edition.

617. Kennedy name to city in Alaska. *Kansas City times* Dec. 27, 1963.
   Bay City changed to John Fitzgerald Kennedy City effective Dec. 20, 1963.

618. Kiska to be known as Narukam and Attu as Atsuta. *New York times* June
26, 1942, p. 7, col. 2.
   Japanese broadcast said renamed by Japs, after landing there June 7, 1942.

619. Kodiak not Kadiak. *National geographic magazine* 12:397-98, Nov. 1901.

With the reversal of a decision by the U.S. Board on Geographic Names, Kadiak became Kodiak.

620. Lake named Rose Teed by army in Alaska; engineers mapping area find one with an hour-glass figure. *New York times* Nov. 29, 1942, p. 32, col. 3.
On Kodiak Island.

621. New names on the International Boundary. *Geographical journal* 62:234-35, Sept. 1923.
A glacier and several peaks.

622. Putnam, G. R. Geographic names in Alaska. U.S. Coast and Geodetic Survey. Annual report 1902-03:1011-16.
List of native names for localities on St. George Island, Bering Sea. Russian or Aleut origin indicated as well as meaning.

623. Ransom, J. Ellis. Derivation of the word "Alaska." *American anthropologist* n.s. 42:550-51, July-Sept. 1940.
Philological study of the word in Aleut.

624. Ransome, Alfred L. & William H. Kerns. Names and definitions of regions, districts and subdistricts in Alaska (used by the Bureau of Mines in statistical and economic studies covering the mineral industry of the territory). Washington, U.S. Bureau of Mines, 1954. 91p. (U.S. Bureau of Mines. Information circular no. 7679)

625. Stewart, George Rippey. Alaska; *In his* Names on the land; a historical account of place-naming in the United States. Rev. and enl. ed. Boston, Houghton Mifflin, 1958. p. 386-412.

626. ——— The name Alaska. *Names* 4:193-204, Dec. 1956.
Presents the general outlines of the process by which Alaska has become a notable name; some details of the process remain to be filled in.

627. Thalbitzer, William. Eskimoiske stednavne fra Alaska til Grønland set i arkaêologieno lys. *Geografisk tidsskrift* 35:137-55. 1932.
"Eskimo place names in Alaska and Greenland in the light of archaeology. Summary in English."—Griffin.

628. U.S. Board on Geographic Names. Decisions. Washington, Dept. of the Interior.
Alaska is included in the following Decision lists: 4301 (July-Oct. 1943); 4401-4402, 4404, 4408 (Jan.-Feb., April, Aug. 1944); 4501-4503, 4510-4512 (Jan.-March, Oct.-Dec. 1945); 4601-4609 (Jan.-Sept. 1946); 4704-4707 (April-July 1947); 4801-4812 (1948); 4903, 4905-4912 (March, May-Dec. 1949); 5003, 5006 (Jan.-June, 1950); 5401 (July 1950-May 1954); 5701 (May 1954-March 1957); 5901- (April 1957-).

629. ——— Decisions on names in Alaska. June 1952. Washington, Dept. of the Interior, 1952. 16p. (*Its* Decision list no. 5204)
"In effect as of May 1952."

630. ——— Decisions on names in Alaska, Saint Lawrence Island. March 1951. Washington, Dept. of the Interior, 1951. 25p. (*Its* Decision list no. 5102)

"Comprises all decisions rendered for Saint Lawrence Island, Alaska, and associated features."

631. U.S. Board on Geographic Names. American Geographical Society. Bulletin 22:326-32. 1890.
Reports formation of the Board, and announces project to prepare Alaskan name list.

632. U.S. Map Information Office. Named and best known mountain peaks in Alaska, 10,000 feet or over. Washington, 1955. 2 l.

633. U.S. Work Projects Administration. Pennsylvania. Geographic names in the coastal areas of Alaska. Comp. under the supervision of the Coast and Geodetic Survey by personnel of Works [sic] Projects Administration, Project OP-765-23-3-7, in the city of Philadelphia, Pa., 1939-40. Washington, 1943. 133p.

634. Wagner, Henry Raup. The cartography of the northwest coast of America to the year 1800. Berkeley, Univ. of California Press, 1937. 2v.
List of maps: 2:273-364.
Place names still in use: 2:371-422.
Obsolete place names: 2:423-525.
Bibliography: 2:527-43.

635. Zeusler, F. A. Alaskan names. United States Naval Institute. Proceedings 67:1428-31, Oct. 1941.

ARIZONA

636. Arizona. Development Board. Historical markers in Arizona. Phoenix, 1958?. 2v.
Information on place-names scattered throughout.

637. Barnes, William Croft. Arizona place names. Tucson, Univ. of Arizona, 1935. 503p. (Arizona. University. General bulletin, no. 2) (*University of Arizona bulletin*, v. 6, no. 1)
Bibliography: p. 502-03.
Review: *American literature* 7:489-90, Jan. 1936.

638. —— Arizona place names. Rev. and enl. by Byrd H. Granger. Illus. by Anne Merriman Peck. Tucson, Univ. of Arizona Press, 1960. 519p.
Bibliographies: p. 397-407.
This edition is expanded from the original 2900 place-names to 7200.
Review: by William Bright, *Journal of American folklore* 75:77-78, Jan. 1962; by T. M. Pearce, *Names* 8:99-100, June 1960.

639. —— Arizona place names. A compilation of the names of Arizona's cities, villages, and settlements, early stage and modern railroad stations, its mountains and canyons, lakes and streams, springs and desert water holes, long forgotten mining towns, military posts and camps; their origin, meaning and history. *Arizona historical review* 5:286-301, Jan. 1933.
Reprinted as the first part of his book, Arizona place names, 1935.

640. Barney, James M. How Apache Leap got its name. *Arizona highways* 11:6-7, 20-21, Aug. 1935.

641. Brandes, Ray. Frontier military posts of Arizona. Globe, Ariz., D. S. King, 1960. 94p.
Descriptions and data relating to the name, origin, and existence of military posts in Arizona. Includes a listing of temporary camps, settler's forts, and place-names which imply military origin.

642. ——— A guide to the history of the U.S. Army installations in Arizona, 1849-1886. *Arizona and the West* 1:42-65, Spring 1959.
Includes list and name information.

643. Brophy, Frank Cullen. In the classical tradition; Of names and places; *In his* Arizona sketch book. Phoenix, Arizona-Messenger Print. Co., 1952. p. 147-51, 289-96.

644. Chapman, H. H. Why the town of McNary moved. *American forests and forest life* 30:589-92, 626, Oct. 1924.
The town of McNary, La., was abandoned and all the inhabitants moved to Cooley, Ariz., rechristened McNary, because of the depletion of the timber stand in Louisiana.

645. DeHarport, David L. Origin of the name, Cañon del Muerto. *El Palacio* 67:95-97, June 1960.

646. Dellenbaugh, Frederick S. Naming the Grand Canyon. *Science* n.s. 77:349-50, April 7, 1933.

647. Feather, Adlai. Origin of the name Arizona. *New Mexico historical review* 39:89-101, April 1964.

648. Fontana, Bernard L. Arizona place names. *Arizona highways* 36:2-5, March 1960.

649. Forrest, Earle Robert. Missions and pueblos of the old Southwest. Cleveland, Arthur H. Clark Co., 1929. 2v.
Spanish mission names in Arizona and New Mexico, with their English equivalents, 1:333-35.

650. Freeman, Merrill P. "Arizona," its derivation and origin. Tucson, 1913. 11p.

651. Goldwyn is honored; Arizona governor names village for film producer. *New York times* Nov. 15, 1939, p. 18, col. 3.
Goldwyn, Ariz., will be a motion-picture set.

652. Granger, Byrd Howell. Early Mormon place names in Arizona. *Western folklore* 16:43-47, Jan. 1957.

653. ——— Grand Canyon place names. Illus. by Anne Merriman Peck. Tucson, Univ. of Arizona Press, 1960. 26p.
A section from William Croft Barnes, Arizona place names. 1960 (see no. 638).

654. —— Methodology used in the revision of Arizona place names. *Names* 10:265-73, Dec. 1962.

655. Hinton, Richard Josiah. 1000 old Arizona mines; with a gallery of old photographs. [Photos from the Rose-Bartholomew collection] Toyahville, Tex., Frontier Book Co., 1962. facsim. (100p.), 101-126p. of illus.
Reproduction, newly paged, of chapters 4 and 5 (p. 72-167) of The hand-book of Arizona. San Francisco, Payot, Upham, 1878.
Includes lists of names of mines with their location, etc.

656. Honor Claude Birdseye's memory. *Kansas City times* March 1, 1965, p. 2.
Claude Birdseye Point.

657. Kelley, E. J. Early mine names were descriptive of events. *Arizona highways* 7:6-7, April 1931.

658. King, Dale S. Desert garden; will Congress change Organ Pipe Cactus National Monument to Arizona Desert National Park? *Arizona highways* 26:28-35, April 1950.

659. Kitt, Edith O. & T. M. Pearce. Arizona place name records. *Western folklore* 11:284-87, Oct. 1952.

660. Lloyd, Elwood. Arizonology (knowledge of Arizona); a compilation of more than two thousand names found on the maps of Arizona, together with information concerning their meaning, history, and many other interesting facts about this wonderful state. Flagstaff, Coconino sun, 1933. 92p.

661. Miller, Joseph. Arizona names and places. *Arizona highways* 19:20-23, 48-49, Sept.-Oct. 1943.

662. Mirkowich, Nicholas. A note on Navajo place names. *American anthropologist* n.s. 43:313-14, April-June 1941.
Lists Navajo names still in use for a few places in Arizona and New Mexico.

663. Newton, Charles H. The reason why place names in Arizona are so named. Phoenix, C. H. Newton Pub. Co., 1954. 47p.

664. Schilling, Frank A. Military posts of the old frontier: Arizona, New Mexico. Historical Society of Southern California. Quarterly 42:133-49, June 1960.
Includes origin and changes of names.

665. Smith, Gusse Thomas. Arizona names, their origin and meaning. *Progressive Arizona and the great Southwest* 6:34, 36, Jan. 1928; 6:27-30, 34, March 1928; 6:33-36, April 1928; 6:35-36, June 1928.

666. —— Priceless names of Arizona. *Progressive Arizona and the great Southwest* 6:21-22, 34, Jan. 1928.

667. The Stories of two Arizona place names: How the Hassayampa River got its name; and How the Colorado River turned red. *New Mexico folklore record* 4:33. 1949-50.
Collected by Walter N. Simons from Tom Larison.

668. Theobald, John & Lillian Theobald. Arizona Territory post offices & postmasters. Phoenix, Arizona Historical Foundation, 1961. 178p.
    Pre-territorial post offices: p. 75-77.
    Post offices, 1863-1912: p. 78-138.
    These lists include some origins and changes of name.

669. Tourist query serves as town name. *Kansas City star* April 22, 1965, p. 16.
    Why, Arizona.

670. U.S. Board on Geographic Names. Decisions. No. 19- . Decisions rendered May 4, 1932. Grand Canyon National Park, Arizona. Washington, Govt. Print. Off., 1932. 16p.

671. Van Valkenburgh, Richard F. & Frank O. Walker. Old placenames in the Navaho country. *Masterkey* (Southwest Museum, Los Angeles) 19:89-94, May 1945.
    Contains a list giving the popular, Spanish, and Navaho names; location; etc.

672. Warner, Robert C. The fortified spring; a good shot gave Pipe Spring its odd name. *Denver post* July 16, 1961, Empire magazine, p. 25.

673. Willson, Roscoe G. The origin of Arizona's name. *Arizona highways* 31:2-5, March 1955.

ARKANSAS

674. Allsopp, Frederick William. Arkansas place names; *In his* Folklore of romantic Arkansas. New York, Grolier Society, 1931. 1:59-107.

675. Arkansas. History Commission. The Arkansas handbook, 1949-50. By Dallas Tabor Herndon. Little Rock, The Commission, 1950. 157p.
    Arkansas counties, how they got their names: p. 144-45.

676. Arkansas. Laws, statutes, etc. Acts and resolutions of the General Assembly. 1881:216-17.
    "Concurrent resolution declaring the proper pronunciation of the name of the state."
    It should be pronounced in three syllables, with final "s" silent, the "a" in each syllable with the Italian sound, and accent on first and last syllables.
    Also in Arkansas. Office of Secretary of State. Biennial report. 1925-26:29-30.
    A short article entitled Arkansas or Arkansaw, including brief summary of the controversy and copy of Concurrent resolution declaring the proper pronunciation of the name of the state.

677. —— General acts and joint and concurrent resolutions and memorials and proposed constitutional amendments of the 44th General Assembly. 1923: 803-04.
    Senate concurrent resolution no. 2. Approved Jan. 26, 1923. Adopting popular name The Wonder State, and declaring The Bear State to be a misnomer.
    Also in Arkansas. Office of Secretary of State. Biennial report 1925-26:12.

A short article entitled Arkansas called "The Wonder State," which includes a copy of Senate concurrent resolution no. 2, 1923.

678. Arkansas divided by two. *New York times* Feb. 28, 1945, p. 13, col. 6-8.
Arkansas House rejects resolution to fix Ark-an-saw-yans as official pronunciation for residents of the state.

679. Blair, Mrs. Herbert. Names of many prominent families given to streets in Batesville. *Independence County chronicle* 2:34-39, Oct. 1960.

680. Branner, John Casper. Some old French place names in the state of Arkansas. *Arkansas historical quarterly* 19:191-206, Autumn 1960.
Reprinted from *Modern language notes* 14:33-40, Feb. 1899.
Also issued as a separate, Baltimore, Md., 1899. 7p.
Review: American Geographical Society. Bulletin 31:94-95. 1899.
cf. article by Raoul Renault, no. 692.

681. Bryson, Fred R. The spelling and pronunciation of Arkansas. *Arkansas historical quarterly* 4:175-79, Autumn 1945.
Originally appeared in the Sunday magazine section of the *Arkansas gazette*, May 13, 1945, under title We call it "Arkansas."

682. Caldwell, Norman W. Place names and place name study. *Arkansas historical quarterly* 3:28-36, Spring 1944.
The author describes the work he has done on a study of place nomenclature in Arkansas. Suggests that the magnitude of the undertaking requires some form of cooperation to carry the study to completion.

683. Chase, Carroll & Richard McP. Cabeen. The first hundred years of United States territorial postmarks, 1787-1887. Arkansas Territory. *American philatelist* 55:147-57, Dec. 1941.
Gives a list of post offices in the area of the present state of Arkansas and six in what became eastern Oklahoma, 1819-36, with notes on some names.

684. Eclectic Society of Little Rock, Ark. Proceedings of the Legislature and of the Historical Society of the State of Arkansas, and the Eclectic Society of Little Rock, Ark., fixing the pronunciation of the name Arkansas. Little Rock, Eclectic Society, 1881. 16p.
Reprinted: In relation to the pronunciation of the name "Arkansas." Arkansas Historical Association. Publications 2:462-77. 1908, with footnote: "Prepared in 1880 by a joint committee from the Eclectic Society and the old members of the then defunct Arkansas Historical Society. Issued at the time in pamphlet form. Because of its value it is reprinted here for permanent preservation."

685. France, Isabel. Fascinating folk names of our hills and hollows. *Ozarks mountaineer* May 1959, p. 5.

686. Gazetteer and business directory of the new Southwest. Embracing all of that region of country—including counties, towns and cities—contiguous to the St. Louis and San Francisco Railway, its divisions and branches, located in southwest Missouri, southeastern Kansas, the eastern portion of the Indian country, and the northwest section of Arkansas. In which is included an abridged directory of leading business houses of St. Louis. St. Louis, United States Directory Pub. Co., 1881. 224p.

687. Hill, Robert T. The pronunciation of "Arkansas." *Science* 10:107-08, Aug. 26, 1887.

688. Martel, Glenn. Origin of Columbia's place names reviewed. *Arkansas historical quarterly* 11:1-14, Spring 1952.
Reprinted from Magnolia, Ark., *Daily banner* June 30, 1951.
Columbia County.

689. Murdock, John. The pronunciation of "Arkansas." *Science* 10:120, Sept. 2, 1887.

690. The Name "Texarkana." *American speech* 2:113, Nov. 1926.

691. The Naming of Jamestown. *Independence County chronicle* 1:16-18, April 1960.
Includes a letter signed J. S. Trimble, which appeared in the *North Arkansas times* June 26, 1869.

692. Renault, Raoul. Some old French place-names in the state of Arkansas. *Modern language notes* 14:191-92, March 1899.
Some corrections of material in article by John Casper Branner (see no. 680).

693. Shelpman, Mrs. Bob. Desha named for distinguished soldier, Franklin W. Desha. *Independence County chronicle* 2:30-33, Oct. 1960.

694. Smackover, Arkansas. *Times-picayune*, New Orleans, Jan. 7, 1951, Dixie, p. 23.
One of a series on unusual place-names in lower Mississippi Valley region.

695. U.S. 88th Congress, 1st session. House. A bill to provide that the Bull Shoals Dam and the Bull Shoals Reservoir, White River Basin in Missouri and Arkansas shall hereafter be known as the "Harry S. Truman Dam" and the "Harry S. Truman Reservoir." H. R. 1094. Jan. 9, 1963. Washington, 1963. 2p.
Introduced by Mr. Hull and referred to the Committee on Public Works.

696. U.S. 88th Congress, 2d session. House. A bill to designate the lake created by the Dardanelle Dam in the State of Arkansas as Lake David D. Terry in honor of the late David D. Terry. H. R. 9748. Jan. 27, 1964. Washington, 1964. 1p.
Introduced by Mr. Mills and referred to the Committee on Public Works.

697. Whaley, Storm. They call it; a guide to the pronunciation of Arkansas place names. n.p., Associated Press, 195?. 48p.

CALIFORNIA

698. Alegría, Fernando. Nombres españoles en California. *Atenea* 100:217-27, marzo 1951.

699. ———— Trail of names. *Americas* 3:33-34, Nov. 1951.

Spanish geographical names in California. Translation of the article above in *Atenea* marzo 1951.

700. Ames, Richard Sheridan. Verdict on California names. *Westways* 26:20-21, 38-39, Dec. 1934.
Based on the Sixth report of the U.S. Geographic Board.

701. Archbald, John. Why "California"? *Overland monthly* 2:437-41, May 1869.
Various derivations considered etymologically.

702. Asbill, Frank M. Place naming in the Wailaki country. *Western folklore* 8:252-55, July 1949.

703. Aschmann, Homer. Miracle mile. *American speech* 32:156-58, May 1957.
Name for the commercial district on Wilshire Blvd., Los Angeles.
In response to article by Mamie Meredith, "Miracle miles" in the U.S.A. (see no. 268).

704. Austin, Herbert D. New light on the name of California. Historical Society of Southern California. Annual publication v. 12, pt. 3, p. 29-31. 1923.

705. Austin, Mary Hunter. Regional place names; *In her* The land of little rain. Photographs by Ansel Adams; introduction by Carl Van Doren. Boston, Houghton Mifflin, 1950. p. 113-24.
The editors attempt to identify places the author mentions, some disguised.

706. Bailey, Gilbert Ellis. The history, origin and meaning of some California towns and places. *Overland monthly* 44:89-93, 199-204, 356-61, 468-78, 558-67, July-Nov. 1904.
Names classified in more than 50 categories, such as church, water, location, color, local peculiarities, soils, trees, animals, minerals, and many others.

707. Ballenger, Hersh. Kingdom of virgins. *Westways* 26:26-27, 40, Sept. 1934.
Recounts the story of Queen Calafia as told in the Spanish romance which is the source of the name California.

708. Bancroft, Hubert Howe. History of California. San Francisco, History Co., 1886. 1:142-46.
A list of places between San Diego and San Francisco as named in Crespi's diary of the first exploration of the California coast by land, with distances, bearings, and latitudes. The present name of each place is noted.

709. Barrett, Samuel Alfred. The ethno-geography of the Pomo and neighboring Indians. Berkeley, University Press, 1908. 332p. (University of California. Publications in American archaeology and ethnology, v. 6, no. 1)
"Includes the locations of the various ancient and modern villages and camp sites. The glossary contains a list of Indian terms from which place-names are derived. The bibliography includes a list of published works in which mention is made of the aboriginal names of peoples or places within the territory under investigation."—Price.

710. Beeler, Madison S. Sonoma, Carquinez, Umunhum, Colma: some disputed California names. *Western folklore* 13:268-77, Oct. 1954.

711. ——— Yosemite and Tamalpais. *Names* 3:185-88, Sept. 1955.

712. Bowman, J. N. Blucher. *Western folklore* 6:179, April 1947.
Land grant, Sonoma County.

713. ——— The elusive Rio Jesus Maria. *Western folklore* 6:73-78, Jan. 1947.

714. ——— The meaning of the name "Sonoma." *California folklore quarterly*
5:300-02, July 1946.

715. ——— The names of land grants in provincial California. *Names* 7:122-
26, June 1959.

716. ——— The names of the California missions. Historical Society of Southern California. Quarterly 39:351-56, Dec. 1957.

717. ——— The names of the Los Angeles and San Gabriel rivers. Historical
Society of Southern California. Quarterly 29:93-99, June 1947.

718. ——— Place names from private land grant cases. *Western folklore*
6:371-75, Oct. 1947.

719. ——— "Quesesosi." *Western folklore* 7:171-73, April 1948.
Supplement to Dorothy H. Huggins's article on the same name, *ibid.* 6:82, Jan.
1947, with additional note by Erwin G. Gudde p. 173.

720. ——— Rio Ojotska—American River. *Western folklore* 6:177, April 1947.
In the early 1830's, Rio Ojotska was a name for the American River.

721. ——— Schoolhouse Creek. *Western folklore* 8:64, Jan. 1949.
In north Berkeley.

722. ——— Spring Valley. *California folklore quarterly* 5:199, April 1946.
San Francisco.

723. ——— Tamalpais. *Western folklore* 6:270-71, July 1947.
Marion County peak.

724. Breeden, Marshall. California place names defined; *In his* The romantic
southland of California. Los Angeles, Kenmore Pub. Co., 1928. p. 184-207.

725. Brentwood, R. G. D. The names of Lake "Taho." *Grizzly bear* 7:5, Oct.
1910.

726. Brewer, William H. The naming of Mount Tyndall. *Sierra Club bulletin*
v. 12, no. 4, p. 443-44. 1927.

727. Brierly, A. A. Dead Horse Meadow. *Western folklore* 8:65, Jan. 1949.

728. Bright, William. Karok names. *Names* 6:172-79, Sept. 1958.
Analysis and classification of 117 Karok village names.

729. ——— Some place names on the Klamath River. *Western folklore*

11:121-22, April 1952.
"From the Karok Indian language."—*American speech.*

730. Brown, Alan K. San Mateo County place-naming. *Names* 12:154-84, Sept.-
Dec. 1964.

731. Brown, Thomas Pollok. Colorful California names, their history and meaning; with a foreword by Nancy Newhall. San Francisco, Wells Fargo Bank American Trust Co., 1957. 45p.
  1st ed. 1934. 28p., with title: California names; rev. eds.: 1935. 28p.; 1954.
44p.; 1955. 44p.

732. Budd, Louis J. The naming of Altruria, California. *Western folklore*
10:169, April 1951.

733. Budge, Belva Adele. A source unit on the origin and meaning of California
place names: original studies drawn from the period of the Spanish missions.
59p.
  Thesis (M.A.) Stanford Univ., 1941.

734. Bumpass Hell is official. Board on Geographic Names says California
approves it. *New York times* Oct. 31, 1948, sec. 1, p. 60.

735. Bunnell, Lafayette H. Origin of names in the Yosemite Valley; *In* Biennial
report of the Commissioners to Manage Yosemite Valley and the Mariposa Big
Tree Grove, 1889-90, p. 9-13. (California. Legislature. Appendix to the Journals of the Senate and Assembly. 29th sess. v. 2, doc. 5. 1891)
  Portion of a manuscript rejected by *Century magazine* because it disproved
their case regarding Yosemite.

736. California. Legislature. Senate. Select Committee on the Derivation and
Definition of the Names of Counties of California. Informe de la Comisión Espe-
cial sobre la derivación y definición de los nombres de los diferentes condados
del estado de California, &c. [San José], H. H. Robinson, [1850]. 20p.

737. ——— Report on the derivation and definition of the names of the several
counties of California, by Mr. Vallejo. [San José], H. H. Robinson, [1850]. 16p.
  Translated from the original by Joseph H. Scull.

738. California. Mining Bureau. Origin of the name California; *In its* Sixth
annual report, 1885-86, pt. 1, p. 8-10. (California. Legislature. Appendix to
the Journals of the Senate and Assembly. 27th sess. v. 4, doc. 2. 1887)
  Quotes from a Spanish romance published in 1521 in which the name California
appears. Refutes idea that this could be the origin of the name.

739. California is restless; her southern cities seek new names, and a special
war rages about Hollywood. *New York times* June 13, 1937, sec. 10, p. 14, col.
1-2.
  Proposed change of Culver City to Hollywood City and of South Pasadena to San
Pasqual.

740. California names with their pronunciation and definition. Pasadena, Wood
& Jones, 1924. 16p.

741. Carlisle, Henry C. San Francisco street names; sketches of the lives of pioneers for whom San Francisco streets are named. San Francisco, American Trust Co., 1954. 26 l.
Limited to names of pioneers who were in San Francisco before 1850.

742. Cerf, Bennett. [Streets named for literary folk, San Diego.] *Saturday review* 39:6, June 23, 1956.
In the Trade winds column.

743. Chapman, Charles Edward. The name "California"; its origin and application. *Grizzly bear* 26:3-5, Dec. 1919.

744. —— New light on origin name "California." *Grizzly bear* 18:5, March 1916.

745. Chase, Carroll & Richard McP. Cabeen. The first hundred years of United States territorial postmarks, 1787-1887. California Territory. *American philatelist* 63:561-67, April 1950.
Includes list of post offices.

746. Coester, Alfred. Names on the land: the name Carquinez. *Western folklore* 6:81-82, Jan. 1947.

747. Conner, E. Palmer. Lost street names of Los Angeles. *Touring topics* 22:57, July 1930.

748. Conrad, Dale. Street names; *In* Conrad, Barnaby. San Francisco: a profile with pictures. New York, Viking Press, 1959. p. 214-24.
Includes a list of typical street names in San Francisco, plus information about them.

749. Cordary, N. J. Off with the old! On with the new! But let's not apply the slogan to street names. *Los Angeles realtor* 10:11, 33-34, June 1931.
Los Angeles street names.

750. The Correct name of Lassen Peak. *Geographical review* 2:464-65, Dec. 1916.

751. Cretser, Emory C. Pudding from Put-In? *Western folklore* 8:64, Jan. 1949.

752. Curletti, Rosario Andrea. Pathways to pavements, the history and romance of Santa Barbara Spanish street names; illus. by Peter Wolf. Santa Barbara, County National Bank & Trust Co., 1950. 87p.

753. Cutter, Donald C. Sources of the name "California." *Arizona and the West* 3:233-44, Autumn 1961.

754. Davidson, George. The origin and the meaning of the name California, Calafia the queen of the island of California, title page of Las Sergas. San Francisco, F. F. Partridge Print., 1910. 50p. (Transactions and proceedings of the Geographical Society of the Pacific. v. 6, pt. 1. ser. 2)
Issued also as a separate.

755. —— Voyages of discovery and exploration on the northwest coast of America from 1539 to 1603. Washington, Govt. Print. Off., 1887. (U.S. Coast

and Geodetic Survey. Report, 1886. Appendix no. 7)
The name "California" (extracted from Coast pilot of California, Oregon and
Washington. 4th ed. 1886): p. 156-57.

756. —— Why San Francisco Bay was so named; *In his* The discovery of San
Francisco Bay. Geographical Society of the Pacific. Transactions and proceedings 2d ser. 4:5-6. 1907.

757. De Ford, Miriam Allen. American ghost towns. *American notes and queries* 4:75-76, Aug. 1944.
Sutterville, California.

758. Diller, J. S. The basis for the official designation of Lassen Peak. *Geographical review* 4:56-58, July 1917.

759. Douglas, Edward Morehouse. California mountain passes. Washington,
Board of Surveys and Maps, Map Information Office, 1929. 3p.

760. —— Gazetteer of the mountains of the State of California. Preliminary
(incomplete) ed. Washington, Map Information Office, Federal Board of Surveys
and Maps, 1929. 63p.

761. Drake, C. M. California names and their literal meanings, also other primary geography names and their meanings; a book for teachers and other curious
people. Los Angeles, Jones Book and Print. Co., 1893. 80p.

762. Dressler, Albert. How some of the mining towns and diggings derived their
names; *In his* California's pioneer mountaineer of Rabbitt Creek. San Francisco,
A. Dressler, 1930. p. 35-36.

763. An Early day romance. *Grizzly bear* 32:6, Jan. 1923.
Contains personal recollections on the origin and meaning of some California
names.

764. Edwards, Clinton R. Wandering toponyms: El Puerto de la Bodega and
Bodega Bay. *Pacific historical review* 33:253-72, Aug. 1964.

765. El Capinero. *Western folklore* 8:370, Oct. 1949.
Signed: E. R. F.
Tulare County.

766. Enochs, Elizabeth. A study of place names in the American River drainage
system, 1848-1854. 1957.
Thesis (M.A.) Sacramento State College, 1957.

767. Evans, Oscar. What's in a name? *Western folklore* 6:174-76, April 1947.
Names of physical features.

768. Farquhar, Francis Peloubet. A footnote on the name California. *California
Historical Society quarterly* 6:167-68, June 1927.
Contains an excerpt from *Notes and queries* 3:289, 519, April 11, June 27, 1857,
on the possibility of the name California being an ingredient used in the making
of fireballs or combustibles.

769. —— Naming America's mountains—the Sierra Nevada of California. *American alpine journal* v. 14, no. 1, p. 131-58. 1964.

770. —— Place names of the High Sierra. San Francisco, Sierra Club, 1926. 128p. (Sierra Club. Publications no. 62)
Enlarged from the *Sierra Club bulletin* 11:380-407; 12:47-64, 126-47. 1923-25.

771. Faull, Harry A. From pathways to freeways, a study of the origin of street names in the city of Pomona. Historical Society of Southern California Quarterly 34:133-46, June 1952.

772. Frickstad, Walter Nettleton. A century of California post offices, 1848-1954. Oakland, 1955. 395p.
A Philatelic Research Society publication.
Part I presents an abstract of the official records of the establishment, discontinuance, and change of name of all post offices operated in California from 1848 to the end of 1954.
Part II consists of 20 official and unofficial lists published on various dates between 1849 and 1859, reporting the offices then operating in California.

773. "Frisco" is now conceded as a term of affection. *New York times* Dec. 2, 1945, p. 12, col. 4.
San Francisco.

774. Gamble, Thomas S. How the cities of southern California were named. *Overland monthly and Out West magazine* 2d ser. 91:57, April 1933.

775. —— The unsung romance of California. *Overland monthly and Out West magazine* 2d ser. 91:39-40, March 1933.
Origin and meaning of various place-names.

776. Gannett, Henry. Place names for application in the Sierra Nevada. *Sierra Club bulletin* 4:239-41, Feb. 1903.
Ideas regarding selection of place-names in the Sierra Nevada.

777. Gardner, J. E. The flag of freedom. *California folklore quarterly* 5:199, April 1946.
Freedom, formerly Whiskey Hill, Santa Cruz County.

778. Gill, R. Bayley. $200.00 for a name. *Western folklore* 6:375, Oct. 1947.
Tecopa, Inyo County.

779. Girgich, Henrietta. Sniktaw Creek. *Western folklore* 7:175, April 1948.
Watkins reversed.

780. Goethe, Charles Matthias. Sierran cabin, from skyscraper; a tale of the Sierran piedmont. Sacramento and San Francisco, Keystone Press, 1943. 185p.
Place names [of ghost towns]: p. 109-17.

781. —— "What's in a name." Tales, historical or fictitious, about 111 California Gold Belt place names. Sacramento, Calif., Keystone Press, c1949. 202p.
Review: by Aubrey Drury, *Western folklore* 9:175-76, April 1950.

782. Goulet, Lucien. Another Dardanelles. *Western folklore* 6:178, April 1947.
Whittaker's Dardanelles, rocky peaks.

783. ——— The Dardanelles once more. *Western folklore* 6:79-81, Jan. 1947.

784. Gregoire, Henri. La Chanson de Roland en l'an 1085. Baligant et Californe
ou l'étymologie du mot "Californie." Academie Royale de Belgique. Classe des
lettres et des sciences morales et politique 5th ser. 25:211-73. 1939.

785. Gregory, Tom. How Santa Rosa received its name. *Grizzly bear* 9:2, Oct.
1911.

786. Gudde, Elizabeth K. Mocho Mountain. *Names* 5:246-48 Dec. 1957.
A typical example of the processes involved in establishing a name of foreign
origin, from the papers of George Davidson.

787. Gudde, Erwin Gustav. The buttes of California. *Western folklore* 6:265-66,
July 1947.

788. ——— California place names, a geographical dictionary. Berkeley, Univ.
of California Press, 1949. 431p.
   Glossary and bibliography: p. 401-29.
   Review: by T. M. Pearce, *Western folklore* 9:82-83, Jan. 1950.

789. ——— California place names: the origin and etymology of current geographical names. Rev. and enl. [*i.e.*, 2d] ed. Berkeley, Univ. of California Press,
1960. 383p.
   1st ed. 1949.
   Incorporates many corrections and additions.
   Glossary and bibliography: p. 357-82.
   Review: by William Bright, *Journal of American folklore* 75:78-82, Jan. 1962;
by Kemp Malone. More about place names, *American speech* 35:210-11, Oct.
1960; by E. Wallace McMullen, *Names* 12:58-64, March 1964; by George R. Stewart,
California Historical Society quarterly 39:364-66, Dec. 1960.

790. ——— Dunderberg, not Dunderberg Peak. *Western folklore* 6:375, Oct.
1947.

791. ——— Hoopa from Whoop-ah? *Western folklore* 6:179, April 1947.
   Valley and Indian reservation, Humboldt County.

792. ——— Literary echoes in California place names. Book Club of California. News-letter v. 14, no. 2. 1949.

793. ——— The name California. *Names* 2:121-33, June 1954.

794. ——— The name of our state. California. Secretary of State. California
blue book 1958:651-52.

795. ——— The names in Death Valley. *Western folklore* 8:160-61, April 1949.

796. ——— The names of California counties. California. Secretary of State.
California blue book 1958:653-61.
   Earlier issues of the California blue book contained repeatedly first the "Vallejo

Report" (see no. 737), then Prentiss Maslin's Origin and meaning of the names of the counties of California (see no. 863). Gudde's account is "based on the results of scholarly research obtained since Maslin published his article."

797. ———— 1,000 California place names: their origin and meaning. 2d rev. ed. Berkeley, Univ. of California Press, 1959. 96p.
1st ed. 1947. 96p.; rev. ed. 1949. 96p.
A popular edition based on the author's California place names.

798. ———— Paradise or Pair o' Dice. *Western folklore* 6:178, April 1947.
Butte County.

799. ———— Place names in the San Francisco Bay counties; *In* California. Dept. of Natural Resources. Division of Mines. Geologic guidebook of the San Francisco Bay counties. San Francisco, 1951. (*Its* Bulletin 154) p. 31-38.

800. ———— The solution of the Islay problem. *California folklore quarterly* 5:298-99, July 1946.
Islais Creek.

801. ———— [Topographic nomenclature]. *California Historical Society quarterly* 28:184-85, July 1949.
Report of talk at Society's meeting.

802. Guinn, James Miller. The passing of our historic street names. Historical Society of Southern California. Annual publication v. 9, pts. 1-2, p. 59-64. 1912-13.
Street names of Los Angeles.

803. ———— The plan of old Los Angeles and the story of its highways and byways. Historical Society of Southern California. Annual publication v. 3, pt. 3, p. 40-50. 1895.
Plan of early streets, origin of street names, changes in names, etc.

804. ———— Some California place names (their origin and meaning). Historical Society of Southern California. Annual publication 7:39-46. 1906.

805. Hale, Edward Everett. The name of California. American Antiquarian Society. Proceedings April 1862, p. 45-53.
Also in *Historical magazine* 6:312-15, Oct. 1862.

806. Hanna, Phil Townsend. The dictionary of California land names. Rev. and enl. ed. Los Angeles, Automobile Club of Southern California, 1951. 392p.
1st ed. 1946. 360p.
Originally published serially in *Westways* v. 31-38, Jan. 1939-March 1946, under title California names—a gazetteer.
Review: by W. W. Robinson, *Pacific historical review* 16:196, May 1947; by Mamie Meredith, *Names* 1:284-86, Dec. 1953.

807. ———— The origin and meaning of some place names of the Death Valley region. *Touring topics* 22:42-43, 54, Feb. 1930.

808. Harrington, John Peabody. A tentative list of the Hispanized Chumashan

place-names of San Luis Obispo, Santa Barbara, and Ventura counties, California. *American anthropologist* n.s. 13:725-26, Oct.-Dec. 1911.

809. Harrison, William Greer. Romance of the word "California." *Overland monthly* 68:443-44, Dec. 1916.

810. Hart, James D. San Francisco streets. *Overland monthly and Out West magazine* 88:49, 59, Feb. 1930.

811. Hartesveldt, Richard J. Place names of Yosemite Valley. Yosemite National Park, Calif., Yosemite Natural History Assoc., 1955. 21p.
Special issue, v. 34, no. 1, Jan. 1955, of *Yosemite nature notes, the monthly publication of the Yosemite Naturalist Division and the Yosemite Natural History Association.*
Includes the names shown on the U.S. Geological Survey's Yosemite Valley special sheet and a few other local names.
"Does not measure up to our standards of popular onomatology."—Erwin G. Gudde, *Names* 3:194, Sept. 1955.

812. Heck, Lewis. California. Congrès international de sciences onomastiques. 5th, Salamanca, 1955. Programme et communications. p. 47.
Résumé of paper on the name California.

813. Hill, Archibald A. California place-names from the Spanish. *American speech* 7:317-18, April 1932; 8:75, April 1933.
Criticism of article by Joseph B. Vasché (see no. 940).

814. Hine, Robert V. The naming of California's utopias. *Western folklore* 12:132-35, April 1953.

815. Hisken, Clara. Tehama—Indian or Aztec? *Western folklore* 8:62-63, Jan. 1949.
Supplemented by information from Dorothy H. Huggins, *ibid.* p. 63-64.

816. Hubbard, Harry D. Vallejo. Ed. by Pauline C. Santoro. Boston, Meador Pub. Co., 1941. 374p.
Naming of important geographical points: p. 75-83.
The discovery of, and the origin of the name, California: p. 165-73.

817. Huggins, Dorothy H. Batiquitos and San Elijo lagoons. *Western folklore* 6:376, Oct. 1947.
San Diego County.

818. —— Butano. *Western folklore* 9:157, April 1950.
San Mateo County. A request for information.

819. —— Carquinez, the strait of the Mud People. *California folklore quarterly* 5:104-07, Jan. 1946.
George R. Stewart disagrees in his article Carquinez again, *ibid.* 5:302-03, July 1946.

820. —— More Dardanelles. *California folklore quarterly* 5:303, July 1946.
Tuolumne County.

821. —— Nicasio and Novato. *Western folklore* 6:270, July 1947.
Marin County.

822. —— The oldest names in new California. *California folklore quarterly*
5:197-98, April 1946.
Mugu Laguna and Mugu Point, Ventura County.

823. —— Place names from the Portola pilgrimage; *In* Essays for Henry R.
Wagner. San Francisco, Grabhorn Press, 1947. p. 65-80.

824. —— Puente. *Western folklore* 6:269-70, July 1947.
Los Angeles County.

825. —— "Quesesosi" or "Guesesosi." *Western folklore* 6:82, Jan. 1947.
Land claim. *cf.* J. N. Bowman's article on the same name, *ibid.* 7:171-73,
April 1948.

826. Hutchinson, W. H. The naming of Cohasset. *Western folklore* 6:266-69,
July 1947.
Butte County.

827. Index to California place names. California. State Library, Sacramento.
Continuing.

828. Island's name changed to Wake. *New York times* April 26, 1942, p. 33, col. 3.
Mullet Island changed for duration of war.

829. Iventosch, Herman. Orinda, California; or, The literary traces in California
toponymy. *Names* 12:103-07, June 1964.

830. James, George Wharton. The various names of Lake Tahoe; *In his* The lake
of the sky, Lake Tahoe. Chicago, C. T. Powner, 1956. p. 56-62.
First published 1915. 2d ed. 1921. Rev. ed. 1928.

831. Jones, Joseph. Street-names of Palo Alto, California. *American speech*
7:273-77, April 1932.
"Names of colleges, authors, trees, prominent citizens, some Civil War gen-
erals, and feminine given names serve as headings under which the street names
are listed."—Price.

832. Karpenstein, Katherine. Amboy to Goffs. *California folklore quarterly*
5:200, April 1946.

833. —— California place name records. *Western folklore* 12:129-32, April
1953.

834. Kelly, Isabel T. Ethnography of the Surprise Valley Paiute. California.
University. Publications in American archaeology and ethnology v. 31, no. 3,
p. 74-75. 1932.
Indian names of the Valley and their meaning.

835. Kniffen, Fred B. Achomawi geography. California. University. Publications in American archaeology and ethnology v. 23, no. 5, p. 297-322. 1928.

Discussion of the areas occupied by different tribes and the meaning of some of the Indian place-names.

836. Kroeber, Alfred Louis. California place names of Indian origin. California. University. Publications in American archaeology and ethnology v. 12, no. 2, p. 31-69. 1916.

837. ———— The ethnography of the Cahuilla Indians. California. University. Publications in American archaeology and ethnology v. 8, no. 2, p. 29-39. 1908.
"Two parallel lists of place-names in the Cahuilla Indian language; one, the original place-name, and second, the present name, or, this being impossible, the location of the name."—Price.

838. ———— Karok towns. California. University. Publications in American archaeology and ethnology v. 35, no. 5, p. 29-38. 1936.
Towns along the Klamath River.

839. ———— Place names; *In his* Handbook of the Indians of California. U.S. Bureau of American Ethnology. Bulletin 78:892-97. 1925.

840. Krutch, Joseph Wood. The forgotten peninsula; a naturalist in Baja California. New York, Sloane, 1961. 277p.
Brief mention of place-names in Baja California, and origin of the name California, p. 56-60.

841. LeConte, J. N. Identification of the great peaks of the southern Sierra. *Sierra Club bulletin* v. 11, no. 3, p. 244-54. 1922.
Includes origin of names.

842. Leland, J. A. C. Cohasset—well named. *Western folklore* 6:377, Oct. 1947.

843. ———— Eastern tribal names in California. *California folklore quarterly* 5:391-93, Oct. 1946.

844. ———— Gualala again. *Western folklore* 7:175, April 1948.
Additional note to the Harriet B. Titus article, Walhalla-Gualala, *ibid.* 6:271, July 1947.

845. ———— The origin of the name "Sequoia." *Western folklore* 6:269, July 1947.

846. ———— Some eastern Indian place names in California. *California folklore quarterly* 4:404-08, Oct. 1945.

847. Lloyd, Elwood. Californology (knowledge of California), a compilation of more than fifteen hundred Spanish, Indian and unusual names found on the maps of California, together with information concerning their meaning, pronunciation and history. Hollywood, Hartwell Pub. Corp., 1930. 55p.

848. The Local name of Lassen Peak. *Geographical review* 3:148, Feb. 1917.

849. Lodian, L. History of the name Kalifornia (California). *Coal trade journal* 40:998, Dec. 4, 1901.

Also in *Book-lover* 3:142, May-June 1902, with title Meaning of the name Kalifornia (California).

850. Loomis, C. Grant. A California story: Yuba City. *Western folklore*
15:194-95, July 1956.
Refers to note in *Yankee notions* 12:111. 1863.

851. Loud, Llewellyn L. Ethnogeography and archaeology of the Wiyot territory. California. University. Publications in American archaeology and ethnology v. 14, no. 3, p. 284-98. 1918.
Gives "the chief Wiyot settlements and their sites, minor settlements and camp sites in 1850; places abandoned previous to 1850; places of mythological interest; and lists of geographical names with maps."—Price.

852. Lovejoy, Ora A. A study of southern California place names. Historical Society of Southern California. Annual publications v. 11, pt. 1, p. 44-50. 1918.

853. Lynch, Frank E. Counties of California; *In his* The pathfinder of the great western empire. Los Angeles, Gem Pub. Co., 1920. p. 15-37.
Derivation of the name is included in the description of each county.

854. McAbee, Forrest L. How Yorkville was named. *Western folklore* 6:177, April 1947.

855. McKenney, J. Wilson. He named Lake Cahuilla. *Desert* 13:11-13, March 1950.

856. McKeon, Thomas J. Some conjectures on place names in Marin County. *Grizzly bear* 57:3, Oct. 1935.

857. McNary, Laura Kelly. California Spanish and Indian place names, their pronunciation, meaning and location. Los Angeles, Wetzel Pub. Co., 1931. 77p.
References: p. 77.

858. Make Japan St. Colin Kelly St. *New York times* Feb. 10, 1942, p. 4, col. 5. San Francisco.

859. Maloney, Alice Bay. Shasta was Shatasla in 1814. *California Historical Society quarterly* 24:229-34, Sept. 1945.

860. Marcou, Jules. Notes upon the first discoveries of California and the origin of its name. U.S. Engineer Dept. Annual report, 1877-78, pt. 3, Appendix NN, p. 1648-51.
"Describes some of the old maps of California and treats of the seventeenth century controversy as to whether California was an island or part of the mainland. Gives various names by which some of the places were known."—Price.

861. Marshall, Martha Lebeaud. A pronouncing dictionary of California names in English and Spanish. San Francisco, French Book Store, 1925. 40p.

862. Maslin, Prentiss. Counties in California; *In* McGroarty, John Steven. California, its history and romance. Los Angeles, Grafton Pub. Co., 1911. p. 309-22.
Data concerning the names and the origin of the counties of California prepared

and published officially by direction of the state legislature in accordance with an act approved Feb. 12, 1903.

863. —— Origin and meaning of the names of the counties of California. California. Secretary of State. California blue book 1907:275-81; 1909:338-44.

864. Masson, Marcelle Saylor. How Dunsmuir was named. *Western folklore* 6:377, Oct. 1947.

865. Maule, William M. Buckeye Creek. *Western folklore* 8:65, Jan. 1949.

866. —— Fales Hot Springs. *Western folklore* 7:174-75, April 1948.

867. —— Folger Peak. *Western folklore* 6:376, Oct. 1947.

868. —— Montgomery Peak. *Western folklore* 6:178, April 1947.

869. —— Why Disaster Peak was so named. *Western folklore* 6:270, July 1947.
Alpine County.

870. Merriam, Clinton Hart. Cop-eh of Gibbs. *American anthropologist* n.s. 31:136-37, Jan.-March 1929.
"Points out the excusable error of George Gibbs in identifying 'Cop-eh' with the stream 'Putes Creek.' "—Price.

871. —— Source of the name Shasta. Washington Academy of Sciences. Journal 16:522-25, Nov. 18, 1926.
Peter Skene Ogden gave name to river now known as Rogue River, and to mountain at head of it, now known as Mount Pitt. Due to break in continuity of local knowledge of the region, name has been transferred to features remote from those upon which originally bestowed. Great mountain and river to which name was transferred are still within or bordering on the territory of the Shasta tribe.

872. Miers, Allan. Bogus in Siskiyou. *Western folklore* 6:376-77, Oct. 1947.

873. Miller, Guy C. College Terrace. *Western folklore* 6:78-79, Jan. 1947.
In Palo Alto.

874. —— Palo Alto. *Western folklore* 7:284-88, July 1948.

875. Moore, Edwin R. Spanish and Indian names in California and the Southwest pronounced and defined. South Pasadena, Vance Print. Co., 1924. 18p.

876. Moreno, Henry Manuel. Moreno's dictionary of Spanish-named California cities and towns; comp. from the latest U.S. postal and parcel zone guides; California blue book; Velazquez dictionary; Southern Pacific & Union Pacific maps and authentic sources. An accurate, ready reference for all schools, newspaper offices, etc. Chicago, Donohue, 1916. 95p.

877. Morley, S. G. Carquinez Straits once more. *Western folklore* 6:271-72, July 1947.
Differs with Alfred Coester, *ibid.* p. 81-82.

878. Mott, Gertrude. A handbook for Californiacs; a key to meaning and pro-
nounciation of Spanish and Indian place names; with foreword by Herbert E. Bolton.
San Francisco, Harr Wagner Pub. Co., 1926. 104p.
   Also published under title Handbook for Californians.
   Authorities consulted: p. 104.
   "Earlier and more nearly correct pronunciation of these many place-names
along with an explanation of the meaning of each."—Review, *American speech*
1:562-63, July 1926.

879. Mountain nicknamed. Baldy is popular name used for peak in California.
New York times Aug. 20, 1959, p. 22.
   Real name Mount San Antonio, probably for St. Anthony of Padua.

880. Murbarger, Nell. The ghost towns of Inyo. Westerners. Los Angeles
Corral. Westerners brand book 11:1-18. 1964.

881. Names, full of meaning, alone remain of early day gold camps. *Grizzly
bear* 38:4, March 1926.

882. Names of old places in Valley Springs region; Names of old places around
West Point. *Las Calaveras* (Quarterly bulletin of the Calaveras County Historical Society) 5:[1-2], July 1957.

883. Names on the land: Hobo Hot Springs. *Western folklore* 6:176-77, April
1947.
   Near Bakersfield.

884. New place names approved. *Sierra Club bulletin* 35:10, Jan. 1950.
   Sierra names approved by U.S. Board on Geographic Names.

885. Nomland, Gladys Ayer & A. L. Kroeber. Wiyot towns. California. University. Publications in American archaeology and ethnology v. 35, no. 5, p. 39-
48. 1936.
   Along Eel River, Mad River, and on Humboldt Bay.

886. Norton, Arthur Lauren. How California received her name. *Los Angeles
County employee* 4:10-12, 45-46, Oct. 1931.

887. Not funny, at home. Cucamonga thinks it's time for a name change. *Kan-
sas City star* Oct. 6, 1958, p. 3.
   A.P. release.
   Considering among other names Arpege, after the perfume.

888. Old meanings of Indian place names overturned. *Grizzly bear* 20:5, Dec.
1916.
   Based on Alfred Louis Kroeber, California place names of Indian origin (see
no. 836).

889. Olmsted, Frederick Law. Place names for California. *Landscape architecture* 13:40-42, Oct. 1922.
   Suggests ways of forming an English place-name, and mentions some names
that have local characteristics and English terminations that could be applied in
the vicinity of Berkeley.

890. Origin and meaning of the names of the counties of California, with county
seats and dates upon which counties were created; *In* California. Constitution.
Constitution of the State of California. 1945-1946, p. 467-79.

891. Oswalt, Robert L. Gualala. *Names* 8:57-58, March 1960.
  A note on the origin of the name Gualala for a small coastal town in Mendocino
County and for the river at whose mouth the town lies.

892. Palmer, Theodore Sherman. Place names of the Death Valley region in
California and Nevada. Los Angeles, Dawson's Book Shop, 1948. 80p.
  Result of National Park Service project.
  Review: by Katherine Karpenstein, *Names* 1:62-63, March 1953.

893. Patton, Annaleone Davis. California Mormons by sail and trail. Salt Lake
City, Utah, Deseret Book Co., 1961. 197p.
  Mormon names in early California; Geographic names associated with or named
by early Mormons: p. 189-90.

894. Peaks in the Sierra named. *Sierra Club bulletin* 34:16, Feb. 1949.
  Five features on east slope of Sierra Nevada named by U.S. Board on Geographic Names.

895. Pearce, Thomas M. Maggie's Peak. *Western folklore* 8:370, Oct. 1949.
  Napa and Sonoma counties. Request for information.

896. Pioneer Dean tells how Tahoe got its name. *Grizzly bear* 26:5, Feb. 1920.

897. Place-name card index. San Diego Public Library.
  Continuing.

898. Place-name file. Los Angeles Public Library.
  A collection of notes on the origin and meaning of California place-names compiled by the Library School of the Los Angeles Public Library under the supervision of Charles Fletcher Lummis.

899. Powers, Stephen. Tribes of California, Yosemite. *Contributions to North
American ethnology* 3:361-68. 1877.
  "Indian names of places or localities in the Yosemite Valley with their signifi-
cance, as well as some legends connected with the names."—Price.

900. Pronunciation of "Los Angeles." *American speech* 25:75, Feb. 1950.
  Signed: H. S.

901. Putnam, George Palmer. Death Valley and its country. New York, Duell,
1946. 231p.
  The name: p. 10-15.

902. Putnam, Ruth & Herbert I. Priestley. California: the name. California.
University. Publications in history v. 4, no. 4, p. 293-365. 1917.

903. The Queen of California. *Atlantic monthly* 13:265-78, March 1864.
  Partly reprinted later in Edward Everett Hale, His level best and other stories.
Boston, Roberts Bros., 1872. p. 234-78.

Contains translations of passages from the Spanish romance said by Hale to be the origin of the name California.

904. Raup, Hallock Floy. Modern California cartography, aids for the map compiler. *Pacific historical review* 15:77-84, March 1946.
Sources for place-names.

905. ——— Place names of the California gold rush. *Geographical review* 35:653-58, Oct. 1945.
Also reprinted.
827 place-names in Trinity, Amador, and Calaveras counties were studied "to ascertain tendencies in geographical nomenclature among the early miners."

906. ——— & William B. Pounds. Northernmost Spanish frontier in California as shown by the distribution of geographic names. *California Historical Society quarterly* 32:43-48, March 1953.

907. Raymenton, H. K. San Diego's street names. San Diego Historical Society. Quarterly 10:24-25, April 1964.

908. Rivera, Adolfo G. Along the highways, meaning of the words you see. *Los Angeles County employee* v. 10, Oct. 1937-Jan. 1938.
A series of articles. Mostly Spanish words.

909. Russell, Richard Joel. Basin Range structure and stratigraphy of the Warner Range, northeastern California. California. University. Publications. Bulletin of the Dept. of Geological Sciences 17:387-496. 1928.
Some material on place-names in northeastern California, p. 392-94.

910. Sánchez, Louis A. "El Capinero" twice more. *Western folklore* 9:155-56, April 1950.
Includes notes by S. G. Morley.

911. Sanchez, Nellie Van de Grift. The name of our beloved California, was it given in derision? *Grizzly bear* 18:8, April 1916.

912. ——— Origin of "California." *Motor land* 33:7, 13, Sept. 1933.
A popular article on the origin of the name in the old Spanish tale, Las sergas de Esplandian.

913. ——— Spanish and Indian place names of California, their meaning and their romance. San Francisco, Robertson, 1930. 343p.
Earlier editions: 1914. 445p.; 1922. 454p.
Review of 1914 ed.: by Charles A. Kofoid, *Dial* 57:497-98, Dec. 16, 1914.

914. Schulz, Paul E. Stories of Lassen's place names. The origins and meanings of the place names in Lassen Volcanic National Park, with relevant annotations. Mineral, Calif., Lassen Volcanic National Park, 1949. 62p.

915. Scott, Fred N. Pronunciation of Spanish-American words. *Modern language notes* 6:435-36, Nov. 1891.

916. Shafer, Robert. The pronunciation of Spanish place names in California.

American speech 17:239-46, Dec. 1942.
Also issued as a separate.

917. Shulman, David. Derivation of California. *New York times* Nov. 20, 1938,
sec. 4, p. 8, col. 5-6; reply by Howard W. Vernon, *ibid.* Nov. 27, 1938, sec. 4,
p. 9, col. 6.

918. Sierra County changes name. *Sierra Club bulletin* 35:11, Jan. 1950.
Names of rivers changed by Sierra County Board of Supervisors.

919. Sierra or Sierras? *Sierra Club bulletin* 32:32, Nov. 1947.
Refers to Sierra Nevada.

920. Sokol, A. E. California, a possible derivation of the name. *California Historical Society quarterly* 28:23-30, March 1949.

921. Steger, Gertrude A. Place names of Shasta County. Bella Vista, The author,
1945. 75p.
Bibliography: p. iii-vi.

922. Stein, David Allen. Los Angeles: a noble fight nobly lost. *Names* 1:35-38,
March 1953.
The pronunciation of Los Angeles.

923. Stephenson, Terry Elmo. Names of places in Orange County. Orange County
Historical Society. Orange County history series 1:45-54. 1931; 2:107-17. 1932.

924. Stewart, George Rippey. Caribou as a place name in California. *California
folklore quarterly* 5:393-95, Oct. 1946.

925. —— More on the name California. *Names* 2:249-54, Dec. 1954.

926. —— Nomenclature of stream-forks on the west slope of the Sierra Nevada. *American speech* 14:191-97, Oct. 1939; 16:312, Dec. 1941.

927. —— Place names; *In his* Donner Pass and those who crossed it. San
Francisco, California Historical Society, 1960. p. 89-90.
Various types of names in the Donner Pass area.

928. —— Three Mendocino names. *Western folklore* 9:154-55, April 1950.

929. Stories behind California's names. I. Indian names. II. Spanish names.
III. American names. *California historical nugget* 1:39-43, 59-66, 79-87,
March-May 1924.

930. Sykes, Godfrey. How California got its name. *Out West magazine* 41:225-
30, June 1915.

931. Teeter, Karl V. Notes on Humboldt County, California, place names of
Indian origin. *Names* 6:55-56, March 1958.
Addenda, *ibid.* 7:126, June 1959.

932. Terrill, Nate. The etymological history of a clam. *Western folklore*

9:264-65, July 1950.
Pismo Beach.

933. Thompson, Betty. Once Hangtown—now Placerville. *Mining world* 10:42, Feb. 1948.

934. Titus, Harriet B. Walhalla-Gualala. *Western folklore* 6:271, July 1947.
Sonoma County. *cf.* J. A. C. Leland's article, Gualala again, *ibid.* 7:175, April 1948.

935. To vote on becoming Distomo. *New York times* Dec. 3, 1944, p. 24, col. 3.
Linda Vista, Calif.

936. Turk, Henry W. Place names along the emigrant trail. *Grizzly bear* 56:5, Feb. 1935; 56:2, March 1935.

937. U.S. Board on Geographic Names. Decisions. Place names, Sequoia National Park, California. Oct. 3, 1928. Washington, Govt. Print. Off., 1928. 11p.

938. —— Decisions. No. 30—June 30, 1932. Yosemite National Park, California. Washington, Govt. Print. Off., 1934. 29p.

939. U.S. Work Projects Administration. Pennsylvania. Geographic names in the coastal areas of California, Oregon and Washington. Comp. under the supervision of the Coast and Geodetic Survey. Washington, 1940. 94p.

940. Vasché, Joseph B. Trends in the pronunciation of the Spanish place-names of California. *American speech* 6:461-63, Aug. 1931.
cf. article by Archibald A. Hill, no. 813.

941. Vasquez, Pablo. Place names on the coast. *La Peninsula, journal of the San Mateo County Historical Association* v. 10, no. 4, p. [16-18], Feb. 1960.
From the foot of the San Pedro Mountain, north of Spanish Town, to the Santa Cruz line on the south.

942. Wagner, Henry Raup. The discovery of California. *California Historical Society quarterly* 1:36-56, July 1922.
Has sections on By whom was the name given and to what was it applied?, and The derivation of the name "California" as applied to the island or peninsula so called.

943. —— The names of the Channel Islands. Historical Society of Southern California. Annual publication v. 15, pt. 4, p. 16-23. 1933.
The islands now known as San Miguel, Santa Rosa, Santa Cruz, and Anacapa.

944. —— Saints' names in California. Historical Society of Southern California. Quarterly 29:49-58, March 1947.

945. Wakefield, Lucy. Hangman's tree. *Grizzly bear* 7:9, June 1910.
Origin of name Hangtown.

946. Walsh, Martin. Can you pronounce the name of your town correctly? *Touring topics* 25:12, 40-41, Sept. 1933.

947. ——— Name pronunciation contest: prize-winning lists of correctly-pronounced California names. *Touring topics* 25:33, Oct. 1933.

948. Wannamaker, Jim. Tail of the dog. *Frontier times* 32 (n.s. no. 2):27, Spring 1958.
Account of how White River in Tulare County got its nickname of Tailholt.

949. Waterman, Thomas Talbot. The village sites in Tolowa and neighboring areas in northwestern California. *American anthropologist* n.s. 27:528-43, Oct.-Dec. 1925.
The names of the Indian villages with their English meanings. Includes some Oregon material.

950. ——— Yurok geography. California. University. Publications in American archaeology and ethnology v. 16, no. 5, p. 177-283. 1920.
Contains several thousand primitive place-names of the Yurok Indians.

951. Wells, Harry Laurenz. California names; words, phrases and place names in common use in the Golden state, spelled, pronounced, defined and explained. Los Angeles, Kellaway-Ide Co., 1940. 96p. (p. 89-96, advertising matter)
1st ed. 1934. 94p.

952. White, Lynn Townsend. Changes in the popular concept of "California." *California Historical Society quarterly* 19:219-24, Sept. 1940.
Briefly traces mention of name California in literature from the 12th century on.

953. Whiting, Joseph Samuel & Richard J. Whiting. Forts of the State of California. [Seattle], 1960. 90p.
Descriptions and data relating to the name, origin, and existence of military and semimilitary establishments in the State of California which have been designated or referred to as forts. Also includes place-names with the word Fort as a part of the name but which are neither military nor semimilitary establishments.

954. Why Little Ovens? *Western folklore* 8:65, Jan. 1949.
Hornitos, Mariposa County.

955. Wishart, Helen Collier. Elsinore—Danish not Spanish. *California folklore quarterly* 5:198-99, April 1946.
Influence of the Shakespeare play.

956. Wood, Beatrice Dawson. Gazetteer of surface waters of California. Prepared under the direction of John C. Hoyt, in cooperation with the State Water Commission and Conservation Commission of the State of California. Washington, Govt. Print. Off., 1912-13. 3v. (U.S. Geological Survey. Water-supply paper 295-297)
A list of all lakes and streams, based on the topographic atlas, the Land Office map, and the official county maps.

957. Wyatt, Roscoe D. Names and places of interest in San Mateo County with pronunciation, history and traditions. Redwood City, Pub. by the San Mateo County Title Co. for the San Mateo County Historical Assoc., 1936. 30p.

958. ——— & Clyde Arbuckle. Historic names, persons and places in Santa
Clara County. San Jose, Calif., San Jose Chamber of Commerce for the California Pioneers of Santa Clara County, 1948. 42p.

COLORADO

959. Baskette, Floyd. Pronunciation guide: Colorado. Comp. by Floyd Baskette,
College of Journalism, University of Colorado, with the cooperation and assistance
of Colorado broadcasters. n.p., n.d. 11p.
   Includes counties, cities and towns, mountain peaks, lakes and reservoirs, mountain passes, rivers, national parks, and national forests.

960. Bean, Luther E. Place names of the San Luis Valley; *In his* Land of the
blue sky people; a story of the San Luis Valley. Monte Vista, Colo., Monte Vista
Journal, 1962. p. 96-97.
   A list.

961. Block, Augusta Hauck. Old Burlington. *Colorado magazine* 19:15-17, Jan.
1942.
   History of a ghost town of Colorado Territory.

962. Brown, Robert Leaman. Jeep trails to Colorado ghost towns. Caldwell,
Idaho, Caxton Printers, 1963. 239p.
   57 settlements representing a cross-section sampling, typical of the various
kinds of ghost camps.

963. Cairns, Mary Lyons. Origin of names of points of interest; *In her* The olden
days. Denver, World Press, 1954. p. 235-39.
   Around Grand Lake.

964. Calhoun, Raymond. The naming of Pikes Peak. *Colorado magazine* 31:98-
105, April 1954.
   Condensed from his thesis, a historical study of Pikes Peak.

965. Cattle crippled crossing creek gave Cripple Creek its name. *Denver post*
July 6, 1952, p. 2A.
   Names of places, mines, and streets in the district.

966. Chase, Carroll & Richard McP. Cabeen. The first hundred years of United
States territorial postmarks, 1787-1887. Colorado Territory. *American philate-
list* 55:362-72, 456-64, 467, March-April 1942.
   Includes list of post offices, 1861-78, with notes on some names.

967. Cline, Platt. Some place names of Mesa Verde. *Mesa Verde notes* (U.S.
National Park Service) 6:11-13, Aug. 1935.

968. Colorado ghost towns. n.p., n.d. [208] 1.
   Manuscript in Denver Public Library. Western History Dept.

969. Colorado place-name series.

Special file in the library of the State Historical Society of Colorado, State Museum, Denver.

970. Crofutt, George A. Crofutt's grip-sack guide of Colorado. A complete encyclopedia of the state. Resources and condensed authentic descriptions of every city, town, village, station, post office and important mining camp in the state. 2d ed. Omaha, Neb., Overland Pub. Co., 1885. 174p.
  1st ed. 1881. 183p.

971. Davidson, Levette J. Colorado cartography. *Colorado magazine* 32:178-90, 256-65, July, Oct. 1955.
  From work of earliest explorers to date. Many place-name notes.

972. —— Colorado place-name studies. *Western folklore* 12:204-08, July 1953.
  Also reprinted as a separate.

973. —— Street-name patterns in Denver. *Names* 2:46-50, March 1954.

974. —— Two Colorado place names. *Western folklore* 11:41-42, Jan. 1952.
  Fairplay and Cripple Creek.

975. —— & Olga Hazel Koehler. The naming of Colorado's towns and cities. *American speech* 7:180-87, Feb. 1932.
  Names grouped according to nationality, physical characteristics, slang phrase, etc.

976. Dawson, John Frank. Place names in Colorado. Why 700 communities were so named. 150 of Spanish or Indian origin. Denver, J. F. Dawson Pub. Co., 1954. 52p.
  Alphabetical. Includes earlier names of many places.
  Review: *Names* 2:208-09, Sept. 1954.

977. Denver. Public Library. Origin of Denver street names; comp. by Anna G. Trimble. 1932?. 15 l.
  Typewritten.

978. Denver. Public Library. Western History Dept. Place-name file on cards.
  Supplemented by extensive clipping file of brief articles from newspapers; also clippings on ghost towns.

979. Dirty Woman's Creek. *Colorado magazine* 25:282-83, Nov. 1948.

980. Eberhart, Perry. Guide to the Colorado ghost towns and mining camps. 2d rev. ed. Denver, Sage Books, 1959. 479p.
  1st ed. 1959. 479p.
  Some 700 towns are mentioned, located in every important mountain-mining area of the state. Only about 100 are still lively towns.

981. Excelsior! *Time* 63:63, May 3, 1954.
  A mountain peak in Colorado to be named Colorado Mines, for the Colorado School of Mines.

982. Farquhar, Francis Peloubet. Naming America's mountains—the Colorado

Rockies. New York, American Alpine Club, 1961. 319-346p.
Reprinted from the *American alpine journal* v. 12, no. 2, p. 319-46. 1961.

983. French, A. A. The why of our street names. *Colorado genealogist* 17:31-33, April 1956.
In Denver.

984. Gannett, Henry. A gazetteer of Colorado. Washington, Govt. Print. Off., 1906. 185p. (U.S. Geological Survey. Bulletin no. 291)
Issued also as House doc. no. 839, 59th Cong., 1st sess.

985. Griswold, Don L. & Jean Griswold. Colorado's century of "cities." With illustrations from the Fred M. and Jo Mazzula collection. Denver, Smith-Brooks Print. Co., 1958. 307p.
Contains many references to changes of name, name forms, and "kiting"—the practice of adding a common word such as city to the specific name, like a tail to a kite.

986. ——— Names in the Leadville district. *Carbonate chronicle* Jan. 2, 1961, p. 7-10.

987. Hafen, LeRoy Reuben. Colorado cities, their founding and the origin of their names. *Colorado magazine* 9:170-83, Sept. 1932.

988. ——— The counties of Colorado; a history of their creation and the origin of their names. *Colorado magazine* 8:48-60, March 1931.

989. ——— Ghost towns—Tarryall and Hamilton. *Colorado magazine* 10:137-43, July 1933.

990. ——— How Colorado got its name. *Denver post* Jan. 4, 1959, Empire magazine, p. 6-7.

991. Hart, John Lathrop Jerome. Fourteen thousand feet, a history of the naming and early ascents of the high Colorado peaks. Denver, Colorado Mountain Club, 1925. 51p.
Supplement to *Trail and timberline* June 1925.

992. Hoskin, H. G. Kit Carson County's ghost towns. *Colorado magazine* 10:69-71, March 1933.

993. Hutton, Tom. Wheat Ridge or Wheatridge? They seem agreed to differ. *Denver post* June 30, 1957, p. 19A.

994. Idema, Jim. New streets, names, numbers slated for Littleton by June. *Denver post* Dec. 18, 1960, p. 24C.
A new street-naming ordinance goes into effect in 1961.

995. Keeton, Elsie. The story of Dead Man's Cañon and of the Espinosas. *Colorado magazine* 8:34-38, Jan. 1931.
Origin of the name of the cañon as told by Henry Priest, pioneer.

996. Kernochan, Mrs. E. L. List of Colorado towns. n.p., n.d. 15 l.

Manuscript in Denver Public Library. Western History Dept.
Emphasis on ghost towns.

997. Koehler, Olga Hazel. Place names in Colorado.
Thesis (M.A.) Univ. of Denver, 1930.

998. Logan, Donna. He has high hope on names. *Denver post* Dec. 21, 1964, p 18.
Robert M. Ormes, Colorado College professor, researching the history of the
state's mountains, complains of many commonplace names and will recommend
names for the more than 200 mountain summits which should receive official
names.

999. Lowry, Maxine. 'X' marks the spot. Lady, how do you feel about Xenon,
Xanadu, Xebec? *Denver post* July 19, 1959, p. 6D.
The problem of finding names that start with "X" to continue the practice of
naming streets in alphabetical order in Denver and suburbs.

1000. McHendrie, A. W. Origin of the name of the Purgatoire River. *Colorado
magazine* 5:18-22, Feb. 1928.

1001. Matthews, Ruth Estelle. A study of Colorado place names. Stanford Univ.,
1940. 412p.
Thesis (M.A.) Stanford Univ., 1940.

1002. Mining claims. *Gilpin County miner*, Central City, Colo., July 13, 1939.
Reprinted in part in *American speech* 17:72, Feb. 1942.
Names of recorded mining locations.

1003. Richie, Eleanor L. Spanish place-names in Colorado. *American speech*
10:88-92, April 1935.

1004. Ring, Edward. Silverheels. *Colorado magazine* 17:27, Jan. 1940.
Story of the naming of Mount Silverheels at Fairplay, Colo.

1005. Shoemaker, Len. National forests. *Colorado magazine* 21:182-84, Sept.
1944.
Changes in name and status of many national parks, particularly those in Colorado.

1006. Some of the lost towns of Kansas. Kansas State Historical Society. Collections 12:426-90. 1911-12.
Includes a list of incorporations, by Kansas men, of towns now within the boundaries of Colorado.

1007. Taylor, Morris F. Trinidad legends. *Colorado magazine* 41:154-57,
Spring 1964.
"There is no good evidence to support the contention that the town was named
after a daughter of Felipe Baca."

1008. Taylor, Ralph C. Colorado, south of the border. Denver, Sage Books,
1963. 561p.
Origin of names [southeastern Colorado]: p. 533-49.

1009. Territory of Colorado; *In* Bancroft, Hubert Howe. History of Nevada,

Colorado and Wyoming. San Francisco, History Co., 1890. p. 401-13; also in U.S. Congress. Congressional globe, 36th Congress, 1st session, 1859-60, p. 1502; 36th Congress, 2d session, 1860-61, p. 639-40, 728-29, 763-66, 792, 833, 1003-05, 1012, 1205-06, 1248, 1274.

Inhabitants of the Pikes Peak region first tried to organize as a county of Kansas, called Arapahoe, Nov. 1858. After many petitions to Congress, a bill for the creation of a new territory was finally introduced and passed, becoming law Feb. 28, 1861. The names Colorado, Jefferson, and Idaho were all considered, but Colorado prevailed.

1010. Toll, Oliver W. Arapaho names and trails; a report of a 1914 pack trip. n.p., 1962. 43p.

Field notes on a pack trip with three Arapaho Indians through the Estes Park-Grand Lake region of Colorado, arranged in order to learn the Arapaho names for the area.

1011. Toll, Roger Wolcott. The mountain peaks of Colorado, containing a list of named points of elevation and topographic details. Denver, Colorado Mountain Club, 1923. 59p.

Supplement to *Trail and timberline* Jan. 1923.

1012. Trager, George L. Some Spanish place-names of Colorado. *American speech* 10:203-07, Oct. 1935.

To record the pronunciation of a number of Colorado place-names of Spanish origin in the mouths of native speakers of English.

1013. U.S. Board on Geographic Names. Decisions. No. 27—June 30, 1932. Rocky Mountain National Park, Colorado. Washington, Govt. Print. Off., 1934. 10p.

1014. —— Decisions. No. 37—Decisions rendered February 7, 1934. Mesa Verde National Park, Colorado. Washington, Govt. Print. Off., 1934. 7p.

1015. U.S. Writers' Program. Colorado. Place names of Colorado towns. *Colorado magazine* v. 17-20, Jan. 1940-May 1943.

An alphabetical series of some 3,000 town names, giving brief history of the name with source.

1016. Vivian, C. H. Ghost camps. *Compressed air magazine* 46:6474-79, July 1941.

Describes several towns that flourished for a time due to mines, but were later abandoned. Gives origin of some of the names.

1017. Wallrich, William Jones. The village of Old San Acacio. *Western folklore* 8:367-68, Oct. 1949.

CONNECTICUT

1018. Allen, Morse. Place-names in Salisbury, Connecticut. *Names* 6:97-111, June 1958.

1019. Caulkino, Frunces Manwaring. History of New London, Connecticut. New London, The Author, 1852. 680p.

"A chapter of names, English and aboriginal, p. 118-25, contains a list of geographic names in the Pequot or Mohegan territory."—Pilling.

1020. Connecticut. General Assembly. Centennial Committee. The one hundredth anniversary of the first meeting of the General Assembly, under the present constitution and the second general legislative reunion. The Capitol, Hartford, Wednesday, May 7, 1919. Comp. by William Harrison Taylor, secretary of the Centennial Committee. Hartford, Pub. by the State, 1919. 188p.

"Connecticut towns in the order of their establishment since 1819; with the origin of their names: p. 177-78."—Griffin.

1021. Dexter, Franklin Bowditch. The history of Connecticut, as illustrated by the names of her towns. Worcester, Mass., Press of C. Hamilton, 1885. 30p.

Reprinted from the American Antiquarian Society. Proceedings n.s. 3:421-48, April 1885.

Also in his A selection from the miscellaneous historical papers of fifty years. New Haven, Tuttle, 1918.

1022. Eno, Joel Nelson. Ancient place-names in Connecticut. *Connecticut magazine* 12:93-96, Jan.-March 1908.

The nomenclature of familiar localities with the derivation and interpretation from the Indian language.

1023. —— The nomenclature of Connecticut towns. *Connecticut magazine* 8:330-35, Dec. 1903.

Three types of names: historical, geographical, and biographical.

1024. Gannett, Henry. A geographic dictionary of Connecticut. Washington, Govt. Print. Off., 1894. 67p. (U.S. Geological Survey. Bulletin no. 117)

Issued also as House miscellaneous doc. v. 57, 53d Cong., 2d sess.

1025. Hawley, Charles W. Old names of Connecticut towns. Stamford Genealogical Society. Bulletin 3:61-63, Feb. 1961.

A compilation which translates obsolete place-names into their present-day geographical identity. Includes only Fairfield County.

1026. Hughes, Arthur H. & Morse Allen. Connecticut place names.

These authors, of Trinity College, Hartford, Conn., have completed a manuscript of 23,000 names, and hope to publish it at an early date.—American Dialect Society. Committee on Place Names. Report. Dec. 1963.

1027. Martin, Stanley. Indian derivatives in Connecticut place-names. *New England quarterly* 12:364-69, June 1939.

"Contains an extensive list of the more frequent prefix and suffix components which enter in the formation of local place names of Indian origin."—*American speech*.

1028. Nine new nicknames pondered by Norwalk. *New York times* July 26, 1960, p. 24, col. 1.

Residents asked to pick a new name to replace Clamtown, which is neither complimentary nor accurate.

1029. Pease, John Chauncey & John Milton Niles. A gazetteer of the States of Connecticut and Rhode-Island. Written with care and impartiality, from original and authentic materials. Consisting of two parts. With an accurate and improved map of each state. Hartford, Printed and pub. by William S. Marsh, 1819. 389p.

1030. Pronunciation across the seas. *Christian Science monitor* Oct. 31, 1955, p. 11.
  Pronunciation of Greenwich.

1031. Republican town erasing "Roosevelt." Stratford, Conn. pushes plan to change name of park. *New York times* Jan. 1, 1940, p. 25, col. 4.

1032. Sanford, Irvin Wilbur. History and explanation of Indian names in Salisbury, Conn.; *In* Rudd, Malcolm Day. An historical sketch of Salisbury, Connecticut. New York, 1899. p. 19-23.

1033. Speck, Frank Gouldsmith. Geographical names and legends at Mohegan. U.S. Bureau of American Ethnology. Annual report 43:253-59. 1925-26.
  Appendix to his Native tribes and dialects of Connecticut, a Mohegan-Pequot diary.
  A record of names in the old Mohegan community on the Thames River.

1034. Trumbull, James Hammond. Indian names of places, etc., in and on the borders of Connecticut: with interpretations of some of them. Hartford, Case, Lockwood & Brainard Co., 1881. 93p.
  Review: *Nation* 32:424-25, June 16, 1881.

1035. Tyler, Clarice E. Topographical terms in the seventeenth century records of Connecticut and Rhode Island. *New England quarterly* 2:382-401, July 1929.
  "These terms provide some interesting illustrations of changes in the English language."—Griffin.

DELAWARE

1036. Dunlap, Arthur Ray. Dutch and Swedish place-names in Delaware. Newark, Del., Pub. for the Institute of Delaware History and Culture by the Univ. of Delaware Press, 1956. 66p.
  A collection of some 132 names of Dutch or Swedish origin, with a discussion of each, based on researches on 17th-century maps and documents.
  Review: by C. A. Weslager, *Names* 5:182-83, Sept. 1957.

1037. ——— An example of dialect in Delaware place names. *American speech* 25:71-72, Feb. 1950.
  Hecklebirnie, dialect word for "hell," and Hackley Barney, both formerly found in Delaware.

1038. ——— More light on "Catenamon." Archaeological Society of Delaware. Bulletin 6:1-5, April 1954.

1039. ——— Names for Delaware. *Names* 3:230-35, Dec. 1955.

1040. ——— & C. A. Weslager. Indian place names in Delaware. Wilmington, Archaeological Society of Delaware, 1950. 61p.
Review: by J. A. C. Leland, *Names* 1:59-61, March 1953; by James B. McMillan, *American speech* 27:190-91, Oct. 1952.

1041. Gannett, Henry. A gazetteer of Delaware. Washington, Govt. Print. Off., 1904. 15p. (U.S. Geological Survey. Bulletin no. 230)

1042. Weslager, C. A. An early American name puzzle. *Names* 2:255-62, Dec. 1954.
Origin of the name Hoere-kil.

1043. ——— Hockessin: another Delaware place-name puzzle. *Names* 12:10-14, March 1964.

DISTRICT OF COLUMBIA

1044. Anthropological Society of Washington, Washington, D.C. Geographic nomenclature of the District of Columbia. A report. Washington, 1893. 29-53p.
James Mooney, chairman of the committee.
From the *American anthropologist* 6:29-53, Jan. 1893.
A system for naming the streets.

1045. Capital street named for MacArthur. *New York times* March 6, 1942, p. 6, col. 1.
President Roosevelt signed bill renaming Conduit Road, Washington, D.C., MacArthur Blvd.

1046. Edwards, Richard. Statistical gazetteer of the State of Maryland, and the District of Columbia. To which is appended a business directory of the federal metropolis and suburbs. Baltimore, J. S. Waters; Washington, W. M. Morrison & Co., 1856. 328p.

1047. Hagner, Alexander Burton. Street nomenclature of Washington City. Columbia Historical Society. Records 7:237-61. 1904.
Suggests names and methods for naming the streets to take the place of the system in use—designation by letters.

1048. Hodgkins, George W. Naming the capitol and the capital. Columbia Historical Society. Records 60-62:36-53. 1960-62.

1049. Maine Avenue again on Washington maps. *New York times* May 15, 1938, sec. 4, p. 6, col. 6.
Congress moves to change name of Water St. to Maine Ave.

1050. Martin, Joseph. A new and comprehensive gazetteer of Virginia, and the District of Columbia. To which is added a History of Virginia from its first settlement to the year 1754: with an abstract of the principal events from that period to the independence of Virginia, written expressly for the work by a citizen of Virginia [W. H. Brockenbrough]. Charlottesville, J. Martin, 1836. 636p.

Also published 1835, and at Richmond without date under title A comprehensive description of Virginia and the District of Columbia.

1051. Mooney, James. Indian tribes of the District of Columbia. *American anthropologist* 2:259-66, July 1889.
Concerning aboriginal place-names and the current names for the same localities.

1052. Tindall, William. Naming the seat of government of the United States; a legislative paradox. Columbia Historical Society. Records 23:10-25. 1920.

1053. Tooker, William Wallace. On the meaning of the name Anacostia. *American anthropologist* 7:389-93, Oct. 1894.

1054. Weekley, Larry. McAuley Park streets perpetuate nuns' names. *Washington post* Feb. 6, 1965, sec. E, p. 1.

FLORIDA

1055. Applegate, Roberta. What's in a name? History in our parks. *Miami herald* June 24, 1962, sec. E, pt. II, p. 17.
In Miami area.

1056. Bloodworth, Bertha Ernestine. Florida place-names. Gainesville, Univ. of Florida, 1959. 260 l.
Thesis—Univ. of Florida.
Bibliography: 1. 256-59.

1057. Boone, Lalia. Florida, the land of epithets. *Southern folklore quarterly* 22:86-92. 1958.
Nicknames of place-names.

1058. Boyd, Mark F. Mission sites in Florida; an attempt to approximately identify the sites of Spanish mission settlements of the seventeenth century in northern Florida. *Florida historical quarterly* 17:255-80, April 1939.
Includes list of names as given in old manuscripts and maps.

1059. Chase, Carroll & Richard McP. Cabeen. The first hundred years of United States territorial postmarks, 1787-1887. Florida Territory. *American philatelist* 56:246-59, Jan. 1943.
Includes list of post offices, 1821-45, with notes on some names.

1060. Corse, Herbert M. Names of the St. Johns River. *Florida historical quarterly* 21:127-34, Oct. 1942.
Bibliographical footnotes.
Four centuries of history are reflected in the changing names of the St. Johns River.

1061. Craig, James C. Origins of street names. Jacksonville Historical Society. Papers 3:7-11. 1954.
Jacksonville, Fla.

1062. Dau, Frederick W. Indian and other names in Florida, their meaning and derivation; *In his* Florida old and new. New York, Putnam, 1934. p. 336.

1063. Drew, Frank. Some Florida names of Indian origin. *Florida Historical Society quarterly* 4:181-82, April 1926; 6:197-205, April 1928.

1064. Drew, Shelley. Place names in ten northeastern counties of Florida. *American speech* 37:255-65, Dec. 1962.

1065. Enumeration of Florida Spanish missions in 1675, with trans. of documents by Mark F. Boyd. *Florida historical quarterly* 27:181-85, Oct. 1948.

1066. Florida. Dept. of Agriculture. The seventh census of the State of Florida, 1945. Nathan Mayo, Commissioner of Agriculture. [Tallahassee, 1946?]. 141p.
Origin and names of Florida counties: p. 7-8.

1067. Hawks, John Milton. The Florida gazetteer, containing also a guide to and through the state; complete official and business directory; state and national statistics. New Orleans, Printed at the Bronze Pen Stfam [sic] Book and Job Office, 1871. 214p.

1068. McMullen, Edwin Wallace. Cape Canaveral and Chicago. *Names* 12:128-29, June 1964.
Report on discussion of the name change of Cape Canaveral to Cape Kennedy at the meeting of the American Name Society in Chicago Dec. 1963.

1069. ——— English topographic terms in Florida, 1563-1874. Gainesville, Univ. of Florida Press, 1953. 227p.
Also published as doctoral thesis, Columbia Univ. and on microfilm, Ann Arbor, University Microfilms, 1950. Publication no. 1877. Abstracted: *Microfilm abstracts* 10:204-05.
Dictionary of topographic terms found in Florida, with bibliography, preceded by an interesting introduction.
Review: by Margaret M. Bryant, *Names* 2:142-43, June 1954.

1070. ——— The origin of the term Everglades. *American speech* 28:26-34, Feb. 1953.
A revised article taken from his doctoral dissertation, above.
cf. James B. McMillan. To the editor. *American speech* 28:200-01, Oct. 1953.

1071. Phillips, Cabell. Canaveral Space Center renamed Cape Kennedy. *New York times* Nov. 29, 1963, p. 1, 20.
References to other newspaper articles on this name change follow:

Protests are mounting on renaming Canaveral. *New York times* Dec. 5, 1963, p. 35.
Cape's name change declared official. *New York times* Dec. 6, 1963, p. 18.
Federal group supported L. B. J. in retitling Cape Canaveral. *Kansas City star* Dec. 6, 1963.
Wright, C. E. Cape Kennedy. Space Center is renamed but city and port retain name Canaveral. *New York times* Dec. 8, 1963, sec. XX, p. 5.
Fail to block "Cape Kennedy"; despite residents' historical pleas, new name is likely to stick; dates from the 1500s. *Kansas City star* Dec. 8, 1963, p. 4AA.
Random notes from all over: Canaveral renamed in a hurry; "Kennedy"

approval reported in 3 hours by Udall—old name lasted centuries. *New York times* Dec. 9, 1963, p. 14.

Kennedy's name to Cape in 3-hour rush request. *Kansas City times* Dec. 12, 1963.

1072.   Read, William Alexander.   Caxambas, a Florida geographic name. *Language* 16:210-13, July 1940.

1073. —— Florida place-names of Indian origin and Seminole personal names. Baton Rouge, Louisiana State Univ. Press, 1934. 83p. (Louisiana State University studies, no. 11)
   Bibliography: p. 80.
   Review: by John R. Swanton, *American speech* 9:218-20, Oct. 1934; by James A. Robertson, *Florida Historical Society quarterly* 13:111-12, Oct. 1934.

1074. —— The Hitchiti name of Silver Springs, Florida. *Modern language notes* 53:513-14, Nov. 1938.
   The Indian name may be freely translated as "wells of light."

1075.   Simpson, James Clarence.   Middle Florida place names. *Apalachee* 1946: 68-77.
   Indian names.

1076. —— A provisional gazetteer of Florida place-names of Indian derivation, either obsolescent or retained, together with others of recent application. Ed. by Mark F. Boyd. Tallahassee, 1956. 158p. (Florida. Geological Survey. Special publication no. 1)
   Review: by E. Wallace McMullen, *Names* 4:249-52, Dec. 1956; by John W. Griffin, *Florida historical quarterly* 35:194, Oct. 1956.

1077.   Tongue-twisting name to stay. *Lincoln (Neb.) evening journal and Nebraska State journal* Aug. 1, 1962, p. 2.
   Pilaklakaha Ave. in Auburndale, Fla.

1078.   Utley, George Burwell.   Origin of the county names in Florida. *Magazine of history* 8:77-81, Aug. 1908.
   Reprinted in Florida Historical Society. Publications quarterly 1:29-35, Oct. 1908.

1079.   Wilkinson, Herbert James.   The Florida place name "Jupiter." *American speech* 13:233-34, Oct. 1938.

GEORGIA

1080.   Cohen, Hennig.   On the word Georgian. *Georgia historical quarterly* 37:347-48, Dec. 1953.
   1735- .

1081.   Ee places in Georgia. *Sun*, New York, March 30, 1938.
   Most of those discussed end in -hatchee, meaning river in the Seminole-Creek language.

1082. Georgia. Dept. of Archives and History. Georgia's official register.
Each issue has section County data, which includes origin of the name of the counties.

1083. Godley, Margaret W. Georgia county place-names.
Thesis (M.A.) Emory Univ., 1935.

1084. Goff, John H. The beaverdam creeks. *Georgia mineral newsletter* 7:117-22, Fall 1954.
Streams in Georgia that now have or formerly had Beaver in their name.

1085. ———— The buffalo in Georgia. *Georgia review* 11:19-28, Spring 1957.
Georgia place-names which contain the word Buffalo.

1086. ———— The Creek village of "Cooccohapofe" on Flint River. *Georgia mineral newsletter* 14:34-35, Spring 1961.
Concerning its location and derivation.

1087. ———— The derivations of Creek Indian place names. *Georgia mineral newsletter* 14:63-70, Summer-Fall 1961.

1088. ———— The devil's half-acre. *Georgia review* 9:290-96, Fall 1955.
Reprinted in *Georgia mineral newsletter* 12:27-29, Spring-Summer 1959.
Deals with Georgia appellations containing the words devil and hell, like Devil's Elbow, Hell's Half Acre.

1089. ———— Hog Crawl Creek. *Georgia mineral newsletter* 7:38-40, Spring 1954.
A study of the name.

1090. ———— The "Hurricane" place names in Georgia. *Georgia review* 18:224-35, Summer 1964.

1091. ———— Old Chattahoochee town, an early Muscogee Indian settlement. *Georgia mineral newsletter* 6:52-54, Summer 1953.
The name and site of the town.

1092. ———— The poor mouthing place names. *Georgia review* 12:440-50, Winter 1958.
Republished in *Georgia mineral newsletter* 12:65-68, Fall 1959.
Place-names that reflect poverty.

1093. ———— Short studies of Georgia place names. *Georgia mineral newsletter* 7:87-88, 124-28, 163-64, Summer-Winter 1954; 8:22-26, 78-81, 122-25, 158-60. 1955; 9:32-36, 75-80, 105-08, 136-40. 1956; 10:32-35, 56-60, Spring-Summer 1957; 11:31-35, 54-59, 131-32, Spring-Summer, Winter 1958; 12:63-65, Fall 1959; 13:35-42, 102-06, 129-38, Spring, Summer, Fall 1960; 14:30-34, Spring 1961; 15:31-33, 95-101, Spring-Summer, Fall-Winter 1962; 16:45-53, 88-97, Spring-Summer, Fall-Winter 1963; 17:55-73. 1964-65.

1094. ———— Some old road names in Georgia. *Emory University quarterly* 14:30-42, March 1958.
Republished in *Georgia mineral newsletter* 11:98-102, Autumn 1958.

1095. —— Ty Ty as a geographic name. *Georgia mineral newsletter* 7:36-38, Spring 1954.

1096. Irvine, William Stafford. Governor Wilson Lumpkin and the naming of Marthasville. *Atlanta historical bulletin* 2:46-56. 1937.

1097. —— Terminus and Deanville, local names of long ago, of the site of Atlanta. *Atlanta historical bulletin* 3:101-19. 1938.

1098. Jones, Billie Walker. Origin of the name Dry Branch, Georgia. *Georgia mineral newsletter* 10:69, Summer 1957.

1099. Lanman, Charles. The falls of Tallulah. *Magazine of history* 19:249-53, Dec. 1914.
Meaning of the name, also of Deer Leap, Hawthorn's Pool, and Hanck's Sliding Pool.

1100. Mitchell, Eugene M. Queer place names in old Atlanta. *Atlanta historical bulletin* 5:22-31, April 1931.

1101. Read, William Alexander. Indian stream-names in Georgia. *International journal of American linguistics* 15:128-32, April 1949; 16:203-07, Oct. 1950.

1102. Sherwood, Adiel. A gazetteer of Georgia; containing a particular description of the state; its resources, counties, towns, villages, and whatever is usual in statistical works. 4th ed., rev. and cor. Macon, Ga., S. Boykin; Atlanta, J. Richards; etc. etc., 1860. 209p.
1st ed. 1827; 2d ed. 1829; 3d ed. 1837 (two printings).

1103. —— A gazetteer of the State of Georgia, by Rev. Adiel Sherwood; biographical sketch by John B. Clark; foreword by President Spright Dowell, Mercer University. The present edition being a facsimile reprint of the original 1827 publication, with a map of Georgia from the 1829 edition and a portrait of the author. Athens, Ga., Univ. of Georgia Press, 1939. 143p.

1104. U.S. 88th Congress, 1st session. House. A bill to designate the lake formed by the Walter F. George Lock and Dam, Alabama and Georgia, as "Lake Chattahoochee." H. R. 2127. Jan. 17, 1963. Washington, 1963. 1p.
Introduced by Mr. Forrester and referred to the Committee on Public Works.

1105. U.S. 88th Congress, 1st session. Senate. A bill to designate the lake formed by the Walter F. George Lock and Dam, Alabama and Georgia, as Lake Eufaula. S. 454. Jan. 23 (legislative day, Jan. 15), 1963. Washington, 1963. 1p.
Introduced by Mr. Hill and Mr. Sparkman and referred to the Committee on Public Works.
An identical bill was introduced in the House as follows:

U.S. 88th Congress, 1st session. House. A bill to designate the lake formed by the Walter F. George Lock and Dam, Alabama and Georgia, as Lake Eufaula. H. R. 3163. Jan. 31, 1963. Washington, 1963. 1p.
Introduced by Mr. Andrews and referred to the Committee on Public Works.

HAWAII

1106. Alexander, William DeWitt. Hawaiian geographic names. U.S. Coast and Geodetic Survey. Report 1901/02, Appendix 7, p. 367-425.
Includes a glossary of the words most frequently occurring in Hawaiian geographic names, p. 396-99.

1107. Bryan, Edwin Horace. Hawaiian place names. Hawaiian annual 1947:255-74.

1108. Cartwright, Bruce. Place names in old Honolulu. *Paradise of the Pacific* 50:18-20, Jan. 1938.

1109. Coulter, John Wesley. A gazetteer of the Territory of Hawaii. Honolulu, Univ. of Hawaii, 1935. 241p. (University of Hawaii. Research publications, no. 11)
References on Hawaiian place-names: p. 238-39.

1110. The Flying trees of Lahaina, Maui. *Paradise of the Pacific* v. 61, Jan. 1949, Travel supp. p. 17.

1111. Helumoa. *Paradise of the Pacific* v. 61, April 1949, Travel supp. p. 22.
Name of coconut grove where Royal Hawaiian Hotel is located, also a street in Waikiki.

1112. Hogue, Charles Edward. Puowaina, consecrated hill. *Paradise of the Pacific* 61:6, 30, Oct. 1949.
From the *Honolulu advertiser*.
In Honolulu.

1113. Honolulu street names rich in lore and history. *Paradise of the Pacific* v. 59, Nov. 1947, Travel supp. p. 5.

1114. Hyde, C. M. Hawaiian poetical names for places. Hawaiian almanac and annual 1887:79-82.

1115. Judd, Henry Pratt. Place names on Oahu. *Paradise of the Pacific* 50:11-12, Feb. 1938.

1116. —— Pronouncing Hawaii's place names. *Paradise of the Pacific* 58:26, Dec. 1944.

1117. Kauai is island of many names. *Paradise of the Pacific* v. 61, Feb. 1949, Travel supp. p. 20-21.

1118. Kelsey, Theodore. The pronunciation of Hawaiian names. *Paradise of the Pacific* 42:25-30, Feb. 1929.

1119. Lindsey, Jessie Higbee. District and county guide of the Territory of Hawaii. Honolulu, 1947. 38p.
Typewritten.

1120. Lyons, C. J. History in Honolulu streets: highway names are full of

meaning. Hawaiian annual 1932:74-76.
As told by C. J. Lyons in the *P. C. advertiser* March 3, 1902.

1121. ——— The meaning of some Hawaiian place-names. Hawaiian almanac and annual 1901:181-82.

1122. [The Naming of the streets of Honolulu]. Hawaiian almanac and annual 1884:73.

1123. Oahu place names. *Paradise of the Pacific* v. 61, Feb. 1949, Travel supp. p. 28.

1124. Obsolete street names. Hawaiian almanac and annual 1897:88-89.
In Honolulu.

1125. Odd named localities. Hawaiian almanac and annual 1906:108.
In Honolulu.

1126. On Hawaiian duplicated place names. Hawaiian almanac and annual 1905: 150-54.

1127. Sandwich vs. Hawaiian Islands. Hawaiian almanac and annual 1923:70-71.

1128. Stewart, George Rippey. Hawaii; *In his* Names on the land; a historical account of place-naming in the United States. Rev. and enl. ed. Boston, Houghton Mifflin, 1958. p. 412-23.

1129. Street name index. Honolulu Municipal Reference Library.
Card file—continuing.

1130. Taylor, Clarice B. & George H. Miranda. Honolulu street names. *Honolulu star-bulletin* Jan. 16-April 21, 1956.

1131. Thrum, Thomas George. Hawaiian place names; *In* Andrews, Lorrin. A dictionary of the Hawaiian language. Rev. by Henry H. Parker. Prepared under the direction of the Board of Commissioners of Public Archives of the Territory of Hawaii. Honolulu, Pub. by the Board, 1922. p. 625-74.

1132. U.S. Board on Geographic Names. Decisions. Washington, Dept. of the Interior.
Hawaii is included in various Decision lists through 1958. Beginning with list no. 5902, Jan. 1959, Hawaii is included in its alphabetical place with the other states.

1133. ——— Decisions on names in Hawaii. July 1954. Washington, Dept. of the Interior, 1954. 50p. (*Its* Decision list, no. 5403)
Contains 966 decisions.

1134. ——— Names approved by the United States Geographic Board on the recommendation of the Advisory Committee on Hawaiian Geographic Names; *In its* Fifth report. Washington, Govt. Print. Off., 1921. p. 362-90.

1135. U.S. Geological Survey. Water resources of Hawaii, 1909-1911. Prepared under the direction of M. O. Leighton by W. F. Martin and C. H. Pierce. Washington,

Govt. Print. Off., 1913. 552p. (Water-supply paper 318)
Meaning of geographic names: p. 498.
Glossary of some geographic names: p. 498-505.
Principal watercourses, by islands: p. 506-09.
Gazetteer: p. 509-36.

1136. U.S. Hydrographic Office. Gazetteer (no. 4). Hawaiian Islands. Nov. 1943. Washington, Govt. Print. Off., 1944. 51p. (H. O. Misc. no. 884. Reprint Sept. 1944 of H. O. Misc. no. 10, 884)

1137. U.S. Office of Geography. Hawaiian Islands; official standard names approved by the United States Board on Geographic Names. Washington, 1956. 89p. (U.S. Board on Geographic Names. Gazetteer no. 24)

1138. Westervelt, W. D. Legendary places in Honolulu. Hawaiian Historical Society. Annual report 1910:10-21.

1139. Wrestling with place names. Hawaiian almanac and annual 1922:82-87.

IDAHO

1140. Baker, Marcus. Survey of the northwestern boundary of the United States, 1857-1861. U.S. Geological Survey. Bulletin 174:58-61. 1900.
Indian names of camps, stations, rivers, etc. along the 49th parallel in Washington, Idaho, and Montana. Based on the work George Gibbs did for the Smithsonian Institution.

1141. Boise City's change of name. *New York times* Aug. 28, 1940, p. 18, col. 7.

1142. Bridger, Clyde A. The counties of Idaho. *Pacific Northwest quarterly* 31: 187-206, April 1940.
Bibliographical footnotes.
Notes on the creation of the counties, and their boundaries at different periods. Includes copies of acts of the first legislature establishing counties; a table of Counties not now in Idaho; Counties in Idaho; and a section on Origin of county names.

1143. Chamberlain, Alexander F. Geographic terms of Kootenay origin. *American anthropologist* n.s. 4:348-50, April-June 1902.
"Concerned with names of places, camp-sites, and stations, along the 49th parallel in British Columbia, Washington, Idaho, and Montana. These names which seem to have been taken from the language of the Kootenay Indians of this region are mentioned in the reports on the boundary survey. The meanings and etymologies are given where possible."—Price.

1144. Elsensohn, Alfreda, *Sister*. Pioneer days in Idaho County. Caldwell, Idaho, Caxton Printers, 1947-51. 2v.
Name Idaho 1:10-16; origin of other names scattered throughout.

1145. Ghost towns; *In* U.S. Federal Writers' Project. Idaho. The Idaho encyclopedia. Caldwell, Idaho, Caxton Printers, 1938. p. 98-114.

1146. Koch, Elers. Geographic names of western Montana and northern Idaho. *Oregon historical quarterly* 49:50-62, March 1948.

1147. Kramer, Fritz L. Idaho place name records. *Western folklore* 12:283-86, Oct. 1953.

1148. —— Idaho town names. Idaho. State Historical Dept. Biennial report 23:14-114. 1951-52.
    Review: by H. M. Lovett, *Names* 1:216-17, Sept. 1953.

1149. New notes on the word "Idaho." *Idaho yesterdays* 2:26-28, Spring 1958.
    Reprinted: Boise, Idaho Historical Society, 1959. [4]p. (Idaho historical series, no. 1)
    Meaning of word unknown.

1150. Rees, John E. Idaho chronology, nomenclature, bibliography. Chicago, Conkey, 1918. 125p.
    Includes the following item; also a section on Idaho nomenclature, p. 52-118.

1151. —— Idaho, its meaning, origin and application. Portland, Ore., Ivy Press, 1917. 12p.
    Reprinted from the *Oregon historical quarterly* 18:83-92, June 1917; also included in the item preceding, p. 46-51.

1152. Talbert, Ernest W. Some non-English place names in Idaho. *American speech* 13:175-78, Oct. 1938.

1153. Territory of Idaho; *In* Brosnan, Cornelius James. History of the State of Idaho. New York, Scribner, 1918. p. 117-22; also in U.S. Congress. Congressional globe, 37th Congress, 3d session, 1862-63, p. 166, 884, 905, 914, 924, 951, 1509, 1513, 1525, 1530, 1542.
    On March 3, 1863, the bill organizing Idaho Territory was passed. There was considerable discussion as to whether the name should be Montana or Idaho, but Idaho was finally chosen.

1154. Todd, C. C. Origin and meaning of the geographic name Palouse. *Washington historical quarterly* 24:190-92, July 1933.
    "A modification of the Indian tribal name Palloatpallahs."—Griffin.

1155. U.S. 88th Congress, 1st session. Senate. A bill to change the name of the Bruces Eddy Dam and Reservoir in the State of Idaho to the Dworshak Dam and Reservoir. S. 850. Feb. 19, 1963. Washington, 1963. 2p.
    Introduced by Mr. Jordan and Mr. Church and referred to the Committee on Interior and Insular Affairs.
    In honor of the late Senator from Idaho.
    Subsequent documents relating to this bill were published as follows:

    U.S. 88th Congress, 1st session. Senate. Changing the name of Bruces Eddy Dam and Reservoir, Idaho, to the Dworshak Dam and Reservoir. Report no. 268, to accompany S. 850. June 19, 1963. Calendar no. 249. Washington, 1963. 2p.
    Submitted by Mr. McNamara, from the Committee on Public Works, without amendment.

    —— [Reprint of the original bill, June 19, 1963, to accompany the report. Report no. 268 and Calendar no. 249 added]. 2p.

U.S. 88th Congress, 1st session. House. An act to change the name of the Bruces Eddy Dam and Reservoir in the State of Idaho to the Dworshak Dam and Reservoir. S. 850. In the House of Representatives June 24, 1963. Washington, 1963. 2p.
Referred to the Committee on Public Works. Passed the Senate June 20, 1963.

——— Changing the name of Bruces Eddy Dam and Reservoir, Idaho, to the Dworshak Dam and Reservoir. Report no 569, to accompany S. 850. July 22, 1963. Washington, 1963. 2p.
Submitted by Mr. Davis, from the Committee on Public Works, without amendment.

——— [Reprint of the act, July 22, 1963, to accompany the report. Report no. 569 and House Calendar no. 109 added]. 2p.

1156. U.S. Federal Writers' Project. Idaho. Idaho, a guide in word and picture. 2d ed. rev. New York, Oxford Univ. Press, 1950. 300p.
1st ed. 1937.
Origin of names: p. 279-86.

1157. Walgamott, Charles Shirley. South Idaho's names; *In his* Six decades back. Caldwell, Idaho, Caxton Printers, 1936. p. 349-58.

ILLINOIS

1158. Ackerman, William K. The origin of names of stations on the line of the Illinois-Central Railroad Company; *In his* Early Illinois railroads. Chicago, Fergus Print. Co., 1884. p. 109-52.
Also published separately, 67p.

1159. Allen, John W. Legends & lore of southern Illinois. Carbondale, Southern Illinois Univ., Area Services Division, 1963. 404p.
Chap. 2, p. 40-51, deals with southern Illinois place-names.

1160. Barge, William D. Illinois county names. *Magazine of history* 9:273-77, May 1909.

1161. ——— The rejected Illinois county names. A paper prepared for the Illinois State Historical Society, and submitted at its annual meeting, Jan. 24, 1906. Chicago, 1906. 34p.
Also in Illinois State Historical Society. Transactions 1906:122-37 (Illinois State Historical Library. Publications 11:122-37. 1906).

1162. ——— & Norman W. Caldwell. Illinois place-names. Illinois State Historical Society. Journal 29:189-311, Oct. 1936.

1163. Beck, Lewis Caleb. A gazetteer of the states of Illinois and Missouri; containing a general view of each state, a general view of their counties, and a particular description of their towns, villages, rivers, &c., &c. With a map, and other engravings. Albany, Printed by C. R. and G. Webster, 1823. 352p.

1164. Briggs, Harold E. Folklore of southern Illinois. *Southern folklore*

quarterly 16:207-17, Dec. 1952.
The origin of the name Egypt, p. 208-09.

`1165. Brown, Donald E. and Frank E. Schooley. Pronunciation guide for Illinois place names. Urbana, Univ. of Illinois, Division of Univ. Broadcasting, College of Journalism and Communications, 1957. 48p.

1166. Chase, Carroll & Richard McP. Cabeen. The first hundred years of United States territorial postmarks, 1787-1887. Illinois Territory. *American philatelist* 56:179-83, Dec. 1942.
Includes list of post offices.

1167. Custer, Milo. The name Bloomington, and the "ington" names. Bloomington, Ill., 1925. 6p. (Central Illinois Historical Society. Publications no. 3)
In general an analysis of the "ington" names; in particular an interpretation of the word Bloomington. Data apply to all Bloomingtons, of which there are several, author says. He often refers to "our Bloomington," meaning Illinois.

1168. Griffith, Will. Egyptian place-names. *Egyptian key* 2:29-31, March 1947.
Some southern Illinois appellations are unusually interesting.

1169. Halpert, Herbert. "Egypt"—a wandering place-name legend. *Midwest folklore* 4:165-68, Fall 1954.
Reprinted in Richard Mercer Dorson, Buying the wind: regional folklore in the United States. Chicago, Univ. of Chicago Press, 1964. p. 295-99.
Discrepancies between the historical explanation of the name Egypt for southern Illinois and the legendary one.

1170. Harris, Jesse W. Illinois place-name lore. *Midwest folklore* 4:217-20, Winter 1954.

1171 ——— The origin of Grand Tower; *In his* article, Myths and legends from southern Illinois. *Hoosier folklore* 5:14, March 1946.
Reported by Lydia Keneipp, Grand Tower.

1172. ——— Wetaug—a place-name puzzle. *Names* 9:126-28, June 1961.

1173. How Egypt got it's [sic] name. *Egyptian key* 2:31, March 1947.

1174. Hubbard, Anson M. A colony settlement, Geneseo, Illinois, 1836-1837. Illinois State Historical Society. Journal 29:403-31, Jan. 1937.
The origin of the name, p. 405-06.

1175. Hubbs, Barbara Burr. Egypt, the story of a name. *Egyptian key* 1:10, April-May 1943.
Egypt and other Egyptian names in southern Illinois.

1176. Illinois. Secretary of State. Official list of counties and incorporated municipalities of Illinois, 1955. Comp. by Charles F. Carpentier, Secretary of State. Printed by authority of the State of Illinois. n.p., n.d. 23p.
Gives many earlier names of places.

1177. Illinois state gazetteer and business directory, for the years 1864-5. Chicago, J. C. W. Bailey, 1864. 820p.

1178. Is Chicago "Skunk-town"? *Masterkey* (Southwest Museum, Los Angeles) 32:10, Jan.-Feb. 1958.
Signed: M R H.

1179. Is given new odor, meaning of "Chicago." *Chicago daily news* Dec. 29, 1955, p. 23.
Prof. Edward Taube stated in a paper read at the 4th annual meeting of the American Name Society that Chicago, meaning "cracked corn makers," stands as a memorial to the Illinois Indians who first occupied the area.

1180. Larsen, Carl. It's a stinking lie—a skunk didn't give Chicago its name. *Chicago sun-times* Dec. 29, 1955, p. 16.
Report on Prof. Edward Taube's paper, The name: Chicago, read at the annual meeting of the American Name Society.

1181. McCulloch, David. Old Peoria. Illinois State Historical Society. Transactions 1901:41-51 (Illinois State Historical Library. Publications 6:41-51)
Mention of early names scattered throughout this brief history of Peoria.

1182. Meyer, Alfred H. & Norma Baumeister. Toponomy in sequent occupance geography: Calumet region. Indiana Academy of Science. Proceedings 54:142-59. 1945.
Reprinted separately, 1945.
"The systematic study of place names, in association with the physical and cultural elements of a region, is often helpful in relating and integrating geographic phenomena. Particularly is this true in a sequent occupance study in which the 'philological fossils,' as relics of the landscape, may be instrumental in reconstructing the historical-geographic reality of a region. The sequent occupance toponomic technique is applied chorographically to the Calumet region of northwestern Indiana and northeastern Illinois."—Abstract.

1183. The Name of Illinois. *Annals of Iowa* 3:523-24, July 1865.
Source of the name is attributed to the French Isle [sic] aux Nois.

1184. Peck, John Mason. A gazetteer of Illinois, in three parts; containing a general view of the state, a general view of each county, and a particular description of each town, settlement, stream, prairie, bottom, bluff, etc.; alphabetically arranged. 2d ed., entirely rev., cor., and enl. Philadelphia, Grigg & Elliott, 1837. 328p.
1st ed.: Jacksonville, R. Goudy, 1834. 376p.

1185. Peterson, Gordon E. Place names of Bond County, Illinois. Abingdon, Ill., 1951.
Unpublished manuscript.

1186. Professor sheds some new light on Indian origin of city's name. *Chicago daily tribune* Dec. 29, 1955, p. 4.
Dr. Edward Taube in a paper read at annual meeting of American Name Society offered as the meaning of the name Chicago "cracked corn makers," derived from an Algonquian tribal name.

1187. Sandham, William R. A lost Stark County town. Illinois State Historical Society. Journal 13:109-12, April 1920.
The story of Osceola and of its founder.

1188. —— The naming of a group of eight Illinois counties created at the same time. Illinois State Historical Society. Journal 25:120-23, April-July 1932.
States the source for the names of the counties and county seats.

1189. Schooley, Frank E. & Donald E. Brown. Pronunciation guide for Illinois towns and cities. Urbana, School of Journalism, Radio Station WILL, Univ. of Illinois, 1948. Unpaged.

1190. Smith, Grace Partridge. Speech currents in "Egypt." *American speech* 17:169-73, Oct. 1942.
Includes notes on place-names of southern Illinois, p. 169 and 173.

1191. —— They call it Egypt. *Names* 2:51-54, March 1954.
The nickname Egypt for the southern portion of Illinois.

1192. Smith, Hermon Dunlap. Des Plaines, Eau Plaine, or Kickapoo. Chicago, 1940. 3p.
Autographic reproduction of typewritten copy. In Newberry Library, Chicago, Ill.

1193. Steward, John Fletcher. Chicago, origin of the name of the city and the old portages. Illinois State Historical Society. Transactions 1904:460-66 (Illinois State Historical Library. Publication no. 9)
Also published separately.

1194. Syfert, Vernon A. The naming of Bloomington. Illinois State Historical Society. Journal 29:161-67, July 1936.

1195. Thompson, Joseph J. Chicagou—the grand chief of the Illinois. *Illinois Catholic historical review* 7:332-37, April 1925.
"Points out in an interesting discussion the meaning in various Indian languages of the protonym of the western metropolis."—Price.

1196. Vogel, Virgil J. Illinois' onion patch: the origin of Chicago's name. *Illinois history* 12:38-41, Nov. 1958.

1197. —— The Indian origin of some Chicago street names. *Chicago schools journal* 36:145-52, March-April 1955.

1198. —— Indian place names in Illinois. Springfield, Illinois State Historical Society, 1963. 176p. (Pamphlet series, no. 4)
Reprinted from Illinois State Historical Society. Journal 55:45-71, 157-89, 271-308, 385-458. 1962.

1199. —— The mystery of Chicago's name. *Mid-America* 40:163-74, July 1958.
A detailed search of original sources and discussions.

1200 —— Some Illinois place-name legends. *Midwest folklore* 9:155-62, Fall 1959.

INDIANA

1201. Bates, Roy M. Paper towns and ghost towns of Allen County. *Old Fort news* 6:1-12, Sept. 1941.
Towns which were platted but never developed, and towns which died leaving little trace of their existence.

1202. Beckwith, Hiram Williams. Indian names of water courses in the State of Indiana. Indiana. Dept. of Geology and Natural History. Annual report 12:37-43. 1882.
Reprinted in part in *American naturalist* 18:101, Jan. 1884.
Includes map, prepared by Daniel Hough, showing Indian names of lakes, rivers, towns, forts, etc. of Indiana.

1203. Bowers, John O. Dream cities of the Calumet. Gary, Calumet Press, 1929. 32p.
Published also in Lake County Historical Association. Publication 10:174-98. 1929.
Early towns which were planned, and in some cases started, but never reached maturity.

1204. Brewster, Paul G. A glance at some Indiana place-names. *Hoosier folklore bulletin* 2:14-16, June 1943.
Grouped into 12 categories.
Additional observations on Indiana place-names, *ibid.* 3:74-76, Dec. 1944.

1205. Brunvand, Jan. Some Indiana place-name legends. *Midwest folklore* 9:245-48, Winter 1959.

1206. Burns, Lee. Some vanished towns of pioneer days. Society of Indiana Pioneers. Yearbook 1940:7-12.

1207. Chamberlain, E. The Indiana gazetteer, or Topographical dictionary of the State of Indiana. 3d ed. Indianapolis, E. Chamberlain, 1850. 440p.
First issued 1849. p. 425-40 differ. Probably a 3d ed. of John Scott's The Indiana gazetteer (see no. 1240).
Gives origin of name of county in most instances.

1208. Cowen, M. V. B. The Indiana state gazetteer and shippers' guide for 1866-7. Lafayette, Rosser, Spring and Cowen, 1866. 428p.

1209. De la Hunt, Thomas James. History lessons from Indiana names. *Indiana history bulletin* v.3, Extra no. 2:43-49, March 1926.

1210. Dunn, Jacob Piatt. Glossary of Indian names and supposed Indian names in Indiana; *In his* Indiana and Indianans. Chicago, 1919. 1:86-97.
This alphabetical list gives the source and significance of the names in Indiana. Practically the same material is to be found in the author's True Indian stories.

1211. ―――― Indiana geographical nomenclature. *Indiana magazine of history* 8:109-14, Sept. 1912.
Offers corrections of article, Indiana geographical nomenclature (see no. 1228).

1212. —— The meaning of "Tassinong." *Indiana magazine of history* 11:348-51, Dec. 1915.
Probably an original Indian place-name, not a corruption of the French tassement.

1213. —— True Indian stories, with glossary of Indiana Indian names. Indianapolis, Sentinel Print. Co., 1908. 320p.
Reprinted 1964 by Lawrence W. Shultz.
Glossary: p. 253-320.
Manuscript notes on which Mr. Dunn based this and the revised glossary in his Indiana and Indianans are in the Indiana State Library. Indiana Division.
Review: *American historical review* 14:628, April 1909.

1214. —— The word Hoosier; *In his* Indiana and Indianans. Chicago, 1919. 2:1121-55.
Suggests a derivation from the word hoozer, also that it was imported by Cumberland Mountain settlers.

1215. —— The word Hoosier, by Jacob Piatt Dunn; and John Finley, by Mrs. Sarah A. Wrigley. Indianapolis, Bobbs-Merrill, 1907. 37p. (Indiana Historical Society. Publications, v. 4, no. 2)
An earlier version appeared in *Indiana magazine of history* 1:86-96, June 1905.

1216. Ellis, Horace. Indiana's map of patriots. *National republic* 20:8-9, 47, July 1932.
"A discussion of place-names of Indiana which have been selected because of the popularity of noted men."—*American speech.*

1217. Feightner, Harold C. Indiana county government. *Indiana history bulletin* 9:262-63, March 1932.
An alphabetical table of the counties, giving origin of name, date of organization, and present county seat.

1218. Fort Wayne. Public Library. Streets of Fort Wayne. Fort Wayne, 1953. 33p.
A condensation, with some additions which bring it up to date, of a speech by Angus C. McCoy before the Quest Club on Nov. 30, 1945.

1219. Guernsey, E. Y. Indiana; the influence of the Indian upon its history, with Indian and French names for natural and cultural locations. Indiana. Conservation Dept. Publication no. 122. 1933. map.

1220. Hodgin, Cyrus Wilburn. The naming of Indiana. Richmond, Ind., Nicholson Print Co., 1903. 16p. (Papers of the Wayne County, Indiana, Historical Society, v.1, no. 1)
On the source and meaning of the name, and of the nickname Hoosier. Includes poem by John Finley, The Hoosier's nest.

1221. Hoffmann, Frank A. Place names in Brown County. *Midwest folklore* 11:57-62, Spring 1961.

1222. "Hoosier" (based on files in Indiana State Library). *Indiana history bulletin* 15:211-12, April 1938.

1223. Indiana. Laws, statutes, etc. A concurrent resolution concerning Indian names of streams and lakes, directing the State Highway Commission to erect suitable markers at all places in the state where state highways cross streams bearing Indian names, and providing for the education of the public in the use of such Indian names; *In* Indiana. General Assembly. Acts 1:1818-19. 1945.

1224. Indiana. State Library. Indiana Division. Origin of names of Indiana counties.
Typewritten. Based on the work of Max Robinson Hyman, William S. Haymond, and—for Indian names—Jacob Piatt Dunn.

1225. Indiana. State Planning Board. Gazetteer of Indiana cities, towns and villages. 1936.
Typewritten. Rev. ed., 1939?, typewritten.

1226. Indiana Board on Geographic Names. Findings. May 1961/June 1962- .
Indianapolis. v. 1- .
Published to date: no. 1-2, May 1961-June 1963.

1227. Indiana county names. *Magazine of history with notes and queries* 2:420-23, Dec. 1905.

1228. Indiana geographical nomenclature. *Indiana magazine of history* 8:70-83, June 1912.
Taken from Henry Gannett, The origin of certain place names in the United States (see no. 133).
cf. article by Jacob Piatt Dunn, Indiana geographical nomenclature, no. 1211.

1229. Indiana Historical Society. Notes on sources of information concerning lost towns.
Card file in the Society library. Supplemented by special card index in the Indiana State Library. Indiana Division.

1230. Kleber, Albert. The naming of Troy, Indiana. *Indiana magazine of history* 44:178-80, June 1948.
The original county seat of Perry County, named *ca.* 1847.

1231. Lanahan, Margaret. "Silopanaidni." *Outdoor Indiana* Dec. 1950, p. 17-18.
The derision which the name Indianapolis met at first, and the suggestion of the *Vincennes sentinel* editor that the name, later copied elsewhere, be spelled backward.

1232. Lockridge, Ross F. Indian names of Indiana streams. *Indiana teacher* April 1945, p. 215-16.

1233. McCoy, Angus C. The streets of Fort Wayne. *Old Fort news* 9:3-25, Dec. 1945.
Origin of the names.

1234. Meyer, Alfred H. & Norma Baumeister. Toponomy in sequent occupance geography: Calumet region. Indiana Academy of Science. Proceedings 54:142-59. 1945.
Reprinted separately, 1945.
"The systematic study of place names, in association with the physical and

cultural elements of a region, is often helpful in relating and integrating geographic phenomena. Particularly is this true in a sequent occupance study in which the 'philological fossils,' as relicts of the landscape, may be instrumental in reconstructing the historical-geographic reality of a region. The sequent occupance toponomic technique is applied chorographically to the Calumet region of northwestern Indiana and northeastern Illinois."—Abstract.

1235. Names of Indiana streams. *Indiana history bulletin* 9:543-45, Aug. 1932.
"Discussion of how streams in Indiana were named."—Griffin.

1236. Nicholson, Meredith. The Hoosiers. 2d ed. New York, Macmillan, 1915.
p. 29-36.
Traces the origin of the term to a date earlier than the use of it in John Finley's poem The Hoosier's nest, a New Year's address for the *Indianapolis journal* 1830.

1237. Osterhus, Grace Buzby. Names of northern Indiana counties reflect pioneer thinking. Society of Indiana Pioneers. Yearbook 1943:12-18.

1238. Place-names index.
On cards, Indiana Historical Society Library. Indexes variant forms of names as found on old maps, in books, etc. Gives location, derivation of name, origin of name, other names for, etc. About 1,000 cards.

1239. Redfield's Indiana railway gazetteer, travelers' guide, and express and shippers' directory, embracing a complete alphabetical gazetteer and travelers' guide, designating express and telegraph offices, railway stations and routes, and giving location, population and full traveling and shipping directions to all points in the state. Indianapolis, D. A. Redfield, 1865. 94p.

1240. Scott, John. The Indiana gazetteer, or Topographical dictionary; containing a description of the several counties, towns, villages, settlements, roads, lakes, rivers, creeks, and springs, in the State of Indiana. 2d ed. carefully rev., cor., and enl. Indianapolis, Douglass and Maguire, 1833. 200p.
1st ed., by John Scott, published in Centreville by John Scott and W. M. Doughty, 1826. 143p.
2d ed. published anonymously. Introduction states that the publishers had purchased copyright of John Scott's gazetteer. The Indiana gazetteer by E. Chamberlain (see no. 1207) is probably a 3d ed. of Scott's.

1241. —— The Indiana gazetteer, or Topographical dictionary. Indianapolis, Indiana Historical Society, 1954. 129p. (Indiana Historical Society. Publications, v. 18, no. 1)
Reprinted from the original edition, 1826.

1242. Short, Oscar D. Origin of the term "Hoosier." *Indiana magazine of history* 25:101-03, June 1929.

1243. Skinner, Hubert M. An echo from the era of the tassements. *Indiana magazine of history* 12:84-88, March 1916.
Skinner upholds his theory of the French derivation of Tassinong as opposed to Jacob Piatt Dunn's.

1244. That word "Hoosier" again. *Indiana history bulletin* 35:88-89, July 1958.
Reprinted from the *Indianapolis journal* with editorial comment.

Includes letter of John Vawter printed in the *Franklin democratic herald* Jan. 19, 1860.

1245. Town balks at its own name. *New York times* Aug. 21, 1937, p. 17, col. 8.
Petitions ask community name be changed from William Williams Corner to Billville.

1246. Tucker, Glenn. Was "Hoosier" a headgear? *Indiana history bulletin* 35: 141-42, Oct. 1958.
Suggests derivation of name from those who wore hats made by Hosier Brothers at the site of Clarksburg, now Rocklane.

1247. Turner, Timothy Gilman. Gazetteer of the St. Joseph Valley, Michigan and Indiana, with a view of its hydraulic and business capacities. Chicago, Hazlitt & Reed, Printers, 1867. 166p.

1248. Wells, George Y. Visit to Mecca (Ind.). Little town keeps its name as a reminder of Moslem settlement many years ago. *New York times* Aug. 31, 1952.

IOWA

1249. Andrews, L. F. The word "Iowa"—what it means. *Annals of Iowa* 3d ser. 2:465-69, July 1896.

1250. Barnes, Arthur M. Pronunciation guide to names of places and state office-holders in Iowa. Prepared in cooperation with the Iowa Radio-Telegraph News Association. 2d ed. Iowa City, State Univ. of Iowa, 1959. 12p.
1st ed. 1948.

1251. Casady, P. M. The naming of Iowa counties. *Annals of Iowa* 3d ser. 2:195-202, July-Oct. 1895.
Abstract of a paper read before the Pioneer Lawmakers' Association of Iowa, Feb. 15, 1894.

1252. Chase, Carroll & Richard McP. Cabeen. The first hundred years of United States territorial postmarks, 1787-1887. Iowa Territory. *American philatelist* 57:582-86, 797-803, May, Aug. 1944.
Includes list of post offices, with notes on some names.

1253. Childs, C. C. Names of Iowa counties. *Iowa historical record* 4:32-37, Jan. 1888.

1254. Cook, Pauline. Classical place names in Iowa. *Classical journal* 41:323-24, April 1946.

1255. Counties and county names; *In* Iowa. Secretary of State. Iowa official register 1909-10:687-716.
Also in Iowa. Secretary of State. Census of Iowa for 1880. Des Moines, 1883. p. 381-421.

1256. Curtis, Samuel Prentis. I-O-W-A. *Annals of Iowa* 10:286-87, Oct. 1872.

A plea that some one, properly qualified, will explain the real meaning of the word Iowa.

1257. Des Moines—origin and meaning. *Iowa historical record* 4:40, Jan. 1888.
    "Father Kempker in his 'History of the Catholic church in Iowa' gives his reasons for interpreting Des Moines as 'river of monks.' "—Price.

1258. Des Moines River. *Annals of Iowa* 3d ser. 10:342, Jan.-April 1912.
    An article quoted from the *Iowa advocate and half-breed journal,* Montrose, Iowa, Aug. 16, 1847, discussing the origin of the name.

1259. Dubuque County place names. *Dubuque telegraph-herald* Sept. 7, 1930.

1260. The Early names of Council Bluffs. *Annals of Iowa* 3d ser. 2:480, July 1896.
    A letter from D. C. Bloomer gives an account of early names of Council Bluffs, especially that of Kanesville.

1261. Eriksson, Erik McKinley. The name of Odebolt. *Palimpsest* 10:432-41, Dec. 1929.

1262. Fitzpatrick, Thomas Jefferson. The place-names of Appanoose County, Iowa. *American speech* 3:39-66, Oct. 1927.

1263. —— The place-names of Des Moines County, Iowa. *Annals of Iowa* 3d ser. 21:56-73, 127-40, 535-52, 604-40, July, Oct. 1937, Jan., April 1939.
    Bibliography: p. 635-40.

1264. —— The place-names of Lee County, Iowa. *Annals of Iowa* 3d ser. 17:13-58, July 1929.
    Bibliography: p. 57-58.

1265. —— The place-names of Van Buren County, Iowa. *Annals of Iowa* 3d ser. 18:12-41, 87-116, July, Oct. 1931.
    Bibliography: p. 113-16.

1266. Fulton, Alexander R. Iowa Indian nomenclature; *In his* The red man of Iowa. Des Moines, Mills & Co., 1882. p. 421-34.

1267. Garver, Frank Harmon. Boundary history of the counties of Iowa. *Iowa journal of history and politics* 7:3-129, Jan. 1909.
    In alphabetical order, the counties of the state are listed with historical data and the old names of those counties with changes.

1268. Glass, Remley J. Iowa-Minnesota townsite towns. *Annals of Iowa* 3d ser. 28:69-70, July 1946.
    Wheelerwood, Hanford, Cartersville, and Dougherty, platted by Iowa and Minnesota townsite company along the railroad right of way in Cerro Gordo County in 1898-99. Includes origin of names.

1269. The Hawk-eye. *Hawk-eye and Iowa patriot,* Burlington, v. 1, no. 14, p. 2, Sept. 5, 1839.

1270. "Hawkeye" the nickname for Iowans. *Annals of Iowa* 3d ser. 31:380-81, July 1952.

1271. Hildreth, W. H. The name "Iowa." *Annals of Iowa* 1:268-69, April 1864. From the *Davenport gazette* April 1860.

1272. Hills, Leon Corning. History and legends of place names in Iowa; the meaning of our map. 2d ed. Omaha, Omaha School Supply Co., 1938. 90p. 1st ed. 1937. 78p.
Key to references in various books consulted and quoted in the book: p. 89-90.

1273. Hoffman, M. M. The first gazetteer on Iowa. *Annals of Iowa* 3d ser. 18: 383-90, July 1932.
Contains information about Jedidiah Morse, The American gazetteer, 1797 (see no. 522) with excerpts of Iowa material.

1274. Honest to goodness, Iowa has real Podunk Center. *Des Moines (Iowa) Sunday Register* April 14, 1963, Iowa sec., p. 1, 3.
Consists of one small building that houses a grocery store, cafe, and family of five; not on the Madison County maps or in the postal guide.

1275. Howe, Samuel Storrs. A memoir of Indian names in Iowa. *Annals of Iowa* 2d ser. 1:3-28, Jan. 1882.

1276. Iowa. University. School of Journalism. Pronunciation guide to Iowa place names, prepared by Arthur M. Barnes. Iowa City, 1948. 2, 8 l.

1277. I-O-W-A. *Annals of Iowa* 10:234-35, July 1872.
Meaning of the name.

1278. An Iowa editor gives a nickname. *Hawk-eye* v. 5, no. 34, Jan. 18, 1844.
James G. Edwards, quoting his own editorial in the *Fort Madison patriot*, March 24, 1838, suggests the name Hawk-eyes, suggested to him by the title of Chief Black Hawk.

1279. Iowa—its original meaning. *Iowa historical record* 1:135-37, July 1885.
A letter from William Phelps to L. F. Ross is quoted, giving his opinion as to the derivation of the name.

1280. Iowa state gazetteer, embracing descriptive and historical sketches of counties, cities, towns and villages to which is added a shippers' guide and a classified business directory. Comp. and ed. by James T. Hair. Chicago, Bailey & Hair, 1865. 722p.

1281. Irish, C. W. Iowa. *Iowa historical record* 1:13-25, Jan. 1885.
The history of the state serves as a background for the evolution of the name.

1282. Johnson, Ava. Choosing a place-name. *Annals of Iowa* 3d ser. 31:538-42, Jan. 1953.

1283. Keyes, Charles R. Des Moines River, and origin of the name. *Annals of Iowa* 3d ser. 3:554-59, Oct. 1898.
Introduces several possible interpretations concerning the source of the name, with reference to historical maps.

1284. Lathrop, H. W. The naming of Lee County. *Iowa historical record* 9:505-08, July 1893.
Credit for this name in Iowa has usually been ascribed to Charles Lee, but the author discusses the possibility that it may have been named after other persons.

1285. Lea, Albert Miller. The book that gave to Iowa its name, a reprint. Iowa City, State Historical Society of Iowa, 1935. 53p.
Also reprinted in *Annals of Iowa* 3d ser. 11:115-67, July-Oct. 1913.
Includes reprint of title page of original: Notes on Wisconsin Territory by Lieutenant Albert M. Lea. Philadelphia, H. S. Tanner, 1836. And of cover-title: Notes on the Wisconsin Territory; particularly with reference to the Iowa District, or Black Hawk purchase.

1286. Ludwig, Mary Culbertson. Namer of towns. *Palimpsest* 29:161-73, June 1948.
Article on John I. Blair, railroader, who named numerous towns for friends and relatives.

1287. Mawrer, Oscar Edward. "I'oway, my I'owa-a-ay." *Atlantic monthly* 147:42 (2d pagination), June 1931.
Concerning the pronunciation of Iowa.

1288. Mereness, Newton D. Early post offices established in Iowa. *Iowa journal of history and politics* 28:34-35, Jan. 1930.

1289. Mott, David C. Abandoned towns, villages, and post offices of Iowa. *Annals of Iowa* 3d ser. 17:435-65, 513-43, 578-99; 18:42-69, 117-48, Oct. 1930-Oct. 1931.
Index to abandoned towns of Iowa, *ibid.* 18:189-220, Jan. 1932.

1290. Mott, Frank Luther. Pronunciation of Iowa. *Palimpsest* 38:100-05, March 1957.
Reprinted from *ibid.* 5:373-77, Oct. 1924.

1291. —— The pronunciation of the word Iowa. *Iowa journal of history and politics* 23:353-62, July 1925.

1292. Murdock, Samuel. Origin of the name of Iowa. *Iowa historical record* 12:458-62, April 1896.
Gives credit for the name to William Brown and Henry R. Schoolcraft, who, as a committee, brought before the legislature of Michigan a bill to organize the County of Iowa, a name derived from an Indian tribe, the Kiowas, meaning "across the river."

1293. The Name "Ottumwa." *Annals of Iowa* 3d ser. 29:503, Jan. 1949. From *Ottumwa courier* Aug. 7, 1948.

1294. The Naming of Floyd County. *Annals of Iowa* 3d ser. 2:398-400, April 1896.
Material assembled by P. M. Casady.

1295. The Naming of Henry County. *Annals of Iowa* 3d ser. 2:364, April 1896.
This article, which discusses the source of the county's name, is condensed from the *Iowa capital,* Des Moines, Nov. 6, 1895.

1296. Naming of Iowa counties. *Annals of Iowa* 3d ser. 36:395-400, Summer 1962.
From Iowa official register, 1909-1910.

1297. The Naming of the city of Davenport. *Annals of Iowa* 3d ser. 2:243-44,
July-Oct. 1895.
Mrs. Maria Peck argues, through the columns of the *Davenport democrat* for
Dec. 1894, that the city was named after Colonel George Davenport.

1298. Naming of Wisconsin and Iowa. *Annals of Iowa* 3d ser. 27:323-24, April
1946.
Naming of the territories described in a letter from Senator George W. Jones,
Iowa, to Charles Aldrich, curator of the Iowa Historical Department, in 1896.

1299. Odd stories disclose how Iowa towns got named. *Annals of Iowa* 3d ser.
36:71-72, Summer 1961.
From *Des Moines register* April 27, 1959.

1300. Organizing the County of Iowa. *Annals of Iowa* 3d ser. 3:224-25, Oct. 1897.
Copy of an act, passed by the legislature of the Territory of Michigan, Oct. 9,
1829, said by Hon. T. S. Parvin to be the first official publication in which the
name Iowa appeared.

1301. Origin of some Iowa place names. *Des Moines tribune* May 4, 17, 1940.

1302. Parvin, Theodore Sutton. The name Iowa. *Iowa historical record* 12:388-
89, Jan. 1896.

1303. Petersen, William J. Naval namesakes of Iowa cities. *Palimpsest* 34:481-
512, Nov. 1953.

1304. —— A town of many names. *Palimpsest* 45:324-30, Sept. 1964.
Reprinted from *ibid.* 20:349-54, Oct. 1939.
Muscatine.

1305. Price, Eliphalet. The origin and interpretation of the names of the rivers
and streams of Clayton County. *Annals of Iowa* 4:707-11, 753-59, July, Oct. 1866;
5:794-800, 842-47, Jan., April 1867.
The sources of some of the names of the rivers and streams are discussed.

1306. Read, Allen Walker. "Liberty" in Iowa. *American speech* 6:360-67, June
1931.
"Historical summary of use of 'Liberty' as a place name."—Griffin.

1307. —— Literary place names. *Palimpsest* 9:450-57, Dec. 1928.
Regarding place-names in Iowa derived from literature, from which something
may be learned of the character of the reading matter of the pioneer Iowan.

1308. —— Observations on Iowa place names. *American speech* 5:27-44,
Oct. 1929.

1309. —— Study of Iowa place names selected from counties A through F.
Thesis (M.A.) Univ. of Iowa, 1926.

1310. Shambaugh, Benjamin F. The naming of Iowa. *Palimpsest* 16:81-86,

March 1935.

His shorter article, The naming of Iowa, was published in *Palimpsest* 5:370-72, Oct. 1924. It includes a paragraph on the use of Hawkeye.

1311. ——— The naming of Iowa. *Palimpsest* 38:97-99, March 1957.

1312. ——— The origin of the name Iowa. *Annals of Iowa* 3d ser. 3:641-44, Jan. 1899.

Bibliography of the name "Iowa": p. 644.

1313. ——— The territorial capital is named. *Palimpsest* 20:139-45, April 1939.

Iowa City.

1314. Signification in 1854 of Iowa and other Indian names. *Annals of Iowa* 3d ser. 15:541-42, Jan. 1927.

Mr. LeClaire, an Indian interpreter of the government, translates several Indian place-names in Iowa. He declares that Iowa means "a place of retreat" rather than "beautiful." The article is from the *Iowa City journal,* reprinted in the *Democratic union,* Keosauqua, Iowa, July 29, 1854.

1315. U.S. 88th Congress, 1st session. House. A bill to designate the dam being constructed and the reservoir to be formed on the Des Moines River, Iowa, as the Red Rock Dam and Lake Red Rock. H. R. 1135. Jan. 9, 1963. Washington, 1963. 2p.

Introduced by Mr. Smith and referred to the Committee on Public Works.

Subsequent documents relating to this bill were published as follows:

U.S. 88th Congress, 1st session. House. Designating the dam being constructed and the reservoir to be formed on the Des Moines River, Iowa, as the Red Rock Dam and Lake Red Rock. Report no. 618, to accompany H. R. 1135. July 30, 1963. Washington, 1963. 3p.

Submitted by Mr. Davis, from the Committee on Public Works, without amendment.

——— [Reprint of the original bill, July 30, 1963, to accompany the report. Report no. 618 and House Calendar no. 115 added]. 2p.

U.S. 88th Congress, 1st session. Senate. An act to designate the dam being constructed and the reservoir to be formed on the Des Moines River, Iowa, as the Red Rock Dam and Lake Red Rock. H. R. 1135. In the Senate Aug. 6, 1963. Washington, 1963. 2p.

Referred to the Committee on Public Works. Passed the House of Representatives Aug. 5, 1963.

——— Designating the dam being constructed and the reservoir to be formed on the Des Moines River, Iowa, as the Red Rock Dam and Lake Red Rock. Report no. 453, to accompany H. R. 1135. Aug. 23, 1963. Calendar no. 429. Washington, 1963. 3p.

Submitted by Mr. McNamara, from the Committee on Public Works, without amendment.

——— [Reprint of the act, Aug. 23, 1963, to accompany the report. Report no. 453 and Calendar no. 429 added]. 2p.

1316. Vizetelly, Frank. Pronunciation of Iowa. *Atlantic monthly* 147:62 (2d

pagination), April 1931.
  Traces the spelling of the name of the Indian tribe, 1689-1905.

1317. Willcockson, Mrs. Edwin. History of the origin of county names of the
State of Iowa. Sigourney, Iowa, 1957. 18 l.
  Typewritten. Copies at Newberry Library, Chicago; D A R Library, Washing-
ton, D.C.; Iowa Historical Society Library, Des Moines; and State Historical
Society Library, Iowa City.

1318. Williams, Ora. Camels gave a name to Iowa. *Annals of Iowa* 3d ser.
32:51-54, July 1953.
  Indianola.

1319. Zwart, Elizabeth Clarkson. How Iowa towns were named. *Des Moines
register* Oct. 14, 1934.

KANSAS

1320. Adams, F. G. County names. *Daily commonwealth,* Topeka, June 17, 1875.

1321. Admire, William Woodford. Origin of name, location of county seat and
date of organization of each county; *In his* Admire's political and legislative handbook for Kansas, 1891. Topeka, Crane, 1891. p. 200-14.

1322. Asks Breidenthal name for Tuttle Reservoir. *Kansas City star* March 30,
1960, p. 2.
  For Willard J. Breidenthal.

1323. Atchison, Topeka and Santa Fe Railway Company. Statement of origin of
names and stations on Panhandle Division of the Atchison, Topeka and Santa Fe
Railway Company. Amarillo, Tex., Office of Assistant General Manager, 1936.
40p.

1324. Barry, Louise. The renaming of Robidoux Creek, Marshall County. *Kansas historical quarterly* 18:159-63, May 1950.
  Previously named Vermillion Creek or West Fork, of Black Vermillion River.

1325. Baughman, Robert Williamson. Kansas in maps. Topeka, Kansas State
Historical Society, 1961. 104p.
  Includes a brief study of the origin and orthography of the name Kansas during
various periods (p. 5-6), and the earliest appearances of the name on maps.

1326. ——— Kansas post offices, May 29, 1828—August 3, 1961. Topeka, Kansas Postal History Society, 1961. 256p.
  Three major parts: 1. Alphabetical list, every known Kansas post office, past
and present; 2. Territorial list, limited to those established before Kansas became a state, Jan. 29, 1861, including pre-territorial offices created prior to
May 30, 1854; 3. County list, all post offices that ever existed within each county.
  Includes name changes.

1327. Beachy, E. B. Dykes. Famous men and heroic deeds recalled by the names of counties in Kansas. *Kansas City times* Dec. 6, 1951, p. 34.

1328. ———— Indians have left their marks on Kansas in unusual and musical names of towns. *Kansas City star* Feb. 23, 1950, p. 22.

1329. ———— Names of Kansas rivers reflect some of the history made on their banks. *Kansas City times* Jan. 17, 1950, p. 22.

1330. ———— Railroad men gave their names to towns which grew on Kansas prairie. *Kansas City star* March 9, 1950, p. 26.

1331. Campbell, W. M. Many mixups occur in Kansas counties; towns and counties of the same names sometimes are found hundreds of miles apart. *Topeka capital* May 4, 1930.

1332. Carney, Alfred. The christening of a Kansas town, Herndon, Kansas. *Aerend* 5:174-75, Summer 1934.

1333. Carruth, W. H. Origin of Kansas names—Foreign settlements. Kansas State Historical Society. Transactions 4:257-58. 1886-88.

1334. Chaffin, J. W. How White Woman Creek got its name; *In* Lawson, O. S. History of Scott County, Kansas: a thesis submitted for the degree of Master of Arts, Colorado State College of Education, 1936. p. 25-26.

1335. Chase, Carroll & Richard McP. Cabeen. The first hundred years of United States territorial postmarks, 1787-1887. Kansas Territory. *American philatelist* 58:616-20, May 1945; 59:57-74, Oct. 1945.
     Includes a list of post offices.

1336. Cobb, Glenn. Fort Scott place names. *Fort Scott daily tribune-monitor* June 4, 1917.

1337. Connelley, William E. Origin of the name of Topeka. Kansas State Historical Society. Collections 17:589-93. 1926-28.

1338. Cooper, F. A. It happened in Kansas, Kansas origin of county names and date of organization. *Kansas business* 7:5, May 1939.

1339. Corley, Wayne E. County and community names in Kansas; how the 105 counties and over 1000 of the communities got their names. Denver, The Author, 1962. 83 l.

1340. Cory, Charles Estabrook. Place names of Bourbon County, Kansas; streams, towns, deserted villages, local place names, townships, etc. Fort Scott, Whiteside Pub. Co., 1928. 63p.

1341. County was named for Indian tribe. *Arkansas City (Kan.) daily traveler* Oct. 25, 1955.
     Arapahoe County.

1342. Cover, Anniejane Hicks. Some place names of Kansas. *Heritage of Kansas*

v. 4, no. 4, Nov. 1960. 63p.
Origin of names in lists under various categories.

1343. Declare 49 Kansas counties named for military chieftains; two changed after officers had joined rebels. *Wichita eagle* Jan. 6, 1931.

1344. Diller, Aubrey. Origin of the names of tributaries of the Kansas River. *Kansas historical quarterly* 21:401-06, Summer 1955.

1345. "Flint Hills" misnomer; a Kansas statistician would call them "Blue Stem." *Kansas City star* April 14, 1929.

1346. Forgotten counties of Kansas; with past and present names of counties. *Wichita eagle* March 27, 1927.

1347. Gannett, Henry. A gazetteer of Kansas. Washington, Govt. Print. Off., 1898. 246p. (U.S. Geological Survey. Bulletin no. 154)

1348. Gazetteer and business directory of the new Southwest. Embracing all of that region of country—including counties, towns and cities—contiguous to the St. Louis and San Francisco Railway, its divisions and branches, located in southwest Missouri, southeastern Kansas, the eastern portion of the Indian country, and the northwest section of Arkansas. In which is included an abridged directory of leading business houses of St. Louis. St. Louis, United States Directory Pub. Co., 1881. 224p.

1349. Geographical names. Clippings. 2v.
Mounted newspaper clippings in Kansas State Historical Society Library.

1350. Gill, Helen Gertrude. The establishment of counties in Kansas. Kansas Historical Society. Transactions 8:449-72. 1903-04.
Thesis (M.A.) Kansas Univ., 1903.
Includes origin of names that have disappeared.

1351. Hardeman, Nicholas P. Camp sites on the Santa Fe trail in 1848 as reported by John A. Bingham. Ed. by Nicholas P. Hardeman. *Arizona and the West* 6:313-19, Winter 1964.

1352. Have old names; creeks near Topeka got designations from Indians; "Shunganunga" meant "The race course" in Indian tongue. *Topeka state journal* Sept. 4, 1926.

1353. Hay, Robert. Kaw and Kansas, a monograph on the name of the state. Kansas State Historical Society. Transactions 9:521-26. 1905-06.

1354. Hickman, Russell K. The name of Topeka. Shawnee County Historical Society. Bulletin 25:3-7, June 1956.

1355. Hill, W. A. Robbers Roost Creek. *Aerend* 8:45-48, Winter 1937.
Includes names of other streams in Rooks County.

1356. Honig, Louis O. Origin of Kansas place-names. n.d. 16p.
Manuscript in the Kansas State Historical Society Library.

1357. How Cawker City got its name. n.p., n.d. Broadside 23x15 cm.
"The naming the new town was settled by a poker game, with E. Harrison Cawker holding the winning hand, hence Cawker City." See frontispiece of this volume for a reproduction of the broadside.

1358. Howes, Cecil. Ghost towns of Shawnee County. Shawnee County Historical Society. Bulletin 1:25-31, Dec. 1946.

1359. —— How counties got their names. *Kansas teacher* 58:46-48, April 1950.

1360. —— Nearly half the Kansas counties named in honor of war heroes. *Kansas City times* Nov. 8, 1939.

1361. —— They tried to spell "Kansas." *Kansas magazine* 1945, p. 98-99.

1362. —— What about the name, Topeka? Shawnee County Historical Society. Bulletin 1:104-08, Sept.-Dec. 1947.

1363. Indian names. *Sumner County press,* Wellington, Jan. 29, 1874.

1364. Indian names in Leavenworth County and their origin. *Leavenworth times* Sept. 14, 1911.

1365. Ingleman, Anna A. Indian place names of Kansas. n.p., 1929. 386 l.
Thesis (M.A.) Kansas Univ., 1929. Microfilm copy in Kansas State Historical Society Library.

1366. Inman, Henry. Counties of Kansas. *Topeka commonwealth* Jan. 12, 1886.

1367. Kansas. University. William Allen White School of Journalism. A pronunciation guide to Kansas place names. Lawrence, 1955. 23p.

1368. Kansas counties. 1939. 15p.
Manuscript in Kansas State Historical Society Library.

1369. Kansas counties named for military men. Kansas. Adjutant General. Biennial report 28:63-64. 1931-32.

1370. Kansas county names. *Magazine of history with notes and queries* 7:343-47, June 1908.

1371. Kurious Kansas. *Kansas abstracter* 16:12, Nov. 1942.

1372. Letters regarding the origin of the names Monravia, Farmington, Arrington, and Hawthorne.
Manuscript file in the Kansas State Historical Society Library.

1373. Lyman, William A. Origin of the name "Jayhawker," and how it came to be applied to the people of Kansas. Kansas State Historical Society. Collections 14:203-07. 1915-18.
Dates from 1859, and was applied then to a Linn County band organized in opposition to Missouri proslavery ruffians.

1374. McCandlish, J. Vernon. The organization dates of the counties of Kansas with information about whom the counties were named. Kansas City, Kan., March 1, 1955. 9 l.
Manuscript in Kansas State Historical Society Library.

1375. McCoy, John Calvin. Indian names of certain Kansas rivers. Kansas State Historical Society. Transactions 4:305-06. 1886-90.
Information in regard to the significance of the names is incorporated in a boundary survey made by the author.

1376. ——— Name of Solomon River and names of other Kansas streams.
Letter on file in the Kansas State Historical Society Library.

1377. Main origin of Ottawa County names. *Tescott news* Dec. 26, 1940.

1378. Many counties are named for non-Kansans. *Topeka journal* Jan. 28, 1942.

1379. Mead, James Richard. Origin of names of Kansas streams. Kansas Academy of Science. Transactions 18:215-16. 1901-02.

1380. ——— The Wichita Indians in Kansas. Kansas State Historical Society. Transactions 8:171-77. 1903-04.
Place-names which originated during the occupancy of this tribe are mentioned on p. 173-75.

1381. Meanings of Topeka, Wakarusa, and Shunganunga. *Topeka mail and Kansas breeze* May 22, 1896, p. 43.

1382. Mechem, Kirke. The mythical jayhawk. Topeka, Kansas State Historical Society, 1944. 12p.
A delightful fantasy tracing the mythical bird, the jayhawk.

1383. Montgomery, Mrs. Frank C. Fort Wallace and its relation to the frontier. Kansas State Historical Society. Collections 17:195-200. 1926-28.
Origin of place-names along the Smoky Hill route.

1384. Moore, Ely. The naming of Osawatomie, and some experiences with John Brown. Kansas State Historical Society. Collections 12:338-46. 1911-12.
Brief mention of the naming of the town by the author's father.

1385. Murdock, Victor. When the country around Wichita was Peketon County. *Wichita eagle magazine* Aug. 29, 1926.
Includes other place-names which have disappeared.

1386. Myers, C. Clyde. Salem: a town that bloomed, then faded. Kansas State Historical Society. Collections 17:384-88. 1926-28.

1387. The Name "Kansas." *Kansas historical quarterly* 20:450-51, May 1953.
Variant forms beginning with Kansa Indian village shown on Marquette's map, about 1673-74. Includes Kansas City.

1388. Names of Ford County's communities preserve for all time the names of pioneers whose efforts founded them. *Dodge City journal* Oct. 22, 1936.

1389. Names of Kansas towns duplicated. *Lawrence journal world* Oct. 13, 1937.

1390. Names of Kansas towns from many sources. *Topeka capital* July 30, 1916.

1391. The Naming of Pittsburg. *Pittsburg headlight* Nov. 18, 1955.
Also in *Pittsburg sun* Nov. 19, 1955.

1392. The Naming of the different counties. Kansas. State Board of Agriculture.
Annual report 4:185-437. 1875.

1393. Nomenclature of Kansas counties. *The Kansas official* Feb.-April 1921.

1394. Old county names. *Daily commonwealth,* Topeka, April 13-14, 1875, p. 2.

1395. Origin of county names; origin of city names. Kansas State Historical So-
ciety. Transactions 7:472-86. 1901-02.
Prepared by the Kansas State Historical Society for the Geographer of the
United States Geological Survey.

1396. Origin of Doniphan County names. *Atchison daily globe* May 24, 1907.

1397. Origin of Doniphan County names. *Troy chief* May 5, 1932.

1398. Origin of names of Bourbon County's streams reveals interesting side-
lights. *Fort Scott tribune,* Anniversary ed., May 30, 1942, p. 68-69.

1399. Origin of names of the stations on the L. K. & W. *Leavenworth times* Jan.
5, 1912.

1400. Peterson, Karl L. Legendary frontier names identify growing list of Midwestern reservoirs. *Kansas City star* June 28, 1964, p. 2G.
Map on p. 1G.

1401. Place-names of Kansas towns.
File of postal cards in Kansas State Historical Society Library, received in response to queries regarding origin of names, 1901-02.

1402. Poetic Indian names remembered by Henry Trinkle. Kansas State Histori-
cal Society. Collections 16:652-53. 1923-25.
Reprinted from *La Cygne weekly journal* June 21, 1895.
The location and source of the Indian names Nop-shin-gah and Ach-a-pon-gah.

1403. Remsburg, G. J. Many Shawnee County names are derived from Indians
and from early settlers. *Topeka capital* July 2, 1922.

1404. ———— Origin of Central branch [Union Pacific R.R. Co.] names. *Atchison
daily globe* Jan. 27, 1909.

1405. ———— Origin of names of county places. *Leavenworth times* Jan. 24, 1907.

1406. ———— Origin of Nemaha County names. *Sabetha herald* Jan. 28, 1909.

1407. Richards, Walter Marvin. Some ghost towns of Kansas. *Heritage of Kansas*
v. 5, no. 1, Feb. 1961. 32p.

1408. Rumpf, Dan B. What's in a Kansas name? *Kansas business magazine* 5:4, March 1937.

1409. Scheffer, Theodore H. Geographical names in Ottawa County. *Kansas historical quarterly* 3:227-45, Aug. 1934.

1410. Schmidt, Heinie. Ashes of my campfire; historical anecdotes of old Dodge City. Dodge City, Kan., Journal, Inc., 1952- . v. 1- .
   Ghost city of Hess named for a child: 1:59-62.

1411. Schoewe, Walter H. Name of river. Kansas Academy of Science. Transactions 54:269-71, 275-76, 281, 309-29, Sept. 1951.
   Names of Kansas streams; Kansas River and Missouri River, with a list of Kansas streams based on Henry Gannett, A gazetteer of Kansas, 1898 (see no. 1347).

1412. Seek to name a city. *Kansas City star* May 1, 1959, p. 6 B.
   Postcard returns favor Overland Park as the name for the new city to be formed from the Mission urban township in Johnson County.
   References to later newspaper articles on this follow:

   Tanquary, E. A. "Kansas City South, Kansas"? *Kansas City star* May 1, 1959, p. 14 D.
   White, Mary W. Oh, please! *Kansas City star* May 6, 1959, p. 12 D.
      Suggests the name Johnson City.
   Overland Park is name of new city. *Kansas City star* May 8, 1959, p. 1.
   Johnson cities set boundaries for 12. *Kansas City star* May 13, 1959, p. 1.

1413. Sibley, George Champlain. Big John's Spring, Council Grove, Diamond of the Plain; *In* Hulbert, Archer Butler. Southwest on the Turquoise Trail. Colorado Springs, Stewart Commission of Colorado College, 1933. p. 111-13.

1414. Some "misplaced" cities; many of the same name as counties located in other counties. *Topeka journal* Nov. 23, 1935.

1415. Some of the lost towns of Kansas. Kansas State Historical Society. Collections 12:426-90. 1911-12.
   Includes a list of incorporations, by Kansas men, of towns now within the boundaries of Colorado.

1416. Station names. *Missouri Pacific lines magazine* 25:9, Feb. 1952; 26:11, Aug. 1952.
   Station names along the Missouri Pacific lines in Kansas.

1417. Stevenson, Andrew. Many towns named in honor of Santa Fe men. *Santa Fe magazine* 22:55-56, Aug. 1928.
   From Illinois to California, but the greatest number are in Kansas.

1418. Stewart, Ora T. Names of Kansas towns reveal romance. *Jayhawk, the magazine of Kansas* 2:5-6, 29, Jan. 1929.

1419. There are many queerly named towns in Missouri and Kansas. *Kansas City star* Aug. 1, 1937.

1420. Three towns in Atchison County named for Indian chieftains. *Atchison globe* June 13, 1916.

1421. Tilghman, Zoe A. Origin of the name Wichita. *American anthropologist* n.s. 43:488-89, July-Sept. 1941.
　　Reply by Mary R. Haas, *ibid.* n.s. 44:164-65, Jan.-March 1942 refutes Tilghman's theory that the name derives from the Creek language.

1422. U.S. 86th Congress, 2d session. House. A bill to designate the Tuttle Creek Reservoir, Kansas, as the Willard J. Breidenthal Reservoir. H. R. 11400. March 28, 1960. Washington, 1960. 2p.
　　Introduced by Mr. George and referred to the Committee on Public Works.
　　Same, 87th Congress, 1st session. House. H. R. 1741, Jan. 4, 1961. 1p. Introduced by Mr. Breeding and referred to the Committee on Public Works.

1423. U.S. 88th Congress, 1st session. House. A bill to designate the Perry Dam and Reservoir, Delaware River, Kansas, as the Ozawkie Dam and Reservoir. H. R. 7645. July 18, 1963. Washington, 1963. 1p.
　　Introduced by Mr. Avery and referred to the Committee on Public Works.
　　An identical bill was introduced as H. R. 7653, July 18, 1963, by Mr. Ellsworth and referred to the Committee on Public Works.

1424. What's in a name? *Progress in Kansas* 1:27-28, March 1935.
　　Origin of names of some Kansas towns, based on a radio talk by Prof. Allen Crafton, Kansas University.

KENTUCKY

1425. Anderson, James Lee. The house that named the town. *American motorist* 24:3, Jan. 1956.
　　Story of the Owings house in Owingsville, Ky.

1426. Bryant, Thomas Julian. Bryant's Station and its founder, William Bryant. *Missouri historical review* 5:150-73, April 1911.
　　Arguments to prove that the name of the pioneer Kentucky fort and of its founder was Bryant, not Bryan.

1427. Casey Jones. *New York times* Oct. 16, 1938, sec. 4, p. 8, col. 1-2; letter Oct. 30, sec. 4, p. 9, col. 7.
　　Pronunciation of Cayce, Ky.

1428. Cleaves, Mildred P. Kentucky towns and their mark. *In Kentucky* 11:39, Winter 1948.

1429. Counties in Kentucky and origin of their names. Kentucky State Historical Society. Register 1:34-37, Jan. 1903.
　　Published by courtesy of the geographer of the Smithsonian Institution.

1430. Creason, Joe. What was that name again? *Louisville courier-journal,* Nov. 20, 1955, Magazine, p. 7-10.
　　Kentucky place-names.

1431. Field, Thomas Parry. A guide to Kentucky place names. In cooperation with Dept. of Geography, University of Kentucky. Lexington, College of Arts and Sciences, Univ. of Kentucky, 1961. 264p. (Kentucky. Geological Survey. Series X. Special publication 5)
Review: by Helen Carlson, *Names* 10:190-92, Sept. 1962.

1432. —— The Indian place names of Kentucky. *Names* 7:154-66, Sept. 1959.
Reprinted in *Filson Club history quarterly* 34:237-47, July 1960.

1433. Grubbs, Millard Dee. Origin of historic place names; *In his* The 4 keys to Kentucky. Louisville, Slater & Gilroy, 1949. p. 227-50.

1434. Haber, Tom Burns. "Gulliver's travels" in America. *American speech* 11:99-100, Feb. 1936.
Lulbegrud Creek in Kentucky named from the "Travels" according to a record made by Daniel Boone.

1435. Halpert, Herbert. Place name stories of Kentucky waterways and ponds, with a note on bottomless pools. *Kentucky folklore record* 7:85-101, July-Sept. 1961.

1436. Halpert, Violetta Maloney. Place name stories about west Kentucky towns. *Kentucky folklore record* 7:103-16, July-Sept. 1961.

1437. Hardy, Emmet Layton. An introduction to the study of the geographic nomenclature of Kentucky's counties, cities, and towns. Lexington, 1949. 119p.
Thesis (M.S.) Univ. of Kentucky.

1438. —— Place names in old Kentucky. *Louisville courier-journal* Dec. 4, 1949, Roto-sec., p. 14; Dec. 18, Roto-sec., p. 28; Jan. 15, 1950, Roto-sec., p. 31; March 12, Roto-sec., p. 14; April 30, Roto-sec., p. 41.

1439. Hazelip, Pauline. Tales of Glasgow Junction: a town is named. *Kentucky folklore record* 6:1-3, Jan.-March 1960.
Names of Glasgow Junction.

1440. Hewitt, John Napoleon Brinton. The name "Kentucky." *American anthropologist* n.s. 10:339-42, April-June 1908.
A thorough treatise on the derivation and meaning of the name.

1441. Keglertown. *Lincoln (Neb.) evening journal and Nebraska state journal* Dec. 12, 1962.
Derived its name from the game of bowls.

1442. Kentucky proud of unique town names. *Cumberland (Md.) evening times* Sept. 18, 1935.

1443. Ladd, Bill. Boaz is Bohz, Bouty Bow-ti and there's no T in Egypt. *Louisville courier-journal* Dec. 7, 1949, sec. 1, p. 9.

1444. Mahr, August C. Shawnee names and migrations in Kentucky and West Virginia. *Ohio journal of science* 60:155-64, May 1960.
The migration of the western half of the Shawnee nation from the Cumberland

River eastward through the wilderness later called Kentucky can be traced by place-names of Shawnee origin.

1445. Plummer, Niel. Guide to the pronunciation of Kentucky towns and cities. Lexington, Univ. of Kentucky, Dept. of Journalism, 1949. 52p.

1446. Rothert, Otto A. Origin of the names Beargrass Creek, The Point, and Thruston Square. *History quarterly* 2:19-21, Oct. 1927.
"Regarding these sections of Louisville."—Griffin.

1447. Scomp, H. A. Kentucky county names. *Magazine of history with notes and queries* 7:144-54, March 1908.

1448. Spence, Dorothy Clark. How Tolu, Kentucky, got its name. *Kentucky folklore record* 7:119-20, July-Sept. 1961.

1449. Stratton, Margaret Barnes. Place-names of Logan County, and oft-told tales. 3d ed. Russellville, Ky., News-Democrat, 1950. 76p.

1450. Swift, Lucie. "Who'd a thought it" and other Paducah place names; ed. by Herbert Halpert. *Kentucky folklore record* 7:117-19, July-Sept. 1961.

1451. Treadway, C. M. City of Irvine was named for brothers who were among early settlers in state. *Lexington leader* April 4, 1957, p. 3.

1452. Trout, A. M. When it comes to naming streets, sky's the limit. *Louisville courier-journal* June 2, 1960, sec. 1, p. 7.

1453. Trout, Allan. Unusual place names in Kentucky. *Louisville courier-journal* March 2, 1950, sec. 2, p. 15; Jan. 11, 1951, sec. 2, p. 15; April 12, sec. 2, p. 17.

1454. ———— What inspired—name of Monkey's Eyebrow? *Louisville courier-journal* Feb. 21, 1951, sec. 2, p. 15; Feb. 28, sec. 2, p. 15; March 21, sec. 2, p. 13; April 16, sec. 2, p. 11.

1455. U.S. Board on Geographic Names. Decisions. No. 31—February 1, 1933. Mammoth Cave National Park, Kentucky. Washington, Govt. Print. Off., 1934. 6p.

1456. U.S. Congress. House. Committee on Interior and Insular Affairs. Abraham Lincoln Birthplace National Historic Site, Hodgenville, Ky. August 24, 1959 ...Mrs. Pfost submitted the following report. To accompany H. R. 5764. Washington, 1959. 3p. (U.S. 86th Congress, 1st session. House. Report no. 986)
    The Committee recommends the enactment of H. R. 5764, with amendments to change the proposed name from Abraham Lincoln's Birthplace to Abraham Lincoln Birthplace National Historical Site.

1457. U.S. Congress. Senate. Committee on Interior and Insular Affairs. Abraham Lincoln Birthplace National Historic Site. August 4, 1959...Mr. Murray submitted the following report. To accompany S. 1448. Washington, 1959. 2p. (U.S. 86th Congress, 1st session. Senate. Report no. 617. Calendar no. 617)
    Recommends that the bill do pass, with amendments to change the proposed name from Abraham Lincoln's Birthplace to Abraham Lincoln Birthplace National Historic Site.

1458. U.S. 88th Congress, 1st session. House. A bill to designate Fishtrap Reservoir, to be created by the dam authorized to be constructed on the Levisa Fork, in Pike County, Kentucky, as "Kennedy Lake" in honor of the late President John F. Kennedy. H. R. 9524. Dec. 19, 1963. Washington, 1963. 2p.
Introduced by Mr. Perkins and referred to the Committee on Public Works.

1459. U.S. 88th Congress, 1st session. Senate. A bill to change the name of the lake formed by Kentucky Dam. S. 462. Jan. 23 (legislative day, Jan. 15), 1963. Washington, 1963. 2p.
Introduced by Mr. Kefauver and Mr. Gore and referred to the Committee on Public Works.
To change the name from Kentucky Lake to Tennessee-Kentucky Lake.
An identical bill was introduced in the House as follows:

U.S. 88th Congress, 1st session. House. A bill to change the name of the lake formed by Kentucky Dam. H. R. 4254. Feb. 26, 1963. Washington, 1963. 2p.
Introduced by Mr. Murray and referred to the Committee on Public Works.

1460. U.S. Laws, statutes, etc. An act to change the name of the Abraham Lincoln National Historical Park at Hodgenville, Kentucky, to Abraham Lincoln Birthplace National Historic Site. Public law 86-231. (United States statutes at large. 86th Congress. 1st session. 1959. v. 73, p. 466)
S. 1448 was approved Sept. 8, 1959.

1461. Woodbridge, Hensley C. Place names; *In his* A tentative bibliography of Kentucky speech. American Dialect Society. Publication 30:31-33, Nov. 1958.
A bibliography of items on place-names in Kentucky.

1462. Woods, Robert E. Heroes of the War of 1812 for whom Kentucky counties are named. Jeffersontown, Ky., 1937. 6p.
Address given at the state meeting of the Daughters of 1812 in Louisville, Ky.

LOUISIANA

1463. Alleman, Elise A. The legend and history of place names of Assumption Parish. 104p.
Thesis (M.A.) Louisiana State Univ., 1936.

1464. Banta, Anna. How Louisiana bayous got their names. Colonists nearly exhausted own vocabularies and then called on Indians. *Times-picayune*, New Orleans, March 11, 1928, p. 2.

1465. Berry, Nora. Place names of Natchitoches Parish. 133p.
Thesis (M.A.) Louisiana State Univ., 1935.

1466. Bonham, Milledge Louis. Clear reference to word "Istrouma" found by Bonham, former L. S. U. professor during research in Paris. *State times*, Baton Rouge, April 10, 1930.

1467. ―― Notes on place names. *American speech* 1:625, Aug. 1926.
In South Carolina and Louisiana.

1468. Bushnell, David Ives. The Choctaw of Bayou Lacomb, St. Tammany Parish, Louisiana. Washington, Govt. Print. Off., 1909. 37p. (Smithsonian Institution. Bureau of American Ethnology. Bulletin no. 48)
Place names in St. Tammany Parish: p. 6-7.

1469. Chapman, H. H. Why the town of McNary moved. *American forests and forest life* 30:589-92, 626, Oct. 1924.
The town of McNary, La., was abandoned and all the inhabitants moved to Cooley, Ariz., rechristened McNary, because of the depletion of the timber stand in Louisiana.

1470. Chase, Carroll & Richard McP. Cabeen. The first hundred years of United States territorial postmarks, 1787-1887. Orleans Territory. *American philatelist* 55:721-25, Aug. 1942; 56:177-79, Dec. 1942.
Includes list of post offices, 1804-12, with notes on some names.

1471. Chase, John Churchill. Frenchmen, Desire, Good Children, and other streets of New Orleans, in words and pictures. New Orleans, R. L. Crager, 1949. 246p.
New Orleans street names related to history.

1472. Douglas, Lillian. Place-names of East Feliciana Parish. 38p.
Thesis (M.A.) Louisiana State Univ., 1930.

1473. Ficklen, John Rose. Origin of the name Louisiana. *Louisiana historical quarterly* 2:230-32, April 1919.

1474. Fitzpatrick, William H. Odd plantation names hint at comedy, tragedy of era living only in memory. *Times-picayune,* New Orleans, Aug. 28, 1938, p. 3.

1475. Grima, Edgar. Les noms géographiques français en Louisiane. Société de Géographie de Québec. Bulletin 8:267-69, sept. 1914.

1476. Halbert, Henry Sale. Bvlbancha, Choctaw word for the town of New Orleans. *Gulf States historical magazine* 1:53-54, July 1902.

1477. Hearn, Lafcadio. The curious nomenclature of New Orleans streets; *In his* Occidental gleanings, sketches and essays now first collected by Albert Mordell. New York, Dodd, 1925. 1:263-75.

1478. Italian names displaced. *New York times* June 16, 1940, p. 34, col. 5.
Street names in Bossier City changed unofficially as result of anti-Italian sentiment.

1479. Krumpelmann, John T. The renaming of Berlin Street and Berlin streets. *American speech* 26:156-57, May 1951.
New Orleans.

1480. Laurent, Lubin F. Origin of certain place names. *Louisiana historical quarterly* 7:327-31, April 1924.
From the parish of St. John the Baptist, the author has procured names of towns and villages for the purpose of studying their source.

1481. Linton, Albert C. New Orleans street names record history. *Illinois Central magazine* 32:5-0, March 1944.

1482. Lorio, E. C. Place-names of Pointe-Coupée Parish. 68p. Thesis (M.A.) Louisiana State Univ., 1932.

1483. McDavid, Raven I., Jr. Berlin Street in New Orleans. *American speech* 24:238, Oct. 1949.
Changed to General Pershing.

1484. Mitchiner, Nantelle. Place names in Louisiana, extraordinary, survey reveals, Bible and literature culled. *Morning advocate*, Baton Rouge, Sept. 4, 1938, p. 16.

1485. —— What's in a name? Many strange place names are found in Louisiana. *Louisiana tourist* (Louisiana Dept. of Commerce and Industry) 1:6, Nov. 1938.

1486. Read, William Alexander. Geographical names; *In his* Louisiana-French. Baton Rouge, Louisiana State Univ. Press, 1931. p. 152-201. (Louisiana State University studies, no. 5)
Also in rev. ed. (photo facsim.), 1963.
Includes three alphabetical lists under the headings: Indian, French, and Spanish. The first supplements the author's Louisiana place-names of Indian origin (see no. 1488).

1487. —— Istrouma. *Louisiana historical quarterly* 14:503-15, Oct. 1931.
The Indian word Istrouma, meaning "red post," is the source of the name Baton Rouge.

1488. —— Louisiana place-names of Indian origin. Baton Rouge, The University, 1927. 72p. (Louisiana State University. University bulletin n.s. v. 19, Feb. 1927)
Bibliography: p. x.
A list of addenda and corrigenda in *Louisiana historical quarterly* 11:445-62, July 1928. Also published separately.

1489. Reynolds, Jack Adolphe. Louisiana place-names of romance origin. 566p. Thesis (Ph.D.) Louisiana State Univ., 1942.

1490. Scroggs, William Oscar. Origin of the name Baton Rouge. Historical Society of East and West Baton Rouge. Proceedings 1:20-24. 1916-17. (Louisiana State University. Bulletin n.s. v. 8, no. 8, Aug. 1917)

1491. Sternberg, Hilgard O'Reilly. The names "False-River" and "Pointe Coupée," an inquiry in historical geography. *Louisiana historical quarterly* 31:598-605, July 1948.

1492. Turner, Sarah Anne. Place-names of Webster Parish. A linguistic, historical study. 93p.
Thesis (M.A.) Louisiana State Univ., 1935.

1493. Villiers du Terrage, Marc, *Baron de*. La Louisiane, histoire de son nom et de ses frontières successives (1681-1819). Paris, Adrien-Maisonneuve, 1929. 74p. (Publications de la Société des Américanistes de Paris)

1494. Walker, Norman M. The geographical nomenclature of Louisiana. *Magazine of American history* 10:211-22, Sept. 1883.

1495. Woods, William S. L'abbé Prévost and the gender of New Orleans. *Modern language notes* 66:259-61, April 1951.
Reply by Leo Spitzer, *ibid.* 66:571-72, Dec. 1951.
Concerning the gender of New Orleans in French.

1496. Wurzlow, Helen Emmelin. There's more than meets the eye in names of bayous. *Times-picayune*, New Orleans, Dec. 12, 1943, p. 11.

MAINE

1497. Ambitious names of Maine towns. *New York times magazine* June 24, 1928, p. 20.

1498. Andrews, L. A. Squeaker Guzzle. *Rudder* 63:18-19, 68, Nov. 1947.
Concerning this island's name and other Maine names.

1499. Ballard, Edward. Geographical names on the coast of Maine. U.S. Coast Survey. Report 1868:243-59.
Also issued as a separate, 1871.
"Full of errors, because Dr. Ballard, though painstaking, relied upon incompetent information."—Eckstorm.

1500. Beck, Horace P. The folklore of Maine. New York, Lippincott, 1957. 284p.
Names on the sea: p. 1-24. Coastal names.

1501. Chadbourne, Ava Harriet. Maine place names and the peopling of its towns. Portland, Me., Bond Wheelwright Co., 1955. 530p.
"An excellent example of sound historical research based on geographical names."—E. K. Gudde.
Review: by Elisabeth K. Gudde, *Names* 4:185, Sept. 1956.

1502. Eckstorm, Fannie Hardy. The Indian names of two Maine mountains. *New England quarterly* 9:132-42, March 1936.
Sowbungy, or Sourbungy, Mountain, and Sowangas Mountain were given Indian names of the golden eagle.

1503. —— Indian place-names of the Penobscot Valley and the Maine coast. Orono, Me., Printed at the Univ. Press, 1941. 272p. (University of Maine studies. Second series, no. 55) (The Maine bulletin, v. 44, no. 4, Nov. 1941)
The Appendix (p. 237-41) includes a reproduction of Joseph Nicolar's article on Penobscot place-names which appeared originally in the *Old Town herald*, of unknown date.
Bibliography: p. 242-54.
Review: *New England quarterly* 16:503-07, Sept. 1943.

1504. ——— Is Kokadjo Indian? *Sprague's journal of Maine history* 13:95-97, April-June 1925.

Kokadjo (an Indian word) is the name of Little Spencer Mountain but is not desirable as a name replacing the old, established names of First, Second, and Third Roach ponds.

1505. Gatschet, Albert Samuel. All around the Bay of Passamaquoddy, with interpretation of its Indian names or localities. Washington, Judd, 1897. p. 16-24.

Reprinted from *National geographic magazine* 8:16-24, Jan. 1897.

Supplemented by an article in the *Eastport sentinel* Sept. 15, 1897.

1506. Gentler place names along Maine's coast. *New York times magazine* Oct. 12, 1930, p. 18.

Replace robust and expressive names given by early settlers.

1507. Greenleaf, Moses. Indian place-names; Indian names of some of the streams, islands, etc., on the Penobscot and St. John rivers in Maine, taken from a letter from M. Greenleaf, esq., to Rev. Dr. Morse. Bangor, Me., Privately printed, 1903. 12p.

Reprinted from American Society for Promoting Civilization and General Improvement of the Indian Tribes of the United States. Report. New Haven, 1824.

Also reprinted in Smith, Edgar Crosby. Moses Greenleaf, Maine's first mapmaker. Bangor, Printed for the De Burians, 1902.

1508. Hayward, John. A gazetteer of the United States, comprising a series of gazetteers of the several states and territories. Maine. Portland, Me., S. H. Colesworthy; Boston, B. B. Mussey, 1843. 92p.

1509. Hubbard, Lucius Lee. Woods and lakes of Maine; a trip from Moosehead Lake to New Brunswick in a birch-bark canoe, to which are added some Indian place-names and their meanings, now first published. New and original illustrations by Will L. Taylor. Boston, J. R. Osgood and Co., 1884. 223p.

Some Indian place-names in northern Maine: p. 192-216.

1510. Kennebunkport keeps name. *New York times* March 8, 1938, p. 21, col. 2; letter March 20, 1938, sec. 4, p. 9, col. 2.

Proposal to change to its original name of Arundel defeated.

1511. McKeon, Ed. Ever hear of K'chi Mugwock? Bangor area abounds in Indian names. *Bangor daily news* Feb. 12, 1959, p. 7.

1512. Maine. State Water Storage Commission. Gazetteer of the rivers and lakes of Maine. Waterville, Sentinel Pub. Co., 1914. 323p. (Fourth annual report, 1913)

"Arranged alphabetically by drainage basins."

1513. Matthews, Albert. Origin of the name of Maine. Cambridge, J. Wilson and Son, 1910. 366-82p.

Reprinted from the Colonial Society of Massachusetts. Publications 12:366-82. 1909.

p. 380-82, note on the name Mariana, the name intended by John Mason for the territory between the Naumkeag and the Merrimac, granted to him in 1621-22.

1514. Maurault, Joseph Pierre Anselme. Histoire des Abenakis, depuis 1605,

jusqu'à nos jours. [Sorel, Qué.], Imprimé à l'atelier typographique de la "Gazette de Sorel," 1866. 631p.
A list of place-names in Maine and Canada, with significations, in Introduction p. ii-vii.

1515. Meaning of the Indian names Penobscot and Kennebec. *Ladies' repository* 24:631, Oct. 1864.
Signed: H. Y. W.

1516. Placentia Islands. *Historical magazine* 10:321, Oct. 1866.
Possible derivation of the name.

1517. Potter, Chandler Eastman. Appendix to the "Language of the Abnaquies" [by William Willis]. Maine Historical Society. Collections 4:185-95. 1856.
More on Abnaqui names of geographic features in Maine.
cf. William Willis, The language of the Abnaquies, or eastern Indians, no. 1528.

1518. Randel, William Peirce. Saco named for Indians. *New York times* Nov. 14, 1937, sec. 4, p. 9, col. 7.

1519. —— Town names of York County, Maine. *New England quarterly* 11:565-75, Sept. 1938.
Bibliographical footnotes.

1520. Sands, Donald B. The nature of the generics in island, ledge, and rock names of the Maine coast. *Names* 7:193-202, Dec. 1959.
Deals with the four groups into which the generics fall and the problem of when elements of binomial toponyms can be considered lexical evidence.

1521. Shaw, Justin H. Kittery, Devon. *Devon and Cornwall notes and queries* 9:48-49, April 1916.
Question concerning origin of name. Had been referred to in Everett Schermerhorn Stackpole, Old Kittery and her families. Lewiston, Me., Press of Lewiston Journal Co., 1903, as derived from Kittery Point near Dartmouth, England.

1522. The Strangest things happen in Maine. *Christian Science monitor* May 25, 1962, p. 4.
"On town names, especially the cosmopolitan—Norway, Belfast—and the abstract—Unity, Freedom."—*American speech.*

1523. Thoreau, Henry David. The Maine woods, arranged with notes by Dudley C. Lunt, illus. by Henry Bugbee Kane. New York, Norton, 1950. 340p.
Appendix, p. 336-40: A list of Indian words; including a short list from William Willis, The language of the Abnaquies. Maine Historical Society. Collections 4:93-117. 1856.
Also in other editions.

1524. True, Nathaniel Tuckerman. Indian names on the Androscoggin. *Historical magazine* 8:237-38, July 1864.
45 names of geographic features in the Abnaki language.

1525. U.S. Board on Geographic Names. Decisions. No. 39—Decisions rendered April 4, 1934. Acadia National Park, Maine. Washington, Govt. Print. Off., 1934. 3p.

1526. Varney, George Jones. A gazetteer of the State of Maine. Boston, B. B. Russell, 1881. 611p.

1527. Whipple, Joseph. A geographical view of the District of Maine, with particular reference to its internal resources, including the history of Acadia, Penobscot River and Bay, with statistical tables, shewing the comparative progress of the population of Maine with each state, list of the towns, their incorporations, census, polls, etc. Bangor, P. Edes, printer, 1816. 102p.

1528. Willis, William. The language of the Abnaquies, or eastern Indians. Maine Historical Society. Collections 4:93-117. 1856.
    Includes Indian names applied to portions of the state, with definitions, p. 103-17.
    Some of these names were included in Henry David Thoreau, The Maine woods (see no. 1523).
    For additional material, see Chandler Eastman Potter, no. 1517.

1529. Wright, Walter W. Norway, Maine. *Norwegian-American studies and records* 15:219-22. 1949.
    Origin of the name; answers the speculations of Dr. Halvdan Koht in v. 13, and his articles in *Nordisk tidende* Sept. 3, 1942 and *Decorah-posten* Sept. 4, 1942.

MARYLAND

1530. Associated Stamp Clubs of the Chesapeake Area. Postal markings of Maryland, 1766-1855. [The Maryland postal history catalog] Ed. by Roger T. Powers. Baltimore, 1960. 100p.
    More than 600 names, with period of operation, of Maryland offices.

1531. Babcock, W. H. Notes on local names near Washington. *Journal of American folk-lore* 1:146-47, July-Sept. 1888.
    The origin and changes of several place-names around Washington.

1532. Baltimore's quaint local names are being lost. *Baltimore American* Feb. 4, 1923.

1533. Berkley, Henry J. Extinct river towns of the Chesapeake Bay region. *Maryland historical magazine* 19:125-34, June 1924.

1534. Bevan, Edith Rossiter. Some Maryland towns have odd place names. *Maryland gardener* 6:619-20, May 1952.

1535. Bouton, E. H. A competition in street naming. *Landscape architecture* 9:125-28, April 1919.
    The winning plan for naming the streets at Sparrows Point.

1536. Bump, Charles Weathers. Indian place-names in Maryland. *Maryland historical magazine* 2:287-93, Dec. 1907.

1537. Collitz, Hermann. Baltimore—what does the name mean? *Johns Hopkins alumni magazine* 22:133-34, Jan. 1934.

1538.	Conowingo known in Indian lore. *Sunday sun,* Baltimore, March 28, 1926, Magazine sec., p. 9.

1539.	Coyle, Wilbur F. Few original names of estates in Baltimore have survived. *Baltimore news* Jan. 22, 1922.

1540.	Craig's business directory and Baltimore almanac for 1842. Baltimore, Craig, 1842. 145p.
   Post offices in Maryland: p. 56-57.

1541.	Edwards, Richard. Statistical gazetteer of the State of Maryland, and the District of Columbia. To which is appended a business directory of the federal metropolis and suburbs. Baltimore, J. S. Waters; Washington, W. M. Morrison & Co., 1856. 328p.

1542.	Fisher, Richard Swainson. Gazetteer of the State of Maryland, comp. from the returns of the seventh census of the United States, and other official documents. To which is added, A general account of the District of Columbia. New York, J. H. Colton; Baltimore, J. S. Waters, 1852. 122p.

1543.	Forgotten names "Below the deadline." *Baltimore American* Feb. 11, 1923.
   South Baltimore.

1544.	Gannett, Henry. A gazetteer of Maryland. Washington, Govt. Print. Off., 1904. 84p. (U.S. Geological Survey. Bulletin no. 231)
   Also in Maryland. Bureau of Industrial Statistics. Report 1908:415-523.

1545.	Gordon, Douglas H. Hero worship as expressed in Baltimore street names. *Maryland historical magazine* 43:121-26, June 1948.

1546.	Harris, William H. How it got that name. Upper Chesapeake Bay and tributaries. Salem, N.J., n.d. 4p.
   Folder issued by Mr. Harris, 127 Seventh St., Salem, N.J., giving information about names of places along Chesapeake Bay and requesting additional information to be published in the *Salem (N.J.) Standard and Jerseyman* (about 1938).

1547.	Heckewelder, John Gottlieb Ernestus. Names given by the Lenni Lenape or Delaware Indians to rivers, streams and places in the now states of New Jersey, Pennsylvania, Maryland, and Virginia. Pennsylvania German Folklore Society. Publications 5:1-41. 1940.
   Published also in American Philosophical Society. Transactions 4:351-96. 1834; Historical Society of Pennsylvania. Bulletin 1:121-35, 139-54, June, Sept. 1847; Moravian Historical Society. Transactions 1872:275-333; as a separate: Bethlehem, [Pa.], H. T. Claude, printer, 1872. 58p.; and in his A narrative of the mission of the United Brethren among the Delaware and Mohegan Indians. Cleveland, Burrows Bros., 1907. p. 523-66.

1548.	How well are you up in Easton history? *Easton (Md.) star-democrat* Feb. 2, 1945.
   Talbot County names.

1549.	Hoye Crest name given highest peak. *Glades star* (Garrett County Historical Society) 2:160, June 30, 1952.

1550. Island's name changed; Potomac Park redesignated to honor architects. *New York times* July 13, 1960, p. 53.
Name of Falls Island changed to Olmsted Island.

1551. Johnson, Gerald W. Place-names. *Evening sun*, Baltimore, July 2, 1931.

1552. —— What's in a name? *Sun*, Baltimore, Oct. 31, 1929.

1553. Kenny, Hamill. Baltimore: new light on an old name. *Maryland historical magazine* 49:116-21, June 1954.
Also reprinted as a separate.
Its Irish provenance and American history and meaning.

1554. —— The origin and meaning of the Indian place-names of Maryland. College Park, Md., 1950, i.e., 1951. 2v.
Thesis (Ph.D.) Univ. of Maryland.

1555. —— The origin and meaning of the Indian place names of Maryland. Baltimore, Waverly Press, 1961. 186p.
Bibliography: p. 161-175.
Review: by C. A. Weslager, *Maryland historical magazine* 56:311-14, Sept. 1961; by V. J. Vogel, *Names* 10:65-69, March 1962; by A. R. Dunlap, *American speech* 37:55-57, Feb. 1962.

1556. Kerney, Ellen. American ghost towns. *American notes and queries* 4:32, May 1944.
Snowhill, and Furnace, Md.

1557. Kuethe, J. Louis. A list of Maryland mills, taverns, forges and furnaces of 1795. *Maryland historical magazine* 31:155-69, June 1936.

1558. —— Maryland place names. *Sun*, Baltimore, Sept. 8, 1940, sec. 2, p. 3.

1559. —— Maryland place names have strange origins. *Sun*, Baltimore, May 23, 1937, sec. 2, p. 2; March 24, 1940.

1560. —— Runs, creeks and branches in Maryland. *American speech* 10:256-59, Dec. 1935.

1561. Marye, William Bose. Place names of Baltimore and Harford counties. *Maryland historical magazine* 25:321-65, Dec. 1930; 53:34-57, 238-52, March, Sept. 1958.

1562. —— The several Indian "Old Towns" on the upper Potomac River. *Maryland historical magazine* 34:325-33, Dec. 1939.

1563. —— Some Baltimore city place names. *Maryland historical magazine* 54:15-35, 353-64, March, Dec. 1959; 58:211-32, 344-77, Sept., Dec. 1963; 59:52-93, March 1964.
Part 2 has subtitle Huntington or Huntingdon, the two Liliendales and Sumwalt Run; Parts 3-4 (Sept. 1963-March 1964) have title and subtitle Baltimore city place names: Stony Run, its plantations, farms, country seats and mills.
Supplementary note by the author, *ibid.* 54:437-38, Dec. 1959.

1564. Maryland. Board of Public Works. Maryland as it is. A good land to live in and raise a family. Opportunities for settlers. Varied resources of land and water. Baltimore, Sun Job. Print. Off., 1903. 168p.
Indian names, county names, towns and localities: p. 113-21.

1565. Maryland. State Planning Commission. Gazetteer of Maryland. Prepared jointly by Maryland State Planning Commission and Department of Geology, Mines and Water Resources. Baltimore, Johns Hopkins Press, 1941. 242p. (Maryland. Geological Survey. Reports v. 14)
"Assistance in the preparation of this report was furnished by the Work Projects Administration project no. 651-25-2089."
Issued also as its Publication no. 33.
Sources of information: p. 237.

1566. The Name "Accident." *Glades star* (Garrett County Historical Society) v. 2, no. 6, p. 85-87, June 30, 1951.

1567. Names. *Eastern Shore magazine* v. 1, Dec. 1937, p. 5; Feb. 1938, p. 4.
Peculiar names found on the Eastern Shore.

1568. Names of neighborhoods in old Baltimore town. *Sun*, Baltimore, Jan. 20, 1907.
On the names of the villages absorbed into Baltimore.

1569. A New name needed for Swastika Road. *Kansas City star* Feb. 5, 1960, p. 8.
A 1920 name in Frederick, Md.

1570. Norris, Walter B. More Maryland place names: "Maryland Point." *Maryland and Delaware genealogist* 1:63, March 1960.

1571. ———— Origin of some interesting Maryland place names. *Maryland and Delaware genealogist* 1:16, Sept. 1959.

1572. The Origin of many of Talbot's geographical names. *Easton (Md.) star-democrat* Dec. 11, 1931.

1573. Rubincam, Milton. Queen Henrietta Maria: Maryland's royal namesake. *Maryland historical magazine* 54:131-48, June 1959.
Biography of the member of the royal family for whom Maryland was named.

1574. Stewart, Richard D. Baltimore day by day. *Baltimore news-post* Nov. 21, 25, 1944.
Other material on place-names appeared from time to time in this column, signed Carroll Dulaney, and also appeared on Sundays in the *Baltimore American.*

1575. Touch of London recurs in old local names. *Baltimore American* Feb. 18, 1923.
Names in old Baltimore.

1576. Truitt, Alfred. They left many mementoes. *Sun*, Baltimore, Feb. 10, 1929.
Indian place-names.

1577. Weird names given estates on city sites centuries ago. *Sun*, Baltimore,

Jan. 23, 1927.
Baltimore place-names.

1578. What's in a name in Maryland. *Evening sun,* Baltimore, Oct. 6, 1944.
Origin of about 40 Maryland place-names.

1579. Wright, Esther Clark. The naming of Monkton Mills. *Maryland historical magazine* 52:248-50, Sept. 1957.
After a Nova Scotia township name.

MASSACHUSETTS

1580. Amory, Thomas C. Report on the names of streets. Massachusetts Historical Society. Proceedings 6:24-40, June 1862.
Street names of Boston. In answer to a letter from the New England Historic Genealogical Society, *ibid.* 6:4-5, April 1862.

1581. Asks Cambridge to drop name of Harvard Square. *New York times* June 29, 1939, p. 8, col. 4.
Proposal to change name to George Washington Square.

1582. Banks, Charles Edward. Capowack. Is it the correct Indian name of Martha's Vineyard? *New England historical and genealogical register* 52:176-80, April 1898.
Algonquin name.

1583. ―――― Martin's or Martha's—What is the proper nomenclature of the Vineyard? *New England historical and genealogical register* 48:201-04, April 1894.

1584. Barrows, Charles Henry. An historical address delivered before the citizens of Springfield in Massachusetts at the public celebration, May 26, 1911, of the two hundred and seventy-fifth anniversary of the settlement; with five appendices, viz: Meaning of Indian local names, The cartography of Springfield, Old place names of Springfield, Unrecorded deed of Nippumsuit, Unrecorded deed of Paupsunnuck. Springfield, Mass., Connecticut Valley Historical Society, 1916. 100p.

1585. Baylies, Francis. The original of local and other names, a letter from Hon. Francis Baylies to Hon. P. W. Leland. Brooklyn, 1879. 24p. (Elzevir Club series, no. 1)
Most of the names are of Massachusetts.

1586. Boston streets well-named. *Magazine of history* 17:93, Aug.-Sept. 1913.

1587. Captain Gosnold's Martha. *New York herald tribune* Sept. 14, 1947.
Origin of name Martha's Vineyard.

1588. Chase, George W. List of dates of incorporation of the towns in Massachusetts, and their historical origin; *In* Massachusetts. Abstract of the Census

of Massachusetts, 1860. Boston, Wright & Potter, 1863. p. 215-37.
    Includes many Indian names of places before incorporation under present form.

1589. De Costa, B. F. Cago de baxos: or, The place of Cape Cod in the old
cartology. *New England historical and genealogical register* 35:49-59, Jan. 1881.
    A study of the various names for Cape Cod appearing on old maps.

1590. Dexter, Ralph W. The relationship of natural features to the place names
of Cape Ann, Massachusetts. Essex Institute. Historical collections 88:141-49,
April 1952.

1591. Dudley, Myron Samuel. Indian names of Nantucket. Nantucket, 1894. 1p.
    A list of names, as found in the various records of Nantucket and adjacent is-
lands as designations of persons and places. The author wished to learn the
English equivalents.

1592. Fay, Joseph Story. Letters on the origin of names prevailing on Vineyard
Sound. Massachusetts Historical Society. Proceedings 12:334-35, Feb. 1873.

1593. ——— The track of the Norseman, a monograph. Boston, C. C. Roberts,
1876. 7p.
    Reprinted in *Magazine of American history* 8:431-34, June 1882.
    Mentions some place-names that author considers of Norse origin and favors
supposition that Hole in such names as Wood's Hole, Holmes's Hole, etc. is a
corruption of a Norse word holl meaning "hill."

1594. Fish tales can't beat lake name. *Rocky Mountain motorist* 31:4, May 1961.
    The lake name with 45 letters: Chargoggagoggmanchauggagoggchaubunagunga-
maugg.

1595. Freeman, Nathaniel. Indian places within, or near the county of Barnstable.
Massachusetts Historical Society. Collections 1:230-32. 1792.

1596. Gahan, Laurence K. Methods of translating Indian place names. Massachusetts Archaeological Society. Bulletin 21:46-47, April-July 1960.
    Language of the Indians of Massachusetts.

1597. Gannett, Henry. A geographic dictionary of Massachusetts. Washington,
Govt. Print. Off., 1894. 126p. (U.S. Geological Survey. Bulletin no. 116)
    Issued also as House miscellaneous doc. v. 27, 53d Cong., 2d sess.

1598. Geographical gazetteer of the towns in the Commonwealth of Massachusetts.
Boston, Greenleaf and Freeman, 1784-85. 98p.
    Issued in parts, appended to the monthly numbers of the *Boston magazine* Oct.
1784-Dec. 1785. Includes only Suffolk County (p. 1-90) and part of Middlesex
County (p. 91-98). "The publisher informs his customers that he is obliged to
suspend the publication of the gazetteer for the present."—Note in *Boston magazine* 2:442, Dec. 1785. It was never completed nor issued as a separate work and
was without a separate title page.
    Ed. probably by Rev. James Freeman. The Society for Compiling a Magazine
in the Town of Boston voted Aug. 20, 1784, "That a committee be appointed to
prepare proposals for collecting a complete geographical gazetteer of the several
towns in the Commonwealth, to be inserted in the magazine." *cf*. Manuscripts of

the Society for Compiling a Magazine, in the collection of the Massachusetts Historical Society.

1599. Green, Samuel Abbott. Observations on the names of certain villages in Massachusetts and New Hampshire. Massachusetts Historical Society. Proceedings 2d ser. 10:465-67, Feb. 1896.
Use of Harbor away from the coastline. Includes Townsend Harbor, Mass.

1600. ——— Remarks on Nonacoicus, the Indian name of Major (Simon) Willard's farm at Groton, Mass. Massachusetts Historical Society. Proceedings 2d ser. 8:209-12, May 1893.

1601. ——— The town of Becket. Cambridge, 1890. 2p.
Remarks by Dr. Green at a meeting of the Massachusetts Historical Society, Jan. 9, 1890.

1602. Harding, William B. Origin of the names of the towns in Worcester County. Worcester, C. Jillson, 1883. 21p.

1603. Hayward, John. A gazetteer of Massachusetts, containing descriptions of all the counties, towns and districts in the commonwealth; also, of its principal mountains, rivers, capes, bays, harbors, islands, and fashionable resorts. To which are added, statistical accounts of its agriculture, commerce and manufactures; with a great variety of other useful information. Rev. ed. Boston, J. P. Jewett & Co., 1849. 452p.
Earlier editions: 1846. 444p.; 1847. 444p.

1604. Hommel, Rudolf. American ghost towns. *American notes and queries* 4:45-46, June 1944.
Dogtown, Mass.

1605. Horsford, Eben Norton. The Indian names of Boston, and their meaning. Cambridge, J. Wilson and Son, 1886. 26p.
Originally published in *New England historical and genealogical register* 40:94-103, Jan. 1886.

1606. Kinnicutt, Lincoln Newton. Indian names of places in Plymouth, Middleborough, Lakeville and Carver, Plymouth County, Massachusetts, with interpretations of some of them. Worcester, Commonwealth Press, 1909. 64p.

1607. ——— Indian names of places in Worcester County, Massachusetts, with interpretations of some of them. Worcester, Commonwealth Press, 1905. 59p.
Names of the Nipmuck tribe.

1608. Lake with a long name. *New York times* June 12, 1938, sec. 11, p. 20, col. 1-2.
Origin of lake name with 45 letters, Chaubunagungamaug for short.

1609. Leland, P. W. Algonquin, or Indian terms as applied to places and things. Old Colony Historical Society. Collections 3:83-103. 1885.

1610. Lucas, J. Landfear. The Mary Ann Rocks, U.S.A. *Notes and queries* 154: 280, April 21, 1928.
Mr. Lucas's supposition as to the origin of the name of the rocks near Cape Cod

is subsequently challenged by Albert Matthews in the May 26, 1928, number of the same magazine, p. 372.

1611. Martha's Vineyard. *New England historical and genealogical register* 12:33, Jan. 1858.

1612. Massachusetts. Secretary of the Commonwealth. Historical data relating to counties, cities and towns in Massachusetts. Prepared by the Secretary of the Commonwealth, Division of Public Records. Boston, Wright and Potter Print. Co., 1920. 73p.

1613. —— Historical data relating to counties, cities and towns in Massachusetts. Prepared by Frederic W. Cook. n.p., 1948. 92p.
Part 1. Counties, containing a list of counties with date of incorporation. Part 2. Existing cities and towns. Part 3. Extinct places.

1614. Massachusetts Geodetic Survey. Massachusetts localities. A finding list of Massachusetts cities and towns; and of villages, certain lesser localities, railroad stations, and post offices whose location is not localized within the appropriate cities and towns by their names, and other generally related material. Arranged for quick reference within one alphabet. Boston, Dept. of Public Works, Offset Print. Division, 1962. 53p. (Massachusetts. Dept. of Public Works. Publication no. 90)
Reprinted 1963. 51p.
Originally published 1938, 78p., as Massachusetts WPA project no. 16565, sponsored by Massachusetts Dept. of Public Works.

1615. Matthews, Albert. The naming of Hull, Massachusetts. Boston, Press of D. Clapp & Son, 1905. 12p.
Reprinted from *New England historical and genealogical register* 59:177-86, April 1905.

1616. Mood, Fulmer. Why the "Vineyard"? *New England quarterly* 6:131-36, March 1933.
Bibliographical footnotes.
Speculations on the origin of the word Vineyard in the name Martha's Vineyard.

1617. Nason, Elias. A gazetteer of the State of Massachusetts. Rev. and enl. by George J. Varney. Boston, B. B. Russell, 1890. 724p.
1st ed. 1874. 576p.

1618. Palmer, Charles James. Berkshire County. Its past history and achievements. n.p., n.d. 24p.
Origin of the names of the towns and villages of Berkshire Co.: p. 11-24.

1619. Poore, Alfred. Groveland localities and place-names. Essex Institute. Historical collections 46:161-77, April 1910.
Compiled in 1854.

1620. Spofford, Jeremiah. A historical and statistical gazetteer of Massachusetts, with sketches of the principal events from its settlement; a catalogue of prominent characters, and historical and statistical notices of the several cities and towns, alphabetically arranged. 2d ed. rev., cor., and a large part rewritten.

Haverhill, E. G. Frothingham, 1860. 372p.
1st ed. published under title A gazetteer of Massachusetts. Newburyport, C. Whipple, 1828. 348p.

1621. Tolman, Adams. Indian relics in Concord. Concord Antiquarian Society. Publications v. 10, n.d.
Place-names, p. 4-13.

1622. Tooker, William Wallace. The name Massachusetts. *Magazine of New England history* 1:159-60, July 1891.
The derivation and meaning of the place-name. Opposes idea in note, *ibid.* 1:13, Jan. 1891, and states article by James Hammond Trumbull (see no. 1623) is best.

1623. Trumbull, James Hammond. Letter on the name Massachusetts. American Antiquarian Society. Proceedings Oct. 21, 1867, p. 77-84.
With remarks by Edward Everett Hale.

1624. U.S. Writers' Program. Massachusetts. The origin of Massachusetts place names of the state, counties, cities, and towns, comp. by workers of the Writers' Project of the Work Projects Administration in Massachusetts. Sponsored by the state librarian of the Commonwealth of Massachusetts. New York, Harian Publications, 1941. 55p.
Bibliography: p. 54-55.

1625. Whitmore, William Henry. An essay on the origin of the names of towns in Massachusetts, settled prior to A.D. 1775. To which is prefixed An essay on the name of the town of Lexington. Boston, Press of John Wilson & Son, 1873. 37p.
Reprinted from Massachusetts Historical Society. Proceedings 12:269-76, 393-419, Oct. 1872, Feb. 1873.
With James Hammond Trumbull's The composition of Indian geographical names (see no. 444) marks the beginning of sound scholarship in place-name studies.

1626. Winship, A. E. Massachusetts names. *Journal of education* (Boston) 48:109-10, 142-43, Aug. 18, Sept. 1, 1898.

1627. Wright, Harry Andrew. Indian deeds of Hampden County, being copies of all land transfers from the Indians recorded in the county of Hampden, Massachusetts, and some deeds from other sources, together with notes and translations of Indian place names. Springfield, Mass., 1905. 194p.
Includes also records of the counties of Hampshire, Worcester, Berkshire, and Franklin, Mass. At the end of each deed, notes are given regarding the meaning or the source of the aboriginal names.

1628. ———— Some vagaries in Connecticut Valley Indian place-names. *New England quarterly* 12:535-44, Sept. 1939.
"Discusses various causes of corruption in Indian place-names."—*American speech.*

MICHIGAN

1629. Armitage, B. Phillis. A study of Michigan's place-names. *Michigan history magazine* 27:626-37, Oct.-Dec. 1943.
Extracted from a paper written for a course in Michigan history at Western Michigan College.
Bibliography: p. 636-37.

1630. Blois, John T. Gazetteer of the State of Michigan, in three parts, with a succinct history of the state, from the earliest period to the present time, with an appendix, containing the usual statistical tables, and a directory for emigrants, &c. Detroit, S. L. Rood & Co., 1840. 418p.
Editions published also in 1838, 1839.

1631. Brotherton, R. A. Meaning of Escanaba. *Inland seas* 4:210-11, Fall 1948.

1632. Brown, Claudeous Jethro Daniels. Lake names. Ann Arbor, Michigan Dept. of Conservation, 1944. 26p. (Michigan. Institute for Fisheries Research, Ann Arbor. Miscellaneous publication no. 2)

1633. Bunker, Norman & Victor F. Lemmer. How Little Girl's Point got its name. *Michigan history* 38:169-73, June 1954.

1634. Butler, Albert F. Rediscovering Michigan's prairies. *Michigan history* 31:267-86, Sept. 1947; 32:15-36, March 1948; 33:117-30, 220-31, June-Sept. 1949.

1635. Carpenter, C. K. Squaw Island—how it received its name. Michigan Pioneer and Historical Society. Historical collections 13:486-88. 1889.
An island in Orion Lake.

1636. Catlin, George B. Biography and romance in Detroit's street names. *Michigan history magazine* 11:604-20, Oct. 1927.

1637. Change of names of counties. Pioneer Society of the State of Michigan. Pioneer collections 1:94. 1877.
A table of changes made by legislative acts, followed by the acts in a section. Reports of counties, towns, and districts, p. 94-518.

1638. Clapp, A. B. Sault Ste. Marie and its names. n.p., n.d. 23p.
Bibliography: p. 7-23.

1639. Davies, Florence. Six Michigan towns (Reading, Plymouth, Bath, Rochester, Manchester, and Oxford) invited to meet "grandmas." *Detroit news* Sept. 18, 1932.
Namesake town association sponsored by the English-speaking Union to encourage exchange of visits between representatives of the cities in the Old and the New World.

1640. Doty, Mrs. W. G. Ann Arbor. *Michigan history magazine* 7:192-98, July-Oct. 1923.
Origin of the name.

1641. Dustin, Fred. Isle Royale place names. *Michigan history magazine* 30:681-722, Oct.-Dec. 1946.

1642. —— Some Indian place-names around Saginaw. *Michigan history magazine* 12:729-39, Oct. 1928.

1643. Dykstra, Lillian. The founding and naming of Ann Arbor. *Michigan history* 40:419-32, Dec. 1956.

1644. Foster, Theodore G. Indian place names in Michigan. *Totem pole* 28:3-4, Jan. 1952; 29:1-6, Aug. 1952.

1645. —— More Michigan place names. *Totem pole* 33:1-3, Nov. 1953; 35:1-6, Feb. 1955.

1646. —— Place-names of Ingham County. *Michigan history magazine* 26:480-517, Autumn 1942.

1647. —— Some Michigan place-names honoring the Navy. *Inland seas* 6:166-68, Fall 1950.

1648. —— Townships in Michigan, an alphabetical list. Lansing, Michigan State Library, 1948. 16p.

1649. —— The Vermont ancestry of some Michigan place names. Vermont Historical Society. News and notes 11:55, 62, March, April 1960.

1650. —— What's in a name. *Lansing state journal.*
A series that appeared *ca.* 1954. Similar series in *Jackson citizen patriot, Kalamazoo gazette,* and *Grand Rapids press,* each dealing with names in the particular paper's circulation area.

1651. Fox, George R. Place names of Berrien County. *Michigan historical magazine* 8:6-35, Jan. 1924.

1652. —— Place names of Cass County. *Michigan history magazine* 27:463-91, Summer 1943.

1653. Gagnieur, William F. Indian place-names. *Michigan history magazine* 9:109-11, Jan. 1925.
Corrections and additions to articles on Indian place-names which appeared in the *Michigan history magazine* in July 1918 and July 1919.

1654. —— Indian place-names in the Upper Peninsula, and their interpretation. *Michigan history magazine* 2:526-55, July 1918.

1655. —— Ketekitiganing (today Lake Vieux Desert). *Michigan history magazine* 12:776-77, Oct. 1928.
A supposition concerning the origin of the Indian place-name Ketekitiganing.

1656. —— Some place names in the Upper Peninsula of Michigan and elsewhere. *Michigan history magazine* 3:412-19, July 1919.

1657. —— Tahquamenon. *Michigan history magazine* 14:557, July 1930.
The possible significance of the old Indian name.

1658. Gerard, William R. Kalamazoo. *American anthropologist* n.s. 13:337-38,

141

April-June 1911.
Gives the derivation and meaning of the word Kalamazoo.

1659. Hamilton, Charlotte. Chippewa County place names. *Michigan history magazine* 27:638-43, Oct.-Dec. 1943.

1660. Hinsdale, Wilbert B. Archaeological atlas of Michigan. Ann Arbor, Univ. of Michigan Press, 1931. 38p. (University Museums, University of Michigan. Michigan handbook series, no. 4)
    Sources: p. 1-3.
    Includes lists of villages, etc.

1661. Indian names. Pioneer Society of the State of Michigan. Pioneer collections 7:136. 1884.
    From the *Detroit gazette* Dec. 6, 1882.
    The original Indian names and their significance are given in a brief note for Saginaw, Shiawassee, and Tittibawassa, Mich.

1662. Inkster prospers. *Lincoln (Neb.) star* Dec. 5, 1959, p. 5.
    Residents being polled on their reaction to changing the name of Inkster (Detroit suburb) to Cherry Hill Heights or Dearborn Hills.

1663. Jenks, William L. History and meaning of the county names of Michigan. Michigan Pioneer and Historical Society. Historical collections 38:439-78. 1912.
    Alphabetical list compiled from this in *Michigan history* 10:646-55, Oct. 1926.

1664. Johnson, William W. Indian names in and about the County of Mackinac. Pioneer Society of the State of Michigan. Historical collections 12:375-81. 1887.
    Translation of the names, and location of the places.

1665. Kelton, Dwight H. Indian names and history of the Sault Ste. Marie Canal. Detroit, Detroit Free Press Print. Co., 1889. 32p.

1666. Langenfelt, Gösta. "Michigander." *American speech* 29:295-96, Dec. 1954.
    Supplement to the Hans Sperber article, *ibid.* 29:21-27.

1667. —— "Michigander": an addendum. *American speech* 31:238, Oct. 1956.

1668. Lanman, James Henry. Indian topographical terms; *In his* History of Michigan. New York, E. French, 1839. p. 260-61.
    Chippewa Indian names with English definitions, obtained from Henry Connor, and supervised by H. R. Schoolcraft.

1669. Leestma, Roger A. Origin of Dutch place names in Allegan and Ottawa counties, Michigan. Michigan Academy of Science. Papers 34:147-51. 1948.

1670. McCormick, William R. Indian names in the Saginaw Valley. Pioneer Society of the State of Michigan. Pioneer collections 7:277. 1884.
    List of the original names, with their meanings, for places and rivers in the Saginaw Valley.

1671. McMullen, Edwin Wallace. Prairie generics in Michigan. *Names* 7:188-90, Sept. 1959.
    The author gives more attention to the Indian names listed in this article, as a

result of a communication from Virgil J. Vogel, in More information on Michigan prairie names, *ibid.* 8:53-56, March 1960.
Addendum, by Virgil J. Vogel, *ibid.* 8:186, Sept. 1960.

1672. Marckwardt, Albert Henry. Wolverine and Michigander. *Michigan alumnus quarterly review* 58:203-08, Spring 1952.
Early history of these names.

1673. May, George S. The meaning and pronunciation of Michilimackinac, general introduction. *Michigan history* 42:385-90, Dec. 1958.
This article introduces the following:

Greenman, Emerson F. The meaning of Michilimackinac. p. 391-92.
Originally published as Michigan Historical Commission. Information series no. 97.
Smith, Emerson R. Michilimackinac, land of the great fault. p. 392-96.
Dever, Harry. Back the attack! It's Mackinac! p. 396-99.
Kelsey, William Kline. Mackinac, not Mackinaw. p. 400-01.
Originally appeared in his column, The Commentator, *Detroit news* Nov. 5, 1957.
Rankin, Ernest H. What is the proper pronunciation of Mackinac? p. 402-05.
Originally appeared in *Mining journal,* Marquette, March 5, 1958.
Marckwardt, Albert Henry. The history of the pronunciation of Mackinac. p. 405-13.

1674. Michigan. Dept. of Conservation. Geological Survey Division. Committee on Geographic Names. Lake gazetteer, Gogebic County, Michigan. Lansing, 1952, *i.e.*, 1954. 50, 27p.

1675. Michigan. Historical Commission. Names of places of interest on Mackinac Island, Michigan, established, designated and adopted by the Mackinac Island State Park Commission and the Michigan Historical Commission.
Descriptive and explanatory notes by Rt. Rev. Monsignor Frank A. O'Brien, president, Michigan Historical Commission. Lansing, Wynkoop, Hallenbeck, Crawford Co., 1916. 86p. (Bulletin, no. 5)

1676. Mikado, Mich. may vote to be Marion Claire. *New York times* Feb. 1, 1942, p. 33, col. 2.

1677. Noggle, Fred D. Origin of the name "Chicaming." *Totem pole* 24:4-5, Jan. 2, 1950.
Berrien County.

1678. Origin and orthography of some of the proper names in the Lake Superior district; *In* U.S. General Land Office. Report on the geology and topography of a portion of the Lake Superior land district, in the State of Michigan. Washington, Govt. Print. Off., 1851. 2:396-400.

1679. Purcell, J. M. "Michigander." *American speech* 31:303-04, Dec. 1956.

1680. Quaife, Milo Milton. Wolverine. *American notes and queries* 3:181-82, March 1944.
Why is Wolverine applied to the people of Michigan?

1681. Rankin, Ernest H. Michilimackinac. *Inland seas* 14:270-76, Winter 1958.
Proper pronunciation: Mackinaw.

1682. Rosalita, S. M. Detroit, the story of some street names; illus. by Charles
Acker, ed. by Joe L. Norris. Detroit, Wayne Univ. Press, 1951. 20p.

1683. Russell, John Andrew. The geographical impress of the races in the
making of Michigan; *In his* The Germanic influence in the making of Michigan.
Detroit, Univ. of Detroit, 1927. p. 358-61.
Influence of the French, English, American, and German inhabitants on the
place-names in Michigan.

1684. Scott, Irving Day. Inland lakes of Michigan. Lansing, Wynkoop, Hallenbeck, Crawford Co., 1921. 383p. (Michigan. Geological and Biological Survey.
Publication 30. Geological series 25)

1685. Sidetracked no longer by its name. *Kansas City star* March 29, 1960, p. 3.
From Detour to De Tour Village to prevent misunderstanding of highway signs.

1686. Smith, C. Henry. Place names: Metamora. *Michigan history magazine*
28:319-20, April 1944.

1687. Smith, Kenneth G. How White Lake was named. *Michigan history magazine* 6:273-76. 1922.

1688. Sperber, Hans. Words and phrases in American politics: Michigander.
American speech 29:21-27, Feb. 1954.
Traces the state nickname to its origin as a personal nickname for Gen. Cass,
meaning "the gander from Michigan."

1689. The Story of a river name. Michigan Archaeological Society. News 2:17-
21, Dec. 1956.
Shiawassee.

1690. Teaboldt, Elizabeth. History of street names in Ypsilanti. Ann Arbor,
1947.
Thesis (M.A.) Univ. of Michigan.

1691. Turner, Timothy Gilman. Gazetteer of the St. Joseph Valley, Michigan
and Indiana, with a view of its hydraulic and business capacities. Chicago, Hazlitt & Reed, printers, 1867. 166p.

1692. Turrell, Archie M. Some place names of Hillsdale County. *Michigan history magazine* 6:573-82. 1922.

1693. Verwyst, Chrysostom. Geographical names in Wisconsin, Minnesota and
Michigan having a Chippewa origin. Wisconsin. State Historical Society. Collections 12:390-98. 1892.
"Cites distortions of names and the source and significance of the correct terminations."—Price.

1694. ⸺ A glossary of Chippewa Indian names of rivers, lakes, and villages.
Acta et dicta 4:253-75, July 1916.

These names are mostly of the Chippewa language, though a considerable number of them are from other Algic dialects.

1695. Wahla, Ed J. Mackin-aw or Mackin-ac? *Totem pole* 24:1-2, Feb. 6, 1950.

1696. Walton, Ivan H. Indian place names in Michigan. *Midwest folklore* 5:23-34, Spring 1955.

1697. Washtenaw County. Pioneer Society of the State of Michigan. Pioneer collections 4:393-94. 1881.
R. V. Williams's interpretation of the name is supplemented by further comments by the editor.

1698. "Wolverine." *American speech* 24:301, Dec. 1949.
Signed: W. G.
Question concerning origin. Refers to note in *Michigan alumnus* March 26, 1949, p. 302.

1699. Wood, Edwin Orin. Historic Mackinac; the historical, picturesque and legendary features of the Mackinac country; illus. from sketches, drawings, maps, and photographs, with an original map of Mackinac Island, made especially for this work. New York, Macmillan, 1918. 2v.
Michilimackinac—application of name and various spellings: 2:563-66.
Indian names in the Mackinac country (taken from Dwight H. Kelton's Indian names of places near the Great Lakes): 2:624-40.

1700. Yost, Fielding H. The Wolverine. *Michigan history magazine* 27:581-89, Oct.-Dec. 1943.

1701. ——— The Wolverine state. *Michigan history magazine* 27:337-39, Spring 1943.
Two popular articles on the question of Michigan's nickname.

MINNESOTA

1702. Baker, James H. Chippewa origin of the name "Minnesota." Minnesota Historical Society. Collections 3:337-38. 1870-80.
"Pointing out that the name is of possible Chippewa origin, Mr. Baker proceeds to discuss its meaning."—Price.

1703. Berthel, Mary W. Place names of the Mille Lacs region. *Minnesota history* 21:345-52, Dec. 1940.

1704. Blegen, Theodore Christian. That name "Itasca." *Minnesota history* 13:163-74, June 1932.
Readers of the articles by Edward C. Gale and Irving H. Hart (see nos. 1713 and 1715) will find further information here.

1705. Brower, Jacob Vradenberg. Nomenclature of Itasca State Park. Minnesota Historical Society. Collections 11:271-79. 1904.
This article traces the word Itasca to its source. Embodied in the report are

lists of traditional and geographical names; names at the Itasca Basin with the names of people who suggested them or of those whose names were used to designate the place; and changed and new names in the region, with sources. This material is the same, except for a slight addition, as that found in an article by the same author which appeared *ibid.* 7:282-89. 1893.

1706. Brown, Calvin L. Some changes in local boundaries and names in Minnesota. *Minnesota history bulletin* 4:242-49, Feb.-May 1922.

1707. Chase, Carroll & Richard McP. Cabeen. The first hundred years of United States territorial postmarks, 1787-1887. Minnesota Territory. *American philatelist* 58:287-97, 420-35, Jan., March 1945.

Includes list of post offices, with notes on some names.

1708. Culkin, William E. North Shore place names. St. Paul, Scott-Mitchell Pub. Co., 1931. 95p.

"This treatise undertakes to give the origin of the place names along the North Shore of Lake Superior between Fond du Lac in Duluth on the southwest and the Pigeon River at the Canadian boundary on the northeast."—p. 13-14.

1709. Davis, Edward W. Taconite: the derivation of the name. *Minnesota history* 33:282-83, Autumn 1953.

The geological term taconite, used for the iron formation of the Mesabi Range, came from an Indian geographic name in Massachusetts.

1710. Explorer names on the land. *Gopher historian* 11:9, Fall 1956.

1711. Flandrau, Charles E. Reminiscences of Minnesota during the territorial period. Minnesota Historical Society. Collections 9:212-15, 219-21. 1898-1900.

"From reminiscences and his knowledge of the Sioux language, the writer gives his own interpretations of the significance of geographical names, some of which are sinking into oblivion, and the origin of the word Itasca."—Price.

1712. Forrest, Robert J. Mythical cities of southwestern Minnesota. *Minnesota history* 14:243-62, Sept. 1933.

An exposé of forgeries in census reports and voting tabulations, and of cities that existed only on the plat books in the speculators' offices.

1713. Gale, Edward C. The legend of Lake Itasca. *Minnesota history* 12:215-25, Sept. 1931.

"The author connects the name with two Indian legends, neither of which is known to-day to the Indians or white inhabitants of the region. Nevertheless, he explains the probability of the relationship."—Price.

1714. Gilfillan, Joseph A. Minnesota geographical names derived from the Chippewa language. Minnesota. Geological and Natural History Survey. Annual report 15:451-77. 1886.

A list of 439 names of rivers, lakes, etc. in Minnesota, and some in the adjoining territories of Dakota and Manitoba, and the State of Wisconsin, in the Ojibway or Chippeway language. The meanings and the English names are given.

1715. Hart, Irving H. The origin and meaning of the name "Itasca." *Minnesota history* 12:225-29, Sept. 1931.

An independent study made by an Iowan, published with the Gale article (see no. 1713) under general title Itasca studies, since they supplement each other in unusual fashion.

1716. Hiebert, John M. Historic names of Minnesota counties. *Gopher historian* 9:14-17, Fall 1954.

1717. Jones, Jefferson. A check list, the territorial post-offices of Minnesota. Bozeman, Mont., The Author, 1949. 16p.

1718. Minnesota. Dept. of Drainage and Waters. Gazetteer of meandered lakes of Minnesota. n.p., 1928. 183p.

1719. Minnesota. State Drainage Commission. Gazetteer of Minnesota streams; *In its* Report of the water resources investigation of Minnesota, 1909-10. St. Paul, McGill-Warner Co., 1910-12. 1:318-43; 2:566-94.

1720. Minnesota. State Geographic Board. Minnesota geographic names.
   Manuscript file in the Minnesota Historical Society Library, started by the Federal Writers' Project.

1721. Minnesota. Something about the names of its counties. *St. Cloud journal-press* Jan. 31, 1878.

1722. Minnesota to rename lakes. *New York times* June 6, 1937, p. 17, col. 3.
   The newly created State Geographic Board will rename the lakes with duplicate names in the Long lakes and Rice lakes.

1723. Moyle, John B. Indian names on a Minnesota map. *Conservation volunteer* (Minnesota Dept. of Conservation) 25:27-31, Jan.-Feb. 1962.
   Nearly all of Chippewa and Dakota (or Sioux) origin.

1724. Neufeld, Jean. Indian names of Minnesota counties. *Gopher historian* 8:15-16, Spring 1954.

1725. Ojibway-Dakota Research Society of Minnesota. Ojibway and Dakota place names in Minnesota; ed. by Mrs. Karen Daniels Petersen. *Minnesota archaeologist* 25:5-40, Jan. 1963.

1726. Rossman, Laurence A. Naming Itasca's lakes. Grand Rapids, Minn., 1931. 10p.

1727. Street names: for St. Anthony and Minneapolis; shown on an early map, what they are called today. *Hennepin County history* 18:8-10, Spring 1959.

1728. Swanson, Roy W. Scandinavian place-names in the American Danelaw. *Swedish-American historical bulletin* 2:5-17, Aug. 1929.
   "A study of place-names of Scandinavian origin in Minnesota, the Danelaw of America."—Griffin.

1729. U.S. Work Projects Administration. Minnesota. Alphabetical index of Minnesota lakes & streams showing identification numbers. Prepared under the direction of the hydrologist of the Division of Water Resources and Engineering of the Department of Conservation by the Work Projects Administration. St. Paul, 1941. 115p.

1730. Upham, Warren. Minnesota county names. *Magazine of history with notes and queries* 8:152-59, 215-18, 285-92, Sept.-Nov. 1908.

1731. —— Minnesota geographic names, their origin and historic significance. St. Paul, Minnesota Historical Society, 1920. 735p. (Collections of the Minnesota Historical Society, v. 17)
Wide coverage of geographical features; includes names of streets and parks in Minneapolis, St. Paul, and Duluth.
Review: by M. R. Gilmore, *Minnesota history bulletin* 3:448-49, Aug. 1920.

1732. Verwyst, Chrysostom. Geographical names in Wisconsin, Minnesota and Michigan having a Chippewa origin. Wisconsin. State Historical Society. Collections 12:390-98. 1892.
"Cites distortions of names and the source and significance of the correct terminations."—Price.

1733. —— A glossary of Chippewa Indian names of rivers, lakes and villages. *Acta et dicta* 4:253-74, July 1916.
These names are mostly of the Chippewa language though a considerable number of them are from other Algic dialects.

1734. Williams, John Fletcher. Origins of Minnesota county names. *St. Paul daily pioneer* March 13, 1870.

1735. Williamson, Andrew W. Minnesota geographical names derived from the Dakota language, with some that are obsolete. Minnesota. Geological and Natural History Survey. Annual report 13:104-12. 1884.

1736. Zumberge, James H. The lakes of Minnesota, their origin and classification. Minneapolis, Univ. of Minnesota Press, 1952. 99p. (Minnesota. Geological Survey. Bulletin no. 35)
Lists of lakes, p. 85-94.

MISSISSIPPI

1737. Bass, Mary Frances. A study of place names of Clarke County, Mississippi. Thesis (M.A.) Univ. of Alabama, 1941.

1738. Cain, Cyril E. The first hundred years of post offices on the Pascagoula River. *Journal of Mississippi history* 11:178-84, July 1949.
Jackson and Greene counties, 1821- .

1739. Chase, Carroll & Richard McP. Cabeen. The first hundred years of United States territorial postmarks, 1787-1887. Mississippi Territory. *American philatelist* 55:220-26, Jan. 1942.
Includes list of post offices, 1803-17, with notes on some names.

1740. Gannett, Henry. The origin of certain place names in the State of Mississippi. Mississippi Historical Society. Publications 6:339-49. 1902.

1741. Halbert, Henry Sale. Choctaw Indian names in Alabama and Mississippi. Alabama Historical Society. Transactions 3:64-77. 1898-99.

1742. —— Origin of Mashulaville. Mississippi Historical Society. Publications 7:389-97. 1903.
An American village that has grown on the site of an ancient Indian village and was named for the Indian chief Moshulitubee.

1743. Mississippi. Dept. of Archives and History. The official and statistical register. 1904- . Nashville, Tenn.
Each issue contains a list of the counties, with date of establishment and origin of name; also article on the meaning of Mississippi; also in 1917:446-47, Indian names of Mississippi, an article condensed from the paper by H. S. Halbert (Dept. reports, 1896-97).

1744. Note on the origin of Natchez. *Louisiana historical quarterly* 14:515, Oct. 1931.

1745. Riley, Franklin L. Extinct towns and villages of Mississippi. Mississippi Historical Society. Publications 5:311-83. 1902.

1746. Seale, Lea Leslie. Indian place-names in Mississippi. Louisiana State University and Agricultural and Mechanical College. Publications n.s. v. 32, no. 1, Jan. 1940. The Graduate School abstracts of theses, session of 1938-1939, p. 5-7.
Abstract.

1747. Spiro, Robert H. Place names in Mississippi. *Mississippi magazine* 1:6-8, Jan. 1955.

MISSISSIPPI VALLEY

1748. Berger, Vilhelm. Amerikanska ortnamn af svenskt ursprung. New York, 1915. 12p.
Swedish names in Minnesota, Iowa, Nebraska, Kansas, and the Dakotas.

1749. Chase, Carroll & Richard McP. Cabeen. The first hundred years of United States territorial postmarks, 1787-1887. The District of Louisiana, The Territory of Louisiana and Missouri Territory. *American philatelist* 55:572-78, 636-40, June-July 1942.
Includes list of post offices, 1804-21, with notes on some names.

1750. —— —— Indiana Territory. *American philatelist* 56:80-86, Nov. 1942.
Includes list of post offices, with notes on some names.

1751. —— —— Michigan Territory. *American philatelist* 56:722-30, Aug. 1943; 57:137-43, Nov. 1943.
Includes list of post offices, with notes on some names.

1752. —— —— The territory northwest of the River Ohio (usually known

as Northwest Territory). *American philatelist* 55:775-82, 809, Sept. 1942.
Includes list of post offices, with notes on some names.

1753. —— —— Wisconsin Territory. *American philatelist* 57:301-05,
387-402, Jan.-Feb. 1944.
Includes list of post offices, with notes on some names.

1754. Conclin, George. A book for all travelers. Conclin's new river guide;
or, A gazetteer of all the towns on the western waters: containing sketches of
the cities, towns, and countries bordering on the Ohio and Mississippi rivers
and their principal tributaries. Cincinnati, U. P. James, 1855. 128p.
Earlier editions 1848, 1849, 1850, 1851. For later editions see Uriah Pierson
James, James' river guide, no. 1763.

1755. Connelley, William E. Origin of Indian names of certain states and rivers.
Ohio archaeological and historical quarterly 29:451-54, Oct. 1920.
"Statements relative to the derivation and meaning of the names of the states of
Iowa, Missouri, Mississippi, Ohio and Kentucky and the rivers Ohio, Mississippi,
Missouri and Neosha."—Griffin.

1756. Craig, Isaac. The Shawanese name for the Ohio. *Magazine of American
history* 8:363-64, May 1882.
The author gives the origin of the place-name and denounces the interpretation
of Colonel John Johnston in Henry Howe's Historical collections of Ohio. Cincinnati, Derby, Bradley & Co., 1847.

1757. Croy, Homer. Let's name the town for me. *Saturday evening post* 218:6,
June 8, 1946.

1758. Cumings, Samuel. The western pilot; containing charts of the Ohio River
and of the Mississippi, from the mouth of the Missouri to the Gulf of Mexico;
accompanied with directions for navigating the same, and a gazetteer; or description of the towns on their banks, tributary streams, etc. also a variety of matter
interesting to travelers, and all concerned in the navigation of those rivers; with
a table of distances from town to town on all the above rivers. Corrected by
Capts. Charles Ross & John Klinefelter. Cincinnati, J. A. & U. P. James, 1854.
140p.
Earlier editions 1825, 1829, 1832, 1834, 1838, 1840, 1843, 1848.
A revised and altered edition of the author's Western navigator. "Cumings'
editions of the 'Navigator' and 'Pilot' were amplifications of The navigator of
Zadock Cramer without acknowledgment of the main source of their material."
—Joseph Sabin, Dictionary of books relating to America 5:126; also L. C. card.

1759. Delanglez, Jean. The Jolliet lost map of the Mississippi. *Mid-America*
28:67-144, April 1946.
The nomenclature of Jolliet's lost map, p. 97-139.

1760. —— El Rio del Espíritu Santo; an essay on the cartography of the Gulf
Coast and the adjacent territory during the sixteenth and seventeenth centuries.
Ed. by Thomas J. McMahon. New York, 1945. 182p. (United States Catholic
Historical Society. Monograph series, 21)
Much of the contents of this monograph appeared in *Mid-America* 25:189-219,
231-49, July, Oct. 1943; 26:62-84, 138-64, 192-220, Jan.-July 1944.
An inquiry, through a study of maps, of what knowledge the best-informed

geographers of the period seem to have had of the Mississippi, and, in particular, whether the river which is labeled Rio del Espíritu Santo on these maps is the Mississippi itself. Concludes that the Mississippi is not the Rio del Espíritu Santo. Contains a table of Nomenclature on four early Spanish maps of the Gulf of Mexico.

1761. Dunn, Jacob Piatt. Names of the Ohio River. *Indiana magazine of history* 8:166-70, Dec. 1912.

1762. Haines, Elijah Middlebrook. Indian names; *In* Blanchard, Rufus. The discovery and conquests of the Northwest. Wheaton, [Ill.], Blanchard, 1879. p. 589-98.
Also in edition published Chicago, Cushing, Thomas & Co., 1880. p. 475-84.

1763. James, Uriah Pierson. James' river guide: containing descriptions of all the cities, towns, and principal objects of interest on the navigable waters of the Mississippi Valley. Illus. with forty-four maps. Rev. ed. Cincinnati, U. P. James, 1871. 128p.
Also published 1856, 1858, 1860, 1869.
Earlier editions published by George Conclin with title A book for all travelers. Conclin's new river guide (see no. 1754).

1764. Kelton, Dwight H. Ancient names of rivers, lakes, etc. Pioneer Society of the State of Michigan. Collections 6:349-51. 1884.
The various names and sources for bodies of water in the northern part of the Middle West.

1765. Read, William Alexander. A Vernerian sound-change in English. *Englische Studien* 47:169-74. 1913.
A study of the pronunciation and spelling of Missouri and Mississippi.

1766. Schultz, William Eben. The Middle West; changes in the term applied to the geographical section commonly known as the Middle West. *American speech* 12:316, Dec. 1937.

1767. Stennett, William H. A history of the origin of the place names connected with the Chicago & North western and Chicago, St. Paul, Minneapolis & Omaha railways, comp. by one who for more than 34 years has been an officer in the employ of the system. Chicago, 1908. 201p.
2d ed. 1908.

1768. Thompson, T. P. Origin of the various names of the Mississippi River. Louisiana Historical Society. Publications 9:92-95. 1916.
The names traced in chronological order from early maps and relations of the beginnings of American history.

1769. Voorhis, Ernest. Historic forts and trading posts of the French and of the English fur trading companies. Ottawa, Dept. of the Interior, National Development Bureau, 1930. 188p.
Alphabetical list of forts and posts, p. 28-181.
"A few of these establishments were located on what is now territory of the United States."—Pref.
Includes map of Mississippi and Ohio valleys showing chain of historic French forts.

1770. Wright, Muriel H. The naming of the Mississippi River. *Chronicles of Oklahoma* 6:529-31, Dec. 1928.

MISSOURI

1771. Adams, Orvyl Guy. Place names in the north central counties of Missouri.
Thesis (M.A.) Univ. of Missouri, 1928.
Includes Carroll, Chariton, Livingston, Linn, Macon, Grundy, Sullivan, Adair, Mercer, Putnam, and Schuyler counties.

1772. Atchison, Anne Eliza. Place names of five west central counties of Missouri.
Thesis (M.A.) Univ. of Missouri, 1937.
Includes Jackson, Lafayette, Platte, Clay, and Ray counties.

1773. Beck, Lewis Caleb. A gazetteer of the states of Illinois and Missouri; containing a general view of each state, a general view of their counties, and a particular description of their towns, villages, rivers, &c., &c. With a map, and other engravings. Albany, Printed by C. R. and G. Webster, 1823. 352p.

1774. Bell, Margaret Ellen. Place names of the southwest border counties of Missouri.
Thesis (M.A.) Univ. of Missouri, 1933.
Includes Wright, Webster, Christian, Douglas, Ozark, Taney, Stone, Barry, and McDonald counties.
Includes manuscript on McDonald County names by Vance Randolph.

1775. Bess, Charles E. Podunk in southeast Missouri. *American speech* 10:80, Feb. 1935.

1776. Bloody Island. *Missouri historical review* 26:389-91, July 1932.
Dueling place in the Mississippi River opposite St. Louis.

1777. Broadhead, G. C. Sniabar. *Kansas City review of science and industry* 5:23-24, May 1881.
A creek.

1778. Campbell, Robert Allen. Campbell's gazetteer of Missouri; from articles contributed by prominent gentlemen in each county of the state, and information collected and collated from official and other authentic sources, by a corps of experienced canvassers, under the personal supervision of the editor. Rev. ed. St. Louis, R. A. Campbell, 1875. 796p.
First published 1874.

1779. Discord about a great name. *New York times* Jan. 3, 1933, p. 22, col. 4.
Editorial on pronunciation of Missouri, following talk by Allen Walker Read before Linguistic Society of America.

1780. Doolittle, Mo., meets the General himself at its formal dedication under his name. *New York times* Oct. 12, 1946, p. 10, col. 2.
Formerly Centerville.

1781. Drums in old Mizzou. *Time* 72:38, Sept. 1, 1958.

Naming the new road to the Missouri University stadium in Columbia, Mo., and the furore it caused.

The Chamber of Commerce proposed to name it Caniff Blvd. in honor of Milton Caniff, cartoonist, creator of the character Miss Mizzou in the comic strip Steve Canyon. This produced much comment, both favorable and unfavorable, much of which illustrates various principles of place-naming.

References to some of the newspaper articles on this controversy follow:

"Gutter tactics" hit by head of C. of C. *Columbia Missourian* July 29, 1958, p. 1-2.

Delugach, Al. Bard and comic strip author involved in street name fuss. *Kansas City star* Aug. 10, 1958, p. 1, 19 A.

Decorum of M. U. city shaken by "Miss Mizzou." *Columbia Missourian* Aug. 11, 1958, p. 8.

Suggests a way to honor Don Faurot. *Kansas City star* Aug. 13, 1958, p. 10 D.

"No name" publicity. *Columbia Missourian* Aug. 14, 1958, p. 4.
Editorial.

Capacity crowd expected at street-naming meeting. *Columbia Missourian* Aug. 16, 1958, p. 1.

Street of no name. *Columbia Missourian* Aug. 20, 1958, p. 4.
Editorial; picture.

Providence wins out over Caniff. *Kansas City star* Sept. 3, 1958, p. 1.

"Caniff obituary." *Columbia Missourian* Sept. 4, 1958, p. 4.
Editorial.

Council selects Providence as inner loop compromise. *Columbia Missourian* Sept. 9, 1958, p. 1.

Letters to the editor. *Columbia Missourian* July 29, 1958, p. 4; Aug. 5, p. 4; Aug. 6, p. 4; Aug. 7, p. 3; Aug. 19, p. 4; Aug. 26, p. 4; Aug. 28, p. 4.

1782. Eaton, David Wolfe. How Missouri counties, towns and streams were named. Columbia, State Historical Society, 1916-18. 5v.

Reprinted from the *Missouri historical review* 10:197-213, 263-87, April, July 1916; 11:164-200, 330-47, Jan., April-July 1917; 13:57-74, Oct. 1918.

1783. Elliott, Katherine. Place-names of six northeast counties of Missouri.
Thesis (M.A.) Univ. of Missouri, 1938.
Includes Marion, Shelby, Lewis, Knox, Clark, and Scotland counties.

1784. Ewing, Martha Kennedy. Place-names in the northwest counties of Missouri.
Thesis (M.A.) Univ. of Missouri, 1929.
Includes Buchanan, Clinton, Caldwell, Daviess, DeKalb, Andrew, Holt, Atchison, Nodaway, Worth, Gentry, and Harrison counties.

1785. Gazetteer and business directory of the new Southwest. Embracing all of that region of country—including counties, towns and cities—contiguous to the St. Louis and San Francisco Railway, its divisions and branches, located in southwest Missouri, southeastern Kansas, the eastern portion of the Indian country, and the northwest section of Arkansas. In which is included an abridged directory of leading business houses of St. Louis. St. Louis, United States Directory Pub. Co., 1881. 224p.

1786. Hamlett, Mayme Lucille. Place-names of six southeast counties of Missouri.

Thesis (M.A.) Univ. of Missouri, 1938.
Includes Pemiscot, Scott, Dunklin, New Madrid, Mississippi, and Stoddard counties.

1787. Harding, Samuel Bannister. Life of George R. Smith, founder of Sedalia, Mo., in its relations to the political, economic, and social life of southwestern Missouri, before and during the Civil War. Sedalia, Mo., Priv. print., 1904. 398p.
The name "Sedalia": p. 291.

1788. Harrison, Eugenia Lillian. The place-names of four river counties in eastern Missouri.
Thesis (M.A.) Univ. of Missouri, 1943.
Includes Franklin, Lincoln, St. Charles, and Warren counties.

1789. How Randolph County was named. *Missouri historical review* 26:215, Jan. 1932.

1790. Johnson, Bernice Eugenia. Place-names in six of the west central counties of Missouri.
Thesis (M.A.) Univ. of Missouri, 1933.
Includes Bates, Cass, Henry, Johnson, St. Clair, and Vernon counties.

1791. Kansas City, North, may get new name. *Kansas City star* March 24, 1961, p. 1, 2 A.

1792. Kiel, Herman Gottlieb. The centennial biographical directory of Franklin County, Missouri. Washington, D.C., 1925. 444p.
Includes a list of geographical names, and a list of post offices.

1793. Leech, Esther Gladys. The place-names of Pike County, Missouri; *In* Ramsay, Robert Lee. Introduction to a survey of Missouri place-names. Columbia, Univ. of Missouri, 1934. p. 60-124.
Bibliography: p. 121-24.

1794. ——— Place-names of six east central counties of Missouri.
Thesis (M.A.) Univ. of Missouri, 1933.
Includes Randolph, Monroe, Audrain, Montgomery, Ralls, and Pike counties.

1795. Leland, J. A. C. Indian names in Missouri. *Names* 1:266-73, Dec. 1953.
Etymology of the Indian names selected from Robert Lee Ramsay, Our storehouse of Missouri place names (see no. 1809).

1796. McDermott, John Francis. Sun or Beausoleil Island? A hidden origin in a place name. *American speech* 32:155-56, May 1957.
Once a stopping place for the fur trader Eugene Pourée *dit* Beausoleil and therefore incorrectly named (*i.e.,* translated) by William Clark and others, 1804- .

1797. Missouri. *Magazine of American history* 29:299, March 1893.
The source and significance of the name Missouri as given by the Indians.

1798. Missouri counties, past and present. *Missouri historical review* 34:498-506, July 1940.
Includes origin of names.

1799.   The Missouri state gazetteer and business directory, containing full and complete descriptions of the cities, towns and villages, with the names and address of the merchants, manufacturers, professional men, etc. etc. St. Louis, Sutherland & McEvoy, 1860. 781p.

1800.   Myers, Robert Lee. Place-names in the southwest counties of Missouri.
Thesis (M.A.) Univ. of Missouri, 1930.
Includes Barton, Jasper, Newton, Cedar, Dade, Lawrence, Polk, and Greene counties.

1801.   O'Brien, Anna. Place-names of five central southern counties of Missouri.
Thesis (M.A.) Univ. of Missouri, 1939.
Includes Dallas, Laclede, Texas, Dent, and Shannon counties.

1802.   Origin of Franklin County names. *Republican tribune,* Union, Aug. 15, 1919.

1803.   Overlay, Fauna Robertson. Place-names of five south central counties of Missouri.
Thesis (M.A.) Univ. of Missouri, 1943.
Includes Benton, Camden, Hickory, Morgan, and Pettis counties.

1804.   Pace, Nadine. Place-names in the central counties of Missouri.
Thesis (M.A.) Univ. of Missouri, 1928.
Includes Callaway, Boone, Howard, Cole, Moniteau, Cooper, and Saline counties.

1805.   Peterson, Karl L. Legendary frontier names identify growing list of Midwestern reservoirs. *Kansas City star* June 28, 1964, p. 2G.
Map on p. 1G.

1806.   Picinich, Donald George. A pronunciation guide to Missouri place names.
Rev. by Robert Lee Ramsay. Columbia, Mo., 1951. 32p. (University of Missouri bulletin, v. 52, no. 35. Journalism series, no. 126)
1st ed. 1951. 24p. (University of Missouri bulletin, v. 52, no. 3. Journalism series, no. 121)

1807.   Pottenger, Cora Ann. Place-names of five southern border counties of Missouri.
Thesis (M.A.) Univ. of Missouri, 1945.
Includes Howell, Oregon, Ripley, Carter, and Butler counties.

1808.   Pronunciation of "Missouri." *Missouri historical review* 26:387-89, July 1932.

1809.   Ramsay, Robert Lee. Our storehouse of Missouri place names. Columbia, Univ. of Missouri, 1952. 160p. (Missouri handbook no. 2) (University of Missouri bulletin, v. 53, no. 34. Arts and science series, 1952, no. 7)
Review: by Hobart M. Lovett, *Names* 1:61-62, March 1953.

1810.   ———   Place-name paragraphs, pub. in the Sunday editions of the *St. Louis Globe-Democrat* May 26, 1946 to September 21, 1947; with an article on the "Place names in Lawrence County" from the Centennial number of the *Lawrence Chieftain,* Mt. Vernon, Mo. July 24, 1947. 36 l.
Photostatic reproduction of a scrapbook, Missouri University Library.

1811. —— The place names of Boone County, Missouri. Gainesville, Fla., American Dialect Society, 1952. 52p. (American Dialect Society. Publication, no. 18)
Review: by Mayme L. Hamlett, *Names* 1:218, Sept. 1953.

1812. —— The place names of Franklin County, Missouri. Columbia, Mo., 1954. 55p. (University of Missouri studies, v. 26, no. 3)
Most of the material used in this study was published in preliminary form in the *Washington Missourian* July 5-Nov. 1, 1951.

1813. —— Progress in the survey of Missouri place-names. Missouri Academy of Science. Proceedings 7:55-65, Oct. 25, 1941.
Survey was begun in 1928. 13 theses completed, covering 90 of 114 counties with remaining counties assigned and in progress.

1814. —— Some secrets of Jefferson County place names. Missouri Historical Society. Bulletin 10:8-26, 406, Oct. 1953, April 1954.
Most of the material used in this study was published in preliminary form in the *Jefferson republic*, De Soto, March 29-July 12, 1951.

1815. —— The study of Missouri place-names at the University of Missouri. *Missouri historical review* 27:132-44, Jan. 1933.
"A report of progress made in the study of Missouri place-names. Five theses include a total of 47 counties and over 3,500 place-names."—Griffin.

1816. —— ; Allen Walker Read, & Esther Gladys Leech. Introduction to a survey of Missouri place-names. Columbia, Univ. of Missouri, 1934. 124p. (University of Missouri studies; a quarterly of research. v. 9, no. 1)
Bibliography of literary sources: p. 39-59.
Bibliography for Pike County place-names: p. 121-24.
An important document in place-name studies—not only an outline of the outstanding university program, but a model to be followed in other states.
Review: *American speech* 9:304-06, Dec. 1934; *Beiblatt zur Anglia* 47:69, March 1936.

1817. Read, Allen Walker. Plans for the study of Missouri place-names. *Missouri historical review* 22:237-41, Jan. 1928.

1818. —— Pronunciation of the word "Missouri." *American speech* 8:22-36, Dec. 1933.
Reprinted in part in Mott, Frank Luther, ed. Missouri reader. Columbia, Univ. of Missouri Press, 1964. p. 17-21.
Includes many references to newspaper articles.

1819. Ross, Mildred E. Nodaway County, Missouri. Maryville, Mo., 1959. 64p. (Northwest Missouri State College studies, v. 23, no. 3, Aug. 1, 1959) (Northwest Missouri State College bulletin, v. 53, no. 8)
Appendix I: Historical guide to the towns: p. 56-63.

1820. Sauer, Carl O. Origin of the name "Ozark." *Missouri historical review* 22:550, July 1928.
Reprinted from his The geography of the Ozark highland of Missouri. Chicago, Univ. of Chicago Press, 1920. p. 5.

1821. Schultz, Gerard. Geographical names of Miller County. *Missouri historical review* 25:540-41, April 1931.
From *Miller County autogram,* Tuscumbia, Aug. 28, 1930.

1822. Shoemaker, Floyd Calvin. Missouri, the name. *Missouri historical review* 38:199-202, Jan. 1944.
From his Missouri and Missourians. Chicago, Lewis Pub. Co., 1943. 1:1-3.

1823. Some lost counties of Missouri. *Missouri historical review* 26:89-91, Oct. 1931; 27:169-70, Jan. 1933.
Why some of the proposed names were changed before they were accepted.

1824. Squires, Monas N. Missouri's abbreviation: Mo. *Missouri historical review* 26:84-85, Oct. 1931.
"Uncritical."—A. W. Read.

1825. Switzler, William F. The real meaning of the word Missouri. *Missouri historical review* 17:231-32, Jan. 1923.
From the *Boonville democrat* Oct. 22, 1897, and the *Kansas City star* Aug. 27, 1922.
A note by J. Walter Fewkes was published in *Missouri historical review* 17:377-78, April 1923.

1826. There are many queerly named towns in Missouri and Kansas. *Kansas City star* Aug. 1, 1937.

1827. Town names reveal much state history. *St. Louis post-dispatch* Sept. 21, 1919.

1828. U.S. 88th Congress, 1st session. House. A bill to provide that the Bull Shoals Dam and the Bull Shoals Reservoir, White River Basin in Missouri and Arkansas shall hereafter be known as the "Harry S. Truman Dam" and the "Harry S. Truman Reservoir." H. R. 1094. Jan. 9, 1963. Washington, 1963. 2p.
Introduced by Mr. Hull and referred to the Committee on Public Works.

1829. Weakley, Janet. Missouri names. *St. Louis globe-democrat* July 8, 1945.

1830. Weber, Frank Thomas Ewing. Place-names of six south central counties of Missouri.
Thesis (M.A.) Univ. of Missouri, 1938.
Includes Miller, Pulaski, Osage, Maries, Phelps, and Gasconade counties.

1831. Welty, Ruth. Place names of St. Louis and Jefferson County.
Thesis (M.A.) Univ. of Missouri, 1939.

1832. Wetmore, Alphonso. Gazetteer of the State of Missouri. With a map of the state. To which is added an appendix, containing frontier sketches, and illustrations of Indian character. With a frontispiece, engraved on steel. St. Louis, C. Keemle, 1837. 382p.

1833. The Word "Missouri." *Missouri historical review* 34:87-93, Oct. 1939.
"A study of the various meanings suggested for the word since Father Marquette's time. 'Muddy Water' as one of these is discredited in favor of 'town of the large canoes.' "—*American speech.*

1834. Zimmer, Gertrude Minnie. Place-names of five southeast counties of Missouri.
Thesis (M.A.) Univ. of Missouri, 1944.
Includes Ste. Genevieve, St. François, Washington, Iron, and Crawford counties.

MONTANA

1835. Baker, Marcus. Survey of the northwestern boundary of the United States, 1857-1861. U.S. Geological Survey. Bulletin 174:58-61. 1900.
Indian names of camps, stations, rivers, etc. along the 49th parallel in Washington, Idaho, and Montana. Based on the work George Gibbs did for the Smithsonian Institution.

1836. Brower, Jacob Vradenberg. Geographic names; *In his* The utmost waters of the Missouri River. American Geographical Society. Bulletin 28:390-91. 1896.
Origin of place-names in the region of the source of the Missouri River.

1837. Bue, Olaf J. A guide to pronunciation of place names in Montana. Missoula, Bureau of Press & Broadcasting Research, School of Journalism, Montana State Univ., 1959. 28p.

1838. Chamberlain, Alexander F. Geographic terms of Kootenay origin. *American anthropologist* n.s. 4:348-50, April-June 1902.
"Concerned with names of places, camp-sites, and stations along the 49th parallel in British Columbia, Washington, Idaho and Montana. These names which seem to have been taken from the language of the Kootenay Indians of this region are mentioned in the reports on the boundary survey. The meanings and etymologies are given where possible."—Price.

1839. Childears, Lucille. Montana place name records. *Western folklore* 13:47-50, Jan. 1954.

1840. ——— Montana place names from Indian myth and legend. *Western folklore* 9:263-64, July 1950.

1841. Grinnell, George Bird. Some Indian stream names. *American anthropologist* n.s. 15:327-31, April-June 1913.
Names of the Gros Ventres of the Prairie Indians, and the Pawnee Indians.

1842. Holtz, Mathilde Edith & Katharine Isabel Bemis. Some Blackfeet legends and Indian names; *In their* Glacier National Park, its trails and treasures. New York, Doran, 1917. p. 191-207.

1843. Koch, Elers. Geographic names of western Montana and northern Idaho. *Oregon historical quarterly* 49:50-62, March 1948.

1844. McClintock, Walter. The old North trail; or, Life, legends and religion of the Blackfeet Indians. London, Macmillan, 1910. 539p.
An Indian recounts to the author the Blackfeet names for rivers, mountains, and other landmarks along the trail, near Helena, Mont. p. 437-40.

1845. McDavid, Raven I., Jr. Hidden "Hell" in "Helena." *American speech* 26:305-06, Dec. 1951.

1846. Mansfield, Michael Joseph. Proposed change of name of Hungry Horse Dam. U.S. Congress. Congressional record v. 109, no. 33, p. 3293, March 4, 1963.
From Hungry Horse Lake to Truman Lake or Truman Reservoir.

1847. Montana. Historical Society. The changing place-names of Glacier National Park; *In its* Blackfeet man: James Willard Schultz. Helena, 1961. (Montana heritage series, no. 12) p. 18-20.
Schultz's endeavors to restore the Indian names, reproduced from his Signposts of adventure.

1848. The Montana almanac. 1957- . Missoula, Montana State Univ.
Origin of Montana place names, an alphabetical list scattered at intervals throughout the various editions (see indexes).

1849. Mundt, Karl E. Two Mobridges in two states. U.S. Congress. Congressional record 105:16816-17, Sept. 7, 1959.
South Dakota, and new town in Montana. Includes origin of name.

1850. Omundson, Don Bert. A study of place names in Missoula County, Montana. Thesis (M.S.) Montana State Univ., 1961.

1851. Pemberton, W. Y. Changing the name of Edgerton County. Montana. Historical Society. Contributions 8:323-27. 1917.
Reasons why the name was changed to Lewis and Clark County.

1852. Rowe, Jesse Perry. The origin of some Montana place names. Missoula, The Author, n.d. 260-313p.

1853. Sanders, Wilbur Edgerton. Montana: organization, name, and naming. The word, its significance, derivation, and historical use. Montana. Historical Society. Contributions 7:15-60. 1910.

1854. Schultz, James Willard. Indian names in Glacier Park. *Outlook* 143:442-44, July 28, 1926.
Gives briefly some of the Blackfeet and Kutenai Indian names for places in the park.

1855. ——— Signposts of adventure; Glacier National Park as the Indians know it. Boston, Houghton, 1926. 224p.
Contents: Introductory; Blackfeet Indian names of the topographical features of Glacier National Park upon its east side; Kutenai Indian names of the topographical features of the west side of Glacier National Park.

1856. Territory of Montana. Montana. Historical Society. Contributions 6:171. 1907; also U.S. Congress. Congressional globe, 38th Congress, 1st session, 1863-64, p. 1168-69, 2510.
Memorial from Territory of Idaho asks that eastern portion of the territory be organized into a new territory to be called Jefferson Territory. Considerable debate as to whether the new territory should be named Jefferson, Douglas, Idaho, or Montana. James M. Ashley's proposal of Montana won out.

1857. U.S. Board on Geographic Names. Decisions. Place names, Glacier National Park, Mont. March 6, 1929. Washington, Govt. Print. Off., 1929. 18p.

1858. U.S. 88th Congress, 1st session. Senate. A bill to designate the lake to be formed by the waters impounded by the Clark Canyon Dam in the State of Montana as Hap Hawkins Lake. S. 142. Jan. 14 (legislative day, Jan. 9), 1963. Washington, 1963. 1p.
Introduced by Mr. Metcalf and Mr. Mansfield and referred to the Committee on Public Works.
Subsequent documents relating to this bill were published as follows:

U.S. 88th Congress, 1st session. Senate. Designating the lake to be formed by the waters impounded by the Clark Canyon Dam, Mont., as Hap Hawkins Lake. Report no. 274, to accompany S. 142. June 19, 1963. Calendar no. 255. Washington, 1963. 4p.
Submitted by Mr. Metcalf, from the Committee on Public Works, without amendment.

—— [Reprint of the original bill, June 19, 1963, to accompany the report. Report no. 274 and Calendar no. 255 added]. 1p.

U.S. 88th Congress, 1st session. House. An act to designate the lake to be formed by the waters impounded by the Clark Canyon Dam in the State of Montana as Hap Hawkins Lake. S. 142. In the House of Representatives June 24, 1963. Washington, 1963. 1p.
Referred to the Committee on Interior and Insular Affairs. Passed the Senate June 20, 1963.

1859. U.S. 88th Congress, 1st session. Senate. Joint resolution to designate the lake to be formed by the waters impounded by the Canyon Ferry Dam, Montana, "Lake Townsend." S. J. Res. 121. Sept. 24, 1963. Washington, 1963. 1p.
Introduced by Mr. Mansfield and Mr. Metcalf and referred to the Committee on Interior and Insular Affairs.
In honor of the city of Townsend and the man for whom it was named, an official of the Northern Pacific Railway Company.

1860. Wolle, Muriel Vincent Sibell. Montana pay dirt; a guide to the mining camps of the Treasure State. Denver, Sage Books, 1963. 436p.
Bibliography: p. 411-16.

NEBRASKA

1861. Abbott, N. C. Lincoln, name and place. Nebraska State Historical Society. Publications 21:8-133. 1930.

1862. Brashier, Mary. Alias a river; behind a river lies a priceless heritage. *Outdoor Nebraska* 37:12-13, 24, Dec. 1959.
Discusses French, Spanish, and Indian names for the Platte River and other rivers in Nebraska.

1863. Broadcast tale of dead cities—Ghost towns of Box Butte County. *Alliance news* March 12, 1931.

1864. Campbell, I. C. G. The Weeping Water legend; an anthology and commentary. Weeping Water, Chamber of Commerce, 1964. 36p.
Legends relating to the origin of the name of Weeping Water, Neb.

1865. Changing Missouri coming back to Rockport—Old river town forgotten for fifty years. *Omaha world-herald* Oct. 20, 1912.

1866. Chase, Carroll & Richard McP. Cabeen. The first hundred years of United States territorial postmarks, 1787-1887. Nebraska Territory. *American philatelist* 59:430-39, 609-17, Feb., April 1946.
Includes a list of post offices, with notes on the origin of some of the names.

1867. Christensen, Arved. A pronunciation guide to Nebraska place names, prepared by Arved Christensen, Wayne B. Wells, Nanci Debord, under the supervision of Paul Schupbach. Lincoln, Univ. of Nebraska, Radio Section, Dept. of Speech, School of Fine Arts, 1953. 48p. (University of Nebraska publication no. 183)

1868. County names, changes made news in early days. *Lincoln (Neb.) Sunday journal and star* May 30, 1954, p. 12-F.

1869. Crowther, Charles L. The pocket gazetteer of the State of Nebraska, with a complete list of counties and principal towns in the same, population, banks, hotels, halls, churches, attorneys at law. Also, a valuable index and original railroad guide to Nebraska, etc., etc. Lincoln, Journal Co., state printers, 1882. 72p.

1870. Early settlers had mania for laying out town sites in Dakota County. *Eagle,* South Sioux City, Aug. 25, 1932.

1871. Eight Mile Grove fades into mists of pioneer past. *Nebraska State journal,* Lincoln, May 5, 1935.

1872. Fairclough, G. Thomas. Notes on some unusual street names in Nebraska City. *American speech* 34:70-71, Feb. 1959; 37:157-58, May 1962.
Refers to article *ibid.* 20:177, Oct. 1945.

1873. Fitzpatrick, Lilian Linder. Nebraska place-names. Lincoln, 1925. 166p. (University of Nebraska studies in language, literature and criticism, no. 6)
Bibliography: p. 148-52.
Review: *American speech* 1:46-48, Oct. 1925; *Michigan history magazine* 10:643-46, Oct. 1926.

1874. —— Nebraska place names [new ed.]. Including selections from The origin of the place-names of Nebraska, by J. T. Link. Ed., with an introduction, by G. Thomas Fairclough. Lincoln, Univ. of Nebraska Press, 1960. 227p. (A Bison book, BB 107)
Fitzpatrick's work, first published 1925, is reprinted in full, with two pages of Errata added. The selections from Link's work, published 1933, include the name of the state, the state's natural features, and some miscellaneous cultural features.
Fairclough says that this edition brings together the most significant work that has been done in the study of Nebraska place-names.
Review: by William Coyle, *Ohio historical quarterly* 70:184-85, April 1961. Contrasts Nebraska names with those in Ohio.

1875. Fontenelle, one of oldest towns. *Arlington review-herald* Sept. 29, 1910.

1876. Gibson, Ron. Possible rift over lake name waning. *Lincoln (Neb.) evening journal* Sept. 9, 1960, p. 26.
Proposals that the lake to be created by the Red Willow Dam near McCook be named for Senators Hugh Butler and George Norris.

1877. Gilmore, G. H. Ghost towns in Cass County, Nebraska. *Nebraska history magazine* 18:181-84, July-Sept. 1937.

1878. Gilmore, Melvin Randolph. The aboriginal geography of the Nebraska country. Mississippi Valley Historical Association. Proceedings 6:317-31. 1912-13.
Aboriginal names of streams and places with an appended list of some place-names as applied by the Dakota, Omaha, and Pawnee, and identified by the English name for the same place.

1879. —— Some Indian place names in Nebraska. Nebraska State Historical Society. Publications 19:130-39. 1919.
Read before the Association of American Geographers, Chicago, Dec. 29, 1914.

1880. Green, Norma Kidd. Ghost counties of Nebraska. *Nebraska history* 43: 253-63, Dec. 1962.

1881. Hamilton, William. Indian names and their meaning. Nebraska State Historical Society. Transactions and reports 1:73-76. 1885.
Appended is a list of Indian names of streams and localities contributed by Henry Fontenelle.
Includes Sac names.

1882. Herman, Dick. That Devil's Nest name is as old as Nebraska. *Lincoln evening journal and Nebraska State journal* July 4, 1962.
Name of a real-estate development in Knox County; also other locations in the United States involving the word devil.

1883. How to say "Beatrice" depends on location. *Lincoln Sunday journal and star* June 2, 1963, p. 7 B.

1884. Jones, Alf D. Origin of the name Omaha, according to the Indian tradition. Nebraska State Historical Society. Transactions and reports 4:151-52. 1892.

1885. Link, John Thomas. The origin of the place names of Nebraska (The toponomy of Nebraska). Lincoln, Printed by authority of the State of Nebraska, 1933. 186p. (Nebraska. Geological Survey. Bulletin 7, 2d ser.)
Issued also as the author's thesis (Ph.D.) Univ. of Nebraska, 1932, under title: The toponomy of Nebraska. Selections also reprinted in Lilian Linder Fitzpatrick, Nebraska place names (see no. 1874).
Bibliography: p. 161-70.

1886. Lost towns of Nebraska. *Nebraska State journal*, Lincoln, March 27, 1910.

1887. Many defunct Richardson County towns tell tale of pioneer ambition. *Nebraska State journal*, Lincoln, June 30, 1935.

1888. Mattes, Merrill J. Chimney Rock on the Oregon Trail. *Nebraska history* 36:1-26, March 1955.
Reviews early travelers' descriptions and notes various names used.

1889. —— Hiram Scott, fur trader. *Nebraska history* 26:127-62, July-Sept. 1945.
A speculative biography of the man for whom Scotts Bluff was named.

1890. Meredith, Mamie. A Nebraska "Podunk." *American speech* 19:74-75, Feb. 1944.
The town of Brock, Neb., formerly known as Podunk.

1891. Miller, John C. Ghost towns in Otoe County. *Nebraska history magazine* 18:185-89, July-Sept. 1937.

1892. Nebraska cities and towns. *Omaha Sunday world-herald* May 30, 1954, Centennial section no. 7. 16p.
An alphabetical listing of Nebraska's incorporated places together with the origins of their names. To be used with caution.

1893. Nebraska in the making. *Elkhorn Valley mirror,* Norfolk, Neb., v. 1, no. 35, Oct. 14, 1926.

1894. "Nebraska place-names" tells when a crick becomes a stream. *Summer Nebraskan* (Univ. of Nebraska) July 11, 1961, p. 2.
Popular article based on Lilian Linder Fitzpatrick, Nebraska place names (see no. 1874).

1895. Nebraska town, county names add up to confused picture. *Lincoln (Neb.) star* Sept. 11, 1958, p. 10.
Duplication of names causes the confusion.

1896. Neu, Irene. The alphabet along the railroad. *California folklore quarterly* 5:200, April 1946.
On the Burlington between Lincoln and Kearney.

1897. New towns in a new state. *Nebraska State journal,* Lincoln, Feb. 21, 1909.

1898. The Old river towns. 3p.
Typescript in Nebraska Historical Society Library.

1899. Omaha's name. *Omaha world-herald* Nov. 22, 1925.

1900. Pangle, Mary Ellen. Place-names in Nebraska. *Journal of American history* 26:177-88. 1932.
Bibliography: p. 187-88.

1901. Phillips, Hazel Spencer. Invincible gambler; folklore. Lebanon, Ohio, Warren County Historical Society, n.d. [4]p. (Folklore series, no. 9)
"Information furnished by Mrs. Thomas Bamber, and Harry B. Allen, Cozad, Nebraska, whose research inspired Mari Sandoz' book Gamblin' Man's Son."
John Jackson Cozad, who established Cozaddale, Ohio, and Cozad, Neb.

1902. Place names. *Michigan history magazine* 10:643-46, Oct. 1926.
The significance of some of the unusual Nebraska names.

1903. Potts, Aartje. Omaha street nomenclature.
Thesis (M.A.) Univ. of Nebraska, 1931.

1904. Ramsey, Basil S. From what source did Cass County derive its name?
Plattsmouth journal March 6, 1913.

1905. Roberts, Martha G. Omaha's namesake: Omaja, Cuba. *Omaha world-herald* Nov. 27, 1955, Magazine, p. 24 G.
In 1906 a homesick railroad foreman from Omaha, Neb., began using the name Omaha in his daily reports. The name was kept for the first settlement in 1906 at Omaja (pronounced Omaha) by the family of Cornelio Plant, Mormons coming from England.

1906. Savage, James W. The christening of the Platte. Nebraska State Historical Society. Transactions and reports 3:67-73. 1892.

1907. Solitary ghosts. *Nebraska history magazine* 18:189-91, July-Sept. 1937.
Supplementary to the articles by G. H. Gilmore and J. C. Miller in the same issue.

1908. Story of DeSoto, one time river boom town. *Omaha world-herald* Oct. 4, 1925.

1909. Taylor, Norm. Nebraska can give Texas run for title of "Brag Capital."
Lincoln (Neb.) Sunday journal and star Sept. 11, 1960, p. 1B, 7B.
Boastful town titles, such as The Best Little City Out West, Home of Famous Men.

1910. Towns of the past are now cornfields. *Omaha world-herald* Feb. 27, 1910.

1911. True, M. B. C. County names. Nebraska State Historical Society. Transactions and reports 4:141-44. 1892.
Brief notes about the counties that were named for the presidents and other eminent men. Also suggests names that might be used in the future.

1912. Turpin, Ted. Surprising thing about Surprise is how early town got its name. *Lincoln (Neb.) evening journal* Dec. 14, 1961.

1913. U.S. Federal Writers' Project. Nebraska. Origin of Nebraska place names. Comp. by the Federal Writers' Project, Works Progress Administration, State of Nebraska; sponsored by the Nebraska State Historical Society. Lincoln, 1938. 28p.

1914. What's in a street name? Commissioners will decide. *Lincoln (Neb.) Sunday journal and star* Oct. 27, 1963.
Problem of whether to give a traffic artery traversing both the northern part of the city of Lincoln and the county a single street name, and, if so, which name of the at least seven names now in use.

NEVADA

1915. Ashbaugh, Don. Nevada's turbulent yesterday; a study in ghost towns. [Los Angeles], Westernlore Press, 1963. 346p. (Westernlore ghost town series, 1)

1916. Averett, Walter R. Directory of southern Nevada place names. Rev. ed. Las Vegas, 1962. 114p.
Also published in a facsimile edition by the Arthur H. Clark Company, Glendale, Calif.
1st ed. 1956. 40 l.
Bibliography: p. 111-14.
Includes towns, railroad sidings, topographic features, springs and waterholes, mines, and some ranches. Special attention to obscure or forgotten names.

1917. Brown, Thomas Pollok. Elko, Nevada. *Western folklore* 9:378-79, Oct. 1950.

1918. Carlson, Helen. Influence of nineteenth-century Nevada railroads on names along the line. *Western folklore* 15:113-21, April 1956.

1919. —— Mine names on the Nevada Comstock lode. *Western folklore* 15:49-57, Jan. 1956.

1920. —— Names of mines on the Comstock.
Thesis (M.A.) Univ. of Nevada, 1955.
Much of this thesis was published as a series of articles in the *Reno evening gazette* May 9-24, 1955.

1921. —— Nevada. *Western folklore* 14:44-49, Jan. 1955.
In the Names and places section. A survey of bibliographical aids.

1922. Chase, Carroll & Richard McP. Cabeen. The first hundred years of United States territorial postmarks, 1787-1887. Nevada Territory. *American philatelist* 56:586-94, June 1943.
Includes list of post offices, with notes on some names.

1923. Chatham, Ronald L. & Paul F. Griffin. How Nevada towns were named; Nevada history has left its mark on the nomenclature of the state. *Nevada highways and parks* v. 17, no. 2, p. 26-31. 1957.
From the research paper of the authors.

1924. Fox, Theron. Nevada treasure hunters ghost town guide. Includes 1881 fold-in map of Nevada with glossary of 800 place names, 1867 map of Nevada. Handy reference to locating old mining camps, ghost town sites, mountains, rivers, lakes, camel trails, abandoned roads, springs and water holes. San Jose, Calif., 1961. 24p.

1925. Frickstad, Walter Nettleton. A century of Nevada post offices, 1852-1957, by Walter N. Frickstad and Edward W. Thrall, with the collaboration of Ernest G. Meyers. Oakland, Calif., 1958. 40p.

1926. Gibby, Patricia Martin. Deeth and Disaster in Nevada. *Western folklore* 11:42, Jan. 1952.
Some place-names.

1927. Grieder, T. G. Beowawe: a Nevada place name. *Western folklore* 19:53-54, Jan. 1960.
In Paiute means "great posterior."
More on Beowawe, A Nevada place name, by K. W. Clarke, *ibid.* 20:112, April 1961.

1928. Hall, Eugene Raymond. Mammals of Nevada. Berkeley, Univ. of California Press, 1946. 710p.
Gazetteer: p. 650-69.

1929. Huggins, Dorothy H. Elko, Nevada. *Western folklore* 8:370, Oct. 1949.
cf. George Rippey Stewart article, *ibid.* 9:156, April 1950.

1930. Leigh, Rufus Wood. Nevada place names, their origin and significance. Sponsors: Southern Nevada Historical Society, Las Vegas; Lake Mead Natural History Association, Boulder City. [Salt Lake City?, 1964]. 149p.
Bibliography: p. 143-44.

1931. Linsdale, Jean M. The birds of Nevada. Berkeley, Cooper Ornithological Club, 1936. 145p. (Pacific coast avifauna no. 23)
List of localities: p. 14-22.

1932. McVaugh, Rogers & F. R. Fosberg. Index to the geographical names of Nevada. [Washington, D.C., 1941] 3 pts. (216 l.) (U.S. Bureau of Plant Industry. Division of Plant Exploration and Introduction. Contributions toward a flora of Nevada, no. 29. June 1, 1941)
Work Projects Administration of Nevada, Projects O. P. 65-2-04-13, W. P. 658; O. P. 165-2-04-21, W. P. 752. Collaborator, University of Nevada.

1933. Nevada. Constitutional Convention, 1864. Official report of the debates and proceedings. San Francisco, F. Eastman, printer, 1866. p. 33-35.
In convention the year before, the name Nevada was chosen for the state after consideration of Washoe, Esmeralda, and Humboldt. Move to change to Washoe in this session was defeated.

1934. Ohmert, Audrey Winifred. The significance of the nomenclature in Washoe County, Nevada. Nevada Historical Society. Biennial report 2:82-95. 1909-10.

1935. Palmer, Theodore Sherman. Place names of the Death Valley region in California and Nevada. Los Angeles, Dawson's Book Shop, 1948. 80p.
Result of National Park Service project.
Review: by Katherine Karpenstein, *Names* 1:62-63, March 1953.

1936. The Significance of the nomenclature in Churchill, Douglas, Lyon, Ormsby, and Storey counties. Nevada Historical Society. Biennial report 3:169-223. 1911-12.
Prepared by students in fulfillment of thesis requirements in the History Department of the State University.
Churchill County, by Vera Ellen Hasch; Douglas, Ormsby, and Storey counties, by Cora Mildred Cleator; Lyon County, by Florence Leslie Bray.

1937. Stewart, George Rippey. Buffalo Meadows, Nevada. *Western folklore* 7:174, April 1948.

1938. —— Elku, Nevada. *Western folklore* 9:156, April 1950.
In answer to Dorothy H. Huggins's article, *ibid.* 8:370, Oct. 1949.

1939. Taylor, Jock. Comstock mystery man. *Westways* 41:11, March 1949.
"On Ebenezer Fenimore (Old Virginia) alleged by Dan de Quille in the *Territorial enterprise*, July 20, 1881, to have named Virginia City."—Writings on American history.

1940. Territory of Nevada; *In* Bancroft, Hubert Howe. History of Nevada, Colorado and Wyoming. San Francisco, History Co., 1890. p. 150-51; also in U.S. Congress. House. Journal, 35th Congress, 1st session, 1857-58, p. 789; U.S. Congress. Congressional globe, 36th Congress, 2d session, 1860-61, p. 120, 897, 1334, 1362.
Delegate Crane wrote to his constituents from Washington in Feb. 1858 that a territorial government was about to be established under name of Sierra Nevada. On May 12, 1858 a bill was introduced to organize the Territory of Nevada. Bills were again introduced in 1860 and 1861, and passed March 2, 1861, organizing the new Territory of Nevada out of the western portion of Utah, then known as the Washoe Mines.

1941. U.S. Writers' Program. Nevada. Origin of place names: Nevada. Nevada State Dept. of Highways, sponsor, and State Dept. of Education, co-sponsor. Reno, 1941. 79p.

NEW ENGLAND

1942. Achorn, Erik. Geographical and place names taken from "A map of the most inhabited part of New England...Nov. 29, 1774." Essex Institute. Historical collections 89:275-87, July 1953.

1943. Baylies, Francis. The original of local and other names, a letter from Hon. Francis Baylies to Hon. P. W. Leland. Brooklyn, 1879. 24p. (Elzevir Club series, no. 1)
Most of the names are of Massachusetts.

1944. Berry, A. B. New England's lost city found. *Magazine of American history* 16:290-92, Sept. 1886.
"The discussion pertains to the origin of the word and the discovery of the location by Prof. Horsford. The city is Norumbega."—Price.

1945. Buchanan, Milton Alexander. Notes on Portuguese place-names in northeastern America; *In* Estudios hispánicos, homenaje a Archer M. Huntington. Wellesley, Mass., 1952. p. 99-104.
Principally Newfoundland; also Labrador, Nova Scotia, New England coast.

1946. Bushnell, David Ives. New England names. *American anthropologist* n.s. 13:235-38, April 1911.
"Contains a copy of a document giving the Indian names of rivers along the New England coast, and the names of the chiefs whose villages occupied their shores. The document is now in the British Museum and was probably written in the early part of the 17th century."—Griffin.

1947. De Costa, B. F. The lost city of New England. *Magazine of American history* 1:14-20, Jan. 1877.
The source and meaning of Norumbega, a name that has ceased to exist. Raises the question as to whether such a city as described did exist.

1948. Douglas-Lithgow, Robert Alexander. Dictionary of American-Indian place and proper names in New England; with many interpretations, etc. Salem, Salem Press, 1909. 400p.
List of Abnaki words (Maine and New Hampshire): p. 387-91.
List of Massachusetts, or Natick, Indian words: p. 393-96.
Bibliography: p. 397-400.

1949. Ganong, William Francis. The origin of the place-names Acadia and Norumbega. Royal Society of Canada. Proceedings and transactions 3d ser. v. 11, sec. 2, p. 105-11. 1917.
"Presents evidence drawn from early maps and records of explorations."— Griffin. See also Ganong's article, Norumbega, *ibid.* v. 25, sec. 2, p. 200-02. 1931, in which he concludes that it was the Indian name for the country between Narragansett Bay and New York, or, more specifically, was used by the Indians of Narragansett Bay for their country.

1950. Hayward, Edward F. The names of New England places. *New England magazine* n.s. 13:345-48, Nov. 1895.
A general article citing the origin of names in the New England states.

1951. Hayward, John. The New England gazetteer; containing descriptions of all the states, counties and towns in New England. Alphabetically arranged. 14th ed. Concord, N.H., I. S. Boyd and W. White; Boston, J. Hayward, 1841. 528p.
1st-9th ed. published 1839; a later ed. published Boston, Parker, Elliott & Co., 1856. 704p.

1952. Huden, John Charles. Indian place names of New England. New York, Museum of the American Indian, Heye Foundation, 1962. 408p. (Contributions from the Museum of the American Indian, Heye Foundation, v. 18)
Bibliography: p. 387-94.
Review: by Hamill Kenny, *Names* 12:234-38, Sept.-Dec. 1964.

1953. Masta, Henry Lorne. Abenaki Indian legends, grammar and place names. Victoriaville, P.Q., La Voix des Bois-Francs, 1932. 110p.
The meaning of Indian names of rivers, lakes, etc., p. 81-105.

1954. Matthews, Albert. The name "New England" as applied to Massachusetts. Colonial Society of Massachusetts. Publications 25:382-90. 1924.

1955. Mitchell, Edwin Valentine. It's an old New England custom. New York, Vanguard Press, 1946. 277p.
To adopt peculiar place names: p. 215-52.

1956. The New England gazetteer. 1902. Boston, Sampson, Murdock & Co., 1902. 1637-1828p.
The gazetteer portion of the New England business directory and gazetteer published separately.

1957. The New England gazetteer, comprising a concise description of the cities, towns, county seats, villages, and postoffices. Boston, Sampson, Davenport & Co., 1885. 182p.

1958. Prince, Thomas. The vade mecum for America: or A companion for traders and travellers: containing I. An exact and useful table, shewing the value of any quantity of any commodity. II. A table of simple and compound interest. III. The names of the towns and counties in the several provinces and colonies of New-England, New-York and the Jersies; as also the several counties in Pensilvania, Maryland and Virginia; together with the time of the setting of their courts. IV. The time of the general meeting of the Baptists and Quakers. V. A description of the principle roads from the mouth of Kennebeck-River in the north-east of New-England to James-River in Virginia. VI. A correct table of the kings and queens of England. Together with several other instructive tables in arithmetick, geography, &c. To which is added, the names of the streets in Boston. Collected & composed with great care & accuracy. Boston, Printed by S. Kneeland and T. Green for D. Henchman, and T. Hancock, 1732. 220p.
  Attributed to Thomas Prince. *cf.* Charles Evans, American bibliography, 3598.

1959. Rafn, Carl Christian. Derivation from the Icelandic of Indian names. Massachusetts Historical Society. Proceedings 8:194-97, Feb. 1865.
  "Cites some Indian names in the New England region and suggests that their origin may have been from words of the ancient Norsemen. Interprets the possible relation between the names in this country and those in the Scandinavian countries."—Price.

1960. Rounds, Stowell. A note on place names in New England. *Names* 6:124-25, June 1958.
  Use of Street in names of hamlets or settlements.

1961. Russell, Francis. Place names in New England. *Nineteenth century and after* 140:284-88, Nov. 1946.

1962. Savage, James. A list of the ancient Indian names of our modern towns, &c.; *In* Winthrop, John. The history of New England from 1630 to 1649. Boston, Phelps and Farnham, 1825-26. 2:392-95.

1963. Sleeper, Myron O. Indian place names in New England. Massachusetts Archaeological Society. Bulletin 10:89-93, July 1949.

1964. Stone, Stuart B. New England names. *Journal of education* (Boston) 81:19, 48, Jan. 7, 14, 1915.
  Brief notes concerning the source of some New England place-names.

1965. Tooker, William Wallace. The significance of John Eliot's Natick and the name Merrimac; with historical and ethnological notes. New York, F. P. Harper, 1901. 56p. (The Algonquian series, no. 10)
  First essay "Read before the American Association for the Advancement of Science, Section H, 1897, and reprinted in the *American anthropologist* 10:281-87, Sept. 1897. Now reprinted with additions."—p. 5.
  Second essay appeared originally in the *American antiquarian* 21:14-16. 1899.

1966. True, Nathaniel Tuckerman. Collation of geographical names in the Algonkin language. Essex Institute. Historical collections 8:144-49, Sept. 1868.
  Also published separately. 6p.

1967. Tuttle, Charles W. Communication on geographical names. Massachusetts Historical Society. Proceedings 16:377-79, Nov. 1878.
Explains the significance of Piscataqua River.

1968. ——— The Piscataqua River. *Magazine of New England history* 1:207, Oct. 1891.
Views on the derivation and meaning of the Indian name.

1969. Verrill, Alpheus Hyatt. Indian names and their meanings; *In his* The heart of old New England. New York, Dodd, 1936. p. 284-91.

1970. Walker, Joseph B. The valley of the Merrimack. New Hampshire Historical Society. Collections 7:414-15. 1863.
Indicates different ways of spelling the name Merrimack and the origin of Monomack as applied to the valley.

1971. Webb's New England railway and manufacturers' statistical gazetteer; containing an interesting sketch of every station, village and city on each railroad in New England, together with a statistical, historical and biographical account of their representative manufacturing establishments. Providence, Providence Press Co., 1869. 568p.

NEW HAMPSHIRE

1972. Alden, Timothy. Indian names of White Hills and Piscataqua River. Massachusetts Historical Society. Collections 2d ser. 2:266-67. 1814.

1973. Ballard, Edward. Indian mode of applying names. New Hampshire Historical Society. Collections 8:446-52. 1866.
With particular reference to New Hampshire. Includes a list of Indian names connected with the valley of the Merrimack, and their meanings.

1974. Brennan, James F. What was the origin of the name of our town? American Catholic Historical Society. Records 26:25-35, March 1915.
Also published separately. 7p.
Peterborough, N.H.

1975. Burt, Frank H. The nomenclature of the White Mountains. *Appalachia* 13:359-90, Dec. 1915; 14:261-68, June 1918.
Bibliography 13:389-90.

1976. Charlton, Edwin Azro. New Hampshire as it is. Claremont, N.H., Tracy and Sanford, 1855. 592p.
3d ed. rev. with an appendix containing additions and corrections for the gazetteer. Claremont, Kenney, 1857. 594, 4p.
Part II, A gazetteer.

1977. Colby, Fred Myron. The nomenclature of some New Hampshire towns. *Magazine of history* 11:145-49, March 1910.

1978. Day, Gordon M. The name Contoocook. *International journal of American*

linguistics 27:168-71, April 1961.
Analysis of this name borne by a lake, a river, and a village in southern New Hampshire.

1979. Edmands, J. Rayner. Topographical contributions. *Appalachia* 5:121-28, June 1888.
Further comments on the system of nomenclature submitted by the Committee on Nomenclature in the article, Nomenclature of the White Mountains (see no. 1995).

1980. Farmer, John. A catechism of the history of New-Hampshire, from its first settlement to the present period; for the use of schools and families. 2d ed. Concord, Hoag and Atwood, 1830. 108p.
The Appendix contains: "A list of the most considerable towns in New-Hampshire; their former name, the time they were settled."

1981. —— & Jacob B. Moore. A gazetteer of the State of New-Hampshire. Embellished with an accurate map of the state, and several other engravings, by Abel Bowen. Concord, J. B. Moore, 1823. 276p.

1982. Fay, Charles E. Our geographical nomenclature. *Appalachia* 3:1-13, June 1882.
Presidential address—general remarks on nomenclature in New Hampshire.

1983. Fogg, Alonzo J. The statistics and gazetteer of New-Hampshire. Containing descriptions of all the counties, towns and villages, statistical tables, with a list of state officers, etc. Concord, D. L. Guernsey, 1874. 674p.

1984. Green, Samuel Abbott. Observations on the names of certain villages in Massachusetts and New Hampshire. Massachusetts Historical Society. Proceedings 2d ser. 10:465-67, Feb. 1896.
Also published separately, Boston, 1896. 3p.
Use of Harbor away from the coastline. Includes Mason Harbor and Dunstable Harbor.

1985. —— Some Indian names. Massachusetts Historical Society. Proceedings 2d ser. 4:373-74, May 1889.
Also published separately, 1889. 3p.
South Eggenocke, Southheaganock, and Souhegan; also Pennichuck.

1986. Hammond, Otis G. New Hampshire county names. *Magazine of history* 9:48-50, Jan. 1909.

1987. Hayward, John. A gazetteer of New Hampshire, containing descriptions of all the counties, towns, and districts in the state; also of its principal mountains, rivers, waterfalls, harbors, islands, and fashionable resorts. To which are added, statistical accounts of its agriculture, commerce and manufactures. Boston, J. P. Jewett, 1849. 264p.

1988. Hunt, Elmer Munson & Robert A. Smith. The English background of some of the Wentworth town grants. *Historical New Hampshire* Nov. 1950, p. 1-52.
The English source of many New Hampshire town names.

1989.   Kearsarge. *Historical magazine* 9:28-29, Jan. 1865.
The various forms of the name with derivation and meaning.

1990.   Martin, Lawrence.   Who named Mount Washington? *Geographical review* 28:303-05, April 1938.
"Points out that although the name was given to Mount Washington, in New Hampshire, some time prior to 1792, the date and occasion of the naming have not been established."—Griffin.

1991.   Mason, Ellen McRoberts.   The North Conway Mount Kearsarge. *Granite monthly* 47:72-74, Feb.-March 1915.
Concerning proposed change of name to Pequawket.

1992.   Merrill, Eliphalet & Phinehas Merrill.   Gazetteer of the State of New-Hampshire.   Comp. from the best authorities.   Exeter, Printed by C. Norris & Co. for the authors, 1817.   218p.

1993.   New Hampshire. Secretary of State.   Manual for the General Court. no. 1-1889- .
Each year includes a record of grants.   A list gives original names, many of which are now obsolete, and present names.   Includes corporate history of the towns, with origin and changes of name.

1994.   New Hampshire. State Planning and Development Commission.   Communities, settlements, and neighborhood centers in the State of New Hampshire.   An inventory prepared by the State Planning and Development Commission, Concord, New Hampshire.   Concord, 1937.   55p.

1995.   Nomenclature of the White Mountains. *Appalachia* 1:7-11, June 1876.
Report of the Committee on Nomenclature of the Appalachian Mountain Club, suggesting a system that might be applied.

1996.   The Origin of some New Hampshire mountain names. *Historical New Hampshire* 11:1-28, April 1955.

1997.   Smith, Robinson V.   New Hampshire Indians have gone but their names at least remain. *Historical New Hampshire* 8:32-36, Oct. 1952.

1998.   U.S. Board on Geographic Names.   Mount Kearsarge and Mount Pequawket, New Hampshire: historical notes relating to the conflicting names of Mount Kearsarge and Mount Pequawket, New Hampshire, submitted to the United States Geographic Board at the suggestion of Senator J. H. Gallinger, together with the decision of the Board in regard thereto.   Comp. by David M. Hildreth, topographer, Post Office Department, member, United States Geographic Board.   Washington, Govt. Print. Off., 1916.   14p. (64th Cong., 1st sess. Senate doc. no. 307)
The U.S. Geographic Board decided that Kearsarge was the proper name of the mountain located in Merrimack County and Pequawket of the one in Carroll County.

NEW JERSEY

1999. Amboy, Kill van Kull, Arthur Kill. *Magazine of American history* 1:197-98, March 1877.
A reply to an inquiry, p. 129, for the meaning of these names.

2000. Becker, Donald William. Indian place-names in New Jersey. Cedar Grove, N.J., Phillips-Campbell Pub. Co., 1964. 111p.
Bibliography: p. 101-03.

2001. Berlin, N.J. is opposed to changing its name. *New York times* Oct. 11, 1944, p. 23, col. 4.

2002. Bisbee, Henry Harold. Place names in Burlington County, New Jersey. Riverside, N.J., Burlington County Pub. Co., 1955. 115p.
Review: *Pennsylvania magazine of history and biography* 80:270-71, April 1956.

2003. Borough of Ho-Ho-Kus insists on hyphens; tells Farley it knows how to spell name. *New York times* Dec. 28, 1939, p. 23, col. 4-5.

2004. Boyer, Charles Shimer. The origin and meaning of place names in Camden County. Camden, 1935. 16p. (Camden County Historical Society. Camden history, v. 1, no. 8)
Reprinted from *West Jersey press* of May 23, 30, and June 6, 13, 1935.

2005. De Costa, B. F. Cabo de arenas; or, The place of Sandy Hook in the old cartology. *New England historical and genealogical register* 39:147-60, April 1885.
A study of various names used on old maps for the geographical feature now called Sandy Hook. Includes a table giving the names appearing on many old maps for Sandy Hook, Connecticut River, Narragansett Bay, Cape Cod, and Cape Breton.

2006. Dulles name to live. New Jersey boulevard will be a memorial. *Kansas City times* May 28, 1959.
The Dumont Borough Council voted to change the name of Sunnyside Blvd. to Dulles Blvd. in honor of John Foster Dulles.

2007. Dunlap, Arthur Ray. Barnegat. *American speech* 13:232-33, Oct. 1938.

2008. Early names of Dover. New Jersey Historical Society. Proceedings n.s. 5:128. 1920.

2009. Eno, Joel Nelson. New Jersey county names. *Magazine of history* 25:111-13, Sept.-Oct. 1917.

2010. GI village named "Distomo." *New York times* June 10, 1946, p. 3, col. 4; June 24, p. 33, col. 5.
Community for veterans opposite the airport in Atlantic City.

2011. Gannett, Henry. A geographic dictionary of New Jersey. Washington, Govt. Print. Off., 1894. 131p. (U.S. Geological Survey. Bulletin no. 118)
Issued also as House miscellaneous doc. v. 9, 53d Cong., 3d sess.

2012. Gordon, Thomas Francis. A gazetteer of the State of New Jersey.

Comprehending a general view of its physical and moral condition, together with a topographical and statistical account of its counties, towns, villages, canals, rail roads &c., accompanied by a map. Trenton, D. Fenton, 1834. 266p.

2013. ——— Indian names, with their signification; *In* Barber, John W. & Henry Howe. Historical collections of the State of New Jersey. New York, Tuttle, 1844. p. 512.

2014. Hampton, George. Places and place names of Cumberland County. *Vineland historical magazine* 9:156-63, Jan. 1924.

2015. Heckewelder, John Gottlieb Ernestus. Names given by the Lenni Lenape or Delaware Indians to rivers, streams and places in the now states of New Jersey, Pennsylvania, Maryland, and Virginia. Pennsylvania German Folklore Society. Publications 5:1-41. 1940.
　　Published also in American Philosophical Society. Transactions 4:351-96. 1834; Historical Society of Pennsylvania. Bulletin 1:121-35, 139-54 June, Sept. 1847; Moravian Historical Society. Transactions 1872:275-333; as a separate: Bethlehem [Pa.], H. T. Claude, printer, 1872. 58p.; and in his A narrative of the mission of the United Brethren among the Delaware and Mohegan Indians. Cleveland, Burrows Bros., 1907. p. 523-66.

2016. Hoboken. *Magazine of American history* 4:312, 468, April, June 1880.
　　Discussion of the possible derivation of the name.

2017. Levittown name change set. *New York times* Dec. 25, 1963, p. 53.
　　To Willingboro, effective Feb. 1, 1964.

2018. Mrs. Brisbane bars use of name for new street. *New York times* Nov. 17, 1938, p. 19, col. 3.
　　Asks Point Pleasant officials not to name new street for her husband, Arthur Brisbane.

2019. Nelson, William. Indian words, personal names, and place-names in New Jersey. Washington, 1902. 183-92p. (Anthropologic miscellanea)
　　Reprinted from *American anthropologist* n.s. 4:183-92, Jan.-March 1902.
　　An "alphabetical list of Indian personal and place-names in New Jersey taken from New Jersey records relating to land transfers prior to 1703. In the original records, 'New Jersey archives, v. 21,' quite a number of the Indian place-names are followed by English interpretations." This list gives the original names and locations of the places. Delaware Indians.

2020. ——— The Indians of New Jersey: their origin and development; manners and customs; language, religion and government. With notices of some Indian place names. Paterson, Press Print. and Pub. Co., 1894. 168p.
　　Delaware Indians.

2021. New Jersey. State Highway Dept. Bureau of Planning and Traffic. Highway Planning Survey Section. An alphabetical listing of local places and incorporated municipalities in the State of New Jersey, showing their incorporated titles and the county in which each is located. In cooperation with the U.S. Department of Commerce, Bureau of Public Roads. [Trenton, New Jersey State Highway Commission, Bureau of Public Information, 1962]. 53p.

2022. Northern Jersey names vary from sublime to ridiculous, noble community titles blush beside Hogwallow, Teetertown and Cat Swamp. *New York times* Dec. 4, 1927, sec. 11, p. 6, col. 6-8.

2023. Pennington, Mary V. Tracing Teaneck. *New York times* Oct. 10, 1935, p. 24, col. 6.
  On derivation of Bogota and Teaneck.

2024. Philhower, Charles A. The origin and meaning of the name Amboy and the word Lenape. Archaeological Society of New Jersey. Bulletin 10:9-10, May 1955.

2025. Salter, Edwin. Origin and signification of geographical names in the counties of Monmouth and Ocean and their vicinity. New Jersey Historical Society. Proceedings 2d ser. 4:18-26. 1875-77.

2026. Schmidt, Hubert G. Some Hunterdon place names, historical sketches about communities and localities in Hunterdon County, New Jersey. Flemington, D. H. Moreau, 1959. 32p.

2027. Sheppard, Cora June. How it got that name; places in Cumberland County. *Vineland historical magazine* 23:52-56, April 1938.
  "Brief notes on the origin of place names."—Griffin.

2028. Stewart, George Rippey. Professor Stewart comments on "Hoere(n)kil." *American speech* 19:215-16, Oct. 1944.
  In correction of the article by A. R. Dunlap, An early place name puzzle: "Hoere(n)-Kil," *ibid.*, 19:112-14, April 1944, the origin of the word is given, and its location in New Jersey rather than in Delaware.

2029. Union may again be "Connecticut Farms." *New York times* July 15, 1946, p. 25, col. 1.

2030. U.S. Army Signal Training Command and Fort Monmouth. Fort Monmouth history and place names, 1917-1961. Fort Monmouth, N.J., [1961?]. 89p.

2031. U.S. Writers' Program. New Jersey. The origin of New Jersey place names. Comp. by workers of the Writers' Program of the Work Projects Administration in the State of New Jersey. Sponsored by New Jersey State Library Commission. n.p., 1939. 41p.
  Indian place names bibliography: 3d prelim. leaf.
  Reissued: New Jersey Public Library Commission, 1945. 33p.

2032. Vermeule, Cornelius C. Some early New Jersey place-names. New Jersey Historical Society. Proceedings n.s. 10:241-56, July 1925; 11:151-60, April 1926.

2033. Weslager, C. A. Robert Evelyn's Indian tribes and place-names of New Albion. Archeological Society of New Jersey. Bulletin 9:1-14, Nov. 1954.
  Nine proper nouns mentioned in a letter by the explorer Robert Evelyn discussed and compared with contemporary accounts and maps.

2034. Will honor late publisher. *New York times* Nov. 25, 1945, p. 24, col. 5.

Five-point intersection to be named Press Plaza in honor of J. Lyle Kinmouth, late publisher of the Asbury Park Press.

2035. Wolfe, Theodore F. More local aboriginal names; some information of great interest regarding the origin and meaning of the names of familiar localities. *Iron era,* Dover, N.J. June 17, 1892.

2036. ―――― Origin of the name Succasunna. New Jersey Historical Society. Proceedings n.s. 9:334-40, Oct. 1924.
    Originally published in the *Iron era,* Dover, N.J. Feb. 27, 1891, with additions in the *Dover index* March 19, 1909.

2037. ―――― Some local aboriginal names; another valuable contribution to Indian nomenclature. *Iron era,* Dover, N.J. Nov. 6, 1891.

NEW MEXICO

2038. Barker, Elliott Speer. What's in a name?; *In his* Beatty's Cabin: adventures in the Pecos high country. Albuquerque, Univ. of New Mexico Press, 1953. p. 151-62.

2039. Barker, S. Omar. Place names―pleasant and puzzling. *New Mexico magazine* 34:30, 46, 48, Aug. 1956.
    Comments on this article in the Mail bag, *ibid.* 34:5, 56, Oct. 1956.

2040. ―――― Road map riddles. *New Mexico magazine* 40:20-21, 38, May 1962.
    Meaning and pronunciation of New Mexico place-names.

2041. Brothers, Mary Hudson. Place names of the San Juan basin. *Western folklore* 10:165-67, April 1951.

2042. Brown, Frances Rosser. How they were named. *New Mexico magazine* 13:27, 41-42, Aug. 1935; 13:28, 37-38, Sept. 1935; 13:28, 39-41, Oct. 1935.

2043. ―――― The Spanish had a name for them. *New Mexico magazine* 20:14, 29-30, Oct. 1942.
    Mountains.

2044. Bryan, Howard. Off the beaten path. *Albuquerque tribune* Sept. 5, 1957, p. 22.
    Origin of Albuquerque and other New Mexican names, some of Moorish or Arabic origin resulting from Moors on Coronado's expedition, according to Rev. Fr. Julius J. Hartmann.

2045. ―――― Some colorful place names in New Mexico. *Western folklore* 15: 285-86, Oct. 1956.
    Reprinted from *Albuquerque tribune* June 4, 1956.

2046. Burnham, Lucy S. New Mexico place-names: Fruitland, The Meadows, Burning Hill. *Western folklore* 10:74-75, Jan. 1951.

2047. Carlson, Helen. Truth or Consequences, New Mexico. *Western folklore* 16:125-28, April 1957.
New name of Hot Springs, derived from radio program.
The voters decided on Jan. 13, 1964, by a vote of 891 to 752, to keep the new name.—*New York times* Jan. 15, 1964, p. 17.

2048. Cassidy, Ina Sizer. New Mexico place name studies. *Western folklore* 14:121-23, April 1955.

2049. ———— New Mexico place names—Taos. *El Palacio* 61:296-99, Sept. 1954.

2050. ———— The story of Sapello, or "Seat Joe." *Western folklore* 12:286-89, Oct. 1953.
Origin of Sapello, N.M.

2051. ———— Taos, New Mexico. *Western folklore* 8:60-62, Jan. 1949.

2052. Chant, Elsie Ruth. The naming of Tucumcari. *New Mexico folklore record* 3:36-37. 1948-49.

2053. Chávez, Angelico, *Fray.* The Albuquerque story. *New Mexico magazine* 34:18-19, 50-51, Jan. 1956.

2054. ———— Albuquerque, what does it mean? *New Mexico magazine* 34:12, 48, July 1956.

2055. ———— Aztec or Nahuatl words in New Mexico place-names. *El Palacio* 57:109-12, April 1950.

2056. ———— Don Fernando de Taos. *Western folklore* 8:160, April 1949.

2057. ———— Neo-Mexicanisms in New Mexico place names. *El Palacio* 57:67-79, March 1950.

2058. ———— New Mexico place-names from Spanish proper names. *El Palacio* 56:367-82, Dec. 1949.
Spanish colonial families whose names became attached to the land.

2059. ———— New Mexico religious place-names other than those of saints. *El Palacio* 57:23-26, Jan. 1950.

2060. ———— Saints' names in New Mexico geography. *El Palacio* 56:323-35, Nov. 1949.

2061. Dike, Sheldon H. The territorial post offices of New Mexico. *New Mexico historical review* 33:322-27, Oct. 1958; 34:55-69, 145-52, 203-26, 308-09, Jan.-Oct. 1959.

2062. Forrest, Earle Robert. Missions and pueblos of the old Southwest. Cleveland, Arthur H. Clark Co., 1929. 2v.
Spanish mission names in Arizona and New Mexico, with their English equivalents, 1:333-35.

2063. 44,000 postmasters will hear about Truth or Consequences. *Albuquerque*

tribune April 3, 1950, p. 6.
   New name for Hot Springs.

2064. Gatschet, Albert Samuel. The navel in local names. *American anthropologist* 6:53-54, Jan. 1893.
   Includes ruin Hálona, one of the Seven Cities of Cibola, on south bank of Zuni River.

2065. Hale, Edward Everett, Jr. French place-names in New Mexico. *French review* 3:110-13, Nov. 1929.
   Also reprinted separately. 6p.

2066. Hardeman, Nicholas P. Camp sites on the Santa Fe trail in 1848 as reported by John A. Bingham. Ed. by Nicholas P. Hardeman. *Arizona and the West* 6:313-19, Winter 1964.

2067. Harrington, John Peabody. The ethnogeography of the Tewa Indians. U.S. Bureau of American Ethnology. Annual report 29:29-636. 1907-08.
   Bibliography: p. 585-87.
   Includes the derivation and meaning of geographical terms and place-names in the Tewa language.

2068. —— Haa´k'o, original form of the Keresan name of Acoma. *El Palacio* 56:141-44, May 1949.

2069. —— Name of Zuñi Salt Lake in Alarcon's 1540 account. *El Palacio* 56: 102-05, April 1949.

2070. —— Old Indian geographical names around Santa Fe, New Mexico. *American anthropologist* n.s. 22:341-59, Oct.-Dec. 1920.
   Also reprinted as a separate.

2071. —— Olivella River. *El Palacio* 56:220-22, July 1949.
   On the name 'O`gha´p'oo`ghe`, meaning Olivella River, applied in the Tewa language to the part of Santa Fe Creek on which Santa Fe stands.

2072. Heck, Lewis. [Letter requesting information as to form of name of a mountain, Chicoma Peak or Tschicoma Peak]. *New Mexico magazine* 36:5, Jan. 1958.

2073. Hewett, Edgar L. Origin of the name Navaho. *American anthropologist* n.s. 8:193, Jan.-March 1906.
   The tribal designation is derived from the Tewa Indian pueblo of Navahú, meaning "the place of great planted fields."

2074. Hill, Robert T. Descriptive topographic terms of Spanish America. *National geographic magazine* 7:291-302, Sept. 1896.
   Prepared for reports to Director of U.S. Geological Survey on geography of Texas-New Mexico region.
   Topographical features as protuberances or mountain forms, plains, declivities, streams, and stream valleys.

2075. Hodge, F. W. Early Spanish bungling of Indian names. *Western folklore* 9:153-54, April 1950.

2076. —— The name "Navahò." *Masterkey* (Southwest Museum, Los Angeles) 23:78, May 1949.
A Tewa pueblo near Santa Clara.

2077. —— Pueblo names in the Oñate documents. *New Mexico historical review* 10:36-47, Jan. 1935.

2078. Jones, William M. Origin of the place-name Taos. *Anthropological linguistics* v. 2, no. 3, p. 2-4. 1960.

2079. Land of Enchantment investigated. *The New Mexican,* Santa Fe, Oct. 10, 1954.
Background of the nickname The Land of Enchantment used on auto license plates.

2080. McHarney, Caryl. What's in a name? Nowhere in the Southwest are place titles more expressive than in New Mexico where three cultures met and mingled. *Denver post* Dec. 4, 1955, Empire magazine, p. 31.

2081. Martinez, Velma. Names under the sun. *New Mexico magazine* 36:24, 46-47, April 1958.

2082. Mirkowich, Nicholas. A note on Navajo place names. *American anthropologist* n.s. 43:313-14, April-June 1941.
Lists Navajo names still in use for a few places in Arizona and New Mexico.

2083. Mitchell, L. B. The meaning of the name Albuquerque. *Western folklore* 8:255-56, July 1949.

2084. New Mexico Folklore Society. Place-name Committee. New Mexico place-name dictionary. 1st-3rd collection. 1949-51. Albuquerque, 1949-51. 3pts.
Each annual collection lists from 138 to 334 names.

2085. —— Report for 1950-51. *New Mexico folklore record* 7:25-26. 1952-53.
Signed by Ina Sizer Cassidy, chairman.

2086. Pearce, Thomas M. "Albuquerque" reconsidered. *Western folklore* 16: 195-97, July 1957.

2087. —— Loving and Lovington: two New Mexico towns. *Western folklore* 8:159-60, April 1949.

2088. —— The lure of names. *New Mexico quarterly* 32:161-77, Autumn-Winter 1962-63.
Includes geographical names in New Mexico, p. 167-72.

2089. —— New Mexico place-name dictionary. *Western folklore* 8:257-59, July 1949.
Discussion of the first collection.

2090. —— The New Mexico place-name dictionary: a polyglot in six languages. *Names* 6:217-25, Dec. 1958.

2091. —— Religious place names in New Mexico. *Names* 9:1-7, March 1961.

2092. ——— Second collection, New Mexico place-name dictionary. *Western folklore* 9:372-78, Oct. 1950.

2093. ——— Some Indian place names of New Mexico. *Western folklore* 10:245-47, July 1951.
From the New Mexico place-name dictionary, third collection.

2094. Rainwater, John R. [Letter regarding spelling of San Augustine Plains]. *New Mexico magazine* 36:5, Aug. 1958.

2095. Reeve, Frank D. Early Navaho geography. *New Mexico historical review* 31:290-309, Oct. 1956.
Fixing the location of certain geographic terms (Cebolleta, Navaho, and Piedra Alumbre or Lumbre) is partly a matter of defining words.

2096. Schilling, Frank A. Military posts of the old frontier: Arizona, New Mexico. Historical Society of Southern California. Quarterly 42:133-49, June 1960.
Includes origin and changes of names.

2097. Simons, Katherine. Street names of Albuquerque. *American speech* 17: 209-10, Oct. 1942.

2098. Sleight, Frederick W. A problem of clarification in ethnographic nomenclature. *El Palacio* 56:295-300, Oct. 1949.
Names of peaks in the Jemez Range.

2099. Standley, Paul Carpenter. The type localities of plants first described from New Mexico. A bibliography of New Mexican botany. Washington, Govt. Print. Off., 1910. 143-246p. (Smithsonian Institution. United States National Museum. Contributions from the United States National Herbarium, v. 13, pt. 6)
Descriptive list of type localities: p. 151-74.

2100. Thatcher, Harold F. & Mary Hudson Brothers. Fabulous La Plata River. *Western folklore* 10:167-69, April 1951.

2101. Trager, George L. The name of Taos, New Mexico. *Anthropological linguistics* v. 2, no. 3, p. 5-6. 1960.

2102. Van Valkenburgh, Richard F. & Frank O. Walker. Old placenames in the Navaho country. *Masterkey* (Southwest Museum, Los Angeles) 19:89-94, May 1945.
Contains a list giving the popular, Spanish, and Navaho names, location, etc.

2103. Where is Reyes Linares? Folklore Society needs 100 more place names to complete listing. *The New Mexican,* Santa Fe, Jan. 4, 1959, p. 5.
Plea for information needed to complete the Dictionary of New Mexico place names.

2104. White, Marjorie Butler. What's in a name? *New Mexico magazine* 38:10-11, 40-42, July 1960.

2105. White, Rose P. New Mexico place names: Roosevelt County. *Western folklore* 9:63-65, Jan. 1950.
Dead Negro Draw and Nigger Hill.

2106 —— The town of Portales, New Mexico. *Western folklore* 8:150-59,
April 1949.

2107. Who knows the name of New Mexico park? *Kansas City star* Feb. 14, 1960,
sec. F, p. 6.
Pancho Villa State Park suggested for new state park established at Columbus,
N.M., to commemorate the 1916 raid by the army of Pancho Villa.

2108. Whole town "Jumping up and down" over proposal. *Hot Springs herald*
March 30, 1950, p. 1.
Proposed change of Hot Springs to Truth or Consequences.

2109. Williamsburg plans vote May 23 on Hot Springs name. *Hot Springs herald*
April 6, 1950, p. 1.
To use name for a city addition changed by original city to Truth or Consequences.

2110. Woods, Dora Elizabeth Ahern. Ghost towns and how to get to them, by
Betty Woods. Maps by M. T. Williams. Scene: New Mexico. Time: the present.
Santa Fe, N.M., Press of the Territorian, 1964. 36p. (Western Americana series,
no. 4)
Includes, in addition, Lucien A. File's copyrighted list of ghost towns, p. 34-36.

2111. Wooton, Elmer Ottis & Paul Carpenter Standley. Flora of New Mexico.
Washington, Govt. Print. Off., 1915. 794p. (Smithsonian Institution. United States
National Museum. Contributions from the United States National Herbarium, v. 19)
Geographic index: p. 755-71.

2112. Young, Robert W. & William Morgan. Navajo place names in Gallup, New
Mexico. *El Palacio* 54:283-85, Dec. 1947.

NEW YORK

2113. Adirondack town looks for a name; iron mining community born of war.
New York times Sept. 13, 1942, p. 21, col. 1.
Suggested Dalliba for Major James Dalliba, founder of iron industry at Morish.
Correct spelling of his name given *ibid*. Sept. 15, 1942, p. 21, col. 3.

2114. Ames, C. H. Poke-o-Moonshine. *Forest and stream* 56:503, June 29, 1901.
Reply to Spears, *ibid*. p. 484.

2115. Armbruster, Eugene L. Gazetteer of Long Island. n.d. 7v.
Manuscript in the possession of the late Long Island historian's family, 263
Eldert St., Brooklyn, N.Y. It includes a very detailed listing of bays, rivers,
towns, and other geographical names with information on the origin of these names.

2116. Asher, Georg Michael. A bibliographical and historical essay on the Dutch
books and pamphlets relating to New-Netherland and to the Dutch West-India Company and to its possessions in Brazil, Angola, etc. as also on the maps, charts,
etc. of New-Netherland . . . Comp. from the Dutch public and private libraries and
from the collection of Frederik Muller in Amsterdam. Amsterdam, N. Israel,
1960. 234, 22, 23p.

1st ed. 1854-67. 2v.
List of names on the maps: 23p. at end.

2117. Ashokan. *Olde Ulster* 4:327, Nov. 1908.

2118. Barker, Elmer Eugene. Origin of name Bouquet River. *Reveille* 1:1, 4, April 1957.

2119. ——— That name—Marcy. *Cloud splitter* 11:10, Nov.-Dec. 1948.

2120. Beacon, N.Y. High School. Sophomore English Class. History and legends of Beacon and vicinity. 1921.
The name Poughkeepsie, p. 22-23.

2121. Beauchamp, William Martin. Aboriginal place names of New York. Albany, New York State Education Dept., 1907. 333p. (New York State Museum. Bulletin 108. Archeology 12)
List of authorities: p. 271-78.

2122. ——— Indian names in New-York, with a selection from other states, and some Onondaga names of plants, etc. Fayetteville, N.Y., Printed by H. C. Beauchamp, 1893. 148p.

2123. Beecher, Willis J. Geographical names as monuments of history. Oneida Historical Society. Transactions 5:9-23. 1889-92. (Publications no. 17)
Those of the ancient country of the Iroquois, with comparison of the country just east of the Iroquois.

2124. Benson, Egbert. Dutch names of places; Dutch names of streets. *Halve maen* (Holland Society of New York) 19:6, July 1944; 19:3, Nov. 1944.
Excerpts from articles written by Egbert Benson (1743-1833) on the nomenclature of the Dutch in Niew Amsterdam, contributed by Hevlyn Dirck Benson, a descendant.

2125. ——— Memoir, read before the Historical Society of the State of New York, December 31, 1816. 2d ed. with notes. Jamaica, H. C. Sleight, 1825. 127p.
1st ed. New-York, W. A. Mercein, 1817. 72p.
Also reprinted from a copy, with the author's last corrections, in New York Historical Society. Collections 2d ser. 2:77-148. 1848. Also published separately, New York, Bartlett & Welford, 1848. 72p.
On the names of places in New York State.

2126. Berger, Meyer. About New York. *New York times* Dec. 18, 1939, p. 20, col. 3-4.
Early names for New York streets.

2127. Birss, John Howard. "Mannahatta." *American speech* 9:154-55, April 1934.
Notes on the appearance of the word.

2128. Blumengarten, Jeannette G. Flatbush place-names. January 1960. 84p.
Thesis (M.A.) Brooklyn College, 1960. On file in the College Library, the Brooklyn Public Library, and the Long Island Historical Society Library.

2129. Board of Geographic Names. New York. State Museum. Museum bulletin

173:13 58, Nov. 1, 1914.

Notice of the creation of the Board, with citation from the law. Includes a glossary, prepared by the Board, of place-names of Albany, Rensselaer, and Schenectady counties.

2130. Boewe, Charles. Mt. Rafinesque. *Names* 10:58-60, March 1962.
Origin of name of this hill near Troy, N.Y.

2131. Bolton, Reginald Pelham. Aboriginal place-names of the county of Westchester. New York, 1942. 67p.

2132. —— Indian paths in the great metropolis. New York, Museum of the American Indian, Heye Foundation, 1922. 280p. (Indian notes and monographs. Miscellaneous, no. 23)
Index of stations on the maps: p. 220-41.
An enlargement of the list in author's New York City in Indian possession. New York, Museum of the American Indian, Heye Foundation, 1920. (Indian notes and monographs, v. 2, no. 7) p. 302-18.

2133. Brinley, C. Coapes. The origin of street names of old West Brighton. *Staten Island historian* 20:1-4, Jan.-March 1959.

2134. Carson, Russell Mack Little. Peaks and people of the Adirondacks. Garden City, N.Y., Doubleday, Page, 1927. 269p.
History of the names of the peaks.

2135. Change of name of Bedloe's Island, N.Y., to Liberty Island. U.S. Congress. Congressional record v. 102, pt. 9, p. 11539, July 2, 1956.
S. J. Res. 114 passed by the Senate.

2136. Changing the name of Bedloe's Island in New York Harbor to Liberty Island. U.S. Congress. Congressional record v. 102, pt. 10, p. 14029-30, July 23, 1956.
Remarks in the House on S. J. Res. 114. Passed.

2137. City draws borders for 87 neighborhoods. Districts mapped as a step to meeting particular needs. *New York times* July 16, 1962, p. 25.
Designation of neighborhoods in New York City for planning purposes, and consideration of historic names for these communities, such as The Village, Bushwick, Tottenville, etc.

2138. Clark, Joshua Victor Hopkins. Onondaga; or, Reminiscences of earlier and later times. Syracuse, Stoddard, 1849. 2v.
Ancient aboriginal names of lakes, streams, and localities in Onondaga County and vicinity, with their meanings, 1:322-26.

2139. Cocks, George William. Old Matinecock. *Nassau County historical journal* 22:1-11, Fall 1961.

2140. Coles, Robert R. Long Island's Indian names. *Long Island forum* 20:145-46, Aug. 1957.
Indian names for Long Island.

2141. —— Some Matinecock place-names. *Long Island forum* 17:207, 218, Nov. 1954.

2142. Colorful rites at lake naming. *Knickerbocker press,* Albany, Aug. 11, 1936.
The naming of Durant Lake.

2143. Constitution Island; origin of its name—neighboring landmarks. American
Scenic and Historic Preservation Society. Annual report 29:123-25. 1924.

2144. Cooper, Susan Fenimore. The Hudson River and its early names. *Maga-
zine of American history* 4:401-18, June 1880.
Traces the historical origin and meaning of the names applied to the Hudson
River by different explorers and settlers.

2145. Cotterell, Harry. Oddly named towns. *New York times* Dec. 18, 1927,
sec. 3, p. 5, col. 6.

2146. Council would honor MacArthur by renaming East River Drive. *New York
times* April 11, 1942, p. 15, col. 3.
New York City.

2147. Crane, Frank W. History written in street names. *New York times* Feb.
22, 1942, sec. 10, p. 1, col. 5, p. 2, col. 5.

2148. Crocker, Elizabeth L. Yesterdays in and around Pomfret, N.Y. Fredonia,
N.Y., 1960-63. v. 1-4.
Early names of places: 4:1-2.

2149. Davis, William Thompson. Staten Island names; ye olde names and nicknames. With map by Charles W. Leng. New Brighton, Natural Science Assoc.,
1896. 76p. (Proceedings of the Natural Science Association of Staten Island,
v. 5, no. 5, Special no. 21, March 14, 1896)

2150. —— Supplement to Staten Island names; ye olde names and nicknames.
New Brighton, Natural Science Assoc., 1903. 91p. (Proceedings of the Natural
Science Association of Staten Island, v. 8, no. 25, Special no. 23)

2151. De Camp, L. Sprague. Pronunciation of upstate New York place-names.
American speech 19:250-65, Dec. 1944.
Includes 13 pages of names with phonetic spelling for each name.

2152. DeKay, James Ellsworth. Indian names of Long Island. Oyster Bay, 1851.
12p.

2153. Derivation of Indian names. *Historical magazine* 2:149, May 1858.
The origin and meaning of Wading River, Quogue, and Peacock Neck on Long
Island.

2154. Devine, Thomas. "Sixth Avenue" preferred. *New York times* Oct. 8, 1962,
p. 22.
A letter to the editor comments on the difficulty in accepting the new name
Avenue of the Americas in New York City.

2155. Disturnell, John. A gazetteer of the State of New York: comprising its
topography, geology, mineralogical resources, civil divisions, canals, railroads
and public institutions; together with general statistics; the whole alphabetically
arranged. Also, statistical tables, including the census of 1840; and tables of

distances. With a new township map of the state. 2d ed. Albany, C. van Benthuy-sen, 1843. 479p.
1st ed. Albany, 1842.

2156. Douglas, Edward Morehouse. Gazetteer of the lakes, ponds, and reservoirs of the State of New York. Washington, Map Information Office, Board of Surveys and Maps, 1928. 45p.
1st ed. 1926. 44p.

2157. ———— Gazetteer of the mountains of the State of New York. Washington, Map Information Office, Board of Surveys and Maps, 1930. 36p.
1st ed. 1927. 36p.

2158. Douglas, Verne. New York City incorrect. *New York times* Feb. 22, 1945, p. 26, col. 7.
Letter pointing out that correct name of the post office is New York, N.Y.

2159. Drake, Leora Wilson. Kanestio; Canisteo, Steuben County; place names in New York State. *Yesteryears* no. 5:58, Oct. 1958.

2160. Dunshee, Kenneth Holcomb. As you pass by. New York, Hastings House, 1952. 270p.
A directory of forgotten streets [in New York City]: p. [272-78].

2161. Dutch proper names in Ulster. *Olde Ulster* 3:239-42, Aug. 1907.

2162. Eardeley, James W. A system of street nomenclature for Greater New York. 1932. 170p.
Manuscript in New York Public Library. Local History Division.

2163. Early names of city's streets were descriptively conferred. *New York times* Nov. 11, 1928, sec. 10, p. 22, col. 7.
Such streets in New York City as Pie Woman's Lane.

2164. Eno, Joel Nelson. New York county names. *Magazine of history* 22:76-82, 127-30, 166-69, March-May 1916; 23:11-15, 126-28, July, Sept. 1916.

2165. ———— A tercentenary history of the towns and cities of New York; their origin, dates, and names, 1614-1914. New York State Historical Association. Proceedings 15:225-64. 1916.

2166. Field, Thomas Warren. Indian, Dutch and English names of localities in Brooklyn. Brooklyn. Common Council. Manual 1868:459-70.
Reprinted in his Historic and antiquarian scenes in Brooklyn and its vicinity. Brooklyn, 1868. p. 49-60, with note calling attention to errors in orthography and signification.

2167. Fillmore, Millard. Inaugural address. Buffalo Historical Society. Publications 1:1-15. 1879.
On the name Buffalo.

2168. First to name square for Truman. *New York times* Oct. 22, 1945, p. 19, col. 6.
Town Lake, N.Y.

2169. Flick, Alexander Clarence. New York place names. New York, Columbia Univ. Press, 1937. 291-332p.
Reprinted from New York State Historical Association. History of the State of New York. v. 10.
Bibliography: p. 330-32.
Classified as Indian, French, Dutch, British, German, Revolutionary, classical, New England, institutional, and nature.

2170. The Founding of the Nieuw Dorp, or Hurley. *Olde Ulster* 1:257-64, Sept. 1905.

2171. French, John Homer. Gazetteer of the State of New York; embracing a comprehensive view of the geography, geology, and general history of the state, and a complete history and description of every county, city, town, village and locality with full tables of statistics. 10th ed. Syracuse, R. P. Smith, 1861. 739p.
Eds. 6-8 published 1860.

2172. Frigand, Sidney J. New York street names. City said to hold its own with Paris in nomenclature. *New York times* Feb. 19, 1962, p. 30.
This letter to the editor, in reply to the Topics column of Feb. 6 (In Paris a street keeps its name), lists unusual names.

2173. Gatschet, Albert Samuel. Origin of the name Chautauqua. *Glen Echo Chautauqua* 1:12, Aug. 1891.

2174. Gay, Alva A. "Madison Avenue." *American speech* 34:232, Oct. 1959.
"A name not only for the large advertising and public relations companies with offices on Madison Avenue, New York, but also, more generally, for all national advertising," p. 232.

2175. Geographic Board rules Liberty Island is Bedloe's. *New York times* Jan. 3, 1940, p. 19, col. 2; editorial Jan. 4, 1940, p. 22, col. 4.

2176. Giles, Dorothy. Polopel Island: Hudson River place-name. *New York folklore quarterly* 11:125-28, Summer 1955.
Suggests explanation of the Dutch name of the island in the Hudson River east of Storm King.

2177. Gilette, Frieda A. Caneadea: Indian place names in New York State. *Yesteryears* no. 3:20-21, Feb. 1958.

2178. Gordon, Thomas Francis. Gazetteer of the State of New York: comprehending its colonial history; general geography, geology, and internal improvements; its political state; a minute description of its several counties, towns, and villages. With a map of the state, and a map of each county, and plans of the cities and principal villages. Philadelphia, Printed for the Author, 1836. 801p.

2179. Graham, Hugh P. Cohoes: place names in New York State. *Yesteryears* no. 4:19, July 1958.

2180. ——— Podunk: place names in New York State. *Yesteryears* no. 6:14, Feb. 1959.

2181. Greenwich intersection named "Village Square." *New York times* Nov. 4,

1939, p. 15, col. 2.
Changed from Jefferson Market Square, New York City.

2182. Haas, Dorothy M. Place names of northern New York. *North country life* 9:42-44, Fall 1955.

2183. Haber, Richard. Gravesend place-names. May 1964. xliii, 239p.
Thesis (M.A.) Brooklyn College, 1964. On file in the College Library, the Brooklyn Public Library, and the Long Island Historical Society Library.

2184. Hadaway, William S. Identification of "Dobbs Ferry." Westchester County Historical Society. Quarterly bulletin 9:16-19, Jan. 1933.

2185. Hale, Edward Everett, Jr. Dialectical evidence in the place-names of eastern New York. *American speech* 5:154-67, Dec. 1929.
Dutch and English words with definitions of such terms as borough, brook, brush, etc. used for parts of place-names.
Errors in Dutch corrected by A. E. H. Swaen, *ibid.* 5:400, June 1930.

2186. Hanford, Franklin. On the origin of the names of places in Monroe County, New York. Scottsville, I. Van Hooser, printer, 1911. 54p. (Publications of the Scottsville Literary Society, no. 5)
Reprinted in Rochester Historical Society. Publication fund series 5:49-77. 1926.

2187. Harris, George Henry. Aboriginal occupation of the lower Genesee country. Rochester, 1884. 96p.
Chapter 5, p. 32-36, Indian place-names of the Genesee area.

2188. ——— Notes on the aboriginal terminology of the Genesee River. Rochester Historical Society. Publications 1:9-18. 1892.

2189. Hauptman, Herbert C. Adirondack place names. *High spots* 9:16-17, Jan. 1932.

2190. ——— By their names. *High spots, the yearbook of the Adirondack Mountain Club* 1939:72-76.
Names in the Adirondacks.

2191. Hawley, L. F. The Chadakoin River. *Names* 3:32-33, March 1955.
Naming the outlet of Chautauqua Lake.

2192. Henry, Mellinger Edward. Old Hudson River town names. *Journal of American folklore* 56:290, Oct.-Dec. 1943.

2193. Historical notice of Kingston and Rondout. *Olde Ulster* 8:353-61, Dec. 1912.
Origin and meaning of Rondout appear in footnote on p. 356. In *ibid.* 9:8-10, Jan. 1913, in continuation of above article, are given former names of Rondout: The Strand, Kingston Landing, and Bolton.

2194. Hoffman, Henry B. Changed house numbers and lost street names in New York of the early nineteenth century and later. New York Historical Society. Quarterly bulletin 21:67-92, July 1937.

2195. Hough, Franklin Benjamin. Gazetteer of the State of New York, embracing a comprehensive account of the history and statistics of the state. With geological and topographical descriptions, and recent statistical tables. Albany, A. Boyd, 1872. 745p.

2196. How famous downtown streets in New York got their names. *Brooklyn eagle* April 15, 1917.

2197. How Old Forge (N.Y.) was named. *Forest and stream* 72:892, June 5, 1909. Short note on the forge used by John Brown (1734-1803).

2198. How the counties got their names. New York (State) Secretary of State. Manual for the use of the Legislature of the State of New York. 1932- . A list appearing in each issue from 1932 on.

2199. Hudson's River. *Magazine of American history* 8:513-14, July 1882. Explains the origin of various names for the Hudson River.

2200. Hull, Raymond. Names on the land in St. Lawrence County. *North country life* 6:32-35, Winter 1952.

2201. In Paris a street keeps its name. *New York times* Feb. 6, 1962, p. 34, col. 3. In the Topics column, the street-naming customs of Paris are contrasted with those of New York City. For reply, see Sidney J. Frigand, New York street names, *ibid.* Feb. 19, 1962, p. 30.

2202. Indian name for Elmira. *Chemung historical journal* 2:199-200, Sept. 1956.

2203. Indians, animals and history. *New York times* Feb. 27, 1961, p. 26L, col. 3. In the Topics column. Theories concerning the origin of the name Coney Island.

2204. Ingraham, Joseph C. To Connecticut; New England Thruway to open direct route from Bronx to Rhode Island. *New York times* Oct. 5, 1958, sec. 2, p. 23, col. 1-4. Includes list of historic names decided on by the New York Legislature for the Thruway and its extensions, such as The Iroquois Trail, The Mohican Path, etc.

2205. An Inquiry into the who's, whens, whys and hows of naming streets in this great city. *New York times* April 25, 1937, sec. 4, p. 9, col. 1. Describes the work of the Aldermanic Committee on Public Thoroughfares, which is the street-naming body for New York City.

2206. Irving and "Gotham." *New York times* Dec. 4, 1962, p. 40. The Topics column, devoted to the nickname Gotham for New York City, first used by Washington Irving in Salmagundi. New York, D. Longworth, 1807-08.

2207. It was once "Bronck's Land." *Americana* 6:1021-22, Oct. 1911. Origin of the name Bronx.

2208. It's Elk Street now, not Elm. *New York times* Feb. 17, 1939, p. 14, col. 5. Elm St. changed to Elk, New York City.

2209. It's still Sixth Avenue to many, but not to its newest tenants. *New York times* Sept. 23, 1962, p. 18 R.

New prestige business concerns on the avenue are using the new name Avenue of the Americas.

2210. Jones, Nathan W. The Esopus Indians and their language. *Olde Ulster* 1:70-75, March 1905.

Place-names given by the Minsi Indians, a tribe of the Delaware Confederacy.

2211. Kalkoen Hoek. *Olde Ulster* 2:338, Nov. 1906.

The name applied to Turkey Point by the Dutch.

2212. Ketchum, William. The origin of the name of Buffalo. Read before the Buffalo Historical Society, April 7, 1863. Buffalo Historical Society. Publications 1:17-42. 1879.

Includes letters on the name of Buffalo from Asher Wright and Nathaniel T. Strong.

2213. Leete, Charles Henry. A study in geographic names. 12p.

Reprint from *Herald-recorder*, Potsdam, N.Y., March 1927.

2214. Leighten, George R. On fitting a name to a street. *New York times magazine* Oct. 21, 1945, p. 16, 53-54.

Reviews attempts to change street names in New York City.

2215. Letters on names for numbered avenues, New York City. *New York times* Dec. 1, 1937, p. 22, col. 6; Dec. 4, p. 16, col. 7; Dec. 7, p. 24, col. 7; Dec. 9, p. 24, col. 7.

2216. Liberman, Elaine A. Williamsburgh place-names. January 1965. 69p.

Thesis (M.A.) Brooklyn College, 1965. On file in the College Library, the Brooklyn Public Library, and the Long Island Historical Society Library.

2217. Liberty Isle idea irks Mr. Curran. *New York times* Aug. 8, 1941, p. 17, col. 4; editorial Aug. 9, p. 14, col. 2; letter Aug. 14, p. 16, col. 7; bill offered, Aug. 15, p. 19, col. 2.

Congress proposes to change name of Ellis Island to Liberty Isle.

2218. Local names from the Dutch. *Olde Ulster* 4:90-92, March 1908.

2219. Lost town of Gates found by woman. *Albany evening news* Feb. 3, 1936.

Gates Township in Saratoga County.

2220. Lounsbury, Floyd G. Iroquois place-names in the Champlain Valley; *In* Interstate Commission on the Lake Champlain basin. Report. Albany, 1960. p. 21-66. (New York State. Legislative document [1960], no. 9)

Based on historical and linguistic research.

2221. Ludwig, John Warner. Alphabet of greatness: Manhattan's street names. New York, 1961. 264 l.

Typescript. Copy in New York Public Library.

2222. —— Street names of Manhattan and the stories they tell. New York,

1953. 170 l.
Typescript. Copy in New York Public Library.

2223. Maar, Charles. Origin of the classical place-names of central New York.
New York State Historical Association. Quarterly journal 7:155-68, July 1926.
"The author places the responsibility for the assignment of the classical names
of the different regions in New York on Simeon De Witt, a surveyor for the state."
—Price.
  cf. note: E. E. Hale, Classical names in New York State. *American speech* 3:
256, Feb. 1928.

2224. McKaig, Thomas H. Place names of western New York. *Niagara frontier*
1:61-68, Autumn 1954.

2225. McKnight, Nellie. Incongruous names; information on the naming of New
York towns is sought. *New York times* Feb. 15, 1928, p. 22, col. 6.
  On name Athens, N.Y., and others.
  Author's second letter appeared *ibid.* March 4, 1928, sec. 3, p. 5, col. 6, men-
tioning Robert Harper, early secretary of the State Land Board, who had hand in
assigning classical names.

2226. Manuel Gonzales, the Spaniard. *Olde Ulster* 6:172-76, June 1910.
  Origin of Sam's Point; Shawangunk Mountains; and The Spanish Mine, near
Ellenville, p. 175.

2227. Marlowe, Nicholas. Bedford-Stuyvesant place-names. January 1963. 69p.
  Thesis (M.A.) Brooklyn College, 1963. On file in the College Library, the
Brooklyn Public Library, and the Long Island Historical Society Library.

2228. Maxwell, Mary Ellis. Camillus: place names in New York State. *Yesteryears* no. 5:1-4, Oct. 1958.

2229. Metropolitan area loses one of its Central Parks. *New York times* Oct. 3,
1936, p. 2, col. 5.
  Central Park, Long Island, changed to Bethpage.

2230. Miller, C. Henriette. Aboriginal place names in Columbia County. n.p.,
19?. 5p.
  "This chapter from my book is intended for those who have not read Ruttenber,
O'Callaghan, or Beauchamp, but who would be well informed."

2231. Miller, Philip Schuyler. By guess and by gosh. *Ad-i-ron-dac* 10:6-7,
March-April 1946.
  The problem of tracing the real story of Adirondack place-names.

2232. —— Those poetic red men. *Cloud splitter* 5:4-5, March 1942.
  There were older, authentic Indian names for Adirondack landmarks, but current Indian names were given by the guides.

2233. —— Why the Bouquet? *Ad-i-ron-dac* 11:4-5, Jan.-Feb. 1947.
  Source of name of Bouquet River.

2234. Milliken, Charles F. Ontario County place names. New York. State Museum. Museum bulletin 253:103-10, July 1924.

An alphabetical list of names which contains brief notes on the meaning of the name and the location of the place.

2235. Mills, Borden H. Charles Fenno Hoffman's Indian place names. *Ad-i-ron-dac* 12:4-7, July-Aug. 1948.

"Quotes passage from Hoffman's Vigil of faith (1845) reproduced in Kachesco, a legend of the sources of the Hudson (1873) and comments on 26 place names included therein."—Writings on American history.

2236. —— Who was John? *Cloud splitter* 11:4-6, Jan.-Feb. 1948.
Reprinted in *Ad-i-ron-dac* 15:97-98, 100, Sept.-Oct. 1951.
Johns Brook was probably named for John Gibbs.

2237. Minsky, Pearl G. Canarsie place-names. January 1963. 116p.
Thesis (M.A.) Brooklyn College, 1963. On file in the College Library, the Brooklyn Public Library, and the Long Island Historical Society Library.

2238. Minton, Arthur. Names of real-estate developments. *Names* 7:129-53, 233-55, Sept.-Dec. 1959; 9:8-36, March 1961.
Most development names cited are from Long Island.

2239. Morgan, Lewis Henry. League of the Ho-dé-no-sau-nee, or Iroquois. New ed. with additional matter. Ed. and annotated by Herbert M. Lloyd. New York, Dodd, 1904. 2v. in 1.
Also published 1901 in 2v. in an edition of 30 copies only.
1st ed. Rochester, 1851. 477p.
Schedule explanatory of the Indian map, giving the corresponding English and Indian names of places, with their meaning: 2:127-39.
Later printings of this title are as follows:

2240. —— League of the Ho-de-no sau-nee, or Iroquois. New Haven, Re-printed by Human Relations Area Files, 1954. 2v. (Behavior science reprints)

2241. —— League of the Iroquois. Introd. by William N. Fenton. New York, Corinth Books, 1962. 477p. (The American experience series. AE 12)

2242. Morris, Robert T. Niagara. *Saturday review of literature* 8:776, 820, June 4, July 2, 1932.
In brief form the author interprets Niagara Falls as meaning "The-waterfall-that-causes-women-to-exclaim 'Gosh!'"

2243. Mountain lake honors Durant. *Albany evening news* Aug. 11, 1936.

2244. The Name of Katskill, or Kaaterskill. *Olde Ulster* 9:309-14, Oct. 1913.

2245. The Name of Kingston and its predecessors. *Olde Ulster* 1:266-68, Sept. 1905.

2246. Name of 6th Ave. to be changed to the Avenue of the Americas. *New York times* Sept. 21, 1945, p. 23, col. 3; Sept. 25, p. 24, col. 7; Sept. 29, p. 17, col. 7; Sept. 30, sec. 8, p. 1, col. 5; Oct. 3, p. 21, col. 1; Oct. 4, p. 22, col. 3; Oct. 22, p. 16, col. 2.
New York City.

2247. Name sources of townships of Monroe County. *Monroe republican,* Rochester, May 1, 1930.

2248. Names of places on Long Island, and their derivations. *Historical magazine* 9:31, Jan. 1865.
Gives the place-names of Jamaica, Hoppogues, and Comac with derivations and meanings.

2249. Naming of streets for veterans scored. *New York times* July 27, 1938, p. 15, col. 4.
Mayor of New York refuses to sign bills calling for changes.

2250. New York Historical Society. Report of the aboriginal names and geographical terminology of the State of New York. Part I.—Valley of the Hudson. Made to the New York Historical Society, by the committee appointed to prepare a map, etc., and read at the stated meeting of the Society, February, 1844. By Henry R. Schoolcraft, chairman. New York, The Society, 1845. 43p.
Published from the Society's Proceedings 1844:77-115. Additional note in the Proceedings p. 119-20.
The report is based on a historical summary of the Indian tribes, including comments on the sources of their place-names, a map showing the location of the tribes after their dispersal, and terminology of the ancient site of Albany.
Comment on the work of the committee appears under title Indian names in *American penny magazine* 1:322, June 28, 1845.

2251. New York (State) Division of Archives and History. Geographic names; *In* New York (State) University. Annual report of the Education Department v. 40, pt. 1, p. 282. 1942-43.
Brief list of names of Adirondack peaks with origin.

2252. New York State Board of Geographic Names. American Geographical Society. Bulletin 46:365. 1914.
A report of the law, chap. 187, 1913, creating the Board. The personnel of the new board is listed in Bulletin 47:47. 1915.

2253. Noyes, Marion F., ed. A history of Schoharie County. Richmondville, N.Y., Richmondville Phoenix, 1954. 130p.
Schoharie County place-names: p. 106-14.

2254. O'Brien, Michael J. The story of old Leary Street, or Cortland Street— the Leary family in early New York history. American Irish Historical Society. Journal 15:112-17, April 1916.
Various names by which Cortland St. has been known, with some history of the family for whom it was at one time named.

2255. Obsolete names of New York. *American historian and quarterly genealogical record* 1:30-36, 66-73, 113-17, 154-60, July 1875-April 1876.
The four issues of the magazine, all that were published, carried the alphabetical series through "Guy Johnson's patent."

2256. Obsolete towns and villages. New York civil list, 1855-88.
Each issue carries a list of towns and villages with changed names.

2257. O'Callaghan, Edmund Bailey. Indian names of places on the Hudson River.

Historical magazine 3:218, July 1859.
"Designates the location of the places and is an extract from the Book of patents, New York."—Price.

2258. Old city streets recalled by deal. *New York times* March 14, 1937, sec. 14, p. 1, col. 1, p. 4, col. 3; letters March 20, p. 18, col. 7; March 30, p. 22, col. 7.
Lower East Side in New York.

2259. Old names for old streets. *New York times* March 17, 1930, p. 22, col. 6.
Editorial on New York City.

2260. On re-naming street and schools. *American city* 60:116, Dec. 1945.
Comments, including an amusing editorial from the *New York times,* on the proposed change of New York's Sixth Ave. to Avenue of the Americas.

2261. Origin of names of New York State counties. New York (State) University. Bulletin to the schools 10:122-23, 158, 170-71, 202, 252, Jan. 15-May 15, 1924.
Comp. by the Committee on Geographic Names, which assumed the duties of the former State Board of Geographic Names.

2262. Origin of place names on the Hudson River. n.d. 7p.
Typewritten manuscript in New York State Library, Albany.

2263. Paltsits, Victor Hugo. The classic nomenclature of western New York. *Magazine of history* 13:246-49, May 1911.
"Simeon De Witt who surveyed the western section of the state has been blamed for bestowing classical place-names on localities. This exonerates him from the heinous deed, and places the responsibility on a committee of four men."—Price.

2264. Parker, Arthur Caswell. Indian episodes of New York State; a drama-story of the Empire State. A booklet of added information about the pictorial map by this name. Rochester, Rochester Museum of Arts and Sciences, 1935. 35p.
Notable Indian names: p. 32-33.

2265. —— Origin and pronunciation of the place name Mahopack. *Mahopack weekly* March 13, 1929.

2266. Pastore, John O. Change in name of Bedloe's Island in New York Harbor to Liberty Island. U.S. Congress. Congressional record v. 102, pt. 1, p. 229-30, Jan. 9, 1956.
Remarks on introduction in the Senate of S. J. Res. 114.

2267. Plaza to be named for Cadman. *New York times* May 10, 1939, p. 25, col. 1.
Brooklyn Bridge Plaza to be changed to S. Parkes Cadman Plaza.

2268. Pollard, Ray F. A jaunt amongst Schoharie County place names and nick-names. *Schoharie County historical review* 14:25-28, Oct. 1950.

2269. —— Names and nicknames in Schoharie County. *Schoharie County historical review* 23:21-22, Spring 1959.
Names and nicknames of communities, roads, hills, turns, creeks, and points.

2270. Post, John J. Old streets, roads, lanes, piers and wharves of New York, showing the former and present names, together with a list of alterations of streets, either by extending, widening, narrowing or closing. In three parts: 1st. Former name and present name or location. 2d. Present name and former name. 3d. Street alterations. New York, R. D. Cooke, 1882. 76p.

2271. Prince, John Dyneley. Some forgotten Indian place-names in the Adirondacks. *Journal of American folklore* 13:123-28, April-June 1900.
Reprinted in his Fragments from Babel. New York, Columbia Univ. Press, 1939. p. 165-71.
Derivation, pronunciation, and meaning of names from the Abenaki dialect.

2272. Pritchard, Georgiana. On the Erie Canal. *New York folklore quarterly* 10:45-47, Spring 1954.
On the origin of certain nicknames and place-names.

2273. Rashkin, Henry. Bay Ridge place names. August 1960. 47p.
Thesis (M.A.) Brooklyn College, 1960. On file in the College Library, the Brooklyn Public Library, and the Long Island Historical Society Library.

2274. Reinstein, Julia Boyer. Cheektowaga: place names in New York State. *Yesteryears* no. 4:38-39, July 1958.

2275. Reynolds, Helen Wilkinson. In regard to the repetition of place names. Dutchess County Historical Society. Year book 18:54-57. 1933.

2276. —— Kromme Elleboog; a seventeenth century place-name in the Hudson Valley. Dutchess County Historical Society. Year book 18:58-68. 1933.

2277. —— Place-names again; something about Staatsburgh-Stoutsburgh-Stoutenburgh and Hyde Park. Dutchess County Historical Society. Year book 19:24-31. 1934.

2278. —— Poughkeepsie; the origin and meaning of the word. Poughkeepsie, 1924. 93p. (Dutchess County Historical Society. Collections v. 1)
Review: *American speech* 1:46-48, Oct. 1925.

2279. Rhodes, Jerome. The form of street addresses. *American speech* 33:116-17, May 1958.
Omission of Street in Manhattan but not in other boroughs of New York.
cf. articles by Allan F. Hubbell, *ibid.* 32:233-34, Oct. 1957, and G. Thomas Fairclough, *ibid.* 33:299-300, Dec. 1958.

2280. Ricard, Herbert F. The origin of community names in Queens Borough; *In* New York (City) Borough of Queens. Historian. Annual report 1:5-15. 1944.

2281. Rubel, Tamara K. Place names in Brooklyn Heights. May 1963. 73p.
Thesis (M.A.) Brooklyn College, 1963. On file in the College Library, the Brooklyn Public Library, and the Long Island Historical Society Library.

2282. Ruttenber, Edward Manning. Atkarkarton-Atharhacton. *Olde Ulster* 3:270-74, Sept. 1907.

2283. —— Footprints of the red men. Indian geographical names in the valley of Hudson's River, the valley of the Mohawk, and on the Delaware: their location and the probable meaning of some of them. Pub. under the auspices of

the New York State Historical Association. Newburgh, Newburgh Journal Print, 1906. 241p.
With New York State Historical Association. Proceedings v. 6. 1906.

2284. Schmauch, W. W. Thoroughfares of the world—the highways and byways of New York. *Economy spectator* 2:1, 3, March 10, 1931; 2:1, 4, April 10, 1931.
The changes in names in old New York.

2285. Schoolcraft, Henry Rowe. Aboriginal nomenclature. *Knickerbocker, or New York monthly magazine* 58:109-14, Aug. 1861.
Origin of Indian names such as Neversink, Sing Sing, Poughkeepsie, etc.

2286. —— Indian names of the islands and bay of New York; *In* Denton, Daniel. A brief description of New York. New ed. New York, William Gowans, 1845. p. 23-27.

2287. —— —— *Broadway journal* 1:138-39, March 1845.

2288. Schuyler, Elizabeth. Reasons for calling New York the Empire State. New York State Historical Association. Proceedings 15:280-88. 1916.

2289. Scott, Charles. Shawangunk, its meaning and origin. *Olde Ulster* 1:19-20, Jan. 1905.

2290. Scott, Charles R. What's in a name, "Bowling Green." *Telephone review* 7:315-18, Nov. 1916.
History of the area from which a new telephone-exchange name was adopted.

2291. Scott, John A. Odd town names; explanation of classical designations in New York State. *New York times* Feb. 19, 1928, sec. 3, p. 5, col. 3.

2292. Scribner, Lynette Langer. North country place names. *Ad-i-ron-dac* 19:32-33, March-April 1955.

2293. —— Some Lake Champlain place names. *Ad-i-ron-dac* 19:50, May-June 1955.

2294. Sea-Cove Beach renamed. *New York times* Feb. 26, 1956, p. 65, col. 1.
The town of Oyster Bay renamed Sea-Cove Beach, in Sea Cliff and Glenwood Landing, the Harry Tappen Beach, to honor Mr. Tappen, who served as town supervisor for twenty years.

2295. Shaw, Ann. What's in a name? *New York folklore quarterly* 14:305-08. 1958.
Significance of some place-names in Westchester County.

2296. Shulman, David. Coney Island's name. *New York times* Sept. 26, 1938, p. 16, col. 6-7.

2297. Simms, Jeptha R. Indian names. *Historical magazine* 3d ser. 1:120-21, Feb. 1872.
The origin and meaning of several aboriginal place-names in the region of the Mohawk Valley.

2298. Skilton, Frank Avery. Military township of Milton original name of the territory known at present as Ghoa. *Advertiser-journal*, Auburn, Aug. 21, 1925.

2299. Smith, Agnes Scott. The Dutch had a word for it. *New York folklore quarterly* 2:165-73, Aug. 1946.
Includes some Dutch place-names.

2300. Smith, Dorothy Guy. Strange names of school districts. *New York folklore quarterly* 1:152-59, Aug. 1945.
More schoolhouses, *ibid.* 2:64-65, Feb. 1946.
cf. also J. C. Storms's article, no. 2309.

2301. Smith, James L. Erin: place names in New York State. *Yesteryears* no. 5:12, Oct. 1958.

2302. Smith, Thelma E. The islands of New York City. New York Public Library. Municipal Reference Library. Notes 36:97-102, 122-23, June, Sept. 1962.

2303. Sources of Wyoming County place names. *Historical Wyoming* 1:21-22, Nov. 1947.

2304. Spafford, Horatio Gates. A gazetteer of the State of New-York: embracing an ample survey and description of its counties, towns, cities, villages, canals, mountains, lakes, rivers, creeks, and natural topography, with an appendix. Albany, B. D. Packard; Troy, The Author, 1824. 620p.
1st ed. Albany, 1813. 334p.

2305. Spears, Raymond Smiley. Adirondack place names. *Forest and stream* 56:403, May 25, 1901.

2306. —— Poke-o-Moonshine. *Forest and stream* 56:484, June 22, 1901.
Possible derivations of the name.
cf. C. H. Ames's article, *ibid.* 56:503, June 29, 1901.

2307. Square honors Col. Conroy. *New York times* Feb. 11, 1945, p. 6, col. 1.
Law signed designating as Col. J. Gardiner Conroy Square the intersection of Flatbush, St. Mark's, and Sixth aves. in Brooklyn.

2308. Stevens, Ruth Perry. Owego Township, Tioga County: place names in New York State. *Yesteryears* no. 4:23-26, July 1958.

2309. Storms, J. C. Why "Doodletown"? *New York folklore quarterly* 3:58-59, Spring 1947.
On a school district name.
cf. Dorothy Guy Smith's article, no. 2300.

2310. Straus, Nathan. Memorials—to whom? *Art news* 60:25, April 1961.
Editorial. Most of the text of an address over Station WMCA, New York, citing examples of the system of naming highways and other public improvements in New York City for people, and suggesting creation of a Commission on Memorials charged with the responsibility of selecting the individuals to be honored.

2311. Streets named for American artists in growing Munsey Park district. *New York times* Aug. 29, 1937, sec. 12, p. 1, col. 2-3.

2312. [Streets named for literary figures in New York City]. New York Public Library. Municipal Reference Library. Notes 36:12-14, Jan. 1962.
In the Knickerbocker scrapbook column.

2313. Strong, Kate Wheeler. Some strange old place-names. *Long Island forum* 15:109, 116, June 1952.

2314. Sugrue, Francis. Joy in Babylon: U.S. approves Sampawams as name of creek. Board on Geographic Names yields to campaign of letter writing; two weekly papers cite Huntington 1694 charter as authority. *New York herald tribune* Oct. 28, 1948.
Formerly popularly known as East Creek.

2315. Swaen, A. E. H. Dutch place-names in eastern New York. *American speech* 5:400, June 1930.
Corrects errors in article by Edward Everett Hale, Jr., *ibid.* 5:154-67, Dec. 1929.

2316. Tallman, Wilfred B. Place names. *South of the mountains* (Tappan Zee Historical Society) v. 4, no. 1, Jan.-March 1960.
Covers Hudson River localities.

2317. Tappan, New York. *Magazine of American history* 8:51, Jan. 1882.
"In the light of more reliable information disclosed in 'Documents relating to the colonial history of New York,' v. 13, this article disputes the interpretation of the origin of the name."—Price.

2318. Thompson, Benjamin Franklin. The Indian names of Long Island. New York Historical Society. Proceedings 1845:125-31.

2319. Thompson, H. H. Adirondack nomenclature. *Field and stream* 10:286-87, July 1905.
A plea for better names for the streams, lakes, and ponds of New York State, with special reference to the Adirondacks.

2320. —— "What's in a name?"—"Millions in it." *American angler* 4:199-200, Sept. 29, 1883.
Signed: H. H. T.
The aquatic nomenclature of New York State, with special reference to the streams, lakes, and ponds of the North Woods.

2321. Thompson, Harold William. Body, boots and britches. Philadelphia, Lippincott, 1940. 530p.
Place-names: p. 449-80.
History, humor, and beauty in New York State's place-names. Includes a list of Indian names with meanings as given by various authorities.

2322. Tianderra. *Magazine of American history* 18:83, July 1887.
Interprets the source of the names Tianderra and Ticonderoga.

2323. Tooker, William Wallace. The Indian names for Long Island, with historical and ethnological notes. New York, F. P. Harper, 1901. 49p. (The Algonquian series, no. 4)
Published originally in Brooklyn daily eagle almanac 1888:55-56; 1889:25-26;

1890:35-37.
Reprinted in *Archaeologist* 2:171-78, June 1894.

2324. ―――― Indian names of places in the Borough of Brooklyn, with historical and ethnological notes. New York, F. P. Harper, 1901. 53p. (The Algonquian series, no. 2)
From Brooklyn eagle almanac 1893:58-60, with corrections and additions.

2325. ―――― Indian place-names in East-Hampton Town, L.I., with their probable significations; *In* East Hampton, N.Y. Records. Sag-Harbor, 1887-1905. 4:i-x.
Also published separately, Sag-Harbor, J. H. Hunt, 1889. x p.

2326. ―――― The Indian place-names on Long Island and islands adjacent, with their probable significations; ed., with an introduction by Alexander F. Chamberlain; pub. for the John Jermain Memorial Library. New York, G. P. Putnam's Sons, 1911. 314p.
Reprinted: Port Washington, N.Y., I. J. Friedman, 1962. 314p. (Empire State historical publications, 6)
Bibliography: p. 303-14.
Review: *American historical review* 17:410-11, Jan. 1912; *Dial* 51:346, Nov. 1, 1911.

2327. ―――― The origin of the name Manhattan, with historical and ethnological notes. With map. New York, F. P. Harper, 1901. 75p. (The Algonquian series, no. 1)
From Brooklyn eagle almanac for 1897, rev. and enl.

2328. ―――― Some Indian fishing stations upon Long Island, with historical and ethnological notes. New York, F. P. Harper, 1901. 62p. (The Algonquian series, VII)
Read before the American Association for the Advancement of Science, Section H, 1894, and published in the Brooklyn eagle almanac for 1895.

2329. ―――― Some Indian names of places on Long Island, N.Y. and their correspondences in Virginia, as mentioned by Capt. John Smith and associates. *Magazine of New England history* 1:154-58, July 1891.

2330. ―――― Some supposed Indian names of places on Long Island. *Long Island magazine* 1:51-54, May 1893.
Names that have been misinterpreted or misunderstood.

2331. Tottenville recovers its name. *Americana* 5:1195, Dec. 1910.
Post-Revolutionary name restored and maintained because of historic sentiment.

2332. Trumbull, James Hammond. Indian names of places on Long Island, derived from esculent roots. *Magazine of American history* 1:386-87, June 1877.

2333. ―――― Long Island Indians. *Magazine of American history* 1:330, May 1877.
The origin and meaning of the former names Punksole or Punk's Hole for what is now Manorville.

2334. Tuomey, Douglas. What's in a name? *Long Island forum* 23:29-30, Feb.

1960.
The derivation of some of the odd names given to points on Long Island by the early settlers.

2335. Tuxedo Club, Tuxedo Park, N.Y. Report to the executive committee of the Tuxedo Club, from the committee appointed to examine into the original historical names of the Tuxedo region; together with a copy of the manuscript map of this portion of New York and New Jersey, made for Washington in the years 1778-1779. New York, 1888. 7p.

2336. Tyler, Alberta V. Cochecton: place names in New York State. *Yesteryears* no. 4:11-13, July 1958.

2337. Ulmann, Albert. Historic events as street names. *New York times* Aug. 2, 1946, p. 18, col. 6.
Use in New York City.

2338. —— A landmark history of New York; also the origin of street names and a bibliography. New ed. New York, Appleton, 1903. 285p.
1st ed. 1901. 285p.
Origin of street names: p. 258-67.

2339. —— A landmark history of New York, including a guide to commemorative sites and monuments. New York, Appleton-Century, 1939. 440p.
Origin of street and place names: p. 421-31.

2340. U.S. Congress. Senate. Committee on Interior and Insular Affairs. Change in name of Bedloe's Island...Report to accompany S. J. Res. 114. June 26, 1956. Washington, 1956. 4p. (U.S. 84th Congress, 2d session. Senate. Report no. 2356. Calendar no. 2380)
Includes references to the disapproval of the change by the U.S. Board on Geographic Names.

2341. U.S. 84th Congress, 2d session. Senate. Joint resolution to change the name of Bedloe's Island in New York Harbor to Liberty Island. S. J. Res. 114. Jan. 9, 1956. Washington, 1956. 2p.
Introduced by Mr. Pastore and referred to the Committee on Interior and Insular Affairs.
Proposes a more appropriate name for the island on which stands the Statue of Liberty and on which the American Museum of Immigration will be built.

2342. U.S. Laws, statutes, etc. Joint resolution to change the name of Bedloe's Island in New York Harbor to Liberty Island. Public law 936. (United States statutes at large. 84th Congress, 2d session. 1956. v. 70, p. 956, Chapter 902)
S. J. Res. 114 became law Aug. 3, 1956.
Newspaper articles that tell the story of this change follow, in chronological order:

Senators favor naming Bedloe's "Liberty Island." *New York times* June 7, 1956, p. 9, col. 4.
A Senate Interior subcommittee adopted a joint resolution to change the name of Bedloe's Island to Liberty Island. Includes list of previous names of the island.

"Liberty Island." *New York times* June 8, 1956, p. 24, col. 3.

Editorial in support of the proposed change.

Bedloes Island change backed. *New York times* June 27, 1956, p. 14, col. 5.
The Senate Interior and Insular Affairs Committee approved changing name.

Liberty Island bill advances. *New York times* July 3, 1956, p. 16, col. 8.
The Senate passed and sent to the House legislation to change the name of
Bedloe's Island to Liberty Island.

Bedloes Island bill gains. *New York times* July 7, 1956, p. 15, col. 4.
The bill to change the name won the approval of a House Interior subcommittee.

Bedloes bill delayed. *New York times* July 11, 1956, p. 31, col. 1.
Several committee members and the Budget Bureau opposed the change, contending it would outdate maps and charts of New York Harbor. U.S. Board on
Geographic Names also opposed.

Statue of Liberty site is voted a new name. *New York times* July 24, 1956, p. 27,
col. 6.
House of Representatives passed and sent to the President the Senate-approved
resolution to change the name of Bedloe's Island to Liberty Island. Lists previous names.

It's Liberty Island now. *New York times* Aug. 4, 1956, p. 17, col. 1.
President Eisenhower signs bill giving new name to Bedloe's Island.

Topics of the Times. *New York times* Aug. 24, 1956, p. 18, col. 4.
Reports unfavorable comments of a citizen on the change from Bedloe's to
Liberty Island.

Statue of Liberty celebrates at 70. *New York times* Oct. 29, 1956, p. 31, col. 6.
Includes mention of the commemoration of the official change of name to Liberty Island by the unveiling of a plaque, presented by the Downtown Manhattan
Association.

Nevins, Allan. Epic of Liberty Island. *New York times* Oct. 28, 1956, sec. 6,
p. 15, 67-69.
A review of the history of immigration, occasioned by the renaming of Bedloe's Island to Liberty Island.

2343. Van Dyne, Maud. Canadice: place names in New York State. *Yesteryears*
no. 4:14-15, July 1958.

2344. Van Epps, Percy M. The place names of Glenville; *In* Glenville, N.Y.
Historian. Report 1:1-4. 1926.
Also in New York State Historical Association. Quarterly journal 9:272-78,
July 1928.

2345. Van Voris, Arthur H. Aboriginal place names in Schoharie County. *Schoharie County historical review* 17:3-8, May 1953.

2346. Ver Nooy, Amy. Place-names and folklore in Dutchess County. *New York folklore quarterly* 20:42-47, March 1964.

2347. Wall, Alexander J. Blackwell's Island. New York Historical Society.
Quarterly bulletin 5:35-42, July 1921.
Reprinted in part in Valentine's manual of old New York 8:341-52. 1924.
Reviewing the Society's protest of the change by New York City to Welfare Island.

2348. Wallkill. *Olde Ulster* 1:183, June 1905.

2349. The Wallkill. *Olde Ulster* 6:341-43, Nov. 1910.

2350. Want towns hyphenated, Ardsley, Croton and Hastings ask "-on-Hudson" spelling. *New York times* April 10, 1948, p. 15.
Favorable decision: U.S. Board on Geographic Names. Decision list no. 4801, p. 11.

2351. Warner, Anne. The counties of the Empire State. *New York folklore quarterly* 12:292-93, Winter 1956.
The counties arranged in a song, used by New York children to learn them.

2352. Weise, A. J. Paanpaack the site of Troy, N.Y. *Magazine of American history* 1:682-83, Nov. 1877.
Origin and source of Paanpaack or Pontpacht which was later changed to Troy.

2353. Weisman, Carl M. Brooklyn from Breukelen and Bruijkleen. *Names* 1:39-40, March 1953.

2354. Wells, Charles F. Streets with celestial names. *New York folklore quarterly* 15:169-71, Autumn 1959.
Streets in Oswego, N.Y., originally named for constellations, later changed.

2355. Whalen, George E. Dover, and how it got its name. Dutchess County Historical Society. Year book 33:38-41. 1948.

2356. What's in a name? *Harper's weekly* 4:147, March 10, 1860.
Why have we not retained the Indian names? Why was the classical dictionary spilt all over western New York?

2357. White, William Pierrepont. New York classical names due to Governor Clinton. *New York times* Feb. 26, 1928, sec. 3, p. 5, col. 1-2.
Clinton presided at meeting in 1790 which supplied designations for towns in bonus grants to soldiers.
Followed by letter of Robert E. Moody in regard to part played by the commissioners of the New York Land Office and quoting from John Franklin Jameson, The American Revolution considered as a social movement. Princeton, N.J., Princeton Univ. Press, 1926. p. 64-65.

2358. Williams, John D. Place names in Sea Gate, Coney Island, Brighton Beach and Manhattan Beach. August 1964. 92p.
Thesis (M.A.) Brooklyn College, 1964. On file in the College Library, the Brooklyn Public Library, and the Long Island Historical Society Library.

NORTH CAROLINA

2359. Abenethy, Edgar. Unusual names. *State magazine* 10:14-15, Jan. 30, 1943.

2360. Battle, Kemp Plummer. Glimpses of history in the names of our counties. *North Carolina booklet* 6:27-48, July 1906.

2361. —— The names of the counties of North Carolina and the history involved in them. Winston, W. A. Blair, 1888. 38p.

2362. —— North Carolina county names. *Magazine of history with notes and queries* 7:208-22, April 1908.

2363. Cooper, Elizabeth Scott. How Ocracoke got its name. *North Carolina folklore* 4:19-21, Dec. 1956.
    The legend of the name in ballad form.

2364. Cumming, William Patterson. Naming Carolina. *North Carolina historical review* 22:34-42, Jan. 1945.
    Part of a study made with the aid of a grant from the Social Science Research Council.

2365. Edwards, Richard. Statistical gazetteer of the states of Virginia and North Carolina; embracing important topographical and historical information, from recent and original sources. With the results of the last census, in many cases to 1855. Richmond, Pub. for the proprietor, 1856. 601p.

2366. Fink, Paul M. Smoky Mountains history as told in place-names. East Tennessee Historical Society. Publications 6:3-11. 1934.

2367. —— That's why they call it . . . The names and lore of the Great Smokies. Jonesboro, Tenn., P. M. Fink, 1956. 20p.

2368. —— & Myron H. Avery. The nomenclature of the Great Smoky Mountains. East Tennessee Historical Society. Publications 9:53-64. 1937.
    An abstracted account under the title Arnold Guyot's explorations in the Great Smokies, in *Appalachia* 2:253-61, Dec. 1936.
    A major portion of the names either originated with or were confirmed as a result of Arnold Guyot's exploration of the region in the period 1856-1860.

2369. Gatschet, Albert Samuel. Onomatology of the Catawba River basin. *American anthropologist* n.s. 4:52-56, Jan.-March 1902.
    Also issued as a separate.

2370. Here's how to start a name collection. *Chicago Sunday tribune* Dec. 1, 1957, pt. 6, p. 12.
    Different categories found in North Carolina.

2371. Lanman, Charles. The Catawba country of North Carolina. *Magazine of history* 19:92-100, Aug.-Sept. 1914.
    Contains source and significance of names of the Ginger Cake Mountain and Roan Mountain in North Carolina.

2372. Lawrence, R. C. Many changes in names. *State magazine* 11:6, March 16, 1944.

2373. Lindbergh Drive no longer. *New York times* June 14, 1941, p. 19, col. 4.
    Lindbergh Drive, Charlotte, changed to Avon Ave.

2374. Mason, Robert L. A famous landmark is in dispute, two states contend over changing the name of Mt. Collins. *New York times* Aug. 31, 1930, sec. 8,

p. 9, col. 2-4.
Mount Kephart desired for peak in Smoky Mountains National Park, but U.S.
Board on Geographic Names refused.

2375. Peak named for Cammerer, Smoky Mountain ridge also honors Park director. *New York times* Feb. 25, 1942, p. 24, col. 2.
Great Smoky Mountains National Park peak named for Arno B. Cammerer.

2376. Reeves, Paschal. Thomas Wolfe's "Old Catawba." *Names* 11:254-56, Dec.
1963.
Thomas Wolfe's fictional name for North Carolina. Derivation of Catawba.

2377. Shellans, Herbert. Table d'hote. Towns, counties and places, North Carolina. *Names* 11:270-71, Dec. 1963.
Names of places listed in the form of a menu for breakfast, luncheon, and dinner.

2378. —— Tarheel place names. *North Carolina folklore* 4:28-32, Dec. 1956.

2379. "Tar Heels." *American speech* 1:355, March 1926.
An explanation, in a talk by Major William A. Graham, April 25, 1915, of how
North Carolinians came to be called by that name.

2380. U.S. Board on Geographic Names. Decisions. No. 28—June 30, 1932.
Great Smoky Mountains National Park, North Carolina and Tennessee. Washington, Govt. Print. Off., 1934. 46p.

2381. U.S. Writers' Program. North Carolina. How they began—the story of
North Carolina county, town and other place names, comp. by workers of the WPA
Writers' Program of the Work Projects Administration in the State of North Car-
olina. Sponsored by North Carolina Dept. of Conservation and Development,
Raleigh, N.C. New York, Harian publications, 1941. 73p.

2382. Weslager, C. A. Place names on Ocracoke Island. *North Carolina historical review* 31:41-49, Jan. 1954.

2383. What's in a name, being a continuation of the origin of various place names
in counties of North Carolina. *State magazine* 11:3, March 18, 1944.

2384. Wilburn, Hiram C. Judaculla place-names and the Judaculla tales. *Southern Indian studies* 4:23-26, Oct. 1952.
Deals with the geographical location and the meaning of natural features and
objects that owe their names and stories to the mythological life and activities
of the giant Judaculla.

2385. Wilson, E. W. Names in the mountains. *State magazine* 10:4, March 13,
1943.

NORTH DAKOTA

2386. "Beaver Lodge"—how an oilfield gets its name. *Wall Street journal* May
12, 1952, p. 1.
In Williams County.

2387. Bessasson, Haraldur. Icelandic place names in Manitoba and North Dakota. Linguistic Circle of Manitoba and North Dakota. Proceedings 2:8-10, May 1960.

2388. Gilmore, Melvin Randolph. Meaning of the word Dakota. *American anthropologist* n.s. 24:242-45, April-June 1922.
    The author considers Dakota to be a derivative of the same root as the Omaha endakutha, and he believes that both words should be taken in the sense of a "peculiar people" rather than in the sense of "friends."

2389. Hughes, Dorothy J. Coined town-names of North Dakota. *American speech* 14:315, Dec. 1939.

2390. Reid, Russell. Name origins of North Dakota cities, towns and counties. *North Dakota history* 13:118-43, July 1946.
    Based on data gathered by the North Dakota Federal Writers' Project. Contains names of the counties, and place-names A-C; apparently no more published.

2391. Spokesfield, Walter Earnest. The history of Wells County, North Dakota, and its pioneers, with a sketch of North Dakota history and the oregin [sic] of the place names. Valley City, N.D., 1929. 804p.

2392. The State Geographic Board report on North Dakota. *North Dakota historical quarterly* 2:53-56, Oct. 1927.
    "Describes the work of the Board and discusses the 'Seven chief places of historical interest in North Dakota' and 'Places of greatest interest in North Dakota.' "—Price.

2393. Thompson, Roy. The naming of Cando. North Dakota. State Historical Society. Collections 3:321-23. 1910.
    "This name is an illustration of a coined word, 'Can-do.' It proved that a small group of men could locate and name, in spite of the opposition of the settlers, the county seat of Towner County, North Dakota."—Price.

2394. Williams, Mary Ann Barnes. Origins of North Dakota place names: Benson, Cavalier, Pembina, Ramsey, Walsh. Washburn, N.D., 1961. 56p.

2395. ———— Origins of North Dakota place names: Cass & Barnes counties. Washburn, N.D., 1959. 20p.

2396. ———— Origins of North Dakota place names: McLean & Burleigh counties. Washburn?, N.D., 1959. 26p.

2397. ———— Origins of North Dakota place names: Morton, Mercer, Oliver, Grant, Sioux counties. Washburn, N.D., 1959?. 34p.

2398. ———— Origins of North Dakota place names: Stutsman, Wells, Foster, Eddy, Kidder counties. Washburn, N.D., 1959. 32p.

2399. ———— Origins of North Dakota place names: Ward, Renville, Burke, Mountrail counties. Washburn, N.D., 1959. 22p.

OHIO

2400. Baker, James W. How our counties got their names. [Columbus, Ohio, Franklin County Historical Society, Center of Science and Industry, 1963]. Unpaged. (Jim Baker's historical handbook series, v. 1)
First published in the *Columbus dispatch.*

2401. Bauman, Robert F. When the Maumee was called the Tawa. An analysis of river terminology during the last quarter of the 18th century. *Northwest Ohio quarterly* 28:60-87, Spring 1956.

2402. Cottingham, Kenneth. The influence of geology in Ohio place-names. *Ohio journal of science* 49:34-40, Jan. 1949.

2403. Coyle, William. A classification of Ohio place-names. *Ohio state archaeological and historical quarterly* 60:273-82, July 1951.

2404. Davis, Harold E. Indian place names in Ohio.
Dictionary containing several hundred names, in preparation. The author is associated with the American University of Washington, D.C.

2405. Dickoré, Marie. Newton first named Mercersberg. Historical and Philosophical Society of Ohio. Bulletin 8:65-67, Jan. 1950.

2406. Dudley, Helen M. The origin of the name of the town of Worthington. *Ohio state archaeological and historical quarterly* 52:248-59, July-Sept. 1943.

2407. Durbin, Mildred G. Naming the Buckeye State. *American forests and forest life* 33:585-86, Oct. 1927.

2408. Errett, Russell. Indian geographical names. *Magazine of western history* 2:51-59, 238-46, May, July 1885.
Names of Algonkin (principally Delaware) and Iroquois origin in Pennsylvania and Ohio. p. 51-59 deal principally with the river names Ohio and Allegheny.

2409. Farrar, William M. Why is Ohio called the Buckeye State? *Ohio archaeological and historical quarterly* 2:174-79, June 1888.

2410. Fitzgerald, Roy G. Ohio's counties; why so named? Historical and Philosophical Society of Ohio. Bulletin 10:157, April 1952.

2411. ──── Warren County named for General Warren. Historical and Philosophical Society of Ohio. Bulletin 10:241, July 1952.

2412. Green, James A. The map of Hamilton County. Columbus, F. J. Heer Print. Co., 1926. 33p.
Reprinted from the *Ohio archaeological and historical quarterly* 35:291-321, April 1926.
Discusses names on the map of Hamilton County.

2413. Hume, Edgar Erskine. The naming of the City of Cincinnati. *Ohio state archaeological and historical quarterly* 44:81-91, Jan. 1935.

2414. Hunt, William Ellis. Meaning of the names Muskingum, Tuscarawas, and

Walhonding; *In his* Historical collections of Coshocton County, Ohio, 1764-1876. Cincinnati, Clarke, 1876. p. 162-63.

2415.   Italy in Ohio. *New York times* July 23, 1943, p. 16, col. 4.

2416.   Jack, Walter. Origin of the names of Ashtabula County townships. Ashtabula County Historical Society. Quarterly bulletin 9:[2-5], March 15, 1962.

2417.   Jenkins, Warren. The Ohio gazetteer and traveller's guide; containing a description of the several towns, townships, and counties, with their water-courses, roads, improvements, mineral productions, etc. etc., together with an appendix, or general register; embracing tables of roads and distances; of post offices, their location and distance from the capital of the state and of the United States; of works of internal improvement; of the several officers of state, their residence, etc.; of the colleges and their officers; of banks, their officers and capital, etc. Rev. ed. with a second appendix, containing the census of the state for 1840, as taken by order of Congress. Columbus, Isaac N. Whiting, 1841. 578p.
   1st ed. 1837. 546p. Also published 1839.
   "Jenkins' Gazetteer is a continuation of Kilbourn's gazetteers, discontinued in 1834, but is almost entirely rewritten, and contains many additions and corrections."—Peter Gibson Thomson, A Bibliography of Ohio. Cincinnati, The Author, 1880.

2418.   Johnston, John. Names of the rivers by the Shawanoese; *In his* Account of the present state of the Indian tribes inhabiting Ohio, in a letter from John Johnston, United States agent of Indian affairs at Piqua, to Caleb Atwater. American Antiquarian Society. Transactions and collections 1:297-99. 1820.

2419.   Kenny, Laurence J. There's a glory in the name "Ohio." *Mid-America* 37:184-86, July 1955.

2420.   Keyerleber, Karl. On the naming of streets. *Cleveland plain dealer* Jan. 27, 1953.
   Street names in Cleveland.

2421.   Kilbourn, John. The Ohio gazetteer, or, Topographical dictionary; being a continuation of the work originally comp. by the late John Kilbourn. 11th ed. rev. and enl. by a citizen of Columbus. Columbus, Scott and Wright, 1833. 512p.
   1st ed. 1816; 3d ed. 1817; 5th ed. 1818; 6th ed. 1819; 7th ed. 1821; 8th ed. 1826; 9th ed. 1829; 10th ed. 1831.

2422.   Lindsey, David. New England origins of Western Reserve place names. *American speech* 30:243-55, Dec. 1955.

2423.   ———   Ohio's Western Reserve, the story of its place names. Cleveland, Press of Western Reserve University and the Western Reserve Historical Society, 1955. 111p.
   Limited to inhabited places: cities, townships, and villages. Does not account for the names of rivers, lakes, or other geographic features.
   Review: by William D. Overman, *Names* 3:261-63, Dec. 1955; by William D. Overman, *Ohio historical quarterly* 65:97-98, Jan. 1956.

2424.   ———   Place names in Ohio's Western Reserve. *Names* 2:40-45, March 1954.

2425. Lotspeich, C. M. Cincinnati. *American speech* 1:226, Jan. 1926.
How Cincinnati escaped being called Losantiville.

2426. McFarland, R. W. The Chillicothes. *Ohio archaeological and historical quarterly* 11:230-31, Oct. 1902.
Identifies five different towns with this Indian name.

2427. Mahr, August C. Indian river and place names in Ohio. *Ohio historical quarterly* 66:137-58, April 1957.
Indian name Ohio does not mean "the Beautiful River"?

2428. Martin, Maria Ewing. Ohio, 1803-1903; "origin of its names." New Straitsville, Ohio, 1903. 16p.
Read before the 5th Ohio State Conference, Daughters of the American Revolution, Oct. 29, 1903.

2429. ———— Origin of Ohio place names. *Ohio archaeological and historical quarterly* 14:272-90, July 1905.

2430. Naming the streets. Historical and Philosophical Society of Ohio. Bulletin v. 4, no. 3, Sept. 1946, p. 23.
Refers to the second ordinance of Cincinnati, which relates to naming the streets and alleys of the town.

2431. Ohio. Dept. of Natural Resources. Division of Water. Gazetteer of Ohio streams, comp. by J. C. Krolczyk. Columbus, 1954. 175p.

2432. Overman, William Daniel. Ohio place names; the origin of the names of over 500 Ohio cities, towns and villages. Akron, The Author, 1951. 86p.

2433. ———— Ohio town names. *Names* 1:115-17, June 1953.

2434. ———— Ohio town names. Introd. by William T. Utter. Akron, Atlantic Press, 1958, c1959. 155p.
The origin of the names of more than 1,200 Ohio cities, towns, and villages.
Review: by G. R. Stewart in *Names* 7:261-65, Dec. 1959.

2435. Peters, Walter August. Place names. *Cleveland plain dealer* Feb. 15, 18, 20, 22, 25, 27, 29, 1924.
A series on the place-names of Greater Cleveland.

2436. ———— The street names of Cleveland and vicinity. *Western Reserve University bulletin* v. 30, no. 7, July 1927. 62p.
Contents: Names of the first stratum, 1792-1853; The second stratum, 1853-1906; The third stratum, 1906-1925; The growth of compounds, The prefixes; The suffixes.

2437. Phillips, Hazel Spencer. Invincible gambler; folklore. Lebanon, Ohio, Warren County Historical Society, n.d. [4]p. (Folklore series, no. 9)
"Information furnished by Mrs. Thomas Bamber, and Harry B. Allen, Cozad, Nebraska, whose research inspired Mari Sandoz' book Gamblin' Man's Son."
John Jackson Cozad, who established Cozaddale, Ohio, and Cozad, Neb.

2438.	Phillips, Josephine E.	The naming of Marietta.	*Ohio state archaeological and historical quarterly* 55:106-37, April-June 1946.

2439.	Raup, Hallock Floy.	Names of Ohio's streams.	*Names* 5:162-68, Sept. 1957.

2440.	——	The names of Ohio's streams.	*Ohio conservation bulletin* 20:10-11, 27, July 1956.

2441.	——	A preliminary study of geographic names in Ohio.	Ohio State Archaeological and Historical Society.	Museum echoes 22:86-88, Nov. 1949.
    Has 35,000 cards on geographic names of places, natural features, state parks and forests, and miscellaneous features in the State of Ohio. Eventually the cards will be transferred to the U.S. Board on Geographic Names.—American Dialect Society, Committee on Place Names, Dec. 1962.

2442.	Redfield's Ohio railway gazetteer, travelers' guide, and express and shippers' directory, embracing a complete alphabetical gazetteer and travelers' guide. Indianapolis, D. A. Redfield, 1865.	94p.

2443.	Richmond, W. Edson.	Place-names in Franklin County, Ohio.	*Ohio state archaeological and historical quarterly* 53:135-59, April-June 1944.
    Also published separately, 1944.	24p.

2444.	Rideout, Mrs. Grant.	Origin of Put-in-Bay.	*Inland seas* 3:195-96, July 1947.

2445.	Ross, Edna.	Some Logan County place-names.	Ed. by Kelsie B. Harder. Chillicothe, Ohio Valley Folk Research Project, Ross County Historical Society, 1962.	8 1.	(Ohio Valley folk publications, n.s. no. 96)
    Bellefontaine, Degraff, Quincy, Spring Hills, and Loganville.

2446.	Rust, Orton Glenn.	A short account of Clark County, Ohio, place names. 2d ed.	Chillicothe, Priv. pub. R. E. Craver and D. K. Webb, 1951.	4 1.

2447.	Scholl, John William.	Shull's Road.	*Ohio state archaeological and historical quarterly* 55:293-94, July-Sept. 1946.
    A letter to the editor gives reasons why Shell's Road on a road map of Montgomery County should be Shull's Road.

2448.	The Towns called Chillicothe.	*Ohio archaeological and historical quarterly* 12:167-79, April 1903.
    A criticism by J. B. F. Morgan of R. W. McFarland's article, The Chillicothes, and McFarland's reply, reprinted from the *Chillicothe news-advertiser* of Jan. 7 and Feb. 2, 1903.

2449.	Waite, Frederick Clayton.	Place names in Lake County and vicinity.	1939.
    Mounted newspaper clippings from the *Willoughby news-herald,* in the Cleveland Public Library.

2450.	——	Sources of the names of the counties of the Western Reserve.	*Ohio state archaeological and historical quarterly* 48:58-65, Jan. 1939.
    Bibliography: p. 65.

2451. Webb, David Knowlton & Emily A. Webb. A list of Ohio place name variations. Chillicothe, Pub. priv., 1951. Unpaged.

2452. The World in Ohio; a philatelist takes postmaster-eye view of odd Buckeye place names. *Cleveland plain dealer* May 27, 1956, Pictorial magazine p. 18.

OKLAHOMA

2453. Brackett, Walter L. Place-names of five northeast counties of Oklahoma. 1943.
Thesis (M.A.) Univ. of Tulsa, 1943.

2454. Brewington, Eugene H. Place names in Oklahoma, their derivation, origin and present status. Oklahoma City, Okla., The Author, 1956. Unpaged.

2455. Chase, Carroll & Richard McP. Cabeen. The first hundred years of United States territorial postmarks, 1787-1887. Indian Territory. *American philatelist* 60:206-20, 902-07, 914-21, Dec. 1946, Aug. 1947; 61:449-55, 468-70, 547-57, March-April 1948.
Includes list of post offices to 1887, with notes on some names.

2456. Encyclopedia of Oklahoma. [Oklahoma City, 1912]. v. 1.
Editor: v. 1, Emmet Starr.
Gives location (by county) and origin of place-names.

2457. Foreman, Grant. Early post offices of Oklahoma. *Chronicles of Oklahoma* 6:4-25, 155-62, 271-98, 408-44, March-Dec. 1928; 7:7-33, March 1929.
A list showing name, location, beginning date, and first postmaster, grouped by boundaries of the Indian tribes, and later by counties of Oklahoma Territory.

2458. Gannett, Henry. A gazetteer of Indian Territory. Washington, Govt. Print. Off., 1905. 70p. (U.S. Geological Survey. Bulletin no. 248)

2459. Gazetteer and business directory of the new Southwest. Embracing all of that region of country—including counties, towns and cities—contiguous to the St. Louis and San Francisco Railway, its divisions and branches, located in southwest Missouri, southeastern Kansas, the eastern portion of the Indian country, and the northwest section of Arkansas. In which is included an abridged directory of leading business houses of St. Louis. St. Louis, United States Directory Pub. Co., 1881. 224p.

2460. Geary, its name and founding. *Chronicles of Oklahoma* 37:245, Summer 1959.

2461. Gibson, Arrell Morgan. Early mining camps in northeastern Oklahoma. *Chronicles of Oklahoma* 34:193-202, Summer 1956.

2462. Gould, Charles Newton. Oklahoma place names. Norman, Univ. of Oklahoma Press, 1933. 146p.
Unpublished revision in manuscript collection, University of Oklahoma Library.
Review: *American speech* 9:66-67, Feb. 1934.

2463. Holloway, O. Willard. Origin of place names at Fort Sill, Oklahoma. Fort Sill, U.S. Army Artillery and Missile School Library, 1957. 11p. (USA A&MS Library. Special bibliography no. 13)
Rev. ed. 1959. 12 l.

2464. Jeffords, Gladys Wheeler & Lena Lockhart Daugherty. Oklahoma's fabulous Indian names. Muskogee, Okla., American Print. Co., 1962. 27p.
Oklahoma place names: p. 16-27.

2465. Meaning of the Creek Indian name Eufaula. *Chronicles of Oklahoma* 40: 310-11, Autumn 1962.
A city in Alabama and Oklahoma.

2466. Mulhall was first called Alfred. *Chronicles of Oklahoma* 36:213, Summer 1958.

2467. Nye, Wilbur Sturtevant. Place names on the Fort Sill reservation; *In his* Carbine and lance; the story of old Fort Sill. Norman, Univ. of Oklahoma Press, 1937. p. 417-19.
Gives derivation.

2468. Oklahoma place-names file.
Card file prepared at the Oklahoma City Public Library.

2469. Origin of county names in Oklahoma. *Chronicles of Oklahoma* 2:75-82, March 1924.

2470. Shirk, George H. First post offices within the boundaries of Oklahoma. *Chronicles of Oklahoma* 26:178-244, Summer 1948.
List, p. 185-244, includes material on names. Includes Oklahoma Territory, p. 237-44.

2471. ——— Oklahoma place names. Norman, Univ. of Oklahoma Press, 1965. 233p.
Bibliography: p. 233.

2472. Tahlequah, Okla. Sequoyah Vocational School. Some Oklahoma place names; or, What's in a name? by the Sooners (grade five). Tahlequah, Okla., n.d. Unpaged.

2473. Taylor, Nat M. How Lookeba got its name. *Chronicles of Oklahoma* 38: 325, Autumn 1960.

2474. Thoburn, Joseph B. The naming of the Canadian River. *Chronicles of Oklahoma* 6:181-85, June 1928.
"The author believes this river was named by voyageurs from Canada."—Price.

2475. Town named for Gene Autry. *New York times* Nov. 6, 1941, p. 12, col. 6.
Berwyn changed to Gene Autry.

2476. Townsend, A. C. Indian Territory ghost towns. *Chronicles of Oklahoma* 21:44-45, March 1943.

2477. U.S. 88th Congress, 1st session. House. Joint resolution designating the navigation channel and canal portion of the Arkansas River navigation and multiple purpose project as the "Robert S. Kerr Seaway." H. J. Res. 82. Jan. 9, 1963. Washington, 1963. 1p.

Introduced by Mr. Edmondson and referred to the Committee on Public Works.

Subsequent documents relating to this joint resolution, and a bill introduced in the Senate, were published as follows:

U.S. 88th Congress, 1st session. Senate. A bill to change the name of Short Mountain Lock and Dam and Reservoir in the State of Oklahoma to Robert S. Kerr Lock and Dam and Reservoir. S. 1173. March 25, 1963. Washington, 1963. 1p.

Introduced by Mr. Monroney and Mr. Edmondson and referred to the Committee on Public Works.

U.S. 88th Congress, 1st session. House. Designating the Short Mountain Lock and Dam and Reservoir, Oklahoma, as the Robert S. Kerr Lock and Dam and Reservoir. Report no. 220, to accompany H. J. Res. 82. April 22, 1963. Washington, 1963. 4p.

Submitted by Mr. Davis, from the Committee on Public Works, with amendments, changing the title of the joint resolution and the name to Robert S. Kerr Lock and Dam and Reservoir.

―――― [Reprint of the original joint resolution, April 22, 1963, with amendments, to accompany the report. Report no. 220 and House Calendar no. 49 added]. 2p.

U.S. 88th Congress, 1st session. Senate. Joint resolution to change the name of Short Mountain Lock and Dam and Reservoir in the State of Oklahoma to Robert S. Kerr Lock and Dam and Reservoir. H. J. Res. 82. In the Senate May 8, 1963. Washington, 1963. 1p.

Referred to the Committee on Public Works. Passed the House of Representatives May 6, 1963.

―――― Changing the name of the Short Mountain Lock and Dam and Reservoir, Oklahoma, to the Robert S. Kerr Lock and Dam and Reservoir. Report no. 273, to accompany H. J. Res. 82. June 19, 1963. Calendar no. 254. Washington, 1963. 3p.

Submitted by Mr. McNamara, from the Committee on Public Works, without amendment. Includes favorable comments of the Bureau of the Budget and the Dept. of the Army on identical bill S. 1173.

―――― [Reprint of the joint resolution, June 19, 1963, to accompany the report. Report no. 273 and Calendar no. 254 added]. 1p.

2478. Wilson, Raymond R. Place-names of six northeast counties of Oklahoma. 1940.
Thesis (M.A.) Univ. of Tulsa, 1940.

2479. Wright, Muriel H. History of Oklahoma emblems, the name Oklahoma. *Chronicles of Oklahoma* 35:349-50, Autumn 1957.

2480. ―――― The name "Ferdinandina" located on the Arkansas River. *Chronicles of Oklahoma* 41:157-59, Summer 1963.

2481. ―――― The naming of Oklahoma. *Chronicles of Oklahoma* 39:335-37, Autumn 1961.

Includes reference to the suggested Territory of Lincoln, in Congressional bills soon after the Civil War.

2482. —— Some geographic names of French origin in Oklahoma. *Chronicles of Oklahoma* 7:188-93, June 1929.
The French traders and trappers gave names to many of the streams and mountains in Oklahoma.

2483. Young, Della I. Names in old Cheyenne and Arapahoe Territory and the Texas Panhandle. Texas Folk-lore Society. Publications 6:90-97. 1927.

OREGON

2484. Abbott, Walter H. Preservation of Indian names. Oregon Historical Society. Quarterly 12:361-68, Dec. 1911.
A plea for the use of Indian names in Oregon.

2485. Axford, Harold. How some Portland areas got their names. *Oregon journal*, Portland, July 17, 1960.

2486. Barker, M. A. R. Klamath texts. Berkeley, Univ. of California Press, 1963. 197p. (University of California publications in linguistics, v. 30)
Klamath place names with map: p. 189-97. Largely adapted from Leslie Spier, Klamath ethnography (University of California publications in American archaeology and ethnology, v. 30, 1930). 92 new place-names added. 45 additional place-names are included in the Dictionary (published separately).

2487. Barry, James Neilson. Early Oregon forts, a chronological list. *Oregon historical quarterly* 46:101-11, June 1945.

2488. Barton, J. Tracy. "Amelia" and "Shirt Tail Gulch" in Mormon Basin. *Oregon historical quarterly* 43:228-31, Sept. 1942.
Information on these two place-names was obtained by Mr. Barton from his grandfather and grandmother, pioneer settlers of that region.

2489. Berlin, Ore., to take the name of Distomo. *New York times* Oct. 5, 1944, p. 1, col. 1.
Editorial p. 22, col. 3; Berlin, Ore., rebels at change of name to Distomo. *New York times* Oct. 11, 1944, p. 23, col. 3; Berlin, Ore., votes not to become Distomo. *New York times* Oct. 12, 1944, p. 15, col. 2.

2490. Bracher, Frederick. "Ouaricon" and Oregon. *American speech* 21:185-87, Oct. 1946.
Additional evidence based on various editions of Lahontan's Nouveaux voyages which supports George Rippey Stewart's findings reported in his article The source of the name "Oregon" (see no. 2530).

2491. Butterfield, Grace & J. H. Horner. Wallowa Valley towns and their beginnings. *Oregon historical quarterly* 41:382-85, Dec. 1940.
The origin of the name of the towns of Joseph, Wallowa, and Lostine is included with a brief account of their early history.

2492. Carney, Bobette. Aloha man disputes story on naming town. *Beaverton Valley news* Nov. 10, 1960.
  Early Aloha, Ore., history.

2493. Chase, Carroll & Richard McP. Cabeen. The first hundred years of United States territorial postmarks, 1787-1887. Oregon Territory. *American philatelist* 56:360-75, March 1943.
  Includes list of post offices, with notes on some names.

2494. Clark, Malcolm H. "Oregon" revisited. *Oregon historical quarterly* 61: 211-19, June 1960.
  "A minority report" to article by Vernon F. Snow *ibid*. 60:439-47, Dec. 1959.

2495. Corning, Howard McKinley. Historical place name sketches. *Oregon journal*, Portland, May 25-Aug. 17, 1950.

2496. Dorsey, James Owen. The gentile system of the Siletz tribes. *Journal of American folk-lore* 3:227-37, July-Sept. 1890.
  Ancient villages and names of tribes living on the Siletz reservation.

2497. Elliott, Thomas Coit. Jonathan Carver's source for the name Oregon. Oregon Historical Society. Quarterly 23:53-69, March 1922.
  "Associates the name used by Major Rogers with the French word for storm, ouragan."—McArthur.

2498. —— The mysterious Oregon. *Washington historical quarterly* 22:289-92, Oct. 1931.
  Discusses four theories: (1) that the name was invented by Major Robert Rogers; (2) that it was an Indian word; (3) that it was the French word ouragan; (4) that it was Rogers's corruption of the Indian "Ouinipigon," the earliest form of the name Winnipeg.

2499. —— Oregon Inlet, Roanoke Island. *Oregon historical quarterly* 32:281-82, Sept. 1931.
  Directing attention to a curious literary error concerning the name Oregon.

2500. —— The origin of the name Oregon. Oregon Historical Society. Quarterly 22:91-115, June 1921.
  This article supplements the article The strange case of Jonathan Carver and the name Oregon (see no. 2501).

2501. —— The strange case of Jonathan Carver and the name Oregon. Oregon Historical Society. Quarterly 21:341-68, Dec. 1920.
  "The name Oregon was used in a book by Jonathan Carver, published in London in 1778, entitled, 'Travels through the interior parts of North America,' as applied to the 'River of the West.' The writer here gives the results of his researches regarding Carver and his book, and suggests sources for Carver's use of the name Oregon."—Griffin.

2502. Galvani, William H. Origin of the name of Oregon. Oregon Historical Society. Quarterly 21:336-40, Dec. 1920.
  Presents the theory that Oregon is a natural linguistic transformation from Aragon, a name that might very likely have been used by early Spanish settlers.

2503. Gatschet, Albert Samuel. The Klamath Indians of southwestern Oregon. *Contributions to North American ethnology* v. 2, pt. 1, p. xxvii-xxxii. 1890.
Contents: Topographic list of camping places, on Klamath Marsh, along Williamson River, around Upper Klamath Lake; Eminences around Upper Klamath Lake; Camping places in Sprague River valley, and the Modoc country.

2504. Glassley, Ray Hoard. Letters to the Editor. *Oregon historical quarterly* 59:255-59, Sept. 1958.
History of the names of some of Oregon's outstanding geographic features—the Willamette River and its tributaries.

2505. Holladay, railway tycoon of early day, gave town name. *Seaside signal* Aug. 24, 1950.
After Ben Holladay's Seaside Hotel.

2506. Holman, Frederick V. Oregon counties; their creations and the origins of their names. Oregon Historical Society. Quarterly 11:1-81, March 1910.
Condensed in *Magazine of history* 13:119-22, March 1911.

2507. Judson, Lewis. Street names of Salem. *Marion County history* 5:17-20, June 1959.

2508. Kraft, Walter C. Heceta: a name with a split personality. *Names* 7:256-60, Dec. 1959.
Discusses two quite different pronunciations for two landmarks on the Oregon coast named for the Spanish explorer Bruno Heceta.
A footnote to above, by John Lyman, *ibid.* 8:87, June 1960.

2509. Lewis, William S. Some notes and observations on the origin and evolution of the name Oregon as applied to the River of the West. *Washington historical quarterly* 17:218-22, July 1926.
Indian origin of the river now named the Columbia.

2510. Lyman, H. S. Indian names. Oregon Historical Society. Quarterly 1:316-26, Sept. 1900.
Aboriginal place-names of the lower Columbia and Willamette rivers.

2511. McArthur, Lewis Ankeny. Earliest Oregon postoffices as recorded at Washington. *Oregon historical quarterly* 41:53-71, March 1940.
Records from the Division of Postmasters' Appointments at the Post Office Dept. in Washington, D.C. Entries by county, from March 9, 1847 to 1855.

2512. —— Oregon geographic names. 3d ed. rev. and enl. Portland, Pub. by Binfords and Mort for the Oregon Historical Society, 1952. 686p.
1st ed. 1928. 450p.; 2d ed. rev. and enl. 1944. 581p.
Originally published in *Oregon historical quarterly* 26:309-423, Dec. 1925; 27: 131-91, 225-64, 295-363, 412-47. 1926; 28:65-110, 163-224, 281-306, March-Sept. 1927. Six supplements to the 1st ed. were published *ibid.* 43:299-317, Dec. 1942; 44:1-18, 176-218, 286-312, 339-60. 1943; 45:42-74, March 1944. Additions after 1944 were published *ibid.* 46:332-52, Dec. 1945; 47:61-98, 196-216, 329-57, 441-64. 1946; 48:34-42, 68-85, 254-63, 322-31. 1947; 49:63-72, 137-47, 222-43, 299-305. 1948; 50:51-53, 134-38, March-June 1949.
Review of 1st ed.: *Canadian historical review* 10:169-70, June 1929; by David W. Hazen, *Oregon historical quarterly* 29:211-13, June 1928.

Review of 2d ed.; by W. Kaye Lamb, *British Columbia historical quarterly* 9: 170-71, April 1945.

2513. —— Oregon place names; pen and ink illustrations by Marilyn Campbell. Portland, Binfords & Mort for the Oregon journal, 1944. 109p.
An abridgment of the author's Oregon geographic names (see no. 2512).

2514. Meyers, J. A. Oregan—River of the slaves or River of the West. *Washington historical quarterly* 13:282-83, Oct. 1922.
"Reasons for thinking that the name Oregon originated from a typographical error in Jonathan Carver's 'Travels through the interior parts of North America in 1766-1768.' "—Price.

2515. Mills, Hazel E. Two Oregon place name items of 1851 and 1856. *Western folklore* 11:214-16, July 1952.
New names for towns, rather than repetition of old names used elsewhere, and Willamette, etc.

2516. Mills, Randall V. Districts and sections in Eugene, Oregon. *Western folklore* 11:213-14, July 1952.

2517. —— Notes on Oregon place names. *Western folklore* 10:316-17, Oct. 1951.

2518. —— Place-name notes from the *"Oregon spectator."* *Western folklore* 9:60-63, Jan. 1950.
Published Oregon City, 1846-

2519. Minto, John. Minto Pass: its history and an Indian tradition; *In his* Rhymes of early life in Oregon and historical and biographical facts. Salem, Ore., Statesman Pub. Co., 1915?. p. 33-40.
This chapter reprinted from the Quarterly of the Oregon Historical Society, v. 4, no. 3, Sept. 1903.
Original names in Independence Valley: p. 38-39.

2520. Monaghan, Robert R. Pronunciation guide to Oregon place names. Eugene, Oregon Assoc. of Broadcasters, 1961. 81p.
Review: by John R. Krueger, *Names* 10:192-94, Sept. 1962.

2521. Oregon Geographic Names Board. Minutes. Portland, 1914?- .
No decision list has been issued.

2522. Payne, Edward R. Oregon territorial post offices and handstamped postal markings. *Oregon historical quarterly* 60:475-88, Dec. 1959.
A draft of this article appeared in the April 1959 *Western express*, quarterly of the Western Cover Collector's Society.
Includes list of post offices with county now in, date established, and whether discontinued, name changed, or current.

2523. Payne, Edwin R. Oregon territorial postmarks. *American philatelist* 64: 531-32, April 1951.
List of post offices. Additions to Carroll Chase-Richard McP. Cabeen's U.S. territorial postmarks, *ibid.* 56:360-75, March 1943.

2524. Pioneer's name selected for proposed new city: Ben Holladay, Old West's king of transportation, top choice of committee. *Parkrose-East County enterprise* March 15, 1961.

Tentative limits of the proposed east Multnomah County city are described in the March 22 issue of the same paper, and the *Beaverton Valley news* editorializes on the proposed city on March 30.

2525. Rees, John E. Oregon—its meaning, origin and application. Oregon Historical Society. Quarterly 21:317-31, Dec. 1920.

The word Oregon is derived from a Shoshone Indian expression meaning "The River of the West," originating from two Shoshone words Ogwa, "river," and Pe-on, "west," or Ogwa Pe-on.

2526. Scott, H. W. Not Majoram: the Spanish word "Oregano" not the original of Oregon. Oregon Historical Society. Quarterly 1:165-68, June 1900.

2527. Snow, Vernon F. From Ouragan to Oregon. *Oregon historical quarterly* 60:439-47, Dec. 1959.

University of Oregon historian evaluates latest interpretation of controversial name.

See also article by Malcolm H. Clark, *ibid.* 61:211-19, June 1960.

2528. Spier, Leslie. Klamath ethnography. Berkeley, Univ. of California Press, 1930. 338p. (University of California publications in American archaeology and ethnology, v. 30)

Settlements: p. 10-21. Lists of Klamath settlement names, with maps.

For additional material based on this, see M. A. R. Barker, Klamath texts, no. 2486.

2529. Steel, William Gladstone. The mountains of Oregon. Portland, D. Steel, 1890. 112p.

Contains several sections on the names of mountains in Oregon and Washington.

2530. Stewart, George Rippey. The source of the name "Oregon." *American speech* 19:115-17, April 1944.

From Ouaricon on the Carte générale de Canada of Lahontan's Nouveaux voyages dans l'Amérique Septentrionale, 1709.

2531. Strozut, George G. Hayesville should have been named Stephensville. *Marion County history* 4:17-20, June 1958.

2532. Swing, William. St. Johns district gets name from hermit. *Portland Oregonian* Jan. 22, 1961.

James John, member of the Bidwell-Bartleson immigrant party of 1841, platted St. Johns, which won official city status in May 1865.

2533. Trumbull, James Hammond. Oregon, the origin and meaning of the name. *Magazine of American history* 3:36-38, Jan. 1879.

Suggests that Carver did not invent the name Oregon, but that he gave the Algonkin equivalent of the name by which he had reason to believe the tribes living near it designated in their unknown language their "Fair River" or "Belle Rivière."

2534. U.S. Board on Geographic Names. Decisions. No. 32—January 4, 1933. Crater Lake National Park, Oregon. Washington, Govt. Print. Off., 1934. 6p.

2535. U.S. Work Projects Administration. Pennsylvania. Geographic names in the coastal areas of California, Oregon and Washington. Comp. under the supervision of the Coast and Geodetic Survey. Washington, 1940. 94p.

2536. Wandering town settles at last. *Omaha world-herald* April 22, 1956.
Shevlin, Ore., a portable lumbering community, has now taken roots.

2537. Witter, Janet Waldrow. Place names in Clackamas County.
Thesis (M.S.) Reed College, 1962.

PENNSYLVANIA

2538. Ammon, John A. Internal Affairs Department aids in quest for derivation of Butler County school name. Pennsylvania. Dept. of Internal Affairs. Monthly bulletin v. 24, no. 6, p. 9-10, May 1956.
Moniteau, from Missouri.

2539. Another Levittown studies possibility of changing name. *New York times* Nov. 24, 1963, p. 24.
Action stems from success of Levittown, N.J., in changing its name to Willingboro.

2540. Beck, Herbert H. The San Domingo Creek, how it was named. Lancaster County Historical Society. Papers 54:63-64. 1950.
On Saunders Lovington, Negro immigrant from Santo Domingo, who died in Lititz, Pa., in 1844.

2541. Bertin, Eugene P. Origins of Lycoming County place names. *Now and then* 7:202-07, Jan. 1944.

2542. Buck, William J. An enquiry into the origin of the names of places in Bucks County. *American notes and queries* 1:88-95, March 1, 1857.

2543. Clark, John S. Selected manuscripts of General John S. Clark, relating to the aboriginal history of the Susquehanna, ed. by Louise Welles Murray. Athens, Pa., 1931. 150p. (Publications of the Society for Pennsylvania Archaeology, v. 1)
Bibliography: p. 133-35.
Contents: pt. I. The Carantouan sites of Champlain's "Voyages" and their identification. pt. II. The Andastes or Susquehannocks. pt. III. Indian names and Susquehannock forts.

2544. The "Commonwealth" and the "Keystone State." *Greater Pittsburgh* 32:9, Oct. 1950.
Why Pennsylvania is called the Keystone State and designated as a commonwealth.

2545. Davison, Elizabeth M. More about the naming of Wilkinsburg. *Western Pennsylvania historical magazine* 25:174-80, Sept.-Dec. 1942.

2546. Dedicates Curie Avenue. *New York times* Jan. 23, 1940, p. 22, col. 3.
Eve Curie dedicates a Philadelphia street to the memory of her parents.

2547. Demorest, Rose. Names of our streets. *Carnegie magazine* 27:27-28, Jan. 1953.
On the origin of the names of some Pittsburgh streets.

2548. Donehoo, George Patterson. The changing of historic place names; with an introduction and glossary of some historic names changed or misspelled in Pennsylvania, by Henry W. Shoemaker. Pub. under the auspices of the Pennsylvania Alpine Club. Altoona, Tribune Press, 1921. 14p.
"A protest against the unnecessary change of names of places. Includes a partial list of historic place names, changed or misspelled, in Pennsylvania."— Griffin.

2549. ——— A history of the Indian villages and place names in Pennsylvania, with numerous historical notes and references. With an introduction by the Hon. Warren K. Moorehead. Harrisburg, Telegraph Press, 1928. 290p.
Bibliography: p. 288-90.
Appendix A: Villages in New York, destroyed by Gen. Sullivan's army, during 1799.

2550. Dubbs, Paul M. Where to go and place-names of Centre County; a collection of articles from the Centre Daily Times, comp. and pub. during 1959-1960. State College, Pa., Centre Daily Times, 1961. 157p.
A listing and discussion of more than 300 place-names.

2551. Errett, Russell. Indian geographical names. *Magazine of western history* 2:51-59, 238-46, May, July 1885.
Names of Algonkin (principally Delaware) and Iroquois origin in Pennsylvania and Ohio. p. 51-59 deal principally with the river names Ohio and Allegheny.

2552. Espenshade, Abraham Howry. Pennsylvania place names. State College, Pa. Pennsylvania State College, 1925. 375p. (Pennsylvania State College. Studies in historical and political science, no. 1)
List of books consulted: p. 341-45.
Classified lists.
Review: *American speech* 1:451-52, May 1926; by Max Förster, *Zeitschrift für Ortsnamenforschung* 4:94-100. 1928.

2553. Fairclough, G. Thomas. The style of street names. *American speech* 33:299-300, Dec. 1958.
In Scranton, Pa., Street and Avenue are always used following the name. Refers to Jerome Rhodes's article, *ibid*. 33:116-17, May 1958.

2554. Feared "Slippery Rock." *New York times* July 27, 1939, p. 21, col. 7.
Motorists mistake Slippery Rock name sign for warning.

2555. Fenton, William N. Place names and related activities of the Cornplanter Senecas. *Pennsylvania archaeologist* 15:25-29, 42-50, 88-96, 108-18. 1945; 16: 42-57, April 1946.

2556. Franklin, Walter M. Impress of early names and traits. Lancaster County Historical Society. Papers 3:45-53. 1898.

2557. Fretz, A. Henry. Bucks County place names. Pennsylvania. Dept. of

Internal Affairs. Monthly bulletin 21:7-15, 29-32, Feb. 1953; 21:18-24, 29-32, March 1953; 21:23-32, April 1953; 21:26-31, May 1953; 21:31-32, June 1953.

2558. Froke, Marlowe D. & Warren G. Bodow. Pronunciation guide to place names in Pennsylvania. [Harrisburg] Pennsylvania Assoc. of Broadcasters, 1962. 86 l.

2559. Gordon, Thomas Francis. A gazetteer of the State of Pennsylvania. Part first, general description of the state; geological construction, canals and railroads, bridges, revenue, expenditures, public debt, &c. Part second, counties, towns, cities, villages, mountains, lakes, rivers, creeks, &c., alphabetically arranged. To which is added a table of all the post offices in the state, their distances from Washington and Harrisburg, and the names of the post masters. Philadelphia, T. Belknap, 1832. 508p.

2560. Grumbine, Lee Leight. The origin and significance of our township names. Lebanon County Historical Society. Historical papers and addresses 1:121-33. 1899.
  Also published separately.
  Lebanon County names.

2561. Hamilton, Hugh. Sir William Penn: his proprietary province and its counties; those of the Commonwealth of Pennsylvania, with the chronology, etymology, and genealogy of the counties. Retiring address of Hugh Hamilton, president (1919) of the Federation of Pennsylvania Historical Societies; delivered at Harrisburg, Pa., January 15th, 1920. Harrisburg, Press of Central Print. and Pub. House, 1920. 14p.

2562. Harding, Julia Morgan. Names of Pittsburgh streets, their historical significance; *In* Daughters of the American Revolution. Allegheny County, Pa. Fort Duquesne and Fort Pitt. n.p., Reed & Witting Press, 1907. p. 40-47.

2563. Heckewelder, John Gottlieb Ernestus. Names given by the Lenni Lenape or Delaware Indians to rivers, streams and places in the now states of New Jersey, Pennsylvania, Maryland, and Virginia. Pennsylvania German Folklore Society. Publications 5:1-41. 1940.
  Published also in American Philosophical Society. Transactions 4:351-96. 1834; Historical Society of Pennsylvania. Bulletin 1:121-35, 139-54, June, Sept. 1847; Moravian Historical Society. Transactions 1872:275-333; as a separate: Bethlehem, [Pa.], H. T. Claude, printer, 1872. 58p.; and in his A narrative of the mission of the United Brethren among the Delaware and Mohegan Indians. Cleveland, Burrows Bros., 1907. p. 523-66.

2564. Hobbs, Herrwood E. The origin of the names of towns and townships in Schuylkill County. Historical Society of Schuylkill County. Publications 6:43-53. 1947.

2565. Hotchkin, Samuel Fitch. A pocket gazetteer of Pennsylvania arranged by counties. Philadelphia, L. R. Hamersly & Co., 1887. 174p.

2566. Huidekoper, A. Indian and French history in western Pennsylvania. *Magazine of American history* 1:683-85, Nov. 1877.
  "The writer cites some of the changes in place-names in western Pennsylvania due to historical causes."—Price.

2567. Kenny, Hamill. Settling Laurel's business. *Names* 9:160-62, Sept. 1961.
The origin of Laurel in the Pennsylvania and West Virginia place-name Laurel Hill.

2568. McKirdy, James. Origin of the names given to the counties in Pennsylvania. *Western Pennsylvania historical magazine* 8:37-58, 104-19, 159-75, 235-56, Jan.-Oct. 1925.
Also published separately, 76p.
Bibliography: p. 74-76.

2569. MacReynolds, George. Place names in Bucks County, Pennsylvania, alphabetically arranged in an historical narrative. 2d ed. Doylestown, Bucks County Historical Society, 1955. 454p.
1st ed. 1942. 474p.
An 80p. pamphlet was issued to members of the Society in 1941 for suggestions and additions.

2570. Mahr, August C. How to locate Indian places on modern maps. *Ohio journal of science* 53:129-37, May 1953.
Delaware or Lenni Lenape Indian names for Pennsylvania localities, from Rev. Johannes Roth's diary, 1772.

2571. Martin, George Castor. Indian names of nearby streams. n.p., Martin & Allardyce, 1911. 4p.
Vicinity of Philadelphia.

2572. Maxwell, Hugh M. Mt. Gretna—origin of the name. Lebanon County Historical Society. Papers and addresses 2:100-03. 1901.

2573. Morley's "Conshohockens" make Conshohocken mad. *New York times* Nov. 26, 1939, p. 38, col. 7.
Citizens protest use of name as expletive in Christopher Morley's book Kitty Foyle.

2574. Morton, John S. A history of the origin of the appellation Keystone State, as applied to the Commonwealth of Pennsylvania; together with extracts from many authorities relative to the adoption of the Declaration of Independence. To which is appended the new constitution of Pennsylvania. Philadelphia, Claxton, Remsen & Haffelfinger, 1874. 190p.
A compilation of newspaper articles and other material in relation to the theory that Pennsylvania was called the Keystone State from the fact that, by the casting vote of one of her delegates in the Continental Congress (John Morton), the unanimous adoption of the Declaration of Independence was secured.

2575. The Naming of Obelisk. Historical Society of Montgomery County. Bulletin 6:177-78, April 1948.

2576. Origin of Delaware County names. Delaware County Historical Society. Bulletin 10:2, Nov. 1957; 11:2, Jan. 1958.
Names of farms or country houses in the neighborhood of Philadelphia.

2577. Origin of some Somerset County names. Pennsylvania. Dept. of Internal Affairs. Monthly bulletin 10:31-32, Nov. 1942.

2578. Pearce, Ruth L. Welsh place-names in southeastern Pennsylvania. *Names* 11:31-43, March 1963.

2579. Pennsylvania. Historical Society. Historical map of Pennsylvania, showing the Indian names of streams, and villages, and paths of travel; the sites of old forts and battle-fields; the successive purchases from the Indians; and the names and dates of counties and county towns; with tables of forts and proprietary manors; ed. by P. W. Sheafer and others. Philadelphia, Historical Society of Pennsylvania, 1875. 26p.

2580. Pennsylvania. State Geographic Board. Decisions, 1923-1926. Altoona, Times Tribune Press, 1926. 8p.
   List of changes, compiled by G. H. Ashley, the Secretary, in April 1926, was published in *American speech* 21:163-64, Dec. 1926.

2581. Pennsylvania. State University. Dept. of Agricultural Economics and Rural Sociology. Alphabetical listing of cities and towns of Pennsylvania and their county locations. University Park, 1961. 38p.

2582. Pennsylvania Historical Review. Gazetteer, post-office, express and telegraph guide. City of Philadelphia. Leading merchants and manufacturers. New York, Historical Pub. Co., 1886. 292p.

2583. Pinkowski, Edward. Chester County place names. Rev. and enl. Philadelphia, Sunshine Press, 1962. 288p.
   1st ed. 1955. 230p.

2584. Prowell, George R. Pennsylvania county names. *Magazine of history* 10:130-36, Sept. 1909; 12:210-19, Oct. 1910; 19:231-38, Dec. 1914.
   Concluded in 24:234-35, May-June 1917 by Joel N. Eno.

2585. Randel, William Peirce. The place names of Tioga County, Pennsylvania. *American speech* 14:181-90, Oct. 1939.

2586. Roberts, Charles R. Place names of Lehigh County and their origin. Lehigh County Historical Society. Annual proceedings 1936:5-12.

2587. Roberts, John M. & Son, Pittsburgh. The story behind the names of western Pennsylvania counties. Pittsburgh, 1948. 55p.
   Reprinted from advertisements in the *Pittsburgh sun-telegraph.*

2588. Russ, William A., Jr. The export of Pennsylvania place names. *Pennsylvania history* 15:194-214, July 1948.
   On the transplanting of Pennsylvania names to the South and West, as a result of the Delaware migration (*ca.* 1765).

2589. Scott, Joseph. A geographical description of Pennsylvania; also of the counties respectively; in the order in which they were established by the Legislature. With an alphabetical list of the townships in each county; and their population in 1800. Philadelphia, Printed by Robert Cochran, 1806. 147p.

2590. Shain, Samson A. Old Testament place names in Berks and neighboring counties. *Historical review of Berks County* 28:51-52, Spring 1963.

2591. ——— Old Testament place names in Lancaster County. Lancaster County Historical Society. Journal 67:184-93, Autumn 1963.
A chapter in book Rabbi Shain is writing on Old Testament place-names in Pennsylvania.

2592. Shoemaker, Henry Wharton. Place names and altitudes of Pennsylvania mountains, an address at the quarterly meeting of the Wyoming Historical and Geological Society, Wilkes-Barre, Pennsylvania, Friday evening, March 9, 1923. Altoona, Times Tribune Press, 1923. 15p.

2593. Spieler, Gerhard G. Pennsylvania Dutch place names. *Pennsylvania Dutchman* 5:5-6, Nov. 1953.

2594. Township names in Delaware County. Delaware County Historical Society. Bulletin 11:[2], March 1958.

2595. U.S. 88th Congress, 1st session. House. A bill to designate the reservoir on the Shenango River above Sharpsville, Pennsylvania, as the George Mahaney Reservoir. H. R. 7368. July 1, 1963. Washington, 1963. 1p.
Introduced by Mr. Weaver and referred to the Committee on Public Works.

2596. Ward, Townsend. Suggestions regarding the production of a correct geographical and historical map of Pennsylvania. Philadelphia, 1875. 7p.
Includes Indian names.

RHODE ISLAND

2597. Best, Mary Agnes. The town that saved a state, Westerly. Westerly, Utter Co., 1943. 283p.
Some general comments on diversity of opinion about the naming of Rhode Island, p. 42-43.

2598. Bicknell, Thomas Williams. Place names in Rhode Island; *In his* The history of the state of Rhode Island and Providence Plantations. New York, American Historical Society, 1920. 3:1200-09.
Includes Indian names, p. 1207-09.

2599. Brigham, Clarence Saunders. Seventeenth century place-names of Providence Plantations, 1639-1700. Providence, 1903. 28p.
Reprinted from Rhode Island Historical Society. Collections 10:373-400. 1902.

2600. Chapin, Howard M. Glocester, R.I. Rhode Island Historical Society. Collections 26:64-65, April 1933.
Why it is spelled without the "u."

2601. Clapp, Roger Tillinghast. How Acid Factory Brook got its name. *Rhode Island history* 5:97-104, Oct. 1946.

2602. Cocumcussoc. Rhode Island Historical Society. Collections 28:25, Jan. 1935.

Meaning of the word as contained in a letter from William B. Cabot which appeared in the *Evening bulletin* of Oct. 3, 1934.

2603. Colorful town not on map. *Lincoln (Neb.) evening journal* Oct. 21, 1959, p. 19i.
Colorful names in the township of Richmond, which itself does not appear on a map.

2604. Gannett, Henry. A geographic dictionary of Rhode Island. Washington, Govt. Print. Off., 1894. 31p. (U.S. Geological Survey. Bulletin no. 115)
Issued also as House miscellaneous doc. v. 27, 53d Cong., 2d sess.

2605. Haley, John Williams. "The Old Stone Bank" history of Rhode Island. Providence, Providence Institution for Savings, 1944. 4:205-10.
Streets and squares of Providence.

2606. Howland, Benjamin B. The streets of Newport, R.I. *Magazine of New England history* 2:77-93, April 1892.

2607. The Influence of birds on Rhode Island nomenclature. Rhode Island Historical Society. Collections 31:72-75, July 1938.

2608. Kohl, J. G. How Rhode Island was named. *Magazine of American history* 9:81-93, Feb. 1883.

2609. List of Indian and other names of places. Rhode Island Historical Society. Collections 3:302-07. 1835.

2610. The Meaning of Indian place names. Rhode Island Historical Society. Collections 22:33-38, April 1929.
An interview with William B. Cabot.
"Notes regarding Algonquin place names in Rhode Island."—Griffin.

2611. Miner, George L. The possible origin of the name Point Judith. Rhode Island Historical Society. Collections 13:103-04, July 1920.
On the possibility of Roger Williams having named the point after Lady Judith Barrington.

2612. Mussolini Street in retreat. *New York times* Jan. 11, 1942, p. 14, col. 6.
Providence considers renaming Mussolini St. Russo St.

2613. The Name Rhode Island. Rhode Island Historical Society. Collections 20:81, July 1927.

2614. Parsons, Charles W. Town-names in Rhode Island. Rhode Island Historical Society. Proceedings 1886-87:42-51.

2615. Parsons, Usher. Indian names of places in Rhode-Island: collected by Usher Parsons, M.D., for the R.I. Historical Society. Providence, Knowles, Anthony & Co., printers, 1861. 32p.
Narraganset names.

2616. Pease, John Chauncey & John Milton Niles. A gazetteer of the states of Connecticut and Rhode-Island. Written with care and impartiality, from original and authentic materials. Consisting of two parts. With an accurate and improved map of each state. Hartford, Printed and pub. by William S. Marsh, 1819. 389p.

2617. Preston, Howard W. Providence street names. Rhode Island Historical Society. Collections 20:69-79, July 1927.
   Lists established 1772 and 1805.

2618. Rhode Island Historical Society. Committee on Rhode Island Geographical and Historic Names in the Indian Language. Report on Indian names in Rhode Island. Rhode Island Historical Society. Proceedings 1890-91:71-79.
   Proposes general rules for the application, spelling, pronunciation, etc. of Indian names.

2619. Rider, Sidney Smith. The lands of Rhode Island as they were known to Caunounicus and Miantunnomu when Roger Williams came in 1636. An Indian map of the principal locations known to the Nahigansets and elaborate historical notes. Providence, The Author, 1904. 297p.
   Concerning the Indian names of places on these lands and the meanings of the same, p. 45-58.

2620. ——— Sowams, now Warren, the first Indian name of a location known to the Plymouth settlers, 16th of March, 1620-1. *Book notes, consisting of literary gossip, criticisms of books and local historical matters connected with Rhode Island* 23:57-63, 65-70, 73-79, 81-87, 97, April 7-June 16, 1906.

2621. Stevens, Mana Lyman. Newport streets. Newport Historical Society. Bulletin 67:1-13, Dec. 1928.

2622. Tooker, William Wallace. Indian geographic names, and why we should study them, illus. by some Rhode Island examples. Rhode Island Historical Society. Publications n.s. 5:203-15, Jan. 1898.

2623. Trumbull, James Hammond. Indian local names in Rhode Island. *Book notes, consisting of literary gossip, criticisms of books and local historical matters connected with Rhode Island* 29:65-68, April 27, 1912.

2624. Tyler, Clarice E. Topographical terms in the seventeenth century records of Connecticut and Rhode Island. *New England quarterly* 2:383-401, July 1929.
   "These terms provide some interesting illustrations of changes in the English language."—Griffin.

2625. U.S. Board on Geographic Names. Official gazetteer of Rhode Island. Comp. by the Rhode Island Geographic Board in cooperation with the United States Geographic Board. Washington, U.S. Govt. Print. Off., 1932. 95p.
   Includes names recommended for adoption as well as obsolete ones.
   Review: *New York times* Jan. 9, 1933, p. 18, col. 3-4.

SOUTH CAROLINA

2626. Bonham, Milledge Louis. Notes on place names. *American speech* 1:625, Aug. 1926.
   In South Carolina and Louisiana.

2627. Cohen, Hennig. A colonial topographical poem. *Names* 1:252-58, Dec. 1953.
A study of the South Carolina place-names, especially rivers, mentioned in the poem "C. W. in Carolina to E. J. at Gosport."

2628. Cumming, William Patterson. Naming Carolina. *North Carolina historical review* 22:34-42, Jan. 1945.
Part of a study made with the aid of a grant from the Social Science Research Council.

2629. Derrick, Barbara. A name for a state. *South Carolina magazine* 13:12, 23-24, Aug. 1950.
Origin of Palmetto State, 1776.

2630. Gatschet, Albert Samuel. Onomatology of the Catawba River basin. *American anthropologist* n.s. 4:52-56, Jan.-March 1902.
Also issued as a separate.

2631. Names in South Carolina. v. 1- . 1954- .
Editor: Claude Henry Neuffer.
Published by the Dept. of English, University of South Carolina. v. 1 consists of no. 1, Spring 1954 and no. 2, Winter 1954; v. 2, 1955 to date, each volume consists of one number, dated Winter.
Material on the geographic names of the state.

2632. Smith, Henry A. M. Some forgotten towns in lower South Carolina. *South Carolina historical and genealogical magazine* 14:134-46, July 1913.

2633. U.S. Writers' Program. South Carolina. Palmetto place names. Comp. by workers of the Writers' Program of the Work Projects Administration in the State of South Carolina. Sponsored and pub. by the South Carolina Education Association. Columbia, Sloane Print. Co., 1941. 158p.

2634. Ware, Owen. How Montmorenci got its name. *South Carolina magazine* 12:34-35, Feb. 1949.
"Story of Count Achille de Caradeux in the Vale of Montmorency (formerly Conway's Valley) S.C., from 1840 to some time before 1870, and the subsequent renaming of the village of Pole Cat."—Writings on American history.

SOUTH DAKOTA

2635. Black Hills names. *South Dakota historical collections* 6:273-74. 1912.
A letter from Valentine T. McGillycuddy, dated 1908, explaining the origin of many names in the Black Hills region, reprinted from the *Rapid City journal*.

2636. Colorful names in Black Hills originated in days of frontier gold rush. *Christian Science monitor* July 11, 1952, p. 6-C.

2637. Diller, Aubrey. Pawnee House: Ponca House. *Mississippi Valley historical review* 36:301-04, Sept. 1949.
Missouri River trading post, 1790's.

2638. Distad, Lucile. A study of place names in Mellette County, South Dakota.
Thesis (M.A.) Univ. of South Dakota, 1943.

2639. Frybarger, Marjorie L. A study of place-names in Meade County, South
Dakota.
Thesis (M.A.) Univ. of South Dakota, 1941.

2640. Gilmore, Melvin Randolph. Meaning of the word Dakota. *American anthropologist* n.s. 24:242-45, April-June 1922.
The author considers Dakota to be a derivative of the same root as the Omaha
endakutha, and he believes that both words should be taken in the sense of a "peculiar people" rather than in the sense of "friends."

2641. Hanson, Agnes J. A study of place-names in Kingbury County, South
Dakota.
Thesis (M.A.) Univ. of South Dakota, 1940.

2642. Harlow, Dana D. A study of place-names in Spink County, South Dakota.
Thesis (M.A.) Univ. of South Dakota, 1944.

2643. Holland, Ann J. A study of place-names in Sanborn County, South Dakota.
Thesis (M.S.) Univ. of South Dakota, 1942.

2644. Hutcheson, Floyd E. A study of place-names in Davison County, South
Dakota.
Thesis (M.A.) Univ. of South Dakota, 1944.

2645. James, Leta May. A study of place-names in Beadle County, South Dakota.
Thesis (M.A.) Univ. of South Dakota, 1939.

2646. Jones, Mildred McEwen. Supplement [Derivation of local place names];
In her Early Beadle County, 1879 to 1900. Huron, S.D., 1961. p. 97-104.

2647. Kleinsasser, Anna. A study of place-names in Charles Mix County, South
Dakota.
Thesis (M.A.) Univ. of South Dakota, 1938.

2648. Molumby, Joseph A. A study of place-names in Clark County, South
Dakota.
Thesis (M.A.) Univ. of South Dakota, 1939.

2649. Mundt, Karl E. Two Mobridges in two states. U.S. Congress. Congressional record 105:16816-17, Sept. 7, 1959.
South Dakota, and new town in Montana. Includes origin of name.

2650. Place names and post offices. *Wi-iyohi* (South Dakota Historical Society)
6:1-6, April 1952; 6:3-6, May 1952; 6:3-6, June 1952; 6:3-6, July 1952; 6:3-6,
Aug. 1952.
List of more than 1900 early South Dakota post offices, with location in a present county, date of founding, and the first and last date the name was found on a
map.

2651. Snyder, Mary P. A study of place-names in Turner County, South Dakota.
Thesis (M.A.) Univ. of South Dakota, 1940.

2652. South Dakota. Legislature. Legislative manual. 190?- . [Pierre].
Some issues compiled by Dept. of Finance.
Each issue contains a list of county names with origin of name.

2653. U.S. 88th Congress, 1st session. Senate. A bill to change the name of
Fort Randall Reservoir in the State of South Dakota to Lake Francis Case. S. 130.
Jan. 14 (legislative day, Jan. 9), 1963. Washington, 1963. 1p.
Introduced by Mr. Mundt and referred to the Committee on Public Works.
In honor of the late Senator of South Dakota.
Subsequent documents relating to this bill were published as follows:

U.S. 88th Congress, 1st session. Senate. Changing the name of Fort Randall
Reservoir, Missouri River, S. Dak., to Lake Francis Case. Report no. 266, to
accompany S. 130. June 19, 1963. Calendar no. 247. Washington, 1963. 3p.
Submitted by Mr. McNamara, from the Committee on Public Works, without
amendment.

—— [Reprint of the original bill, June 19, 1963, to accompany the report.
Report no. 266 and Calendar no. 247 added]. 1p.

U.S. 88th Congress, 1st session. House. An act to change the name of Fort
Randall Reservoir in the State of South Dakota to Lake Francis Case. S. 130.
In the House of Representatives June 24, 1963. Washington, 1963. 1p.
Referred to the Committee on Public Works. Passed the Senate June 20, 1963.

—— Changing the name of Fort Randall Reservoir, Missouri River, S. Dak.,
to Lake Francis Case. Report no. 567, to accompany S. 130. July 22, 1963.
Washington, 1963. 3p.
Submitted by Mr. Davis, from the Committee on Public Works, without amendment.

—— [Reprint of the act, July 22, 1963, to accompany the report. Report
no. 567 and House Calendar no. 107 added]. 1p. An identical bill was introduced
in the House as follows:

U.S. 88th Congress, 1st session. House. A bill to change the name of Fort Ran-
dall Reservoir in the State of South Dakota to Lake Francis Case. H. R. 1578.
Jan. 10, 1963. Washington, 1963. 1p.
Introduced by Mr. Berry and referred to the Committee on Public Works.

2654. U.S. 88th Congress, 1st session. Senate. A bill to change the name of the
Big Bend Reservoir in the State of South Dakota to Lake Sharpe. S. 131. Jan. 14
(legislative day, Jan. 9), 1963. Washington, 1963. 1p.
Introduced by Mr. Mundt and referred to the Committee on Public Works.
In honor of M. Q. Sharpe, the late Governor of South Dakota.
Subsequent documents relating to this bill were published as follows:

U.S. 88th Congress, 1st session. Senate. Changing the name of Big Bend Reservoir, S. Dak., to Lake Sharpe. Report no. 269, to accompany S. 131. June 19,
1963. Calendar no. 250. Washington, 1963. 3p.
Submitted by Mr. McNamara, from the Committee on Public Works, without
amendment.

—— [Reprint of the original bill, June 19, 1963, to accompany the report.
Report no. 269 and Calendar no. 250 added]. 1p.

U.S. 88th Congress, 1st session. House. An act to change the name of the Big
Bend Reservoir in the State of South Dakota to Lake Sharpe. S. 131. In the

House of Representatives June 24, 1963. Washington, 1963. 1p.
Referred to the Committee on Public Works. Passed the Senate June 20, 1963.

—— Changing the name of Big Bend Reservoir, S. Dak., to Lake Sharpe.
Report no. 568, to accompany S. 131. July 22, 1963. Washington, 1963. 3p.
Submitted by Mr. Davis, from the Committee on Public Works, without amendment.

—— [Reprint of the act, July 22, 1963, to accompany the report. Report no.
568 and House Calendar no. 108 added]. 1p.
An identical bill was introduced in the House as follows:

U.S. 88th Congress, 1st session. House. A bill to change the name of the Big
Bend Reservoir in the State of South Dakota to Lake Sharpe. H. R. 1577, Jan.
10, 1963. Washington, 1963. 1p.
Introduced by Mr. Berry and referred to the Committee on Public Works.

2655. U.S. Writers' Program. South Dakota. South Dakota place names, enl.
and rev. Comp. by workers of the Writers' Program of the Work Projects Administration in the State of South Dakota. Sponsored by the Department of English,
University of South Dakota. Vermillion, Univ. of South Dalota, 1941. 689p.
Bibliography: p. 679-84.
A preliminary series of six pamphlets was issued in 1940. These, with corrections and additions, together with new material, form the one-volume edition of
the complete work.
More than 6000 place-names are treated topically.
The project was supervised by Dr. Edward C. Ehrensperger, Head of the English
Dept., who also conducted the graduate research program at the University.

TENNESSEE

2656. Bible, Jean. Town named for first lady. Dandridge, Tenn., bears Martha
Washington's maiden name. *New York times* June 11, 1961, p. XX 13.

2657. Chase, Carroll & Richard McP. Cabeen. The first hundred years of United
States territorial postmarks, 1787-1887. Territory of the United States south of
the River Ohio. *American philatelist* 58:203-07, Dec. 1944.
Includes list of post offices, with notes on the proposed state of Franklin and
some names.

2658. Coppock, Paul R. History in Memphis street names. West Tennessee
Historical Society. Papers 11:93-111. 1957.

2659. Fink, Paul M. Smoky Mountains history as told in place-names. East
Tennessee Historical Society. Publications 6:3-11. 1934.

2660. —— Some east Tennessee place names. Tennessee Folklore Society.
Bulletin 7:40-50, Dec. 1941.

2661. —— That's why they call it... The names and lore of the Great Smokies.
Jonesboro, Tenn., P. M. Fink, 1956. 20p.

2662. —— & Myron H. Avery. The nomenclature of the Great Smoky Mountains. East Tennessee Historical Society. Publications 9:53-64. 1937.
An abstracted account under the title Arnold Guyot's explorations in the Great Smokies, in *Appalachia* 2:253-61, Dec. 1936.
A major portion of the names either originated with or were confirmed as a result of Arnold Guyot's exploration of the region in the period 1856-1860.

2663. Flowers, Paul. Place names in Tennessee. West Tennessee Historical Society. Papers 14:113-23. 1960.

2664. Irwin, Ned. The legend of Eve Mills. Tennessee Folklore Society. Bulletin 14:28-30, June 1948.
Monroe County.

2665. McWhorter, A. W. Classical place names in Tennessee. *Word study* 9:7-8, Nov. 1933.

2666. Martin, Daniel S. A guide to street naming and property numbering. Nashville, Tennessee State Planning Commission, 1951. 47p. (Publication no. 230)

2667. Mason, Robert L. A famous landmark is in dispute, two states contend over changing the name of Mt. Collins. *New York times* Aug. 31, 1930, sec. 8, p. 9, col. 2-4.
Mount Kephart desired for peak in Smoky Mountains National Park, but U.S. Board on Geographical Names refused.

2668. Montgomery, James R. The nomenclature of the upper Tennessee River. East Tennessee Historical Society. Publications 28:46-57. 1956.

2669. Morris, Eastin. The Tennessee gazetteer, or topographical dictionary; containing a description of the several counties, towns, etc. To which is prefixed a general description of the state, and a condensed history from the earliest settlements down to the convention in 1834. With an appendix, containing a list of the practising attorneys at law in each county; principal officers of the general and state governments; times of holding courts; and other valuable tables. Nashville, W. H. Hunt & Co., 1834. 178p.

2670. Patton, Eugene E. First territory named for Washington. *D. A. R. magazine* 86:139-40, 251, Feb. 1952.
Washington District, N.C. (the later State of Tennessee), established Dec. 3, 1776.

2671. Peak named for Cammerer, Smoky Mountain ridge also honors Park director. *New York times* Feb. 25, 1942, p. 24, col. 2.
Great Smoky Mountains National Park peak named for Arno B. Cammerer.

2672. Swint, Henry Lee. Ezekiel Birdseye and the free state of Frankland. *Tennessee historical quarterly* 3:226-36, Sept. 1944.
Proposals for creating a new nonslave state, to be called Frankland, from the mountain counties of Tennessee, Virginia, North Carolina, and Georgia.

2673. Tennessee blue book. Nashville, Secretary of State.
The origin of county names—a section in each issue 1961-62 to date, including the Special edition for young readers.

2674. U.S. Board on Geographic Names. Decisions. No. 28—June 30, 1932. Great Smoky Mountains National Park, North Carolina and Tennessee. Washington, Govt. Print. Off., 1934. 46p.

2675. U.S. 88th Congress, 1st session. Senate. A bill to change the name of the lake formed by Kentucky Dam. S. 462. Jan. 23 (legislative day, Jan. 15), 1963. Washington, 1963. 2p.
Introduced by Mr. Kefauver and Mr. Gore and referred to the Committee on Public Works.
To change the name from Kentucky Lake to Tennessee-Kentucky Lake.
An identical bill was introduced in the House as follows:

U.S. 88th Congress, 1st session. House. A bill to change the name of the lake formed by Kentucky Dam. H. R. 4254. Feb. 26, 1963. Washington, 1963. 2p.
Introduced by Mr. Murray and referred to the Committee on Public Works.

2676. Williams, Samuel C. The first territorial division named for Washington. *Tennessee historical magazine* n.s. 2:153-64, April 1932.
Priority of the County of Washington, N.C. (now in the State of Tennessee) as the first locality in the United States to bear the name of Washington.

TEXAS

2677. Aarts, Dorothy. Ghost towns of the republic of Texas. n.p., 1939. 22p.
Bibliography: p. 5.

2678. "Abused Spanish" place names in Texas. *American speech* 19:238, Oct. 1944.
Signed C. D. P.
Bunavista, Tex., a name which is a "fermentation of petroleum industry and abused Spanish."

2679. Anderson, John Q. From Flygap to Whybark: some unusual Texas place names. Texas Folklore Society. Publications 31:73-98. 1962.
Bibliography: p. 95-98.

2680. ——— Texas stream names. Texas Folklore Society. Publications 32: 112-47. 1964.
Bibliography: p. 132-34.

2681. Benson, Nettie Lee. San Saba. *Southwestern historical quarterly* 51:88-89, July 1947.

2682. Bolton, Herbert Eugene. The native tribes about the East Texas missions. Texas State Historical Association. Quarterly 11:249-52, April 1908.
Full treatment of the name Texas.

2683. Bryson, Artemisia Baer. Contrasting American names compared with the Spanish names found in Texas. *American speech* 3:436, June 1928.

2684. Cameron, Minnie B. County of Bexar. *Southwestern historical quarterly*

53:477-79, April 1950.
Corrects material in correspondence of Mrs. Cameron, *ibid.* 49:275, Oct. 1946.

2685. Carlisle, Mrs. George F. The origin of some of the Dallas street names. Local History & Genealogical Society [Bulletin] 3:16, May 1957.

2686. Curtis, Albert. Fabulous San Antonio. San Antonio, Naylor, 1955. San Antonio street names: p. 280-87.

2687. Davis, Jeff. Around the plaza. *San Antonio light* June 9, 1936. A newspaper article on curious geographical names in Texas.

2688. Dienst, Alex. The naming of Metheglin Creek, Bell County. Texas Folklore Society. Publications 3:208-09. 1924.

2689. Dobie, James Frank. How the Brazos River got its name. Texas Folklore Society. Publications 3:209-17. 1924.

2690. —— Stories in Texas names. *Southwest review* 21:125-36, 278-94, 411-17, Jan., April, July 1936.
Also in Texas Folk-lore Society. Publications 13:1-78. 1937.
Sources: p. 70-78.
"Folk origins of many Texas place names."—*American speech.*

2691. Edwards, Roy. Cut 'n Shoot, Texas. *Western folklore* 18:33-34, Jan. 1959.
Legends about this name, not a town, but a community and a state of mind.

2692. Emmett, Chris. Shanghai Pierce: a fair likeness. Norman, Univ. of Oklahoma Press, 1953. 326p.
There shall be no town naming to the exclusion of my perpetuity: p. 110-18.
Railroad stations named for members of the Telferner, Hungerford, and Pierce families.

2693. Fulmore, Zachary Taylor. The history and geography of Texas as told in county names. Rev. ed. Austin, S. R. Fulmore, 1926. 225p.
1st ed. 1915. 312p.

2694. —— —— Austin, Steck Co., 1935. 312p. (Original narratives of Texas history and adventure)
A facsimile reproduction of the original edition of 1915.

2695. Gannett, Henry. A gazetteer of Texas. 2d ed. Washington, Govt. Print. Off., 1904. 177p. (U.S. Geological Survey. Bulletin no. 224. Series F, Geography, 36)
1st ed. 1902. 162p. (Bulletin no. 190. Series F, Geography, 28)

2696. Geiser, Samuel Wood. Ghost-towns and lost-towns of Texas, 1840-1880. *Texas geographic magazine* 8:9-20, Spring 1944.
Works cited: p. 20.
Lists more than a thousand ghost towns.

2697. Gibson, Freda. Local place names. West Texas Historical and Scientific Society. Publications 1:37-41. 1926. (Sul Ross State Teachers College. Bulletin 21)

2698. Glasgow, William J. On the confusion caused by the name El Paso. *Pass-word* (El Paso Historical Society) 1:65-67, May 1956.

2699. Gray, Glenn Arthur. Gazetteer of streams of Texas. Washington, Govt. Print. Off., 1919. 267p. (U.S. Geological Survey. Water-supply paper 448)

2700. The Handbook of Texas. Walter Prescott Webb, editor-in-chief, H. Bailey Carroll, managing editor, Llerena B. Friend, Mary Joe Carroll, Louise Nolen, editorial assistants. Austin, Texas State Historical Assoc., 1952. 2v.
Includes origin of name and other information about many Texas place-names (arranged alphabetically).

2701. Hayes, Robert M. East Texas miscellany. *Dallas morning news* July 8, 1960, sec. I, p. 15.
Texas town names: Slocum, Cash, and Po-Boy.

2702. Haynes, Harry. Death of early towns in Washington County: what changes time has wrought. *Dallas morning news* Aug. 17, 1902, p. 4, col. 4-5.

2703. ——— Towns gone: some places in Washington County of which nothing but dim memory remains, the sites even having been lost. *Dallas morning news* Sept. 12, 1902, p. 6, col. 6-7.

2704. ——— Towns of Washington County: origin, date and reason of establishment, and how the names were suggested. *Dallas morning news* Sept. 1, 1902, p. 6, col. 6-7.

2705. Hill, Frank P. Plains names. *Panhandle-Plains historical review* 10:36-47. 1937.
Bibliography: p. 47.

2706. Hill, Robert T. Descriptive topographic terms of Spanish America. *National geographic magazine* 7:291-302, Sept. 1896.
Prepared for reports to Director of U.S. Geological Survey on geography of Texas-New Mexico region.
Topographical features as protuberances or mountain forms, plains, declivities, streams, and stream valleys.

2707. Home city has Nimitz Parkway. *New York times* Dec. 24, 1944, p. 18, col. 3. Fredericksburg, Tex., street named for Admiral Chester W. Nimitz.

2708. King, Dick. Ghost towns of Texas. San Antonio, Naylor, 1953. 140p.

2709. Knight, Ona. Street names of Palestine. *Junior historian* (Texas) 9:19-21, 23, March 1949.
Sketches of persons after whom streets were named.

2710. McCampbell, Coleman. Texas history as revealed by town and community name origins. *Southwestern historical quarterly* 58:91-97, July 1954.
A sampling of names taken from The handbook of Texas. Austin, Texas State Historical Assoc., 1952. 2v.

2711. McGregor, Stuart. Spanish-named Texas streams. *Dallas news* March 29, 1961, p. 3.

2712. Madison, Virginia & Hallie Stillwell. How come it's culled that? Place names in the Big Bend country. Albuquerque, Univ. of New Mexico Press, 1958. 129p.

2713. —— Place names in the Big Bend of Texas. *Western folklore* 14:200-05, July 1955.

2714. Martin, George Castor. Some Texas stream and place names. San Antonio, N. Brook, 1947. 15p.

2715. Massengill, Fred I. Texas towns; origin of name and location of each of the 2,148 post offices in Texas. An interesting compilation of nomenclature running the whole gamut of human interest and sympathies, including religion, history, sports, ranch life and personalities all properly classified for your convenience, entertainment and to add to the sum total of useful knowledge. Terrell, Tex., 1936. 222p.

2716. Morgan, Paul. Texas ballads and other verses. Dallas, Tardy Pub. Co., 1934. 173p.
    Introduction (place names of Texas): p. 9-51.

2717. Norvell, Claudia W. Texas. Author's ed. Dallas, Southwest Press, 1933. 79p.
    A search for the meaning of the name Texas through a study of the Indians of Texas.

2718. Origin of the name of Texas. *Magazine of American history* 7:67, 149, July, Aug. 1881; 8:145-46, 158, 167, Feb., March 1882.
    "A discussion of the source and significance of the name with various interpretations by different authors."—Price.

2719. Origins of names of Texas cities, towns, mountains, rivers and physiographic divisions. Texas almanac and state industrial guide 1936:109-18.
    A revision and amplification of a list of cities and towns published in Texas almanac 1926:338-46.

2720. Payne, L. W., Jr. How medicine mounds of Hardeman County got their names. Texas Folk-lore Society. Publications 3:207-08. 1924.

2721. —— Indian Bluff on Canadian River. Texas Folk-lore Society. Publications 3:205-06. 1924.
    Legend in name.

2722. Pope, Harold Clay. The lighter side of Texas place naming. *Western folklore* 13:125-29, April 1954.

2723. —— Western history in Texas names. *True West* 3:29-31, Sept.-Oct. 1955.

2724. Price, Armstrong. Place names in Texas. *Texas geographic magazine* 8:31-34, Autumn 1944.

2725. Sanders, John Barnette. The postoffices and post masters of Nacogdoches County, Texas, 1845-1930. Center, Tex., 1964. 12p.

2726. ———— The postoffices and post masters of Panola County, Texas, 1845-1930. Center, Tex., 1964. 12p.

2727. ———— The postoffices and post masters of Sabine County, Texas, 1845-1930. Center, Tex., 1964. 7p.

2728. ———— The postoffices and post masters of San Augustine County, Texas, 1845-1930. Center, Tex., 1964. 6p.

2729. ———— The postoffices and post masters of Shelby County, Texas, 1845-1930. Center, Tex., 1964. 16p.

2730. Sebree, Mac. What's in a name? Just about everything. *Austin (Tex.) statesman* Feb. 14, 1959, p. 3.
How U.S. oil fields get their names; picturesque examples.

2731. Smith, Victor J. How Dead Horse Canyon got its name. Texas Folk-lore Society. Publications 3:209. 1924.

2732. Somes, Evelyn. Some place names and Mexican superstitions of the Balmorhea neighborhood. West Texas Historical and Scientific Society. Publications 2:53-54. 1928. (Sul Ross State Teachers College. Bulletin, extra no., Jan. 1, 1928)

2733. Sperry, Omer E. Place names. West Texas Historical and Scientific Society. Publications 8:18-22. 1938. (Sul Ross State Teachers College. Bulletin v. 19, no. 4)
Within area of proposed Big Bend National Park.

2734. Strecker, John Kern. Animals and streams; a contribution to the study of Texas folk names. Waco, Tex., Baylor Univ., 1929. 23p. (Contributions to folklore, no. 2)

2735. Strickland, Rex W. Ghost towns of Texas. *Southwestern historical quarterly* 47:410, April 1944.

2736. Texas towns of historic interest that have been abandoned or remain small towns today. "Ghost" towns and "lost" towns. Texas almanac and state industrial guide 1936:119-24.

2737. Tilloson, Cyrus. Place names of Nueces County. *Frontier times* 26:175-78, April 1949.

2738. Tolbert, Frank X. At "Sanphilop" by the Brazos. *Dallas morning news* Oct. 25, 1959, sec. III, p. 1.
Pronunciation of Sanfelipe.—*American speech.*

2739. ———— Dialogue heard in city of Cuney. *Dallas morning news* Oct. 30, 1960, p. I-18.
"The all-Negro town of Cuney was named for Norris Wright Cuney, Negro Republican leader."—*American speech.*

2740. ———— Earl of Clarendon inspired the name? *Dallas morning news* July

11, 1961, sec. IV, p. 1.
Origin of the name Clarendon.—*American speech*.

2741. —— Last rail stop on way to Hades. *Dallas morning news* Feb. 10, 1959, sec. 4.
The Texas place-names Ditty-Waw-Ditty and Cheesy (Chiesa).

2742. —— Nixon, Kennedy look good to Little Hope. *Dallas morning news* Oct. 30, 1960, p. I-15.
"On the name of the Texas town, Little Hope."—*American speech*.

2743. —— A phantom fort in Jones County. *Dallas morning news* Nov. 8, 1960, sec. 4, p. 1.
The origin of the name of Fort Phantom Hill, Texas.—*American speech*.

2744. —— Why does Montell always count 75? *Dallas morning news* April 24, 1961, sec. IV, p. 1.
On the Texas town named after Captain Charles S. de Montel.—*American speech*.

2745. Town renamed Truman; was Mesquite Tap, Texas. *New York times* Nov. 23, 1945, p. 9, col. 2.

2746. Two place-name pronunciations. *American speech* 4:156-57, Dec. 1928.
Staunton, Va., and Houston, Tex.

2747. U.S. 88th Congress, 1st session. House. A bill to designate the McGee Bend Dam and Reservoir on the Angelina River, Texas, as the Sam Rayburn Dam and Reservoir. H. R. 7594. July 16, 1963. Washington, 1963. 1p.
Introduced by Mr. Brooks and referred to the Committee on Public Works. Subsequent documents relating to this bill were published as follows:

U.S. 88th Congress, 1st session. House. Designating the McGee Bend Dam and Reservoir on the Angelina River, Texas, as the Sam Rayburn Dam and Reservoir. Report no. 581, to accompany H. R. 7594. July 25, 1963. Washington, 1963. 2p.
Submitted by Mr. Davis, from the Committee on Public Works, without amendment.

—— [Reprint of the original bill, July 25, 1963, to accompany the report. Report no. 581 and House Calendar no. 112 added]. 1p.

U.S. 88th Congress, 1st session. Senate. An act to designate the McGee Bend Dam and Reservoir on the Angelina River, Texas, as the Sam Rayburn Dam and Reservoir. H. R. 7594. In the Senate August 6, 1963. Washington, 1963. 1p.
Referred to the Committee on Public Works. Passed the House of Representatives August 5, 1963.

2748. U.S. 88th Congress, 1st session. House. Joint resolution to designate the lake to be formed by the waters impounded by Sanford Dam, Canadian River project, Texas, as "Lake Meredith." H. J. Res. 442. May 20, 1963. Washington, 1963. 1p.
Introduced by Mr. Rogers and referred to the Committee on Interior and Insular Affairs.
Reintroduced in the 89th Congress, 1st session, as H. J. Res. 95.
In honor of A. A. Meredith.

2749. Van Demark, Harry. Texas county names. *Texas monthly* 5:309-15, April 1930.

2750. Walter, Ray A. The town of Mexia. *Southwestern historical quarterly* 62: 108-09, July 1958.
Origin of name.

2751. What's in a name. *Texas municipalities* 10:160, Nov. 1923.
Comment on and analyses of a series of articles running in the *Dallas news*, Sunday supplement, on How Texas towns got their names.

2752. Williams, J. W. Ghost towns in the Wichita Falls area. *Southwestern historical quarterly* 47:311-12, Jan. 1944.

2753. Williamson, Lela. How Devil's River received its name. West Texas Historical and Scientific Society. Publications 1:43. 1926. (Sul Ross State Teachers College. Bulletin 21)

2754. Willis, Roystein E. Ghost towns of the south plains. Lubbock, 1941. 82p. Thesis (M.A.) Texas Technological College.

2755. Young, Della I. Names in the old Cheyenne and Arapahoe Territory and the Texas Panhandle. Texas Folk-lore Society. Publications 6:90-97. 1927.

UTAH

2756. Bero, John A. Utah place names. *Utah humanities review* 2:79-80, Jan. 1947.
Only five cities in Utah derive their names from the Book of Mormon, and only four have Biblical names.

2757. Chamberlin, Ralph V. Place and personal names of the Gosiute Indians of Utah. American Philosophical Society. Proceedings 52:1-13, Jan. 1913.

2758. Gannett, Henry. A gazetteer of Utah. Washington, Govt. Print. Off., 1900. 43p. (U.S. Geological Survey. Bulletin no. 166)

2759. Hunt, Charles B. Geology and geography of the Henry Mountains region, Utah. Washington, Govt. Print. Off., 1953. 234p. (U.S. Geological Survey. Professional paper, no. 228)
Derivation of place names: p. 21-24.

2760. Leigh, Rufus Wood. Five hundred Utah place names, their origin and significance. Salt Lake City, Deseret News Press, 1961. 109p.
A pocketbook excerpted from his full-length book manuscript, Indian, Spanish, and government survey place names of the Great Basin and Colorado plateaus.

2761. —— Lake Bonneville, its name and history. *Utah historical quarterly* 26:150-59, April 1958.
Excerpt from a book manuscript, Place names of the Great Basin and Colorado plateaus.

2762. Phillips, Maxine Brown. The strange new language of a magic land. *Denver post* March 14, 1965, Empire magazine, p. 6-9.
An article on the Glen Canyon National Recreation Area with emphasis on the place-names in it.

2763. Roylance, Ward Jay. Derivation of county names; *In his* Materials for the study of Utah's counties. Salt Lake City, 1962. p. 17-18.
Extracted from Facts about Utah. Utah Tourist & Publicity Council, 1962. 4th printing, rev.

2764. Thompson, Grant & Don Dunn. Udy Hot Springs: a bogey. *Western folklore* 18:166, April 1959.

2765. U.S. Board on Geographic Names. Decisions. No. 38—Decisions rendered April 4, 1934. Zion National Park, Utah. Washington, Govt. Print. Off., 1934. 6p.

2766. U.S. 88th Congress, 1st session. Senate. Joint resolution to designate the lake to be formed by the waters impounded by the Flaming Gorge Dam, Utah, and the recreation area contiguous to such lake in the states of Wyoming and Utah, as "O'Mahoney Lake and Recreation Area." S. J. Res. 17. Jan. 15, 1963. Washington, 1963. 2p.
Introduced by Mr. McGee and others and referred to the Committee on Interior and Insular Affairs.
Subsequent documents relating to this joint resolution, and related joint resolutions introduced in the House, were published as follows:

U.S. 88th Congress, 1st session. House. Joint resolution to designate the lake to be formed by the waters impounded by the Flaming Gorge Dam, Utah, and the recreation area contiguous to such lake in the states of Wyoming and Utah, as "O'Mahoney Lake and Recreation Area." H. J. Res. 293. Feb. 28, 1963. Washington, 1963. 2p.
Introduced by Mr. Aspinall and referred to the Committee on Interior and Insular Affairs.

U.S. 88th Congress, 1st session. Senate. Designating the lake to be formed by the waters impounded by the Flaming Gorge Dam, Utah, in the states of Wyoming and Utah, as "Lake O'Mahoney." Report no. 279, to accompany S. J. Res. 17. June 19, 1963. Calendar no. 260. Washington, 1963. 5p.
Submitted by Mr. Jackson, from the Committee on Interior and Insular Affairs, with amendments, as recommended by the Dept. of the Interior, to restrict the name to the lake, and designate it as Lake O'Mahoney.

—— [Reprint of the original joint resolution, June 19, 1963, with amendments, to accompany the report. Report no. 279 and Calendar no. 260 added]. 2p.

U.S. 88th Congress, 1st session. House. Joint resolution to designate the lake to be formed by the waters impounded by the Flaming Gorge Dam, Utah, as "Ashley Lake." H. J. Res. 604. July 31, 1963. Washington, 1963. 1p.
Introduced by Mr. Burton and referred to the Committee on Interior and Insular Affairs.
In honor of William Henry Ashley (1778-1838), a fur trader, explorer, and Congressman.

—— Providing designations for the lake to be formed by the waters impounded by Flaming Gorge Dam. Report no. 879, to accompany S. J. Res. 17,

Oct. 30, 1963. Washington, 1963. 4p.

Submitted by Mr. Rogers, from the Committee on Interior and Insular Affairs, with amendments, that that portion of the lake in Utah be known as Lake Ashley and the portion in Wyoming as Lake O'Mahoney. Two members of the Committee dissented. The Committee considered S. J. Res. 17, H. J. Res. 293, and H. J. Res. 604 simultaneously.

―――― [Reprint of S. J. Res. 17, Oct. 30, 1963, with amendments, to accompany the report. Report no. 879 and House Calendar no. 161 added]. 2p.

2767. U.S. Writers' Program. Utah. Origins of Utah place names. 3d ed. Comp. and written by Utah Writers' Project, Work Projects Administration. Sponsored and pub. by Utah State Dept. of Public Instruction. Salt Lake City, 1940. 47p. (American guide series)

1st ed. 1938. 29p.; 2d ed. 1938. 36p.; comp. and written by U.S. Federal Writers' Project. Utah.

2768. Utah Tourist and Publicity Council. Facts about Utah. 2d printing rev. Salt Lake City, 1959. 114p.

Frequently reprinted, revised.

Counties, with origin of name: p. 46-52.

VERMONT

2769. Abbott, Susie A. Place names in Peacham. *Vermont quarterly* n.s. 20:291-94, Oct. 1952.

2770. Allen, Morse. Connecticut and Vermont town names. *Vermont history* n.s. 22:273-78, Oct. 1954.

Influence of Connecticut.

2771. Billings, Agnes B. Ripton—the derivation of the name. *Vermont history* n.s. 22:305, Oct. 1954.

2772. Caldwell, Renwick K. The man who named Vermont. *Vermont history* n.s. 26:294-300, Oct. 1958.

Dr. Thomas Young.

2773. Changes in town names, from Thompson's Gazetteer, p. 200, 1842 ed. *Vermont quarterly* n.s. 21:239, July 1953.

2774. Clement, John. Naming Vermont in 1763?. Vermont Historical Society. Proceedings n.s. 1:83-92. 1930.

"An examination of the Sherburne town records with a map of Killington and Rutland, dated 1774."—Griffin.

2775. Dale, George N. Place names in northeastern Vermont. *Vermont quarterly* n.s. 21:145-48, April 1953.

2776. ―――― Towns in Essex County named for famous men. *Vermont quarterly* n.s. 20:204-07, July 1952.

2777. Dean, James. An alphabetical atlas, or, Gazetteer of Vermont; affording a summary description of the state, its several counties, towns, and rivers. Calculated to supply, in some measure, the place of a map; and designed for the use of offices, travellers, men of business, &c. Montpelier, Printed by Samuel Goss for the author, 1808. 43p.

2778. George, Noah J. T. A pocket geographical and statistical gazetteer of the State of Vermont. Embellished with diagrams. To which is prefixed a particular description of the City of Washington, and a large number of statistical tables of the United States. Comp. from the most recent authorities and personal observation. Haverhill, N.H., S. T. Goss, 1823. 264p.

2779. Hartwell, Florence B. Old names of Vermont towns. *Vermont history* n.s. 24:71-72, Jan. 1956.

2780. Hayward, John. A gazetteer of Vermont: containing descriptions of all the counties, towns, and districts in the state, and of its principal mountains, rivers, waterfalls, harbors, islands, and curious places. To which are added statistical accounts of its agriculture, commerce and manufactures; with other useful information. Boston, Tappan, Whittemore and Mason, 1849. 216p.

2781. Huden, John Charles. Historical Champlain maps. *Vermont history* n.s. 27:34-40, 85-87, 191-93, Jan.-July 1959.
Includes identification of names on early maps and modern names that correspond with the map names.

2782. —— Indian place-names in Vermont. *Vermont history* n.s. 23:191-203, July 1955.
Additional Indian place-names, *ibid.* n.s. 24:168-69, April 1956.

2783. —— Indian place names in Vermont. Burlington, Vt., The Author, 1957. 32p. (Monograph no. 1)
Review: by Hamill Kenny, *Names* 6:119-23, June 1958; by G. M. Day, *New England quarterly* June 1958, p. 273-74.

2784. —— Iroquois place-names in Vermont. *Vermont history* n.s. 25:66-76, Jan. 1957.

2785. Hudson, Verne R. The naming of Marshfield, Vt. *Vermont history* n.s. 23:56-57, Jan. 1955.

2786. Johnston, Thesba N. & others. Vermont town names and their derivations. *Vermont quarterly* n.s. 20:260-78, Oct. 1952; 21:10-16, 101-17, 188-99, Jan.-July 1953.

2787. McAleer, George. A study in the etymology of the Indian place name, Missisquoi. Worcester, Mass., Blanchard Press, 1906. 102p.
Bibliography: p. 101-02.
"In his little volume will be found all that is known of the history of the word, with the opinions and discussions of all authorities from the earliest to the most recent,—practically every etymology that has ever been suggested is recorded, and the list of them is an object lesson in the difficulties as well as the 'ease' of etymologizing."—*Review of historical publications relating to Canada* 11:199. 1906.
In the *Review of historical publications relating to Canada* 15:92. 1910, this

author is criticized for a further study, The etymology of Missisquoi. Addenda. Worcester, Mass., The Author, 1910. 39p., as being careless in references and etymologies.

2788. Prentice, E. Parmalee. A name and its meaning. *Vermont quarterly* n.s. 19:30-34, Jan. 1951.
Equinox Mountain.

2789. Roberts, Gwilym R. Where did Poultney get its name. Vermont Historical Society. News and notes 11:82, July 1960.

2790. Rouillard, Eugène. Missisquoi, origine et signification de ce nom. Société de Géographie de Québec. Bulletin 4:248-51, Oct. 1910.
About the name of a bay of Lake Champlain in Quebec and a river in northern Vermont.

2791. Rubicam, Harry C. Grafton, Vt.—the source of its name. *Vermont history* n.s. 22:54, Jan. 1954.

2792. Thompson, Zadock. A gazetteer of the State of Vermont; containing a brief general view of the state, a historical and topographical description of all the counties, towns, rivers, &c. Montpelier, Pub. by E. P. Walton and the author, E. P. Walton, printer, 1824. 310p.
Reprinted in his History of Vermont. Burlington, Chauncey Goodrich, 1842; also in 1853 ed.

2793. Vermont. *New England historical and genealogical register* 16:346, Oct. 1862.
Naming Vermont.

2794. Ward, Merlin B. Moretown, Vt.—the source of its name. *Vermont history* n.s. 22:54, Jan. 1954.

VIRGINIA

2795. Ashton, Betty Parker. Rapidan or Rapid Anne? Name of river is puzzling. *Richmond (Va.) times-dispatch* Nov. 1, 1959, p. D-3, col. 1-3.
Probably named for Queen Anne.

2796. Berkeley, Francis L. "Purton." *Virginia magazine of history and biography* 43:150-52, April 1935.
Origins and associations of the name of an estate in Gloucester County.

2797. Brown, Alexander Crosby. Wolf Trap, the baptism of a Chesapeake Bay shoal. *Virginia magazine of history and biography* 59:176-83, April 1951.

2798. Burrill, Meredith F. Terminology of Virginia's geographic features. Virginia Geographical Society. Bulletin 9:12-20, March 1957.

2799. Cridlin, William Broaddus. A history of colonial Virginia, the first permanent colony in America, to which is added the genealogy of the several shires

and counties and population in Virginia from the first Spanish colony to the present time. Pageant ed. Richmond, Williams Print. Co., 1923. 181, 13p.
Plantations, shires, counties by date of foundation, and source of name.

2800. Crouch, Kenneth Elwood. Bedford has one of seven schools named for women. *Bedford (Va.) bulletin-democrat* June 25, 1964, p. 6.
Includes origin of the name of Staunton River.

2801. ———— The Hocomawananch River. Bedford, Va., 1957. 6 l.
Reprinted from the Oct. 3, 1957 issue of the *Bedford (Va.) democrat.*
Is the river which is to be dammed Roanoke or Staunton? Earlier reference to a name for the river is the Indian name Hocomawananch.

2802. ———— The names of the streams and mountains in Bedford County, Virginia. Bedford, Va., 1959. 6 l.
From the *Bedford (Va.) democrat* issue of May 7, 1959, with title Bedford's streams, mountains have many picturesque names.

2803. ———— New map of post-annexation Bedford adds many streets. *Bedford (Va.) democrat* Oct. 13, 1960, sec. 2, p. 2.
Names of new streets in the town added by Jan. 1960 annexation, and some changes of names within the town due to that annexation.

2804. ———— Place names of Bedford County, their origins and outside associations. *Bedford (Va.) bulletin-democrat* Jan. 31, 1963, sec. 3, p. 6; Feb. 7, sec. 2, p. 4; Feb. 14, sec. 3, p. 5; Feb. 21, sec. 2, p. 6.

2805. ———— Research on Moneta's name leads to Italy, Indian tribe. *Bedford (Va.) bulletin-democrat* Oct. 24, 1963, p. 6.
Theory of origin of this place-name in Bedford community.

2806. ———— Should it be Huddleston or Huttleston? Some history. *Bedford (Va.) bulletin-democrat* Sept. 6, 1962, sec. 2, p. 1, col. 1-2.
More on the same, under title Huttleston Rogers stories evoke interest of family, *ibid.* Sept. 13, 1962, p. 5.
Station on the old Virginia Railway named for its builder, H. Huttleston Rogers, but misspelled.

2807. ———— Street names in the town of Bedford, Virginia. Bedford, Va., 1958. 3 l.
Reprinted from the *Bedford (Va.) democrat* issues of Dec. 11 and 23, 1958.

2808. ———— That name Staunton River: official views and history. *Bedford (Va.) bulletin-democrat* Sept. 5, 1963, p. 6.
Historical background concerning the name of the river which makes Staunton River High School a suitable name for a new school on the south side of Bedford County.

2809. Dramatic history of Albemarle is reflected in quaint names. *Daily progress,* Charlottesville, July 1, 1937, p. 7.

2810. Edwards, Richard. Statistical gazetteer of the states of Virginia and North Carolina; embracing important topographical and historical information, from recent and original sources. With the results of the last census, in many cases

to 1855. Richmond, Pub. for the proprietor, 1856. 601p.
Earlier edition: Richmond, 1855. 469p. Did not include North Carolina.

2811. Evans, C. W. Newport News, origin of the name. *Virginia magazine of history and biography* 55:31-44, Jan. 1947.

2812. First town named Washington. *New York times* May 30, 1949, p. 26.
Claim of Washington, Va., "surveyed and plotted by George Washington, Aug. 4, 1749."

2813. Gannett, Henry. A gazetteer of Virginia. Washington, Govt. Print. Off., 1904. 159p. (U.S. Geological Survey. Bulletin no. 232)

2814. Gerard, William R. Some Virginia Indian words. *American anthropologist* n.s. 7:222-49, April-June 1905.
"The derivation and meaning of certain place-names in Virginia. It contains the author's answer to a criticism of his opinions by William Wallace Tooker in Oct.-Dec. 1904 of this same magazine."—Price.

2815. ———— The Tapehanek dialect of Virginia. *American anthropologist* n.s. 6:313-30, April-June 1904.
Deals with the derivation of the language and some place-names.
Criticized by W. W. Tooker, *ibid.* Oct.-Dec. 1904.

2816. Gilliam, Charles Edgar. Ajacan, the Algonkian name for Hampton Roads, Virginia. *Names* 6:57-59, March 1958.

2817. ———— The Algonquian term—Ajacan—its Indian and Spanish meaning. Archeological Society of Virginia. Quarterly bulletin 12:[2-11], Dec. 1957.

2818. ———— Ethnic significance of the term: Appomattoc. Archeological Society of Virginia. Quarterly bulletin 7:[11-12], March 1953.
Concerned only with the use of this term within the area of the Powhatan tribal country Appomattoc.

2819. ———— Geoethnology—Apamatuck (Mattica) and/or Appamattucks: the chief villages of the Appomattoc, 1607-1691. Archeological Society of Virginia. Quarterly bulletin 4:[8-9], June 1950.
Earlier spellings and meaning of the name Appomattox.

2820. ———— "Harrican" in colonial Virginia records. *Virginia magazine of history and biography* 50:337-44, Oct. 1942.
References in colonial records to variant spellings of Hurricane as a place-name.

2821. ———— Indicated portals of safe entry into Appomattoc. Archeological Society of Virginia. Quarterly bulletin 7:[14-15], June 1953.

2822. ———— Pagan Creek: ethnology of name. Archeological Society of Virginia. Quarterly bulletin 14:9, March 1960.

2823. ———— Tsenakcommacah. Archeological Society of Virginia. Quarterly bulletin 9:[4-7], March 1955.
Meaning of name.

2824. Gordon, J. W. French place-names in Virginia.
Thesis (M.S.) Univ. of Virginia, 1933. "Deposited in the Virginia room of the University Library; one copy may be borrowed."—*American speech*.

2825. Green, Bennett Wood. Word-book of Virginia folk-speech. Richmond, W. E. Jones' Sons, 1912. 530p.
Includes Virginia names of places.

2826. Heckewelder, John Gottlieb Ernestus. Names given by the Lenni Lenape or Delaware Indians to rivers, streams and places in the now states of New Jersey, Pennsylvania, Maryland, and Virginia. Pennsylvania German Folklore Society. Publications 5:1-41. 1940.
Published also in American Philosophical Society. Transactions 4:351-96. 1834; Historical Society of Pennsylvania. Bulletin 1:121-35, 139-54, June, Sept. 1847; Moravian Historical Society. Transactions 1872:275-333; as a separate: Bethlehem [Pa.], H. T. Claude, printer, 1872. 58p.; and in his A narrative of the mission of the United Brethren among the Delaware and Mohegan Indians. Cleveland, Burrows Bros., 1907. p. 523-66.

2827. Hench, Atcheson L. Virginia county names. *American speech* 19:153, April 1944.
In Piedmont, Va., the custom is to omit the word county whenever the speaker wishes to.

2828. Hummel, Ray Orvin. A list of places included in 19th century Virginia directories. Richmond, Virginia State Library, 1960. 153p. (Virginia. State Library, Richmond. Publications, no. 11)

2829. Johnson, Thomas Cary. How Albemarle got its name. *Magazine of Albemarle County history* 16:20-24. 1957-1958.

2830. Kemper, Charles E. Home names in the Valley. *Virginia magazine of history and biography* 45:353-56, Oct. 1937.
A partial list, with brief notes, of names of the homes of prominence in the Valley of Virginia, given and used prior to the Civil War.

2831. Kinnier, C. L. The renaming of Arlington streets. *Arlington historical magazine* 1:41-51, Oct. 1959.
Describes the work of Arlington's Street Names Committee, appointed in 1932, and the system worked out for relieving confusion in street and highway names in Arlington County.

2832. Long, Charles Massie. Virginia county names; two hundred and seventy years of Virginia history. New York, Neale Pub. Co., 1908. 207p.
Authorities consulted: 1 page at end.

2833. Lynchburg, Va. Ordinances, etc. Ordinance naming and describing streets of the city of Lynchburg, Va., amended to August 26, 1958. n.p., 1958. 66p.

2834. McJimsey, George Davis. Topographic terms in Virginia. New York, Columbia Univ. Press, 1940. 151p. (American speech. Reprints and monographs, no. 3)
Appeared serially in *American speech* 15:3-38, 149-79, 262-300, 381-419. 1940.
Bibliography of works cited: p. 141-47.

"A topographic term is not a place name: it is not a proper name used to designate a specific topographic feature. It is merely a word or phrase applied to a group of topographic features which possess essentially the same characteristics. This study is concerned with proper names only when they supply significant topographic information."—Introd.

cf. Henry Bosley Woolf, The DAE and topographic terms. *American speech* 17: 177-78, Oct. 1942, which records words from McJimsey's list not found in the Dictionary of American English.

2835. Martin, Joseph. A new and comprehensive gazetteer of Virginia, and the District of Columbia. To which is added a History of Virginia from its first settlement to the year 1754: with an abstract of the principal events from that period to the independence of Virginia, written expressly for the work by a citizen of Virginia [W. H. Brockenbrough]. Charlottesville, J. Martin, 1836. 636p.
   Also published 1835, and at Richmond without date under title A comprehensive description of Virginia and the District of Columbia.

2836. Milbourne, Mrs. V. S. The founding of Luray and the origin of its name. *William and Mary College quarterly historical magazine* 2d ser. 10:142-44, April 1930.

2837. Moore, J. Brewer & Bruce S. Trant. Street renaming is no cinch, but it solves a lot of problems, as the colorful experience of Portsmouth, Va., demonstrates. *American city* 77:82-84, Aug. 1962.

2838. The New Newport News. *Richmond (Va.) times-dispatch* Sept. 13, 1957, p. 12.
   On the place-name.

2839. Origin of the name of Newport News. *William and Mary College quarterly historical magazine* 9:233-37, April 1901.

2840. Percy, Alfred. Old place names, West Central Piedmont & Blue Ridge Mountains. Madison Heights, Va., Percy Press, 1950. 22, 5p.

2841. Quarles, Garland R. The streets of Winchester, Virginia: the origin and significance of their names. Winchester, Va., Farmers and Merchants National Bank, n.d. 47p.

2842. Raitt, Nathan S. The "whys" of the word; place names of Virginia. Virginia Association of Assessing Officers. News-bulletin 1961, no. 4, p. 5.

2843. Robinson, Morgan Poitiaux. Virginia counties: those resulting from Virginia legislation. Virginia. State Library. Bulletin 9:1-283. 1916.
   Includes alphabetical, chronological, and geographical arrangement; genealogical arrangement; origin of county names; texts of Acts of Assembly (concerning counties) not in the Virginia statutes edited by William Waller Hening. Richmond, 1810-23; bibliography.

2844. Rogers, P. Burwell. Changes in Virginia names. *American speech* 31:21-24, Feb. 1956.
   Names of persons and places undergoing changes in pronunciation.

2845. —— Indian names in tidewater Virginia. *Names* 4:155-59, Sept. 1956.

2846. —— Place names on the Virginia Peninsula. *American speech* 29:241-56, Dec. 1954.
Between the James and the York rivers.

2847. —— Tidewater Virginians name their homes. *American speech* 34: 251-57, Dec. 1959.
A study of patterns in naming homes.

2848. Some Virginia names and their meanings. *Virginia magazine of history and biography* 11:317-21, Jan. 1904.

2849. A Street is named for Harmon Killebrew. *Kansas City times* June 18, 1959, p. 28.
A street in Springfield, Va., was named for the baseball player.

2850. [Street names of Fredericksburg, Va.]. *New York times* Jan. 22, 1960, p. 26.
A full Topics of the Times column.

2851. Tooker, William Wallace. Derivation of the name Powhatan. *American anthropologist* n.s. 6:464-68, July-Sept. 1904.
"The generally accepted etymology and translation as given by the late Dr. Trumbull for the word Powhatan, 'falls in a stream,' is erroneous."—Price.

2852. —— The Kuskarawaokes of Captain John Smith. *American anthropologist* 6:412-13, Oct. 1893.
The derivation and meaning of the name Roanoke.

2853. —— Meaning of some Indian names in Virginia. *William and Mary College quarterly historical magazine* 14:62-64, July 1905.

2854. —— The names Chickahominy, Pamunkey, and the Kuskarawaokes of Captain John Smith; with historical and ethnological notes. New York, F. P. Harper, 1901. 90p. (The Algonquian series, no. 9)
1st essay from *American anthropologist* 8:257-63, July 1895, with additions and corrections.
2d essay also published in *American antiquarian* 17:289-93, Sept. 1895.
3d essay from *American anthropologist* 6:409-14, Oct. 1893.

2855. —— The Powhatan name for Virginia. Lancaster, Pa., New Era Print. Co., 1906. 23-27p.
Reprinted from *American anthropologist* n.s. 8:23-27, Jan.-March 1906.

2856. —— Some Indian names of places on Long Island, N.Y. and their correspondences in Virginia, as mentioned by Capt. John Smith and associates. *Magazine of New England history* 1:154-58, July 1891.

2857. —— Some more about Virginia names. *American anthropologist* n.s. 7:524-28, July-Sept. 1905.
Reprinted separately, 1905.
Adds further information to the etymology of names given in the author's answer to William R. Gerard *ibid*. Oct.-Dec. 1904.

2858. —— Some Powhatan names. *American anthropologist* n.s. 6:670-94, Oct.-Dec. 1904.

A criticism of the opinions of William R. Gerard as found *ibid.* April–June 1904.

2859. Trumbull, James Hammond. Indian names in Virginia. *Historical magazine* 2d ser. 7:47-48, Jan. 1870.

2860. Two place-name pronunciations. *American speech* 4:156-57, Dec. 1928. Staunton, Va., and Houston, Tex.

2861. U.S. Board on Geographic Names. Decisions. No. 35—Decisions rendered April 5, 1933. Shenandoah National Park, Virginia. Washington, Govt. Print. Off., 1934. 13p.

2862. ——— Decisions. No. 36—Decisions rendered April 5, 1933. Names in the vicinity of Shenandoah National Park, Virginia. Washington, Govt. Print. Off., 1934. 4p.

2863. Virginia. Division of Planning and Economic Development. Index of the surface waters of Virginia. Rev. March 1951. n.p., 1951. 59 l.
   1st ed. 1949.
   Lists the names and approximate locations of the surface waters of Virginia.
   Kenneth E. Crouch has added to a few copies two typewritten sheets of additions and corrections for Bedford County.

2864. Virginia. Division of Water Resources. Index of the surface waters of Virginia. Rev. Jan. 1960. Richmond, 1960. 66p.
   Incorporates the additions for Bedford County made by Kenneth E. Crouch.

2865. Virginia Place Name Society. Occasional papers, no. 1- . Charlottesville, Univ. of Virginia, 1961- .
   1961, no. 1, Feb. 17. A preliminary bibliography of Virginia place-name literature, by Gary S. Dunbar.
   1961, no. 2, Sept. 20. Virginia place names, 1676. [Reproduction of a portion of Notes to accompany a facsimile of John Speed's A map of Virginia and Maryland, 1676, published by the McGregor Library, Univ. of Virginia, 1961].
   1961, no. 3, Dec. Analysis of Virginia place-names as to origin, by John E. Manahan.
   1962, no. 1, Jan. 30. Some notes on bison in early Virginia, by Gary S. Dunbar [including list of buffalo place-names on U.S. Geological Survey topographic sheets]. Addenda to Virginia place-name bibliography.
   1962, no. 2, June 18. Ah Sid, by N. Harvey Deal. Yellow Jacket town, by Chas. Edgar Gilliam. A note on the place-name Blacks and Whites (present Blackstone, Va.), by Virginia Jordan.
   1962, no. 3. For this number, members received copies of Index of the surface waters of Virginia (listed, entry above, under Virginia. Division of Water Resources).
   1962, no. 4, Aug. 8. Meadow Branch, the stream east of Monticello, lately called Tufton Branch, with some notes on the nearby surface waters, by J. C. Wyllie.
   1963, no. 1, March 25. Manassas Gap, by David Alan Williams.
   1963, no. 2, Oct. 8. Totier Creek, a first-families-of-Albemarle place name, by John Cook Wyllie.
   1964, no. 1, Oct. 7. The mountains of Virginia, comp. from a card list in the Division of Water Resources and arranged for publication by Brad Gunter, Lee W. Finks, and N. Harvey Deal.

2866. Virginians name new city. *New York times* June 28, 1962, p. 29.
The new city, to be named Chesapeake, became official on Jan. 1, 1963, with the merger of South Norfolk and Norfolk County.

WASHINGTON

2867. Baker, Marcus. Survey of the northwestern boundary of the United States, 1857-1861. U.S. Geological Survey. Bulletin 174:58-61. 1900.
Indian names of camps, stations, rivers, etc. along the 49th parallel in Washington, Idaho, and Montana. Based on the work George Gibbs did for the Smithsonian Institution.

2868. Bechly, Ernst Carl. Map of Washington Territory west of the Cascade Mountains (as of 1870), being a composite of maps of 1859, 1865, and 1870. Showing counties, forts, Indian reservation, roads, R. R. surveys, trails, etc., including data when created or founded, also meaning of words. Chehalis, Wash., 1952. map 125 x 92 cm.

2869. Bowman, J. A. Washington nomenclature. A study. *Washington historical quarterly* 1:5-13, Oct. 1906.

2870. Brier, Warren J. How Washington Territory got its name. *Pacific Northwest quarterly* 51:13-15, Jan. 1960.

2871. Chamberlain, Alexander F. Geographic terms of Kootenay origin. *American anthropologist* n.s. 4:348-50, April-June 1902.
"Concerned with names of places, camp-sites, and stations along the 49th parallel in British Columbia, Washington, Idaho, and Montana. These names which seem to have been taken from the language of the Kootenay Indians of this region are mentioned in the reports on the boundary survey. The meanings and etymologies are given where possible."—Price.

2872. Chase, Carroll & Richard McP. Cabeen. The first hundred years of United States territorial postmarks, 1787-1887. Washington Territory. *American philatelist* 61:871-74, Aug. 1948; 62:362-69, 686-91, Feb., June 1949; 63:43-50, 276-85, Oct. 1949, Jan. 1950.
Includes list of post offices to 1887, with notes on a few names.

2873. Colbert, Mildred. Naming and early settlement of Ilwaco, Washington. *Oregon historical quarterly* 47:181-95, June 1946.

2874. Collins, Josiah. Tacoma vs. Rainier. *Nation* 56:329-30, May 4, 1893.

2875. Connelly, Dolly. Mighty Joe Morovits: real-life Bunyan. *Sports illustrated* 18:52-57, Jan. 7, 1963.
Story of the mountain man whose name is immortalized in landmark names.

2876. Conover, C. T. Many Puget Sound names were given by Wilkes Porter. *Seattle times* Nov. 22, 1956.

2877. Conover, Charles Tallmadge. Mount Rainier or Mount Tacoma? Brief summary of the essential facts in this historic controversy. *National magazine* 48:223-24, 237-38, June 1919.

2878. [Coones, S. F.]. Dictionary of the Chinook jargon, as spoken on Puget Sound and the Northwest, with original Indian names for prominent places and localities, with their meanings. Seattle, Lowman & Hanford Stationery & Print. Co., [1891]. 38p.

2879. Correspondence relative to the Indian names of the great mountain. Mount Rainier or Tacoma. Conducted by Mr. Benjamin L. Harvey. Washington State Historical Society. Publications 2:440-64. 1907-14.

2880. Costello, Joseph A. The Siwash, their life legends, and tales; Puget Sound and Pacific Northwest. Seattle, Calvert Co., 1895. 169p.
Seattle names included.

2881. Craven, Arthur J. Mount Baker—its name and first explorer. *Mazama* 6:33-44, Dec. 1920.

2882. Davidson, George. The name "Mt. Rainier." *Sierra Club bulletin* 6:87-99, Jan. 1906.
Proposed reasons on which the club accepted Mount Rainier.

2883. Denman, A. H. Mount Tacoma—its true name. U.S. Congress. Congressional record 72:10871-73, June 16, 1930.
Historical article on the origin of the Indian name Tacoma for Mount Rainier.

2884. ——— The name. Tacoma, Mt. Tacoma Club, 1924. 10p.
In connection with the effort to change the name of Mount Rainier.

2885. ——— The name of Mount Tacoma; urging the official removal from America's most sublime mountain of the name Rainier and the perpetuation by official adoption of the original Indian name therefor in its most appropriate, euphonious and generally accepted form—Tacoma. Embodying also the research of Judge James Wickersham and the "Brief" of John B. Kaiser, S. W. Wall, Benjamin L. Harvey, W. N. Allen and Walter J. Thompson. Tacoma, Rotary Club, Kiwanis Club, etc., 1924. 93p.
The "Brief" also issued separately; see Tacoma. Justice to the Mountain Committee, no. 2938.

2886. Eells, Myron. Aboriginal geographic names in the State of Washington. *American anthropologist* 5:27-35, Jan. 1892.

2887. Fish, Byron. Ranger named many state peaks, streams. *Seattle times* Dec. 5, 1955, p. 22.
Work of Albert Hale Sylvester of U.S. Geological Survey and U.S. Forest Service. *cf.* Sylvester's article on his work in *American speech* 18:241-52, Dec. 1943.

2888. ——— Some peaks' names Picturesque; others just plain "Baldies." *Seattle times* Nov. 22, 1955, p. 4.

2889. Gibbs, Rafe. The mountain with two names. *American mercury* 30:39-40, June 1955.
Mount Rainier.

2800. Gudde, Erwin Gustav. Okanagan place names. *Western folklore* 8:161-62, April 1949.
Refers to article by A. G. Harvey, Okanagan place names, no. 3269.

2891. Hanford, Thaddeus. The local nomenclature of the Territory. *Washington standard*, Olympia, Jan. 13, 1866, p. 1; Jan. 27, p. 1.
Signed: Philopatris.
Prefers Indian names; also recommends the name Tacoma for the Territory.

2892. Hanson, Howard A. The naming of Elliott Bay. Shall we honor the chaplain or the midshipman? *Pacific Northwest quarterly* 45:28-32, Jan. 1954.
Bay on which Seattle is located. Named for Midshipman Elliott rather than for chaplain, both of Wilkes expedition, 1841.

2893. Hazeltine, Jean. The discovery and cartographical recognition of Shoalwater Bay. *Oregon historical quarterly* 58:251-63, Sept. 1957.

2894. Himes, George Henry. Tyrrell's name should be saved. *Washington historical quarterly* 10:182-84, July 1919.
Justifies Tyrrell for the prairie in Thurston County rather than Hawk's Prairie.

2895. Hitchman, Robert. Color names, surnames, and place names. *Western folklore* 9:372, Oct. 1950.

2896. —— Corruption of French names in Lewis County, Washington. *Western folklore* 9:156-57, April 1950.

2897. —— The Irishman in name-origin stories. *Western folklore* 8:366, Oct. 1949.
Discounts Irishman's connection with naming of Osoyoos and Okanogan (Okanogan: "spelled thus on most maps").

2898. —— Sedro-Woolley, Washington. *Western folklore* 8:369-70, Oct. 1949.
Skagit County.

2899. —— Venturesome stories lie behind the names on the frontierland they called Washington. *American heritage* 4:42-43, 65-67, Summer 1953.

2900. Indians named Puyallup, and this is why! *Chicago tribune* Dec. 18, 1955, pt. 6, p. 10R.

2901. Ketchum, Verne L. The naming of Mount Hood. *Mazama* 13:42-45, Dec. 1931.

2902. Kids to rename streets of town. *Denver post* Nov. 11, 1964, p. 12.
Because of confusion in the names of streets in Milton, Wash., students in fifth and sixth grades were asked to rename the streets, using consecutive numbers one way and alphabetical names the other.

2903. Kingston, C. S. Juan de Fuca Strait: origin of the name. *Pacific Northwest quarterly* 36:155-66, April 1945.

2904. Landes, Henry. A geographic dictionary of Washington. Olympia, F. M.

Lamborn, public printer, 1917. 346p. (Washington. Geological Survey. Bulletin no. 17)

2905. A List of mountain peaks and altitudes of the State of Washington; Prominent mountain passes in Washington. *Mountaineer* 1:141-46, Nov. 1908.

2906. Löfgren, Svante. Swedish place names of Washington State. American Swedish Historical Foundation. Chronicle 3:17-27, Autumn 1956-Winter 1956-57.
   Originally written for *Svenska posten,* Seattle, "several years ago."

2907. Lummis, Charles Fletcher. Editorials on changing the name of Mt. Rainier. *Out west* 23:367-68, 494-95, Oct., Nov. 1905.

2908. McAdie, Alexander. Mt. Rainier or Mt. Tacoma—which?; *In his* Alexander McAdie, scientist and writer. Charlottesville, Va., M. R. B. McAdie, 1949, i.e., 1950. p. 183-86.
   Reprinted from *Sierra Club bulletin* 9:95-98, June 1913.
   Supports George Davidson's argument that the name Rainier should not be changed.

2909. McArthur, Lewis Ankeny. Early Washington post offices. *Washington historical quarterly* 20:129-33, April 1929.
   A few Washington offices included in the book of Oregon records in the Post Office Dept. For period Jan. 1850-Sept. 1853.

2910. McDonald, Lucile. Explorers of 1791 gave many Spanish names to San Juans. *Seattle times* Nov. 6, 1955, p. 2.
   The San Juan Islands were given many Spanish names by the explorers in 1790-91, seeking a supposed passage through the North American continent. Among the names placed on their charts were Sucia ("dirty," for the bad weather), Mal Abrigo ("poor shelter," which became Matia), and Carmela (Mount Baker).

2911. —— Vaughn named for settler of 1852. *Seattle Sunday times* Sept. 7, 1958.

2912. Meany, Edmond Stephen. Dropping the "h" from Port Townsend. *Washington historical quarterly* 24:49-52, Jan. 1933.
   Origin and history of the name.

2913. —— Indian geographic names of Washington. Seattle, Hyatt-Fowells School, 1908. 20p.

2914. —— Name of Mount Saint Helens. *Washington historical quarterly* 15:124-25, April 1924.

2915. —— Origin of Washington geographic names. Seattle, Univ. of Washington Press, 1923. 357p.
   Originally published in *Washington historical quarterly* v. 8-14, 1917-23. The book has additional information.
   Review: *American speech* 1:397, April 1926; *American historical review* 29:614-15, April 1924.

2916. —— Place names and elevations in Mount Rainier National Park; *In his*

Mount Rainier, a record of exploration. New York, Macmillan, 1916. p. 302-25.
This list is not included in his book, Origin of Washington geographic names.

2917. —— Three cities of Washington, origin of their names. Seattle, Univ.
of Washington Press, n.d. 7p.
Reprinted from the *Washington historical quarterly.*
The three cities are Seattle, Spokane, and Tacoma.

2918. —— Vancouver's discovery of Puget Sound; portraits and biographies
of the men honored in the naming of geographic features of northwestern America.
New York, Macmillan, 1915. 344p.

2919. Meeker, Ezra. Who named Tacoma? Address to the Washington Historical Society, at Tacoma, January 22d, 1904. n.p., 1905. 8p.
Gen. McCarver named Tacoma, address by Thomas W. Prosch to the Washington Historical Society, at Tacoma, October 4, 1905: p. 4-8. Prosch points out
many errors and misstatements in Meeker's paper.

2920. Merriam, Clinton Hart. Shall the name of Mount Rainier be changed?
Statement by C. Hart Merriam before the United States Geographic Board, May
11, 1917. Washington, Govt. Print. Off., 1917. 10p.
Opposes the proposal to change the name to Mount Tacoma.

2921. Mount Rainier keeps its name. *New York times* June 13, 1937, sec. 10,
p. 25, col. 3.

2922. The Naming of Mount Hood. *Geographical journal* 75:173, Feb. 1930.

2923. Oliphant, J. Orin. Notes on early settlements and on geographic names of
eastern Washington. *Washington historical quarterly* 22:172-202, July 1931.
Forms an appendix to Edmond Stephen Meany's Origin of Washington geographic
names (see no. 2915), although Oliphant was interested in assembling data relating to early settlements in one area of Washington.

2924. Olympia, Wash. Chamber of Commerce. The great myth—"Mount Tacoma";
Mount Rainier and the facts of history. Issued by the Olympia Chamber of Commerce and the Thurston County Pioneer and Historical Society. Olympia, 1924.
31p.

2925. Petite, Irving. Adventures in state names; Anna Cortez is Anacortes.
Seattle argus May 3, 1957.

2926. —— How names do change! *Seattle times* July 31, 1955, p. 7.
Street-name changes in Seattle.

2927. Piper, Charles Vancouver. Flora of the state of Washington. Washington,
Govt. Print. Off., 1906. 637p. (Smithsonian Institution. United States National
Museum. Contributions from the United States National Herbarium, v. 11)
Geographical index: p. 619-22.

2928. Prosch, Thomas Wickham. McCarver and Tacoma. Seattle, Lowman &
Hanford Print. Co., 1906. 198p.
History of naming the city of Tacoma, p. 162-67.

2929. —— Seattle and the Indians of Puget Sound. *Washington historical quarterly* 2:303-08, July 1908.
Claims that the city was named for Chief Seattle, not Sealth.

2930. Relander, Click. Geographic names and nomenclature; *In his* Drummers and dreamers. Caldwell, Idaho, Caxton Printers, 1956. p. 286-319.
Pertaining to the Columbia River and the adjoining area from Pasco to Vantage, Washington, including Wanapum names of old native villages, campsites, and landmarks.
Review: by Walter C. Kraft, *Names* 5:186-87, Sept. 1957.

2931. Rundell, Hugh A. Washington names; a pronunciation guide of Washington State place names. 2d ed. Pullman, Wash., Radio Station KWSC and the Extension Service, Institute of Agricultural Sciences, Washington State University, 1959. 78 l.
Includes counties and cities. A supplement dealing with names of rivers, parks, mountains, etc., will be published at a later date.

2932. Smith, Charles Wesley. The naming of counties in the State of Washington. Seattle, 1913. 15p. (Bulletin of the University of Washington. University studies, no. 6)
Reprinted from the *Magazine of history* 10:9-16, 79-85, July, Aug. 1909.

2933. Smith, Francis E. Pacific coast place names in the State of Washington. *Americana* 20:23-30, Jan. 1926.

2934. Snowden, Clinton A. Mount Tacoma or Mount Rainier; *In his* History of Washington. New York, Century History Co., 1909. 4:249-54.
Long controversy over the name of the peak Rainier is impartially reviewed.

2935. Steel, William Gladstone. The mountains of Oregon. Portland, D. Steel, 1890. 112p.
Contains several sections on the names of mountains in Oregon and Washington, particularly on the name Tacoma.

2936. Strong, William Duncan. Wakemap: a Columbia River site mispronounced. *American antiquity* 21:410, April 1956.
This Indian archaeological site should be given the Indian rather than the anglicized pronunciation.

2937. Sylvester, Albert Hale. Place-naming in the Northwest. *American speech* 18:241-52, Dec. 1943.
An account by the retired supervisor of the Wenatchee National Forest of his assignment of names to topographical features in the Forest. A rare and entertaining firsthand account.

2938. Tacoma. Justice to the Mountain Committee. Brief submitted to the United States Geographic Board urging the official removal from America's most sublime mountain of the name Rainier and the perpetuation by official adoption of the original Indian name therefor in its most appropriate, euphonious and generally accepted form—Tacoma. May 2, 1917. Tacoma, The Committee, 1917. 77, 24p.
Authorities consulted: p. 72-77.
Proceedings of the Tacoma Academy of Science, Feb. 8, 1893, paper by Hon. James Wickersham, Is it "Mt. Tacoma," or "Rainier"? 24p. at end.

2939. Tacoma or Rainier? *Americana* 18:474-77, Oct. 1924.

2940. Taylor, William H. Mount Si Trail dedicated. *Washington historical quarterly* 22:213-15, July 1931.
Story of Josiah Merritt, "Uncle Si," for whom the mountain was named.

2941. Territory of Washington; *In* Meany, Edmond Stephen. History of the State of Washington. New York, Macmillan, 1924. p. 156-58; also in U.S. Congress. Congressional globe, 32d Congress, 2d session, 1852-53, p. 540-42, 1039, 1046.
Bill introduced for organization of Territory of Columbia. After discussion on name it was passed as Territory of Washington.

2942. Todd, C. C. Origin and meaning of the geographic name Palouse. *Washington historical quarterly* 24:190-92, July 1933.
"A modification of the Indian tribal name, Palloatpallahs."—Griffin.

2943. U.S. Board on Geographic Names. Before the United States Geographic Board, in the matter of the proposal to change the name of Mount Rainier. Statement of C. T. Conover, representing numerous citizens of the State of Washington in favor of retaining the present name, and oral presentation by C. T. Conover and Victor J. Farrar, May 2, 1917. Statement of C. Hart Merriam, a member of the United States Geographic Board, before said body, May 11, 1917. The decision, May 11, 1917. Addenda: statement by John Muir, statements by Dr. C. M. Buchanan, statement by Edwin Els, statement by H. B. McElroy. Seattle, Lowman & Hanford Co., 1924. 74p.
1st ed. 1917. 58p.

2944. ――― Decisions. No. 29—June 30, 1932. Mount Rainier National Park, Washington. Washington, Govt. Print. Off., 1934. 14p.

2945. ――― Decisions on Washington place names. *Washington historical quarterly* 10:79-80, 185-89, Jan., July 1919.

2946. ――― Report of United States Geographic Board on S. J. Res. 64, a joint resolution to change the name of "Mount Rainier" to "Mount Tacoma" and for other purposes. Washington, Govt. Print. Off., 1924. 8p.

2947. U.S. Work Projects Administration. Pennsylvania. Geographic names in the coastal areas of California, Oregon and Washington. Comp. under the supervision of the Coast and Geodetic Survey. Washington, 1940. 94p.

2948. Waterman, Thomas Talbot. An essay on geographic names in the State of Washington. *American anthropologist* n.s. 24:481-83, Oct.-Dec. 1922.
An unfavorable review of Edmond Stephen Meany's article in the *Washington historical quarterly* v. 8, 1917.

2949. ――― The geographical names used by the Indians of the Pacific coast. *Geographical review* 12:175-94, April 1922.
"This paper is interesting in that it demonstrates convincingly that these primitive peoples (and presumably others) are acquainted with the world only as a very limited area, that they have few or no names for the larger elements of the landscape, a mountain range, for example, is nameless as a whole, but that, on the other hand, every minute natural object has a specific name. In this may be found

an explanation of the nature of many primitive place names."—Oscar Diedrich von Engeln. The story key to geographic names. New York. Appleton, 1924. p. xii.

2950. Wickersham, James. Is it "Mt. Tacoma" or "Rainier"; what do history and tradition say? Tacoma, Puget Sound Print. Co., 1893. 16p. (Tacoma Academy of Science. Proceedings, February 6, 1893)
   2d ed., Tacoma, News Pub. Co., 1893. 34p. (Tacoma Academy of Science. Proceedings)
   Also included in Tacoma. Justice to the Mountain Committee. Brief submitted to the United States Geographic Board... (see no. 2938).

WEST VIRGINIA

2951. Bowman, E. L. Origin of counties given for entire state. *Glenville democrat* June 12, 1930.

2952. Carpenter, Charles. Our place names. *West Virginia review* 6:422, 440, Aug. 1929.

2953. Chrisman, Lewis H. The origin of place names in West Virginia. *West Virginia history* 7:77-88, Jan. 1946.

2954. ——— The origin of the names of the county seats of West Virginia. *West Virginia review* 8:44-45, 62, Nov. 1930.

2955. Counties of West Virginia take names from early statesmen. *Cumberland (Md.) evening times* June 20, 1939.

2956. Gannett, Henry. A gazetteer of West Virginia. Washington, Govt. Print. Off., 1904. 164p. (U.S. Geological Survey. Bulletin no. 233)

2957. Indian names—early geography of West Virginia. West Virginia. Dept. of Archives and History. Biennial report 1:251-68. 1904-06.
   Includes Indian names of West Virginia rivers, and the names of places on early maps.

2958. Johnston, Ross B. U.S. Board accedes to West Virginia wishes. *West Virginia history* 16:48, Oct. 1954.
   Tygart Valley, and Tygart Valley River.

2959. Kenny, Hamill. Cheat River and the "Horn papers." *American speech* 28:65-66, Feb. 1953.

2960. ——— Settling Laurel's business. *Names* 9:160-62, Sept. 1961.
   The origin of Laurel in the Pennsylvania and West Virginia place-name Laurel Hill.

2961. ——— The synthetic place name in West Virginia. *American speech* 15:39-44, Feb. 1940.

2962. ——— West Virginia place names, their origin and meaning including the nomenclature of the streams and mountains. Piedmont, W. Va., Place Name

Press, 1945. 768p.
Reprinted in 1960 by the West Virginia University Library in a special limited edition for West Virginia schools.
Review: by E. G. Gudde, *American speech* 21:206-08, Oct. 1946.

2963. Laidley, W. S. Former names of West Virginia towns. *West Virginia historical magazine quarterly* 3:255, July 1903.
List of 21 changed names.

2964. Mahr, August C. Shawnee names and migrations in Kentucky and West Virginia. *Ohio journal of science* 60:155-64, May 1960.
The migration of the western half of the Shawnee Nation from the Cumberland River eastward through the wilderness later called Kentucky can be traced by place-names of Shawnee origin.

2965. Maxwell, Claude W. Indian names in West Virginia. *West Virginia review* 2:286, 291, May 1925.

2966. Miller, Aaron. How Kettle Run was named. *West Virginia folklore* 10:4-5, Fall 1959.

2967. Myers, Sylvester. The counties of West Virginia; *In his* History of West Virginia. Wheeling, 1915. 2:1-14.

2968. ——— Rivers of West Virginia and how they were named; *In his* History of West Virginia. Wheeling, 1915. 2:395-408.
From West Virginia archives and history.

2969. Names of Gilmer County towns have interesting origin. *Glenville pathfinder* Dec. 27, 1934.

2970. Norona, Delf. Wheeling; a West Virginia place-name of Indian origin. Moundsville, W. Va., West Virginia Archeological Society, 1958. 38p. (West Virginia Archeological Society. Publication series no. 4) (Wheeling, W.Va., Oglebay Institute. Mansion Museum Committee. Publication no. 1)

2971. Price, R. N. Place names in Pocahontas County, West Virginia. *Pocahontas times*, Marlinton, March 28, 1940.

2972. Summers, George W. State place names honor many noted Virginians. *Charleston (W.Va.) daily mail* Nov. 5, 1939.

2973. West Virginia. Constitutional Convention, 1861-1863. Debates and proceedings. Huntington, Gentry Bros., 1939?. 1:81-107.
The debate was on the first section of the constitution, which read: The State of Kanawha shall be and remain one of the United States of America. Move to strike out Kanawha, debated and carried. Moved to insert Alleghany, Columbia, New Virginia, West Virginia. These motions withdrawn and a vote taken by roll call, each answering with name preferred. Results: West Virginia-30; Kanawha-9; Western Virginia-2; Allegheny-2; Augusta-1.

2974. West Virginia. University. School of Journalism. Pronunciation guide to West Virginia place names. Morgantown, 1951. 51p.
Foreword signed: Paul Krakowski.

WISCONSIN

2975.　Ahnapee's new name. *Milwaukee sentinel* Aug. 13, 1897.

2976.　Banta, George. The significance of "Neenah." *Wisconsin magazine of history* 5:419-20, June 1922.
　"Neenah was originally a Winnebago village and its name was Wee-nah-pe-ko-ne, which was modified into 'Neenah.' "—Griffin.

2977.　Barton, Albert O. Where Wisconsin names originated. *Wisconsin archeologist* n.s. 26:84-85, Dec. 1945.

2978.　Bisson, Camille. Eau Claire and Eau Galle rivers. *Wisconsin magazine of history* 16:216-18, Dec. 1932.
　The story of the early names of the rivers.

2979.　Bleyer, Henry W. Derivation of the name Milwaukee. *Magazine of western history* 6:509-11, Sept. 1887.

2980.　Brunson, Alfred. Wisconsin geographical names. Wisconsin. State Historical Society. Annual report and collections 1:110-15. 1854.

2981.　Calkins, Hiram. Indian nomenclature of northern Wisconsin, with a sketch of the manners and customs of the Chippewas. Wisconsin. State Historical Society. Annual report and collections 1:119-26. 1854.
　Contains Chippewa names of streams, falls, and rapids.

2982.　Cassidy, Frederic Gomes. Folklore in place-names. *Badger folklore* 1:21-22, April 1948.

2983.　――――　"Koskonong," a misunderstood place-name. *Wisconsin magazine of history* 31:429-40, June 1948.
　Applied to parts of Dane County, 1820- .

2984.　――――　The naming of the "Four Lakes." *Wisconsin magazine of history* 29:7-24, Sept. 1945.
　Dane County.

2985.　――――　The place-names of Dane County, Wisconsin, with a foreword by Robert L. Ramsay. The secretary's report. [Greensboro?, N.C.], 1947. 255p. (Publication of the American Dialect Society, no. 7)
　Review: by A. R. Dunlap, *American speech* 23:52-55, Feb. 1948, particularly helpful in discussing methods to be used in such studies.

2986.　Cole, Harry Ellsworth. Baraboo and other place names in Sauk County, Wisconsin. Baraboo, Wis., Baraboo News Pub. Co., 1912. 50p.

2987.　Doty, J. D. Indian names in Wisconsin. *National intelligencer,* Washington, Dec. 19, 1840, p. 2.
　From the *New York American.*
　Pleads for standardized spelling of Indian names, and appends a list of Wisconsin names.

2988.　The Egg war. *Wisconsin then and now* 10:8, Oct. 1963.

Origin of the name Egg Harbor as recalled by Elizabeth Baird in v. 14 of the *Wisconsin historical collections*.

2989. Hathaway, Joshua. Indian names. Wisconsin. State Historical Society. Annual report and collections 1:116-18. 1854.
12 names in the Chippewa language, with meanings and etymologies.

2990. The History in our county names. *Badger history for boys and girls* 3:10-13, 28, Feb. 1950.

2991. How the names came, story of Wisconsin and their titles. *Milwaukee sentinel* Dec. 1895.

2992. Hunt, John Warren. Wisconsin gazetteer, containing the names, location, and advantages of the counties, cities, towns, villages, post offices, and settlements, together with a description of the lakes, water courses, prairies, and public localities, in the State of Wisconsin. Alphabetically arranged. Madison, B. Brown, printer, 1853. 255p.

2993. Indian names of our Wisconsin lakes. *Wisconsin archeologist* n.s. 4:164-65, July 1925.
An effort should be made to recover from present members of tribes as many as possible of the aboriginal designations, now largely unknown.

2994. Kellogg, Louise Phelps. Memorandum on the spelling of "Jolliet." *Wisconsin magazine of history* 1:67-69, Sept. 1917.
Prepared for submission to the Committee on State Affairs of the Wisconsin Assembly in April 1917. As a result, the bill which provided that the name Joliet be given to a state park at the mouth of the Wisconsin River was amended by substituting the spelling Jolliet.

2995. ——— Organization, boundaries and names of Wisconsin counties. Madison, The Society, 1910. 183-231p.
From Wisconsin. State Historical Society. Proceedings 57:183-231. 1909.

2996. Kuhm, Herbert W. Indian place-names in Wisconsin. *Wisconsin archeologist* 33:1-157, March-June 1952.
An alphabetical list.

2997. Legler, Henry Eduard. Origin and meaning of Wisconsin place-names; with special reference to Indian nomenclature. Wisconsin Academy of Sciences, Arts and Letters. Transactions 14:16-39. 1903.
Also reprinted separately.
Bibliography: p. 36-39.

2998. Naming of Wisconsin and Iowa. *Annals of Iowa* 3d ser. 27:323-24, April 1946.
Naming of the territories described in a letter from Senator George W. Jones, Iowa, to Charles Aldrich, curator of the Iowa Historical Department, in 1896.

2999. Nichols, Phebe Jewell. Wisconsin—what does it mean? *América indígena* 8:171-76, July 1948.
On the Menominee origin of the name.

3000. Origin of name Wisconsin. *Annals of Iowa* 3d ser. 31:367, July 1952.

3001. Origin of the word "Winnequah." *Wisconsin magazine of history* 1:196-97, Dec. 1917.
An explanation for the source of the name given to the point projecting into Lake Monona.

3002. Rouillard, Eugène. Les Iles des Douze Apôtres. Société de Géographie de Québec. Bulletin 12:40, janv. 1918.

3003. Schafer, Joseph. Testing traditions—I. Naming Wisconsin valley towns. *Wisconsin magazine of history* 7:238-42, Dec. 1923.
Avoca, Muscoda, Boscobel.

3004. Skinner, Alanson Buck. Some Menomini place names in Wisconsin; *In his* Material culture of the Menomini. New York, Museum of the American Indian, Heye Foundation, 1921. (Indian notes and monographs. Miscellaneous, no. 20) p. 382-90.
List obtained from John V. Satterlee.
Some of these names were published in the *Wisconsin archeologist* 18:97-102, Aug. 1919.

3005. Smith, Alice E. Stephen H. Long and the naming of Wisconsin. *Wisconsin magazine of history* 26:67-71, Sept. 1942.
Origin and earliest use of word Wisconsin for the territory.

3006. Smith, Huron H. Indian place names in Wisconsin. Milwaukee. Public Museum. Yearbook 10:252-66. 1930.
A list giving derivation and meaning, with several authorities quoted for each name.

3007. Some very odd names; Wisconsin towns that are badly handicapped. *Milwaukee sentinel* Jan. 3, 1897.

3008. Taylor, Stephen. How Mineral Point came by its sobriquet of "Shake-rag-under-the-hill." Wisconsin. State Historical Society. Collections 2:486. 1856.

3009. That's diggin' pretty deep. *Wisconsin then and now* 11:[8], Dec. 1964.
Names of towns and diggings in the mining country, in the form of a sonnet, from a pamphlet titled The home of the Badgers, by Oculus [Josiah Bushnell Grinnell]. Milwaukee, Wilshire & Co., 1845. 36p.

3010. Thwaites, Reuben Gold. Badger Indian names. *Milwaukee sentinel* Oct. 5, 1898.

3011. —— Origin of the term "Badger." Wisconsin. State Historical Society. Proceedings 1907:303-04.
Explanation as given by Moses M. Strong in the *State journal*, Madison, Dec. 10, 1879.

3012. Thwaites, Mrs. Reuben Gold. Indian nomenclature in Wisconsin. *Milwaukee sentinel* June 9, 1898.
Classified as distinctive names derived from fish, birds, animals, water, etc.

3013. Towns shed colorful names to gain dignity in Wisconsin. *Peoria star* Feb. 15, 1939.

3014. U.S. Board on Geographic Names. Decisions. No. 33—October 4, 1933. Names in Sawyer County, Wisconsin. Washington, Govt. Print. Off., 1934. 10p.

3015. U.S. Federal Writers' Project. Wisconsin. Wisconsin Indian place-name legends. Wisconsin centennial issue. Dorothy Moulding Brown. Madison, D. M. Brown, 1948. 30p. (Wisconsin folklore publications)
Published in 1936 under title: Wisconsin Indian place legends. 50p.

3016. Verwyst, Chrysostom. Geographical names in Wisconsin, Minnesota, and Michigan, having a Chippewa origin. Wisconsin. State Historical Society. Collections 12:390-98. 1892.
"Cites distortions of names and the source and significance of the correct terminations."—Price.

3017. —— A glossary of Chippewa Indian names of rivers, lakes and villages. *Acta et dicta* 4:253-74, July 1916.
These names are mostly of the Chippewa language though a considerable number of them are from other Algic dialects.

3018. Vogel, Virgil J. Wisconsin's name: a linguistic puzzle. *Wisconsin magazine of history* 48:181-86, Spring 1965.

3019. What's in a name. *Hobbies* 57:28, May 1952.
Name changes in Wisconsin.

3020. Wheeler, E. P. Geographical names of Chippewa origin.
Manuscript in possession of the State Historical Society of Wisconsin.

3021. White, H. H. French and Indian names in Wisconsin. *Sheboygan Falls news* May 1898.
Reprinted in the Carnival edition of the *Milwaukee sentinel* May 1898.

3022. Wisconsin. State Historical Society. List of post offices in Wisconsin.
A file of 4,000 cards listing alphabetically the names of all post offices established in Wisconsin, and a chronological listing from the first in 1821 to the end of 1917. Available in the Society's Manuscript Division.

3023. Witherell, B. P. H. Reminiscences of the Northwest, XV. Indian names. Wisconsin. State Historical Society. Collections 3:337. 1857.

3024. Woodbury, Jack E. Names, names, names. *Badger history* 12:8-9, Sept. 1958.

WYOMING

3025. Bass, Mabel. What's in a name. *Annals of Wyoming* 32:164-66, Oct. 1960.
Jay Em, named for Jim Moore.

3026. Brock, J. Elmer. How the Chugwater got its name. Westerners. Denver Posse. Brand-book v. 7, no. 5, p. 10, May 1951.

3027. Carter, W. A. List of names in Uinta County, Wyoming. July 1929. Manuscript in the State Historical Department of Wyoming.

3028. Chittenden, Hiram Martin. The Yellowstone National Park. Cincinnati, Clarke, 1895.
The various editions of this contain a chapter on geographic names in Yellowstone Park, and a map index giving all the names in the park.

3029. Clough, Wilson Ober. Some Wyoming place names. *Southern folklore quarterly* 7:1-11, March 1943.

3030. —— Some Wyoming place names. Somewhat enlarged from a paper read before the Western Folklore Conference, University of Denver, July 9, 1942. n.p., 1943. 22p.

3031. Edwards, Elsa Spear. Geographic names, Sheridan County, Wyoming. June 1929.
Manuscript in the State Historical Department of Wyoming.

3032. Emery, Raymond C. A dictionary of Albany County place-names. 115p. Thesis (M.S.) Univ. of Wyoming, 1940.

3033. Frémont, John Charles. [Letter]. *Annals of Wyoming* 30:173-74, Oct. 1958.
Letter to Herman G. Nickerson acknowledging Legislature's designation of his name to a county. March 22, 1884.

3034. Hagen, Mary. Turn left at Spring Creek. *American forests* 70:30-31, 57-59, Sept. 1964.
Names of streams in Wyoming.

3035. Hebard, Grace Raymond. Early history of Washakie County, Wyoming. 1924.
Manuscript in the State Historical Department of Wyoming.

3036. How Powder River shibboleth began. *Wyoming tribune* July 17, 1931.

3037. How Rawlins was named. *Wyoming tribune* July 28, 1931.

3038. Jackson Hole correct way to say it. *Pinedale roundup* Dec. 19, 1929.

3039. King, Norman D. Old Wyoming postoffices. *Annals of Wyoming* 29:157-59, Oct. 1957.
Origins of the names.

3040. Lacy, Bessie Elizabeth. Place names [in Fremont County]; *In* Wyoming. University. Extension Classes Dept. Fremont County and its communities. 1952. p. 67-71.
Bibliography: p. 71.

3041. Linford, Dee. Wyoming stream names. *Annals of Wyoming* 15:163-74,

254-70, 413-16, April, July, Oct. 1943; 16:71-74, Jan. 1944.
Reprinted from *Wyoming wild life magazine.*

3042. —— Wyoming stream names. Cheyenne, 1944. 33p. (Wyoming Game
and Fish Commission. Bulletin no. 3)

3043. Massicotte, E. Z. Le nom géographique Laramie. *Bulletin des recherches
historiques* 40:730-31. 1934.
"A note on the origin of the name Laramie in Wyoming. Lists various people
called Laramie, including French traders, 1788-1810, and raises the question as
to whether the name could have come from one of these or the descendants of one
of them."—Griffin.

3044. Mokler, Alfred James. Wyoming Board compiled list of geographic names.
Casper tribune herald Feb. 9, 1930.

3045. Naming of Slick Creek. *Worland grit.* n.d.

3046. Our mountains bear their names. *Pinedale roundup* Aug. 25, 1932.

3047. Owen, William O. The naming of Mount Owen. *Annals of Wyoming* 5:72-
77, Oct. 1927-Jan. 1928.

3048. Pence, Mary Lou & Lola M. Homsher. The ghost towns of Wyoming. New
York, Hastings House, 1956. 242p.

3049. Place names of Natrona County and their derivation as told by a historian.
Manuscript in the State Historical Department of Wyoming.

3050. Powder River nothing else. *Wyoming tribune* Dec. 3, 1928.

3051. Ridings, Reta W. Wyoming place names, comp. from clippings in University of Wyoming library. 1940. 77p.
Manuscript in the University library.

3052. Seminoe Range is not namesake of Seminole Indians. *Wyoming tribune*
Feb. 19, 1922.

3053. Sioux Indians claim they name Rawhide Buttes. *Lusk herald* July 4, 1929.

3054. Tale of the Crazy Woman, Wyoming. *Omaha world-herald* Jan. 22, 1929.

3055. Tensleep named by Indian tribe. *Wyoming tribune* Dec. 2, 1931.

3056. Territory of Wyoming; *In* Bancroft, Hubert Howe. History of Nevada,
Colorado and Wyoming. San Francisco, History Co., 1890. p. 739-40; also in
U.S. Congress. Congressional globe, 38th Congress, 2d session, 1864-65, p. 116;
40th Congress, 2d session, 1868, p. 1143, 2792-2802, 4322, 4344-45, 4352, 4380.
The first bill to provide temporary government for the Territory of Wyoming,
introduced in Congress in 1865, rested in committee. In 1868 there was considerable discussion as to choice of name, Lincoln, Cheyenne, Shoshonee, and Arapaho
also being proposed. James M. Ashley defended Wyoming.

3057. Titus, C. L. Derivation of name, Telephone Canyon. March 13, 1930.

Letter to the Wyoming State Historian which is in the State Historical Department of Wyoming.

3058. U.S. Board on Geographic Names. Decisions. No. 8—Decisions rendered June 3, 1931. Grand Teton National Park, Wyoming. Washington, Govt. Print. Off., 1931. 5p.

3059. —— Decisions. Yellowstone National Park, Wyoming, May 7, 1930. Washington, Govt. Print. Off., 1930. 26p.

3060. —— Decisions rendered Aug. 10, 1937: Yellowstone National Park, Wyoming. Washington, Govt. Print. Off., 1938. 11p.

3061. U.S. 88th Congress, 1st session. Senate. Joint resolution to designate the lake to be formed by the waters impounded by the Flaming Gorge Dam, Utah, and the recreation area contiguous to such lake in the states of Wyoming and Utah, as "O'Mahoney Lake and Recreation Area." S. J. Res. 17. Jan. 15, 1963. Washington, 1963. 2p.
Introduced by Mr. McGee and others and referred to the Committee on Interior and Insular Affairs.
Subsequent documents relating to this joint resolution, and related joint resolutions introduced in the House, were published as follows:

U.S. 88th Congress, 1st session. House. Joint resolution to designate the lake to be formed by the waters impounded by the Flaming Gorge Dam, Utah, and the recreation area contiguous to such lake in the states of Wyoming and Utah, as "O'Mahoney Lake and Recreation Area." H. J. Res. 293. Feb. 28, 1963. Washington, 1963. 2p.
Introduced by Mr. Aspinall and referred to the Committee on Interior and Insular Affairs.

U.S. 88th Congress, 1st session. Senate. Designating the lake to be formed by the waters impounded by the Flaming Gorge Dam, Utah, in the states of Wyoming and Utah, as "Lake O'Mahoney." Report no. 279, to accompany S. J. Res. 17. June 19, 1963. Calendar no. 260. Washington, 1963. 5p.
Submitted by Mr. Jackson, from the Committee on Interior and Insular Affairs, with amendments, as recommended by the Dept. of the Interior, to restrict the name to the lake, and designate it as Lake O'Mahoney.

—— [Reprint of the original joint resolution, June 19, 1963, with amendments, to accompany the report. Report no. 279 and Calendar no. 260 added]. 2p.

U.S. 88th Congress, 1st session. House. Joint resolution to designate the lake to be formed by the waters impounded by the Flaming Gorge Dam, Utah, as "Ashley Lake." H. J. Res. 604. July 31, 1963. Washington, 1963. 1p.
Introduced by Mr. Burton and referred to the Committee on Interior and Insular Affairs.
In honor of William Henry Ashley (1778-1838), a fur trader, explorer, and Congressman.

—— Providing designations for the lake to be formed by the waters impounded by Flaming Gorge Dam. Report no. 879, to accompany S. J. Res. 17. Oct. 30, 1963. Washington, 1963. 4p.
Submitted by Mr. Rogers, from the Committee on Interior and Insular Affairs, with amendments, that that portion of the lake in Utah be known as Lake Ashley

and the portion in Wyoming as Lake O'Mahoney. Two members of the Committee dissented. The Committee considered S. J. Res. 17, H. J. Res. 293, and H. J. Res. 604 simultaneously.

—— [Reprint of S. J. Res. 17, Oct. 30, 1963, with amendments, to accompany the report. Report no. 879 and House Calendar no. 161 added]. 2p.

3062. Wyoming place names. *Annals of Wyoming* 14:158-61, 227-39, 322-24, April, July, Oct. 1942; 15:85-90, Jan. 1943.

CANADA

3063. Armstrong, George Henry. The origin and meaning of place names in Canada. Toronto, Macmillan, 1930. 312p.
  Authors and works consulted: p. 312.
  Review: *Canadian historical review* 12:319-20, Sept. 1931.

3064. Association of Dominion Land Surveyors. Memorandum, prepared by the Executive Committee of the Dominion Land Surveyors Association, in accordance with a resolution regarding geographical nomenclature and orthography in Canada, passed at the annual meeting held at Ottawa, March 15th and 16th, 1886. Association of Dominion Land Surveyors. Report of proceedings 5:49-60. 1888.
  Also printed separately, Montreal, J. Lovell and Son, 1888. 12p.
  Suggests ways to correct errors and inconsistencies through compilation of a complete geographical dictionary by a government official, the Surveyor General, and in so doing follow the recommended system of nomenclature.

3065. Audet, Francis J. Variations des noms géographiques du Canada. Société de Géographie de Québec. Bulletin 15:290-301. 1921; 16:29-36. 1922.
  Gives past and present names.

3066. Baker, Edna. Prairie place names. Toronto, Ryerson Press, 1928. 28p. (The Ryerson Canadian history readers no. 3)
  "One of a series of readers designed to present historical facts to young Canadians."—Price.

3067. Barbeau, Marius. Legend and history in the oldest geographical names of the St. Lawrence. *Canadian geographical journal* 61:2-9, July 1960.

3068. ——— Légende et histoire dans les plus anciens noms géographiques du

Saint-Laurent. Congrès international de toponymie et d'anthroponymie. 3d, Brussels, 1949. v. 2, Actes et Mémoires. 1951. p. 404-11.

3069. —— Les noms les plus anciens sur la carte du Canada. *Revue trimestrielle canadienne* 35:243-55, automne, 1949.
Based on 16th-century maps.

3070. —— Les plus anciens noms du Saint-Laurent. *Revue de l'Université Laval* 3:649-57, avril 1949.

3071. The Bay of Fundy. *Historical magazine* 10:321, Oct. 1866.
A note on the origin of the name Fundy.

3072. Bedard, Avila. La traduction des noms géographiques. *Le parler français* (Société du Parler Français au Canada) 13:263-72, fév. 1915.
"The author's subject is really the translation into English of names originally French, and he criticizes the Geographic Board of Canada which prescribes that usage is to prevail in cases where both French and English equivalents are found."
—*Review of historical publications relating to Canada* 20:213-14. 1915.

3073. Bell, Charles Napier. Some historical names and places of the Canadian North-west. A paper read before the Society on the evening of 22d January, 1885. Winnipeg, Manitoba Free Press Print, 1885. 8p. (Manitoba. Historical and Scientific Society. Transactions no. 17)

3074. Bourgeois, François. Les noms géographiques dans les Provinces Maritimes. Société de Géographie de Québec. Bulletin 7:336-52, nov. 1913.

3075. Bourinot, John George. Canadian historic names. *Canadian monthly* 7: 289-300, April 1875.
"A general article on the history of place-names, particularly in regard to the effect of Indian nomenclature and legends of different localities on present day English names."—Price.

3076. Brant-Sero, J. Ojijateckha. Indian place names in Mohawk, collected by J. O. Brant-Sero and Chief Alexander Hill. Toronto. Ontario Provincial Museum. Annual archaeological report 1898:171-72.
List of Canadian and American names with their Indian equivalents and meanings.

3077. Buchanan, Milton Alexander. Early Canadian history. Royal Society of Canada. Transactions 3d ser. v. 42, sec. 2, p. 31-57, May 1948.
The name Canada, p. 52-53. Concludes "Cartier's definition of the word must be accepted."

3078. —— Notes on Portuguese place-names in north-eastern America; *In* Estudios hispánicos, homenaje a Archer M. Huntington. Wellesley, Mass., 1952. p. 99-104.
Principally Newfoundland; also Labrador, Nova Scotia, New England coast.

3079. Burns, E. L. M. Their name is Mud. *Beaver* outfit [*i.e.*, volume] 267:14-19, June 1936.
A member of the Geographic Board of Canada describes something of the procedure and problems of straightening out the confusion of duplicate and trite names for lakes, streams, and mountains.

3080. Burwash, Armon. Concerning a few well known Indian names. Toronto. Ontario Provincial Museum. Annual archaeological report 1913:34-36.

3081. —— Concerning some Indian place-names in Canada. *Ottawa naturalist* 32:153-55, Feb. 1919.
Indicates source of name by tribe.

3082. Canada. Dept. of Mines and Technical Surveys. Geographical Branch. Selected bibliography of Canadian toponymy. Ottawa, 1964. 27p. (*Its* Bibliographical series, no. 30)

3083. Canada. Geographic Board. Meaning of Canadian city names, by R. Douglas. Ottawa, F. A. Acland, 1922. 21p.
Reprinted from its Report 17:34-52. 1919/21.
Translation: Histoire des noms de quelques cités canadiennes. Société de Géographie de Québec. Bulletin 17:242-49, 304-15, sept., nov. 1923; 18:33-41, janv. 1924; reprinted separately: Ottawa, F. A. Acland, 1923. 22p.

3084. —— Nomenclature of the mountains of western Canada, approved on the 2nd April, 1918. Ottawa, J. de L. Taché, 1918. 4p.
Also published in its Report 16:33-34. 1917/19.

3085. —— Report, containing all decisions. v. 1-19. 1898-1927. Ottawa.
Report year varies.
no. 1-11, 1898-1912, Supplement to the Annual report of the Dept. of Marine and Fisheries. Marine; no. 12-19, 1913-27, Supplement to the Annual report of the Dept. of the Interior.
Reports for 1898-1919/21 issued in the Sessional papers of the Parliament.
Some reports are cumulative from 1898.
Supplements to the various reports were published in the *Canada gazette* from time to time and were incorporated in the next report.
Each report includes a list of the members of the Board; the bylaws; the decisions, and from 1904 on an index to the decisions; the rules of nomenclature; and a record of the routine work of the Board.
Review: *Review of historical publications relating to Canada* 16:125-26. 1912; of v. 1: by Henry Gannett, *National geographic magazine* 10:519-20, Nov. 1899.

3086. Canada. Permanent Committee on Geographical Names. Principles and procedures. Ottawa, Dept. of Mines and Technical Surveys, Geographical Branch, 1963. 6, 6p.
In English and French. The French is in a separate part, inverted.

3087. Canada. *Historical magazine and notes and queries concerning the antiquities, history and biography of America* 1:153, 188, 217, 315, 349, May-Nov. 1857; 2:23-24, Jan. 1858; 3:192, June 1859.
In the Notes and queries column.
Various explanations of the origin of the word.

3088. Canadian Broadcasting Corporation. A guide to the pronunciation of Canadian place names. Rev. ed. Toronto, 1959. 32p.
Originally part of the CBC's Handbook for announcers, published 1942.

3089. Caron, Abbé Ivanhoe. Les noms géographiques de la Rivière Ottawa in 1686. Société de Géographie de Québec. Bulletin 11:4-10, janv. 1917.

3090. Carrière, Gaston. Essai de toponymie oblate canadienne. *Revue de l'Université d'Ottawa* 28:364-94, 522-31, juil./sept.-oct./déc. 1958; 29:92-108, 233-46, janv./mars-avril/juin 1959.

3091. Chicanot, E. L. A mine of any other name would sound more sweet; a plea for reform in the matter of Canadian nomenclature. *Canadian mining journal* 57: 598-99, Nov. 1936.

3092. Corry, J. H. Some Canadian cities; meaning and origin of names. *Canadian geographical journal* 26:297, June 1943; 27:17, 263, July, Dec. 1943; 28:40, Jan. 1944.

3093. Dauzat, Albert. Le nom du Canada. *Revue internationale d'onomastique* 3:81-82, juin 1951.

3094. Daviault, Pierre. Les noms de lieux au Canada. Royal Society of Canada. Transactions 3d ser. v. 42, sec. 1, p. 42-52, May 1948.
   Discussion of this article by W. H. Alexander in *Western folklore* 8:259-60, July 1949.

3095. Davies, B. On the origin of the name "Canada." *Canadian naturalist and geologist* 6:430-32, Dec. 1861.

3096. Dawson, Samuel Edward. The Saint Lawrence basin and its border-lands, being the story of their discovery, exploration and occupation. London, Lawrence and Bullen, 1905. 451p.
   Also published New York, Stokes, 1905, with title The Saint Lawrence, its basin & border-lands. 451p.
   The origin and meaning of the word Acadia: p. 249-50.

3097. Delaney, G. F. Current problems in Canadian geographic nomenclature. *Canadian surveyor* 9:6-12, Jan. 1947.

3098. ——— Problems in cartographic nomenclature. *Canadian surveyor* 16: 254-63, Nov. 1962.
   Summary in French on p. 263.
   Discusses the desirability of a more serious and systematic approach to map nomenclature on the part of cartographers. Gives examples of difficulties caused by the existence of several languages in an area.

3099. Denys, Nicolas. The description and natural history of the coasts of North America (Acadia). Trans. and ed., with a memoir of the author, collateral documents, and a reprint of the original by Wm. F. Ganong. Toronto, Champlain Society, 1908. 625p.
   Extensive place-name footnotes.

3100. Desbois, Paul. Noms géographiques. Société de Géographie de Québec. Bulletin 7:180-83, 215-23, 285-91, mai-sept. 1913.
   "Notes on the origin and correct form of certain geographical names of Canada."
   —Griffin.

3101. Donovan, Frank P., Jr. Named for railroad presidents. *Railroad magazine* Feb. 1965, p. 24-27.
   Communities in the United States and Canada that were named for railroad presidents.

3102. Douglas, Robert. Notes on mountain nomenclature; coming of age of the Geographic Board of Canada. *Canadian alpine journal* 10:32-37. 1919.

3103. ——— The place-names of Canada. *Scottish geographical magazine* 36: 154-57, July 15, 1920.
A paper read in Ottawa, Feb. 4, 1920, at the annual meeting of the Association of Dominion Land Surveyors. Discusses the principles which underlie a system of nomenclature for Canada.

3104. Elliott, Aaron Marshall. On the word "Canada." *British American magazine* 1:490-93. 1863.

3105. ——— Origin of the name "Canada." *Modern language notes* 3:327-45, June 1888.
Elliott's theory, which traces the word to a Spanish origin, is disposed of by Walter Bell Scaife, Historical notes on certain geographical names (see no. 3180).

3106. Falconer, Robert. What is implied in the term Canadian. *English review* 41:595-604, Oct. 1925.
The history of Canada has given the term Canadian a distinctive meaning, more suitable than the name Americans as used by inhabitants of the United States.

3107. Fraser, J. Keith. Canadian Permanent Committee on Geographical Names. *Geographical bulletin* (Canada. Dept. of Mines and Technical Surveys. Geographical Branch) 21:130-34, May 1964.
A brief history of the organization and work of the Committee and its predecessors, with a list of guiding principles for place-names.

3108. Frémont, Donatien. Des noms français pour nos centres français. Société de Géographie de Québec. Bulletin 16:222-24. 1922.
Plea to preserve the significant French names of western Canada.

3109. Ganong, William Francis. Crucial maps in the early cartography and place-nomenclature of the Atlantic coast of Canada. With an introduction, commentary, and map notes by Theodore E. Laying. Toronto, Univ. of Toronto Press in co-operation with the Royal Society of Canada, 1964. 511p. (Royal Society of Canada. Special publications no. 7)
Reprint of material originally published in Royal Society of Canada. Proceedings and transactions 3d ser. v. 23, sec. 2, p. 135-75; v. 24, sec. 2, p. 135-88; v. 25, sec. 2, p. 169-203; v. 26, sec. 2, p. 125-79; v. 27, sec. 2, p. 149-95; v. 28, sec. 2, p. 149-294; v. 29, sec. 2, p. 101-29; v. 30, sec. 2, p. 109-29; v. 31, sec. 2, p. 101-30. 1929-37.
"Traces the evolution of the cartography and place-nomenclature of the Atlantic coast of Canada, with the associated parts of Newfoundland and New England, from the time of the first discoveries down to the inauguration of our modern geography by Champlain, 1526-1600."—Griffin. Discusses in particular the Cosa map of 1500; the Third decade, 1520-1530, the Homem maps, and the Fagundes voyages; maps of Maggiolo, 1527, and Verrazano, 1524 and 1529; maps of 1535 to 1542; the compiled or composite maps from 1526 to 1600; the geography and cartography of the Cartier voyages; the Mercator world chart of 1569; and Transition from the Mercator chart to the cartographical works of Champlain.

3110. ——— The history of certain geographical names; *In his* The cartography of the Gulf of St. Lawrence, from Cartier to Champlain. Royal Society of Canada. Proceedings and transactions v. 7, sec. 2, p. 51-55. 1889.

3111. —— An organization of the scientific investigation of the Indian place-nomenclature of the Maritime Provinces of Canada. Royal Society of Canada. Proceedings and transactions 3d ser. v. 5, sec. 2, p. 179-93; v. 6, sec. 2, p. 179-99; v. 7, sec. 2, p. 81-106; v. 8, sec. 2, p. 259-93; v. 9, sec. 2, p. 375-448. 1911-15.

In addition to material on specific words includes a summary of "methods of exact scientific analysis." The Indian groups are Micmac, Maliseet, Passama-quoddy, a division of the Maliseets, and the Penobscots.

3112. —— The origin of the place-names Acadia and Norumbega. Royal Society of Canada. Proceedings and transactions 3d ser. v. 11, sec. 2, p. 105-11. 1917.

"Presents evidence drawn from early maps and records of explorations."—Griffin. See also author's article Norumbega, *ibid.* v. 25, sec. 2, p. 200-02. 1931, in which he concludes that Norumbega was the Indian name for the country between Narragansett Bay and New York, or, more specifically, used by the Indians of Narragansett Bay for their country. See also his Acadia, *ibid.* p. 202-03, which develops argument stated *ibid.* v. 9, sec. 2, p. 439-48. 1915.

3113. Geographical names in the Canadian North. *Arctic* 3:72, 195, April, Dec. 1950; 4:144, Sept. 1951; 5:63-64, 132, March, July 1952; 6:280, Dec. 1953; 8:77, Winter 1955; 9:272-75. 1956: 10:61-62, 123-28. 1957; 11:64-66, 127-32, 193-94, 257. 1958; 13:65-66, 142-44, 208, 276. 1960; 14:133-38, 204-08, 269-74, June, Sept., Dec. 1961.

Adopted by Canadian Board on Geographical Names for official use in the Northwest Territories, the Yukon, and northern Quebec.

3114. Guinard, Joseph Étienne. Les noms indiens de mon pays. Leur signification, leur histoire. Montréal, Rayonnement [1960]. 197p.

3115. Hamilton, P. St. C. Origin of Canadian place names. *MacLean's magazine* 38:35, Aug. 1, 1925.

3116. Harrington, John Peabody. Our state names. Smithsonian Institution. Annual report 1954:373-88.

Reprinted as: Smithsonian Institution. Publication 4205. 1955.

Includes Canadian names of Indian origin: p. 387-88.

3117. Harrisse, Henry. The discovery of North America; a critical, documentary, and historic investigation, with an essay on the early cartography of the New World, including descriptions of two hundred and fifty maps or globes existing or lost, constructed before the year 1536; to which are added a chronology of one hundred voyages westward, projected, attempted, or accomplished between 1431 and 1504; biographical accounts of the three hundred pilots who first crossed the Atlantic; and a copious list of the original names of American regions, caciqueships, mountains, islands, capes, gulfs, rivers, towns, and harbours. London, H. Stevens and Son; Paris, H. Welter, 1892. 802p.

Reprinted Amsterdam, N. Israel, 1961. 802p.

Geographical index, p. 751-84.

3118. Hawkes, Arthur. Town christeners in the West. *Canadian magazine* 37:

72-78, May 1911.
"Some interesting examples of the origin of place-names in Canada, especially along the railroad lines."—Price.

3119.   Holmer, Nils Magnus.   Indian place names in North America.   Cambridge, Harvard Univ. Press, 1948.   44p.   (American Institute in the University of Upsala. Essays and studies on American language and literature)

3120.   How, D.   Who called it that?   Devout Indians and loyal Englishmen; stray Portuguese and footloose Frenchmen—they all left a mark on our map.   *MacLean's magazine* 61:19, 31-32, July 1, 1948.

3121.   Indian place names in western Canada.   *Canadian pictorial* 10:18-19, June 1915.
Signed: Max McD.

3122.   Johnson, Alexander.   Origin of the name of Canada; *In his* Our semi-jubilee and Canada.   Royal Society of Canada.   Proceedings and transactions 2d ser. 12: lxi-lxiii.   1906.

3123.   Johnson, George.   Place-names of Canada, read before the Ottawa Scientific Society, Dec. 3rd, 1897.   Ottawa, E. J. Reynolds, 1898.   xxxvii p.
Also published in Ottawa Literary and Scientific Society.   Transactions 1:27-62. 1897-98.

3124. ———   Place-names of Canada: Selkirk.   *Canadian magazine* 13:395-406, Sept. 1899.
Names commemorating the Earl of Selkirk.

3125. ———   Place-names of Canada: the Carletons.   *Canadian magazine* 12: 289-95, Feb. 1899.
Places, streets, etc. named in memory of Sir Guy Carleton.

3126.   Jones, Cyril Meredith.   Indian, pseudo-Indian place names in the Canadian West.   Winnipeg, Ukrainian Free Academy of Sciences, 1956.   19p.   (Ukrainian Free Academy of Sciences.   Series: Onomastica, no. 12)

3127.   Kelton, Dwight H.   Indian names of places near the Great Lakes.   Detroit, Mich., Detroit Free Press, 1888.   55p.
Most of the names are derived from the Ojibway, Cree, and Delaware languages.
Review: by A. S. Gatschet, *Journal of American folk-lore* 2:69, Jan.-March 1889; by D. G. Brinton, *American antiquarian* 11:68, Jan. 1889.

3128.   Kirkconnell, Watson.   Canadian toponymy and the cultural stratification of Canada.   Winnipeg, Ukrainian Free Academy of Sciences.   1954.   16p.   (Ukrainian Free Academy of Sciences.   Series: Onomastica, no. 7)

3129.   Krahn, Cornelius.   Mennonite names of persons and places.   *Mennonite life* 15:36-38, Jan. 1960.
In North and South America.
For a complete list of Mennonite villages, see article Villages in v. 4 of Mennonite encyclopedia.   1959.

3130.   Lacourcière, Luc.   Toponymie canadienne; *In* Société du Parler Français

au Canada. Études sur le parler français au Canada. Québec, Les Presses Universitaires Laval, 1955. p. 199-220.
Observations on Canadian place-names.

3131. Lanctot, Gustave. Nouvelle-France ou Canada. *Revue d'histoire de l'Amérique française* 14:171-72, sept. 1960.

3132. Lanos, J. M. What's in a name? *Queen's quarterly* 17:44-57, July-Sept. 1909.
A plea for regeneration in the practice of name giving in the United States and Canada. Article deals largely with place-names in western Europe, showing how beautiful and appropriate is the terminology used by the Anglo-Saxons, Northmen, and Celts.

3133. Laurent, Joseph. Etymology of Indian names by which are designated certain tribes, towns, rivers, lakes, etc.; *In his* New familiar Abenakis and English dialogues. Quebec, Printed by L. Brousseau, 1884. p. 205-22.

3134. Leechman, Douglas. The father of place names. *Beaver* outfit [*i.e.*, volume] 285:24-30, Autumn 1954.
Dr. Robert Bell, 1841-1917, of Geological Survey, named more than 3000 topographic features.

3135. Loveless, Edna. Geographic names. *Canadian surveyor* 8:21-23, April 1946.
Meaning of a few names.

3136. Maclean, John. Bungay and others. *Beaver* 4:397-99, Aug. 1924.
Indian place-names on the prairies.

3137. MacMillan, Donald Baxter. Eskimo place names and aid to conversation. Washington, Hydrographic Office, U.S. Navy, 1943. 154p. (H. O. Miscel. no. 10,578)
A list of Eskimo names, with meaning, found on northern maps and charts, for Labrador, Hudson Bay, Baffin Land, Greenland, Ellesmere Land, p. 7-77.

3138. Maheux, A. Les noms de lieux. Société de Géographie de Québec. Bulletin 16:234-39. 1922.
General survey of the subject—the act of commemorating historical and religious persons or natural locations.

3139. Masta, Henry Lorne. Abenaki Indian legends, grammar and place names. Victoriaville, P.Q., La Voix des Bois-Francs, 1932. 110p.
The meaning of Indian names of rivers, lakes, etc., p. 81-105.

3140. Masters, D. C. A name for the Dominion. *Mitre* 54:23-26, Trinity 1947.
Controversy over name before passing of British North America Act.

3141. Maurault, Joseph Pierre Anselme. Historie des Abenakis, depuis 1605 jusqu'à nos jours. [Sorel, Qué.], Imprimé à l'atelier typographique de la "Gazette de Sorel," 1866. 631p.
A list of place-names in Maine and Canada, with significations, in introduction p. ii-vii.

3142. Meadows-Wood, P. D. Canadian city names. *United empire* n.s. 13:651-53, Oct. 1922.

3143. Miller, Emile. Nos noms de lieux. Société de Géographie de Québec. Bulletin 4:205-07, sept. 1910.
Many places have been named after the saints.

3144. Naming new towns big task in Canada. *New York times* Nov. 18, 1934, sec. 8, p. 12, col. 3.
In choosing place-names near international boundary, Canada cooperates with U.S. Geographic Board. Very brief description of work of Canadian Geographic Board.

3145. No passport for Canada. *New York times* June 16, 1940, sec. 10, p. 24, col. 4.
Origin of some place-names.

3146. O Tupona. *Newsweek* 30:46, Oct. 20, 1947; 30:2, Nov. 3, 1947.
Names that were considered for Canada. Based on article by D. C. Masters (see no. 3140).

3147. Origine de quelques noms canadiens. *Bulletin des recherches historiques* 11:145, 183, 215, 242, 269, 277, 309, mai-oct. 1905; 12:77, mars 1906.
A list giving very brief notes on origin of names.

3148. Pacifique, Père. Le pays des Micmacs. Liste de 2500 noms géographiques des Provinces Maritimes (l'ancienne Acadie), de la Gaspésie et de Terreneuve en langue micmaque avec la signification quand elle est connue, les noms correspondants en anglais ou en français et de copieuses notes historiques et géographiques; contient cinq cartes regionales, selon les anciens districts. Montréal, l'Auteur, 1934; *In his* Études historiques et géographiques. Ristigouche, Co. Bonaventure, 1935. p. 175-321.
Also reprinted separately: Montréal, l'Auteur, 1934. 176-321p.; another printing has label pasted over imprint on title page: Sainte-Anne de Ristigouche, Co. Bon., 1935.
Originally published in Société de Géographie de Québec. Bulletin 21:111-17, 165-85. 1927; 22:43-55, 140-45, 270-77. 1928; 23:37-45. 1929; 25:96-106. 1931; 27:51-64. 1933; 28:105-47. 1934. The book corrects many typographical errors that appeared in the articles.
Includes place-names with English equivalents.

3149. Palmer, P. E. By any other name. *Canadian geographical journal* 36:149-51, March 1948.
Wide variety of generic and proper names given to similar physical features.

3150. ——— The Canadian Board on Geographical Names. *Names* 1:79-84, June 1953.
A brief summary of the organization and work of the Board, by the chairman.

3151. Patterson, R. M. Names and the unnamed spaces. *Canadian magazine* 74: 13, 30, July 1930.
Too often place-names are ugly and pointless.

3152. Pease, Mary Agnes. There's something in a name. *MacLean's magazine*

52:65, April 15, 1939; 52:49, May 1, 1939; 52:77, May 15, 1939; 52:49, June 1, 1939; 52:49, June 15, 1939.

Series of articles on whys and wherefores of Canadian place-names. Includes Canada, Nova Scotia, New Brunswick, Prince Edward Island, and St. Lawrence River.

3153. Price, Esther Frances. Guide to material on place-names in the United States and Canada. Urbana, Ill., 1934. 250p.

Thesis (M.A.) Univ. of Illinois, 1934. On file in the University Library.

3154. Prowse, George Robert Farrar. Exploration of the Gulf of St. Lawrence, 1499-1525. Winnipeg, 1929. 23p.

List of place names: p. 21-23.

3155. Prud'homme, L. A. Dans l'ouest canadien. Société de Géographie de Québec. Bulletin 5:136-39, mars 1911.

Lakes, rivers, portages, and forts.

3156. Rand, Silas Tertius. A first reading book in the Micmac language: comprising the Micmac numerals, and the names of the different kinds of beasts, birds, fishes, trees, &c. of the Maritime Provinces of Canada. Also, some of the Indian names of places, and many familiar words and phrases, trans. literally into English. Halifax, Nova Scotia Print. Co., 1875. 108p.

Micmac place-names: p. 81-104.

3157. —— Micmac place-names in the Maritime Provinces and Gaspé Peninsula recorded between 1852 and 1890. Collected, arranged and indexed by Lieut.-Col. Wm. P. Anderson. Ottawa, Printed at the Surveyor General's Office, 1919. 116p.

Publication of the Geographic Board of Canada.

3158. —— Micmac place names in the Maritime Provinces of Canada, copied from Rand's manuscripts, and supplemented by help from other sources; *In his* Rand's Micmac dictionary from phonographic wordlists. Charlottetown, P.E.I., Patriot Pub. Co., 1902. p. 177-92.

3159. Reade, John. The history of Canadian geographical names. *New Dominion monthly* 11:344. 1873.

Also in *Maple leaves*, Quebec, 1873.

3160. —— The testimony of names of places. *Rose-Belford's Canadian monthly* 1:602-04, Nov. 1878.

The source of some of the names in North America.

3161. Reynolds, Horace. Fish names land. *Christian Science monitor* Dec. 11, 1957, p. 8.

"The Basque word baccallaóa (Spanish bacallao), meaning codfish, may have come from the Indians. It once was the name of all the French territory north of the St. Lawrence."—*American speech.*

3162. Robinson, Percy James. Potier—places aux français (from Mss. in Municipal Library, Montreal). *Bulletin des recherches historiques* 48:365-68, déc. 1942.

Indian names with French equivalents in Potier's list.

3163. Roe, Frank Gilbert. Buffalo place-names; *In his* The North American buffalo. Toronto, Univ. of Toronto Press, 1951. p. 817-28.
Also miscellaneous references in index: Place-names.

3164. Rouillard, Eugène. L'invasion des noms sauvages. *Bulletin du parler français au Canada* 7:162-70, janv. 1909; 8:97-100, nov. 1909.

3165. ———— Un nom géographique: la Baie des Chaleurs. Société de Géographie de Québec. Bulletin 9:210-11. 1915.
Plea for name to be recognized as it was historically known, instead of the proposed translation Chaleur Bay.

3166. ———— Noms géographiques de la Province de Québec et des Provinces Maritimes empruntés aux langues sauvages; avec carte indiquant les territoires occupés autrefois par les races aborigènes; étymologie, traduction et orthographie. Québec, Marcotte, 1906. 110p. (Publications de la Société du Parler Français au Canada)
Auteurs et ouvrages consultés: p. 5-6.
"A large proportion of the interpretations of New Brunswick place-names in Rouillard's work although credited to Father Bourgeois (of St. Joseph's College, Memramcook) are identical with those in my earlier work (in these Transactions) on New Brunswick place-names, and were evidently taken from that work, though without the customary acknowledgement, by Father Bourgeois."—William Francis Ganong. An organization of the scientific investigation of the Indian place-nomenclature of the Maritime Provinces of Canada. Royal Society of Canada. Proceedings and transactions 3d ser. v. 5, sec. 2, p. 180. 1911.

3167. ———— Noms sauvages; étymologie. Québec, É. Marcotte, 1905. 17p.
Reprinted from *Bulletin du parler français au Canada*.

3168. ———— Noms sauvages; étymologie et traduction. Société de Géographie de Québec. Bulletin 5:410-22, nov. 1911; 6:31-42, janv. 1912.
"A collection of geographical names of the Province of Quebec and the Maritime Provinces, supplementary to the author's 'Noms géographiques' published in 1906."—Griffin.

3169. ———— Quelques noms géographiques. Société de Géographie de Québec. Bulletin 11:91-95, mars 1917.
The history and origin of the Baie du Tonnerre, Rivière Dalmas, French names in the Baie James, Tracadie.

3170. Roy, Pierre Georges. D'où vient le nom de "Nouvelle France"? Société de Géographie de Québec. Bulletin 12:79-80, mars 1918.

3171. ———— Quelques forts du régime français. *Bulletin des recherches historiques* 54:5-14, 35-46, janv.-fév. 1948.

3172. ———— Quelques noms de France. Société de Géographie de Québec. Bulletin 12:57-58, janv. 1918.

3173. Rudnyckyj, Jaroslav B. Canadian place names of Ukrainian origin. 3d ed. Winnipeg, Ukrainian National Home Assoc., 1957. 89p. (Ukrainian Free Academy of Sciences. Series: Onomastica, no. 2)
In Ukrainian. The Ukrainian forms are accompanied by their transliterated

English forms.

An English version, at least in part, of this appeared in the author's Studies in onomastics. 1958. (Onomastica no. 15)

1st ed. 1949; 2d ed. 1951.

Review: by Yar Slavutych, *Names* 6:254-55, Dec. 1958.

3174. —— Classification of Canadian place-names. Congrès international de sciences onomastiques. 4th, Uppsala. Mémoires. 1952. v. 2, pt. 2, p. 453-57.

Also reprinted separately.

3175. —— Slavic toponymic neologisms in Canada. *Canadian Slavonic papers* 1:89-92. 1956.

Descriptive names, abbreviated names, other forms of names.

3176. —— Studies in onomastics. Winnipeg, Ukrainian Free Academy of Sciences, 1956-58. 2v. (Ukrainian Free Academy of Sciences. Series: Onomastica, no. 11, 15)

v. 1, Canadian Slavic namelore; in Ukrainian with English summary. "In this treatise (v. 1), the author presents a full scheme of the types of namelore illustrating his theoretical classification with the material gathered among Slavic settlers in Canada, in 1949-55."

v. 2 is composed of ten of his papers dealing with toponymic problems, etymologies of place-names, etc., mostly Ukrainica, but including some of interest to Canadian and American researchers.

Review of v. 2: by Yar Slavutych, *Names* 8:61-62, March 1960.

3177. —— ed. Ukrainian-Canadian folklore. Texts in English translation. Winnipeg, Ukrainian Free Academy of Sciences, 1960. 232p. (Ukrainica occidentalia, v. VII [5])

Short articles on origin of various place-names, p. 174-83.

3178. Scadding, Henry. Sir Joseph Banks again. Queen Charlotte and some local names, a supplemental note. Toronto, 1890?. 4p.

3179. —— Some lapsed names in Canadian local nomenclature. Canadian Institute. Proceedings n.s. 1:33-38. 1898.

3180. Scaife, Walter Bell. Historical notes on certain geographical names. Canada; *In his* America: its geographical history, 1492-1892. Baltimore, Johns Hopkins Press, 1892. p. 83-88.

Disposes of theory advanced by Aaron Marshall Elliott, Origin of the name "Canada" (see no. 3105), that the name Canada originated from a Spanish word, and traces use of the name on maps from 1548 to 1630.

3181. Sebert, L. Geographic place names. *Canadian surveyor* 15:113-17, March 1960.

Principles of transliteration and representation on maps of place-names in Canada and elsewhere.

3182. Shepherd, Paul. Too many Pine lakes, a story of the troubles dogging the Geographic Board of Canada. *Forest and outdoors* 44:24-25, July 1948.

Repetition of names.

3183. Sherwin, Reider Thorbjorn. The Viking and the red man; the Old Norse

origin of the Algonquin language. New York, Funk & Wagnalls, 1940-48. 5v.
  Algonquin place names: 1:254-310; 2:162-78; 3:155-61; 4:172-208; 5:170-99.
  Bibliography of principal sources of Algonquin place names: 1:331; 2:191.

3184. Skelton, Isabel. The name "Canada." *Canadian magazine of politics, science, art and literature* 57:312-14, Aug. 1921.
  Various names suggested for Canada at the time of the Confederation of the provinces in 1864-65.

3185. Skinner, Charles M. Some odd names of places across the border. *Current literature* 25:41, Jan. 1899.
  An extract from his Myths and legends beyond our borders. Gives origin and meaning.

3186. Skinner, L. B. Map nomenclature. *Canadian surveyor* 12:274-77, July 1954.
  The story behind the names, including work of the Canadian Board on Geographical Names.

3187. Stewart, George Rippey. Names of wild animals for natural features in the United States and Canada. *Revue internationale d'onomastique* 12:282-92, déc. 1960.
  Estimated that about 40,000 natural features in the United States bear the names of wild animals; in Canada, about 10,000.

3188. Strathglass, Allan. Odd Canadian place names. *MacLean's magazine* 40: 17, 76-77, June 1, 1927.

3189. Stursberg, Peter. The strange place names of Canada. *Saturday night, Canada's magazine of business and contemporary affairs* 76:17-18, Aug. 19, 1961.

3190. Tanguay, C. Étude sur les noms. Royal Society of Canada. Proceedings and transactions 1st ser. v. 1, sec. 1, p. 119-29. 1883.

3191. Thomson, D. Walter. There's magic in a name. *MacLean's magazine* 41:3-5, 54, June 1, 1928.

3192. U.S. Board on Geographic Names. Decisions. Washington, Dept. of the Interior.
  Canada is included in the following Decision lists: 4301 (July 1943-Oct. 1943); 4404, 4406-4407 (April, June-July 1944); 4701-4703 (Jan.-March 1947); 4801-4806 (Jan.-June 1948); 4905-4906 (May-June 1949); 5007 (Nov. 1950).

3193. ⸺ Decisions on names in Canada. August 1953. Washington, Dept. of the Interior, 1953. 78p. (*Its* Cumulative decision list no. 5304)
  "In effect as of July 1953."

3194. Van Steen, Marcus. Our heritage of fascinating place-names. *Imperial oil review* 43:9-11, April 1959.

3195. Velyhorskyi, Ivan. The term and name "Canada." Winnipeg, Ukrainian Free Academy of Sciences, 1955. 30p. (Ukrainian Free Academy of Sciences. Series: Onomastica, no. 10)
  In Ukrainian with summary in English.

3196. Voorhis, Ernest. Historic forts and trading posts of the French and of the English fur trading companies. Ottawa, Dept. of the Interior, National Development Bureau, 1930. 188p.

Alphabetical list of forts and posts, p. 28-181.

"A few of these establishments were located on what is now territory of the United States."—Pref.

Includes map of Mississippi and Ohio valleys showing chain of historic French forts.

3197. Walton, Ivan H. Origin of names on the Great Lakes. *Names* 3:239-46, Dec. 1955.

Names of the lakes and their connecting waterways, with some mention of surrounding territory.

3198. Whitcher, A. H. Geographical nomenclature. n.p., 1893. 67-72p.

Reprinted from Proceedings of the Association of Dominion Land Surveyors.

3199. Wightman, F. A. Maritime provincialisms and contrasts—place-names. *Canadian magazine of politics, science, art and literature* 39:168-72, June 1912.

Indicates in a general way the types of names peculiar to each province and in contrast to the others.

3200. Wilkins, Ernest Hatch. Ar Cadie. *Modern language notes* 73:504-05, Nov. 1958.

Offers a different explanation of the process by which Arcadie became Acadie from that discussed in the following article.

3201. ———— Arcadia in America. American Philosophical Society. Proceedings 101:4-30, Feb. 15, 1957.

A well-documented study tracing the use of the name Arcadia and all its various spellings from earliest maps and journals to place-names in the United States, Canada, and South America today. All derive from the name of a novel Arcadia, by Jacopo Sannazzaro, written *ca.* 1485.

3202. Wintemberg, W. J. The Crimean War and some place names of Canada. Royal Society of Canada. Proceedings and transactions 3d ser. v. 21, sec. 2, p. 71-79. 1927.

Place- and street names which perpetuate the names of battles and of some of the cities and fortresses bombarded and captured during the Crimean War, also some of the officers' names.

3203. ———— Early names of the Ottawa River. Royal Society of Canada. Proceedings and transactions 3d ser. v. 32, sec. 2, p. 97-105. 1938.

CANADA—GAZETTEERS

3204. Allen, William Frederick. Gazetteer of railway stations in the United States and the Dominion of Canada. Designating telegraph, express, post, and money-order offices, with the population. Also, a list of the counties and county towns of the several states, with the date at which the several courts are held, together with much other valuable statistical information. Comp. from information obtained from official sources. Philadelphia, National Railway Publication Co., 1874. 412p.

3205. Bouchette, Joseph. The British dominions in North America; or, A topographical and statistical description of the provinces of Lower and Upper Canada, New Brunswick, Nova Scotia, the islands of Newfoundland, Prince Edward, and Cape Breton. Including considerations on land-granting and emigration; and a topographical dictionary of Lower Canada: to which are annexed the statistical tables and tables of distances. London, Longman, Rees, Orme, Brown and Green, 1831. 2v.

   v. 2 published by H. Colburn and R. Bentley.

   Also published 1832, without the "Topographical dictionary of Lower Canada" found in the ed. of 1831.

   The "Topographical dictionary of the Province of Lower Canada" also published separately (see no. 3492).

3206. Canada. Permanent Committee on Geographical Names. Gazetteer of Canada. Special supplement. no. 1- . Ottawa, Dept. of Mines and Technical Surveys, Geographical Branch, 1964- .

   no. 1. A list of named glaciological features in Canada, comp. by C. F. Stevenson.

3207. —— Gazetteer of Canada. Supplement. no. 1- . Decisions of the Canadian Permanent Committee on Geographical Names, Jan./June 1963- . Ottawa, Dept. of Mines and Technical Surveys, Geographical Branch, 1964- .

   Published to date: no. 1-3, Jan./June 1963—Jan./June 1964.

   In English and French.

   The demand for available up-to-date information resulted in the decision to publish semiannual supplements to the gazetteers.

   Arranged by province.

   The following volumes have been published in the Gazetteer of Canada series: Southwestern Ontario, British Columbia, Manitoba, New Brunswick, Saskatchewan, Alberta, Northwest Territories and Yukon (provisional), Prince Edward Island, Nova Scotia, Ontario. These volumes will be found listed separately in the appropriate province section of Canada, entered under the agency's earlier name: Canada. Board on Geographical Names.

3208. Canada. Post Office Dept. Canada official postal guide, comprising the chief regulations of the Post Office, rates of postage and other information, together with an alphabetical list of post offices in Canada. Quebec, etc., 1855- .

   Title varies: 1855-73, List of post offices in Canada; 1875-78, Canadian official postal guide.

3209. —— Canada official postal guide, 1952. Part II. List of post offices in Canada arranged alphabetically, corrected to 1st Dec. 1950. Ottawa, 1952. 194p.

3210. —— List of post offices in Canada. Liste des bureaux de poste du Canada. Oct. 1, 1954- . (Loose-leaf)

   Formerly included in Canada official postal guide.

   Kept up to date by monthly supplements.

3211. —— List of post offices with revenues. Liste des bureaux de poste avec leur recettes. 1954/55- . (Annual)

3212. —— Table of post offices in Canada and the name of the postmasters, on the 1st of January, 1854. Quebec, Printed by Lovell & Lamoureux, 1854. 75p.

3213. Davenport, Bishop. A history and new gazetteer, or geographical dictionary, of North America and the West Indies. Comp. from the most recent and authentic sources. A new and much improved ed. New York, S. W. Benedict & Co., 1842. 592p.

Earlier editions published in Baltimore, Philadelphia, and Providence, 1832, 1833, 1835, 1836, 1838 under title A new gazetteer.

3214. —— A pocket gazetteer, or Traveller's guide through North America and the West Indies; containing a description of all the states, territories, counties, cities, towns, villages, seas, bays, harbors, islands, capes, railroads, canals, &c. connected with North America, and the West Indies, to which is added a large amount of statistical information, relating to the population, revenue, debt, and various institutions of the United States. Comp. from the most recent and authentic sources. Baltimore, Plaskitt & Co., 1833. 468p.

Also published in Trenton, N.J.
Other editions published 1834, 1838.

3215. Forbes, H. A. Gazetteer of northern Canada and parts of Alaska and Greenland. Ottawa, Geographical Bureau, 1948. 75 l.

3216. Lovell's gazetteer of the Dominion of Canada, containing the latest and most authentic descriptions of over 14,850 cities, towns, villages and places in the provinces of Ontario, Quebec, Nova Scotia, New Brunswick, Prince Edward Island, Manitoba, British Columbia, Alberta, Saskatchewan, and the new districts of the North-west territories, Yukon, Franklin, Mackenzie, Keewatin, and Ungava; together with Newfoundland; besides general information, drawn from official sources, as to names, locality, extent, etc., of over 3,000 lakes and rivers; with a table of routes. Ed. with an intro. by G. Mercer Adam. 4th issue, carefully rev. Montreal, J. Lovell and Son, 1908. 973p.

1st ed. published under title Lovell's gazetteer of British North America. Montreal, 1873. 2v.

Also published Montreal, 1881. 533p.; Montreal, 1895. 675p.

3217. McAlpine, C. D. The gazateer [sic] of the Maritime Provinces, for 1878-79. Containing routes for summer travel through the towns of Nova Scotia, New Brunswick, Cape Breton, and P. E. Island. Saint John, C. D. McAlpine, 1878. 240p.

3218. McAlpine's gazetteer of Nova Scotia, New Brunswick, Prince Edward Island and Newfoundland; a geographical and historical data of provinces and cities—location of towns, villages and hamlets—barristers, hotels, express offices and banks. Halifax, McAlpine Pub. Co., 1911. 649p.

Also published 1904, 1133p., under title McAlpine's maritime and Newfoundland gazetteer for Nova Scotia, New Brunswick, Prince Edward Island, and the island of Newfoundland.

3219. The North-American and the West-Indian gazetteer. Containing an authentic description of the colonies and islands in that part of the globe, shewing their situation, soil, produce, and trade; with their former and present condition. Also an exact account of the cities, towns, harbours, ports, bays, rivers, lakes, mountains, number of inhabitants, &c. Illus. with maps. 2d ed. London, G. Robinson,

1778. 218p.
1st ed. London, G. Robinson, 1776. 220p.

3220. Rowell, George P. & Co. Geo. P. Rowell & Co.'s gazetteer, containing a statement of the industries, characteristics, population and location of all towns in the United States and British America, in which newspapers are published. New York, G. P. Rowell & Co., 1873. 243p.

3221. Upham, Warren. Altitudes between Lake Superior and Rocky Mountains. Washington, Govt. Print. Off., 1891. 229p. (U.S. Geological Survey. Bulletin no. 72)
By places along railway lines, including supplementary lists, with indexes for Hills and mountains; Lakes; Towns and stations.

3222. White, G. D. On first looking into the Gazetteer of Canada. *Canadian forum* 39:80-81, July 1959.
Comments on some of the names listed.

3223. White, James. Altitudes in the Dominion of Canada. By James White assisted by George H. Ferguson. 2d ed. Ottawa, Mortimer Co., printers, 1915. 603p.
Published for Canada Commission of Conservation
1st ed., by James White, Ottawa, Printed by S. E. Dawson, 1901. 266p. For the Geological Survey of Canada.
Supplemented by the author's Dictionary of altitudes in the Dominion of Canada (see no. 3224).
Arranged by order of stations under names of railroads.

3224. ——— Dictionary of altitudes in the Dominion of Canada. 2d ed. Ottawa, Mortimer Co., printers, 1916. 251p.
Published for Canada Commission of Conservation.
1st ed. Ottawa, Printed by S. E. Dawson, 1903. 143p. For the Dept. of the Interior.
Supplements the author's Altitudes in the Dominion of Canada (see no. 3223).
Arranged alphabetically under provinces and territories for easier use.

3225. White, William. Post office gazetteer of the Dominion of Canada; comp. from official records, by permission of the Postmaster General. Montreal, J. Lovell, 1872. 174p.

ALBERTA

3226. Alberta's place-names of colorful origin. *Within our borders* March 1, 1954.

3227. Canada. Board on Geographical Names. Gazetteer of Canada: Alberta. Ottawa, 1958. 96p.
Sixth volume of the Gazetteer of Canada series.

3228. Canada. Dept. of the Interior. Dominion Parks Branch. Through the heart of the Rockies & Selkirks, by M. B. Williams. Ottawa?, 1921. 105p.

Place names and altitudes in Rocky Mountains Park: p. 91-95; in Yoho Park: p. 95-97; in Glacier Park: p. 97-99; in Mount Revelstoke Park: p. 100. The first two are from a paper by James White, read before the Royal Society of Canada, 1916; the last two are from Arthur O. Wheeler, The Selkirk Mountains (see no. 3307).

Same in 2d ed. 1924. 110p. p. 95-104.

In 4th ed. 1929. 112p.: Place names and altitudes in Banff Park: p. 97-101; in Yoho Park: p. 101-03; in Glacier Park: p. 103-05; in Mount Revelstoke Park: p. 106.

3229. Canada. Geographic Board. Place names of Alberta. Pub. for the Geographic Board by the Department of the Interior. Ottawa, F. A. Acland, printer, 1928. 138p.

3230. Chrapka, George. How Hairy Hill got its name. *Alberta folklore quarterly* 2:34, March 1946.

3231. Dawson, George M. Blackfoot names of a number of places in the Northwest Territory, for the most part in the vicinity of the Rocky Mountains. Canada. Geological Survey. Report of progress 1882-84:158c-167c.

Names in the list were received from J. C. Nelson, who with A. P. Patrick was engaged in the surveys. Names in the vicinity of the Bow and the Belly rivers, now in Alberta Province.

3232. Dempsey, H. A. Blackfeet place-names. *Alberta historical review* 4:29-30, Summer 1956.

3233. Edmonds, W. Everard. Broad horizons. Toronto, Musson, 1919. 224p.
Place names in southern Alberta, historical sketch: p. 173-78.

3234. Edwards, Ralph W. Mount Eisenhower. *Canadian geographical journal* 32:59-62, Feb. 1946.
Mountain renamed in honor of Gen. Eisenhower.

3235. Godsal, F. W. Origin of the name Crow's Nest Pass. *Canadian alpine journal* 12:184-85. 1922.

3236. ———— Origin of the name "Kicking Horse Pass." *Canadian alpine journal* 14:136. 1924.

3237. How Wetaskiwin received its name. *Alberta folklore quarterly* 2:13-14, March 1946.

3238. Mike Mountain Horse. Medicine Rock, Lethbridge. *Alberta folklore quarterly* 1:133, Dec. 1945.

3239. Thorington, J. Monroe. An interpretation of some old map names in the vicinity of the Kananaskis Pass. *Canadian alpine journal* 13:245-50. 1923.
Further comment, by A. O. Wheeler, *ibid.* p. 250-51.
Some names of mountains on early maps that cannot be identified.

3240. Tyrrell, Joseph Burr. Report on a part of northern Alberta and portions of adjacent districts of Assiniboia and Saskatchewan; *In* Canada. Geological and Natural History Survey. Annual report 1886, pt. E.

Appendix IV. Cree and Stoney Indian names for places within the area of the accompanying map, p. 172-76.

3241. White, James. Place-names in the Rocky Mountains between the 49th parallel and the Athabaska River. Royal Society of Canada. Proceedings and transactions 3d ser. v. 10, sec. 2, p. 501-35. 1916.

3242. Williams, Mabel Berta. Origin of name of Jasper National Park; *In* Canada. Dept. of the Interior. Dominion Parks Branch. Jasper National Park. Ottawa, F. A. Acland, 1928. p. 7-8.
Place names and altitudes: p. 145-62.

3243. ——— Place names and altitudes; *In* Canada. Dept. of the Interior. Dominion Parks Branch. Waterton Lakes National Park, Alberta, Canada. Ottawa, F. A. Acland, 192?. p. 44-45.

BRITISH COLUMBIA

3244. Akrigg, G. P. V. British Columbia place names. *Western folklore* 12:44-49, Jan. 1953.
Bibliography: p. 48-49.
A survey of the work done so far in the study of British Columbia place-names, together with some note of what remains to be done, and what resources are available.

3245. Atkinson, Reginald N. Changes in Okanagan place-names. Okanagan Historical Society. Report 15:21-24. 1951.

3246. Audet, Francis J. Noms géographiques français en Colombie anglaise. Société de Géographie de Québec. Bulletin 16:80-82. 1922.

3247. Boas, Franz. Geographical names of the Kwakiutl Indians. New York, Columbia Univ. Press, 1934. 83p. (Columbia University contributions to anthropology v. 20)
"The names show 'the cultural life and line of development' of these Indians; careful linguistic treatment of the nomenclature."—*American speech.*

3248. Brent, Maria. Indian place names. Okanagan Historical Society. Report 13:20-21. 1949.
Vernon district.

3249. British Columbia. Lands Dept. Geographic Division. Geographical gazetteer of British Columbia. Victoria, Printed by C. F. Banfield, 1930. 291p.

3250. Buckland, F. M. Kelowna—its name. Okanagan Historical Society. Report 6:45. 1935; 17:100. 1953.
6:45. 1935, reprinted from v. 1, 1925.

3251. Burrard, Gerald. The naming of Burrard Inlet. *British Columbia historical quarterly* 10:143-49, April 1946.

3252. Canada. Board on Geographical Names. Gazetteer of Canada: British Columbia. Ottawa, 1953. 641p.
Second volume of the Gazetteer of Canada series.

3253. Canada. Dept. of the Interior. Dominion Parks Branch. Through the heart of the Rockies & Selkirks, by M. B. Williams. Ottawa?, 1921. 105p.
Place names and altitudes in Rocky Mountains Park: p. 91-95; in Yoho Park: p. 95-97; in Glacier Park: p. 97-99; in Mount Revelstoke Park: p. 100. The first two are from a paper by James White, read before the Royal Society of Canada, 1916; the last two are from Arthur O. Wheeler, The Selkirk Mountains (see no. 3307).
Same in 2d ed. 1924. 110p. p. 95-104.
In 4th ed. 1929. 112p.: Place names and altitudes in Banff Park: p. 97-101; in Yoho Park: p. 101-03; in Glacier Park: p. 103-05; in Mount Revelstoke Park: p. 106.

3254. Canadian peaks named for "Big 3." *New York times* Nov. 15, 1944, p. 6, col. 1.
Peaks north of Finlay River in the northeastern corner of the Peace River block and British Columbia have been named after Roosevelt, Churchill, and Stalin.

3255. Chamberlain, Alexander F. Geographic terms of Kootenay origin. *American anthropologist* n.s. 4:348-50, April-June 1902.
"Concerned with names of places, camp-sites, and stations, along the 49th parallel in British Columbia, Washington, Idaho, and Montana. These names which seem to have been taken from the language of the Kootenay Indians of this region are mentioned in the reports on the boundary survey. The meanings and etymologies are given where possible."—Price.

3256. Chamberlin, Rollin T. Cariboo Mountains, a correction. Geographical Society of Philadelphia. Bulletin 26:121-22, April 1928.
A derogatory article on the Geographic Board of Canada because it changed several names given to peaks in the Cariboo Mountains by the author and Allen Carpe, who made the first ascents.

3257. Crane, Charles Allen. Vernon, Enderby and O'Keefe. Okanagan Historical Society. Report 8:14. 1939.

3258. Daly, Reginald A. The nomenclature of the North American Cordillera between the 47th and 53d parallels of latitude. *Geographical journal* 27:586-606, June 1906.
Bibliography: p. 604-06.
A systematic nomenclature is needed for this vast mountain system so that the geology may be more adequately described. Varying definitions used for the mountain ranges, systems, etc. are included.

3259. Dawson, George M. Notes on the Shuswap people of British Columbia. Royal Society of Canada. Proceedings and transactions v. 9, sec. 2, p. 3-44. 1891.
List of 220 place-names in the Shuswap country, British Columbia. 1. Shuswap names of places on the Kamloops sheet of the geological map of British Columbia. 2. Shuswap names of places beyond the limits of the Kamloops sheet, p. 40-44. 3. Shuswap names of inhabited villages.

3260. Firth, Major. Geographical place names in British Columbia. *Canadian surveyor* 9:2-6, April 1948.

3261. Florin, Lambert. Ghost town trails. Maps and drawings by David C. Mason. Seattle, Superior Pub. Co., 1963. 192p.
Bibliography: p. 190.
A roster of known ghost towns: p. 191-92.
Includes western states of the United States, and British Columbia.

3262. Foote, Elsie. Kettle River. Okanagan Historical Society. Report 9:68. 1941.

3263. Gibson, Rex. What's in a name? *Canadian alpine journal* 38:82-84. 1955.
Principles for naming mountains in British Columbia.

3264. Goodfellow, John C. Princeton place names; a paper read before the Similkameen Historical Association, July 26th, 1936. Okanagan Historical Society. Report 7:10-16. 1937.

3265. Gudde, Erwin Gustav. Okanagan place names. *Western folklore* 8:161-62, April 1949.
Refers to article by A. G. Harvey, Okanagan place names (see no. 3269).

3266. Haggen, R. W. Origin of place names in Boundary District, B.C. 1945.
Manuscript in British Columbia Provincial Archives, Victoria.

3267. Harbron, John D. Spaniards on the coast, the eighteenth century Spanish explorers left many place names that are found in British Columbia today. *Beaver* outfit [*i.e.*, volume] 288:4-8, Summer 1957.

3268. Harvey, A. G. The mystery of Mount Robson. *British Columbia historical quarterly* 1:207-26, Oct. 1937.

3269. —— Okanagan place names: their origin and meaning. Okanagan Historical Society. Report 12:193-223. 1948.

3270. —— The place name "Armstrong." Okanagan Historical Society. Report 13:153-55. 1949.
Later information than that in his article *ibid*. 12:197. 1948.

3271. An Historical gazetteer of Okanagan—Similkameen. Okanagan Historical Society. Report 22:123-69. 1958.
A second article appeared, Looking back to the Historical gazetteer in O. H. S. 22 (1958).
Two corrections, an addition, and a comment *ibid*. 23:97-98. 1959.

3272. Kennard, H. B. Indian place names. Okanagan Historical and Natural History Society. Report 3:16-17. 1929.

3273. Kerr, James. British Columbia coast names; their significance today. *National review* 124:229-32, March 1945.

3274. —— British Columbia place names. *Canadian geographical journal* 2:153-70, Feb. 1931.

3275. ———— The coast names of British Columbia. *United empire* 39:296-97, Nov.-Dec. 1948.

3276. Knowles, J. B. Origins of Kelowna street names. Okanagan Historical Society. Report 18:93-97. 1954.

3277. Laing, F. W. Geographical naming record, established and other names. 1938.
Manuscript in British Columbia Provincial Archives, Victoria.

3278. ———— Scotty Creek and Scottie Creek. Okanagan Historical Society. Report 9:56-63. 1941.

3279. Lamb, W. Kaye. Burrard of Burrard's Channel. *British Columbia historical quarterly* 10:273-79, Oct. 1946.
Disagrees with theory advanced in Gerald Burrard's article, *ibid.* 10:143-49, April 1946.

3280. Longstaff, F. V. Captain George Vancouver, 1792-1942; a study in commemorative place-names. *British Columbia historical quarterly* 6:77-94, April 1942.
"Summarizes the history of the place-names which commemorate Captain George Vancouver."—*Geographical journal* 101:95-96, Feb. 1943.

3281. Lucas, E. A. The place names of British Columbia. *Canadian forum* 1: 209-11, April 1921.

3282. Manning, Helen B. Cariboo place names. 1943.
Manuscript in University of British Columbia. Dept. of History, Vancouver.

3283. Martin, Stuart J. Vernon street-names. Okanagan Historical Society. Report 13:156-61. 1949.

3284. Meany, Edmond Stephen. The name of Mount Robson a puzzle. *Washington historical quarterly* 19:20-30, Jan. 1928.

3285. Meek, R. J. Spanish explorers left their mark on Canada. *Saturday night* 63:20, Oct. 4, 1947.
"The Canadian west coast and adjacent islands are sprinkled with many names commemorating voyages of Spanish explorers."—*Canadian historical review.*

3286. Morice, A. G. The northern interior of British Columbia and its maps. Royal Canadian Institute. Transactions 12:25-39. 1920.
The author writes of the deplorable state of the official maps and the application of names on them.

3287. Mount Keogan named for pioneer. Okanagan Historical Society. Report 20:24-25. 1956.
Michael Keogan.

3288. Nelson, Denys. Place names of the delta of the Fraser. 2v.
Typewritten manuscript in the University of British Columbia Library, Vancouver.

3289. —— Some origins of place names of greater Vancouver. *Museum notes* (Art, Historical and Scientific Association of Vancouver, B.C.) 3:5-10, Sept. 1928.

3290. New names on the International Boundary. *Geographical journal* 62:234-35, Sept. 1923.
  A glacier and several peaks.

3291. Norris, L. Some place names. Okanagan Historical Society. Report 2:33-37. 1927; 4:31-32. 1930: 6:133-58. 1935; 8:50-53. 1939; 17:118-24. 1953.

3292. Pemberton, C. C. Discovery and naming of the "Strait of Juan de Fuca." British Columbia Historical Association. Report and proceedings 4:33-36. 1929.

3293. Place names. Okanagan Historical Society. Report 21:40. 1957.

3294. Place names—their significance. The year book of British Columbia, ed. by R. E. Gosnell, 1897:74-83.
  A list.

3295. Richthofen, E. von. The Spanish toponyms of the British Columbia coast, with sideglances at those in the states of Washington, Oregon, and Alaska. Winnipeg, Ukrainian Free Academy of Sciences, 1963. 22p. (Ukrainian Free Academy of Sciences. Series: Onomastica, no. 26)

3296. Rosoman, Graham. The naming of Enderby. Okanagan Historical Society. Report 6:219. 1935.

3297. Schell, Ruth. Penticton streets. Okanagan Historical Society. Report 26:96-99. 1962.

3298. Schultz, James Willard. Signposts of adventure; Glacier National Park as the Indians know it. Boston, Houghton Mifflin, 1926. 224p.
  Contents: Introductory; Blackfeet Indian names of the topographical features of Glacier National Park upon its east side; Kutenai Indian names of the topographical features of the west side of Glacier National Park.

3299. Sismey, Eric. Okanagan—what does it mean? Okanagan Historical Society. Report 28:96-97. 1964.

3300. Stewart, D. K.; G. B. Latimer & H. H. Whitaker. Penticton street names honouring old-timers. Okanagan Historical Society. Report 15:198-202. 1951.

3301. Tassie, G. C. Some place-names. Okanagan Historical Society. Report 10:34-38. 1943.

3302. Thorington, J. Monroe. The climber's guide. *Canadian alpine journal* 38:85. 1955.
  To naming mountains in British Columbia.

3303. Wagner, Henry Raup. The cartography of the northwest coast of America to the year 1800. Berkeley, Univ. of California Press, 1937. 2v.
  List of maps: 2:273-364.
  Place names still in use: 2:371-422.

Obsolete place names: 2:423-525.
Bibliography: 2:527-43.

3304. Walbran, John T. British Columbia coast names, 1592-1906; to which are added a few names in adjacent United States territory; their origin and history, with map and illustrations. Ottawa, Govt. Print. Bureau, 1909. 546p.
Published for Geographic Board of Canada.
Review: *Review of historical publications relating to Canada* 14:115-18. 1910.

3305. Watson, Robert. Victoria's early names. *Beaver* outfit [*i.e.*,volume] 263:32, June 1932.

3306. West, Robert. Mountain names in Mt. Revelstoke Park. *Canadian alpine journal* 42:49. 1959.

3307. Wheeler, Arthur O. The Selkirk Mountains; a guide for mountain climbers and pilgrims. Winnipeg, Stovel Co., 1912. 191p.
Source of name is given for all geographical points mentioned.

3308. White, James. Place-names in the Rocky Mountains between the 49th parallel and the Athabaska River. Royal Society of Canada. Proceedings and transactions 3d ser. v. 10, sec. 2, p. 501-35. 1916.

3309. ——— Place names in vicinity of Yellowhead Pass. *Canadian alpine journal* 6:143-58. 1914-15.
"Numerous names and their derivations have been investigated by the author who also discusses the interpretations by other authors."—Price.

3310. Wolfenden, Madge. The naming of Holland Point. *British Columbia historical quarterly* 18:117-21, Jan.-April 1954.

MANITOBA

3311. Bessasson, Haraldur. Icelandic place names in Manitoba and North Dakota. Linguistic Circle of Manitoba and North Dakota. Proceedings 2:8-10, May 1960.

3312. Canada. Board on Geographical Names. Gazetteer of Canada: Manitoba. Ottawa, 1955. 60p.
Third volume of the Gazetteer of Canada series.

3313. Canada. Geographic Board. Place-names of Manitoba. Pub. for the Geographic Board by the Dept. of the Interior. Ottawa, J. O. Patenaude, acting King's Printer, 1933. 95p.

3314. Cole, George E. Flin Flon—the name; alliteration and music blend in making a good name for a great mine. *Canadian mining journal* 70:63-71, March 1949.
Origin of name of mine in northern Manitoba.

3315. Evans, W. Sanford, Statistical Service. Manitoba place guide. Winnipeg, 1945. 41p.
To accompany the Manitoba population maps. 1945.

3316. McKay, Henry. What's in the name of Manitoba. *Beaver* outfit [*i.e.*, volume] 261:102, Dec. 1930.
Derived from Cree word meaning "The Spirits' Narrows."

3317. Manitou Baa. *Beaver* outfit 287:54, Summer 1956.
Meaning of name for lake.
Disagrees with George Henry Armstrong's definition in his The origin and meaning of place names in Canada (see no. 3063).

3318. Prud'homme, L. A. Le nom de Manitoba. *Revue canadienne* n.s. 8:23-26, juil. 1911.
Review: *Review of historical publications relating to Canada* 16:56. 1911: "... the author explains the origin of the name of the province of Manitoba; he finds it not in the language of the Salteaux who now surround Lake Manitoba, but in the Sioux word Minnetoba, which signifies 'water-prairie.'"

3319. Rouillard, Eugène. Le nom de Manitoba. Société de Géographie de Québec. Bulletin 9:310-11. 1915.
Traces name to aboriginal sources.

3320. Tyrrell, Joseph Burr. Algonquian Indian names of places in northern Canada. Royal Canadian Institute. Transactions 10:213-31, May 1914.
Reprinted separately: Toronto, Univ. Press, 1915.
"During his travels in remote parts of Canada, the writer made a large collection of place names which he presents in four columns. The first lists the Indian name, the second contains the meaning of the names that have been determined, the third includes the names in use on the latest Canadian maps, and the last gives the approximate positions of the places designated."—Price.
Manitoba and District of Patricia, Ontario.
Review: *Review of historical publications relating to Canada* 19:208. 1914.

NEW BRUNSWICK

3321. Bird, Will R. Nova Scotia and New Brunswick names. *MacLean's magazine* 41:54, 56, 58, 60, 63, June 1, 1928.

3322. Canada. Board on Geographical Names. Gazetteer of Canada: New Brunswick. Ottawa, 1956. 84p.
Fourth volume of the Gazetteer of Canada series.

3323. Froidevaux, Henri. À propos de Tracadie. Société de Géographie de Québec. Bulletin 12:158, mai 1918.

3324. Ganong, William Francis. Further suggestions upon nomenclature of unnamed or badly named places in New Brunswick. Natural History Society of New Brunswick. Bulletin 4:321-22. 1901.

3325. —— The Geographic Board of Canada. *Science* n.s. 25:307-08, Feb. 22, 1907.
Criticism of the Board for disregarding local usage and following abstract principles as shown in New Brunswick examples in the Board's sixth report.

3326. —— A monograph of the place-nomenclature of the Province of New Brunswick. Royal Society of Canada. Proceedings and transactions 2d ser. v. 2, sec. 2, p. 175-289. 1896.

Published separately as Contributions to the history of New Brunswick, no. 2, 1896.

Includes: An essay toward an understanding of the principles of place-nomenclature; The historical development of the place-nomenclature of New Brunswick; A dictionary of the place-names of New Brunswick; Sources of information.

Supplemented by information appearing in the author's A monograph of historic sites in the Province of New Brunswick, *ibid.* 2d ser. v. 5, sec. 2, p. 213-357. 1899. (Contributions, no. 4); and his A monograph of the origins of settlements in the Province of New Brunswick, *ibid.* 2d ser. v. 10, sec. 2, p. 3-185. 1904. (Contributions, no. 6)

Also supplemented by his Additions and corrections to monographs on the place-nomenclature, cartography, historic sites, boundaries and settlement-origins of the Province of New Brunswick, *ibid.* 2d ser. v. 12, sec. 2, p. 3-157. 1906. (Contributions, no. 7)

3327. —— The naming of St. Andrews—a miss. *Acadiensis* 2:184-88, July 1902.

3328. —— Notes on the natural history and physiography of New Brunswick. Natural History Society of New Brunswick. Bulletin 6:199-204. 1910.

The local nomenclature of the Muniac, Miramichi, and Cains rivers.

3329. —— The origin of the major Canadian place-names of Fundy and Miramichi. Royal Society of Canada. Proceedings and transactions 3d ser. v. 20, sec. 2, p. 15-35. 1926.

3330. —— Origin of the place-name Pabineau. *Acadiensis* 1:88-89, April 1901.

3331. —— The origin of the place-names in Inglewood Manor. *Acadiensis* 3:7-18, Jan. 1903.

3332. Hind, Henry Youle. A preliminary report on the geology of New Brunswick. Fredericton, G. E. Fenety, printer, 1865. 293p.

"Origin of the names of certain rivers and places in New Brunswick, containing a short vocabulary of the Micmac and Milicete languages, p. 257-59. Names of places and rivers derived from the Abenaquis language, p. 260-61."—Pilling.

3333. Kain, S. W. Indian names in New Brunswick. *St. John sun* Jan. 14, 1886.

A list of the meanings of 20 Indian place-names—Micmac and Maliseet—in Maine and New Brunswick.

3334. New Brunswick Historical Society. Loyalist souvenir; one hundred and fiftieth anniversary of the landing of the Loyalists in the Province of New Brunswick, 1783-1933. Saint John, New Brunswick Historical Society, 1933. 31p.

Some New Brunswick place names: p. 22-28.

3335. Rouillard, Eugène. À travers le Nouveau-Brunswick, quelques vocables gèographiques. Société de Géographie de Québec. Bulletin 14:275-92, nov. 1920.

NEWFOUNDLAND

3336. Canada. Dept. of Mines and Technical Surveys. Geographical Branch.
A list of the place names of the island of Newfoundland with their geographical
positions, comp. from the 10-mile map of Newfoundland pub. by the Dept. of
Natural Resources, Newfoundland, 1941. Ottawa, 1950. 59 l.

3337. Cants, Ernesto do. Quem deu o nome ao Labrador? (Breve estudo) 3. ed.
Porto, Officinas do Commercio do Porto, 1907. 23p.
At head of title: Extrahido do Archivo dos açores, 12:353.

3338. Churchill name to be given to river in Canada. *Kansas City times* Feb. 6,
1965, p. 1.
To rename Hamilton River and its Falls for Sir Winston Churchill.

3339. Forbes, Alexander. Notes on place names; *In his* Northernmost Labrador
mapped from the air. New York, American Geographical Society, 1938. p. 236-
43.

3340. Harrington, Michael Francis. Newfoundland names. *Atlantic advocate*
47:71-77, Oct. 1956.
Groups named by the English, Irish, and Scottish; French, Spanish, and Portuguese; original Indian names; changes made by Nomenclature Board.

3341. Harrisse, Henry. Découverte et évolution cartographique de Terre-Neuve
et des pays circonvoisins, 1497-1501-1769; essais de géographie historique et
documentaire. London, Henry Stevens, Son and Stiles; Paris, H. Welter, 1900.
420p.
La cartographie américano-dieppoise. Nomenclature de La Nouvelle-Écosse:
p. 214-22.
Nomenclature chronologique du Labrador, de Terre-Neuve et de la région
adjacente depuis la découverte jusqu'à la fin du XVIe siècle: p. 355-66.

3342. Horwood, Harold. Fumigating the map. *Atlantic advocate* 49:69, April
1959.
Changes in salty Newfoundland place-names being made by the Canada Post
Office Dept.

3343. Howley, Michael Francis. Newfoundland name-lore. *Newfoundland quarterly* v. 32-39, Oct. 1932-March 1940.
Republished from *ibid*. Oct. 1901-Dec. 1914.

3344. Keenleyside, H. L. Place-names of Newfoundland. *Canadian geographical
journal* 29:255-67, Dec. 1944.

3345. Kirwin, William. Labrador, St. John's and Newfoundland; some pronunciations. Canadian Linguistic Association. Journal 6:115-16, Fall 1960.
Variant pronunciations of these place-names.

3346. Le Messurier, Henry William. The early relations between Newfoundland
and the Channel Islands. *Geographical review* 2:449-57, Dec. 1916.
Many place-names on Newfoundland are of Channel Islands origin, proving that
an intimate connection existed between the people of the Channel Islands and the
early history of Newfoundland.

3347. Miffin, Robert James. Some French place names of Newfoundland. *American speech* 31:79-80, Feb. 1956.

3348. Munn, W. A. Nomenclature of Conception Bay. *Newfoundland quarterly* 33:14-16, Dec. 1933.

3349. Newfoundland 1941. Hand book, gazetteer, and almanac; an annual reference book, ed. by J. R. Smallwood. St. John's, Long Brothers, n.d. 324p.
Gazetteer: p. 67-150.

3350. A nomenclature board for Newfoundland. *Geographical journal* 92:478-79, Nov. 1938.
A board—to be the ultimate authority in respect to pronunciation and spelling of all place-names—has been provided for through the Nomenclature Board Act, 1938.

3351. Noms géographiques canadiens. *Bulletin des recherches historiques* 31: 268, juil. 1925.
Baie des Châteaux, and Chéticamp.

3352. Picturesque place names. *Newfoundland quarterly* 53:3, Sept. 1954.

3353. Place names being changed. *Newfoundland quarterly* 53:41, March 1954.
Signed: Wayfarer.

3354. Rouillard, Eugène. Le Cap Chouart. Société de Géographie de Québec. Bulletin 13:54. 1919.
History of name found on 17th- and 18th-century maps of northern coast of Labrador.

3355. ——— Toponymie de la côte nord du Saint-Laurent et du Labrador Canadien. Société de Géographie de Québec. Bulletin 7:208-12, juil. 1913.

3356. Rouleau, Ernest. A gazetteer of the island of Newfoundland, based on the maps (1:50,000) of the National topographic system pub. by the Dept. of Mines and Technical Surveys, Ottawa. April 1961. Montreal, 1961. 245 1.

3357. ——— Index to the geographical names appearing on the map of Newfoundland (1955), pub. by the Dept. of Mines and Resources of Newfoundland. Montreal, 1961. 34p.

3358. Seary, E. R. The anatomy of Newfoundland place-names. *Names* 6:193-207, Dec. 1958.
This paper was presented in Nov. 1957 as an address to the St. John's Branch of the Humanities Association of Canada.
Newfoundland place-names are being studied systematically, as part of an investigation into Newfoundland linguistics conducted by members of the English Dept. of the Memorial University of Newfoundland under the direction of the present writer.

3359. ——— The French element in Newfoundland place names. Canadian Linguistic Association. Journal 4:63-69, Fall 1958.

3360. ——— The French element in Newfoundland place names; a paper read before the Canadian Linguistic Association on June 11th, 1958. Winnipeg, 1958. 16p. (Ukrainian Free Academy of Sciences. Series: Onomastica, no. 16)

3361. —— Linguistic variety in the place names of Newfoundland. *Canadian geographical journal* 65:146-55, Nov. 1962.

3362. —— Toponomy of the island of Newfoundland, check-list. St. John's, Memorial Univ. of Newfoundland, 1959- . v. 1- .
    Contents: v. 1. Sources, I. Maps. 1959. 153p.; v. 2. Names, I. The Northern Peninsula. 1960. 69p.

3363. Story, G. M. Research in the language and place-names of Newfoundland. Canadian Linguistic Association. Journal 3:47-55, Oct. 1957.
    Place names: p. 47-50.
    The arrangement of the completed work will follow that of the English Place-Name Society.

3364. What's in a name? *Newfoundland quarterly* 53:3, March 1954.

3365. Wheeler, Everett Pepperrell. List of Labrador Eskimo place names. Ottawa, Minister of Resources and Development, 1953. 105p. (National Museum of Canada. Bulletin, no. 131. Anthropological series, no. 34)

3366. White, James. The "Valley River" of Labrador. *Geographical journal* 70:287-89, Sept. 1927.
    Disagrees with assignment of names made in Frizzell, Varick. Explorations in the Grand Falls region of Labrador, *ibid.* 69:332-40, April 1927.

NORTHWEST TERRITORIES

3367. Arctic islands named after Queen Elizabeth. *World affairs* (Toronto) 19: 15, March 1954.
    Includes Ellesmere, Devon, Melville, Axel Heiberg, Bathurst, Prince Patrick, etc.—the northern half of Canadian Arctic Archipelago.

3368. Baird, Patrick Douglas. Baffin Island expedition, 1950, a preliminary report. *Arctic* 3:131-49, Dec. 1950.
    New names, p. 149. Adopted by the Canadian Board on Geographical Names.

3369. —— Baffin Island expedition, 1953, a preliminary field report. *Arctic* 6:227-51, Dec. 1953.
    New names, p. 251. Approved by the Canadian Board on Geographical Names.

3370. Becher, Alexander Bridport. The voyages of Martin Frobisher. Royal Geographical Society. Journal 12:1-28. 1842.
    A list of places named by Frobisher, p. 16-19. Voyage was for the purpose of finding the Northwest Passage. Names in area of Frobisher Strait, etc.

3371. Bell, Charles Napier. The great lone land, some historical names and places in the North West. *Canadian antiquarian and numismatic journal* 12:34-51, Jan. 1885.

3372. Boas, Franz. The Central Eskimo. U.S. Bureau of American Ethnology. Report 6:399-675. 1884-85.
Eskimo geographical names used, with English significations: p. 662-66.

3373. ―― Ortsnamen. *Petermanns Mitteilungen* Ergänzungsband 17. 1884-85, Ergänzungsheft 80:90-95.
A list of Eskimo place-names in Baffin Island, followed by a shorter list of the English names with Eskimo equivalents.

3374. Canada. Board on Geographical Names. Gazetteer of Canada: Northwest Territories and Yukon. Provisional. Ottawa, 1958. 89p.
Seventh volume of the Gazetteer of Canada series.

3375. Chipman, Kenneth G. & John R. Cox. Eskimo place names; *In* Canada. Dept. of Naval Service. Report of the Arctic expedition, 1913-18. Ottawa, F. A. Acland, 1918-28. 11:37B-42B.
Translation and etymology verified by D. Jenness, ethnologist of the expedition.

3376. Debenham, Frank. Place-names in the Polar regions. *Polar record* 3:541-52, July 1942.

3377. Hall, Charles Francis. Narrative of the second Arctic Expedition. Washington, Govt. Print. Off., 1879. 644p. (45th Cong., 3d sess. Senate. Ex. doc. 27)
Contains lists of names to accompany sketch maps, as told to Hall by the Innuit who made the map, as follows:
Innuit names of the Northeast coast of Fox Channel, by the Innuit Oong-er-luk: p. 354; Innuit names of Admiralty Inlet, by Oong-er-luk: p. 355; Names around Pond's Bay, by the Innuit Papa: p. 370; Names of King William's Land and the adjacent country, by the Innuit In-nook-poo-zhee-jook: p. 398.

3378. Hattersley-Smith, G. Northern Ellesmere Island, 1953 and 1954. *Arctic* 8:2-36, Winter 1955.
New names, p. 33.

3379. Manning, Thomas Henry. Eskimo place names of Southampton Island. *Geographical journal* 88:241-42, Sept. 1936.
Although new English names have proved satisfactory and have been accepted by the Geographic Board of Canada, Eskimo names are used by the inhabitants. A list is included.

3380. ―― Explorations on the east coast of Hudson Bay. *Geographical journal* 109:58-75, July 1947.
List of new names used on accompanying map and approved by the Geographic Board of Canada: p. 75.

3381. ―― The Foxe Basin coasts of Baffin Island. *Geographical journal* 101: 225-51, May-June 1943.
New names submitted to the Geographic Board of Canada: p. 248-49.

3382. ―― Narrative of a second Defence Research Board expedition to Banks Island, with notes on the country and its history. *Arctic* 9:3-77. 1956.
Geographical names, p. 66-68. Adopted by the Canadian Board on Geographical Names. Other official names, p. 72-74.

3383. —— Narrative of an unsuccessful attempt to circumnavigate Banks Island by canoe in 1952. *Arctic* 6:171-97, Oct. 1953.
New names, p. 196-97. Approved by the Canadian Board on Geographical Names.

3384. —— Notes on the coastal district of the eastern Barren Grounds and Melville Peninsula from Igloolik to Cape Fullerton. *Canadian geographical journal* 26:84-105, Feb. 1943.
New names given by the British Canadian-Arctic Expedition: p. 87.

3385. Naming of Arctic islands. *Arctic* 2:125, Sept. 1949.
Prince Charles Island in Foxe Basin, and Mackenzie King Island for the southern part of Borden Island.

3386. Naming of northern weather stations. *Arctic* 2:125, Sept. 1949.
Four postwar weather stations established jointly by the Canadian and United States governments in the Canadian Arctic.

3387. "Nattilik" or "Inuit Nunaga" may show up on maps soon. *Lincoln (Neb.) evening journal and Nebraska State journal* Nov. 14, 1962, p. 20.
The Northwest Territories to be split in two, the western section to be called the Territory of Mackenzie, the eastern to have a name chosen by the Eskimo inhabitants.

3388. Parry, Sir William Edward. Journal of a second voyage for the discovery of a northwest passage from the Atlantic to the Pacific; performed in the years 1821-22-23, in His Majesty's ships Fury and Hecla, under the orders of Captain William Edward Parry. London, John Murray, 1824. 571p.
Also published New York, E. Duyckinck, 1824. 464p.
Esquimaux names of places: p. 570-71 (London ed.).

3389. Petitot, Émile Fortuné Stanislas Joseph. On the Athabasca District of the Canadian North-West Territory. Royal Geographical Society. Proceedings n.s. 5:633-55, Nov. 1883.
Contains a number of geographic names.

3390. Prud'homme, L. A. Noms historiques de la langue française au Nord-ouest canadien. Société de Géographie de Québec. Bulletin 9:195-209, 283-93, 348-64, juil.-nov. 1915.

3391. Queen Elizabeth Islands. *Polar record* 7:334, Jan. 1955.
Summarized from *The Times*, London, Feb. 6, 1954.

3392. Rasmussen, Knud Johan Victor. Iglulik and Caribou Eskimo texts. Copenhagen, Gyldendal, 1930. 160p. (Report of the 5th Thule expedition 1921-24. The Danish expedition to Arctic North America in charge of Knud Rasmussen. v. 7, no. 3)
Iglulik texts. Place names according to Eskimo sketch maps from the Igluling-miut: p. 89-99.
Caribou texts. Place names according to sketch maps from Caribou Eskimos: p. 146-60.

3393. —— Netsilik Eskimos, social life and spiritual culture. Copenhagen, Gyldendal, 1931. 542p. (Report of the 5th Thule expedition 1921-24. The Danish expedition to Arctic North America in charge of Knud Rasmussen. v. 8, no. 1-2)

The Seal Eskimos and their country. Eskimo topography: p. 91-113. Around territory of Boothia Isthmus, Netsilik Lake, and Adelaide Peninsula.

3394. Ross, *Sir* John. Narrative of a second voyage in search of a north-west passage, and of a residence in the Arctic regions during the years 1829, 1830, 1831, 1832, 1833. Including the reports of James Clark Ross and the discovery of the northern magnetic pole. London, A. W. Webster, 1835. 2v.

[v. 2] is Appendix, with 120, cxliv, lxiv p.

Place-names are listed in v. 2, pt. 3, p. lii-lxiv, in groups as follows: Latitudes and longitudes, from the N. E. Cape to Gulf of Boothia and King William IV Sea; Latitudes and longitudes of places in Baffin's Bay, determined 1818, 1833; Sir Edward Parry's first voyage; Sir Edward Parry's second voyage; From Sir John Franklin's chart; Sir John Franklin's first journey; From Captain Beechy's chart.

3395. Rouillard, Eugène. Chronique de géographie. Société de Géographie de Québec. Bulletin 16:170-71. 1922.

Decision of Canadian Geographic Board to assign the name Breynat à la Pointe de la Rive, in District of Mackenzie, in honor of bishop thereof.

3396. ―――― Dans l'extrême Nord du Canada. Société de Géographie de Québec. Bulletin 8:195-200, juil. 1914.

3397. Rowley, Diana. Stefansson Island. *Arctic circular* 5:46-53, Oct. 1952.

3398. Sutton, George Miksch. The exploration of Southampton Island, Hudson Bay. Pittsburgh, Pa., Carnegie Institute, 1932-36. 7 pts. (Memoirs of the Carnegie Museum, v. 12)

Includes notes on place-names, in pt. 1, sec. 2, p. 8-23.

3399. Thibert, Arthur. Dictionary; English-Eskimo, Eskimo-English. Ottawa, Research Center of Amerindian Anthropology, Univ. of Ottawa, 1954. 174p.

Geographical names of places in the Arctic: p. 163.

3400. White, James. Place-names―Northern Canada. Canada. Geographic Board. Report 9:231-455. 1910.

Also published separately, 1911. 224p.

A partial report of this study, which deals especially with the names conferred by the explorers in the far north, was published in Royal Society of Canada. Proceedings and transactions 3d ser. v. 4, sec. 4, p. 37-40. 1910.

Review: *Review of historical publications relating to Canada* 16:126. 1912.

3401. Wordie, J. M. An expedition to north west Greenland and the Canadian Arctic in 1937; note on names. *Geographical journal* 92:415-18, Nov. 1938.

The region was mapped and new names proposed.

3402. Wright, John. South-east Ellesmere Island. *Geographical journal* 95:278-91, April 1940.

Coastal names: p. 288-89.

NOVA SCOTIA

3403. À propos du mot "Acadie." Société de Géographie de Québec. Bulletin 11:298, sept. 1917.

3404. Bird, Will R. Nova Scotia and New Brunswick names. *MacLean's magazine* 41:54, 56, 58, 60, 63, June 1, 1928.

3405. Brown, Thomas J. Place-names of the Province of Nova Scotia. Halifax, Royal Print. & Litho. Ltd., 1922. 158p.

3406. Canada. Board on Geographical Names. Gazetteer of Canada: Nova Scotia. Ottawa, 1961. 192p.
Ninth volume of the Gazetteer of Canada series.

3407. Dawson, Robert MacGregor. Nova Scotian place-names. Linguistic Circle of Manitoba and North Dakota. Proceedings 1:10-12, May 1959.

3408. ———— Place names in Nova Scotia. A paper read before the Linguistic Circle of Manitoba and North Dakota on May 16th, 1959. Winnipeg, Ukrainian Free Academy of Sciences, 1960. 16p. (Onomastica, no. 19)

3409. Frame, Elizabeth. A list of Micmac names of places, rivers, etc., in Nova Scotia. Cambridge, Mass., John Wilson and Son, 1892. 12p.

3410. Froidevaux, Henri. Origine du mot "Acadie." Société des Américanistes de Paris. Journal n.s. 12:267-68. 1920.

3411. Ganong, William Francis. The origin of the East-Canadian place-names Gaspé, Blomidon, and Bras d'Or. Royal Society of Canada. Proceedings and transactions 3d ser. v. 22, sec. 2, p. 249-70. 1928.

3412. Harrisse, Henry. Découverte et évolution cartographique de Terre-Neuve et des pays circonvoisins, 1497-1501-1769; essais de géographie historique et documentaire. London, Henry Stevens, Son and Stiles; Paris, H. Welter, 1900. 420p.
La cartographie américano-dieppoise. Nomenclature de La Nouvelle-Écosse: p. 214-22.
Nomenclature chronologique du Labrador, de Terre-Neuve et de la région adjacente depuis la découverte jusqu'à la fin du XVIe siècle: p. 355-66.

3413. Hill, George W. Nomenclature of the streets of Halifax. Nova Scotia Historical Society. Collections 15:1-22. 1911.

3414. Maclellan, W. E. Origin of Pictou's name. *Dalhousie review* 2:251-53, July 1922.

3415. Noms géographiques canadiens. *Bulletin des recherches historiques* 31: 268, juil. 1925.
Baie des Châteaux, and Chéticamp.

3416. Nova Scotia. Dept. of Mines. Gazetteer of Nova Scotia; a geographical dictionary giving names and locations of places in alphabetic order. Comp. by Eva E. Duncan. Halifax, 1958. 199p.

3417. —— Index of geographical names appearing on new map of the Province of Nova Scotia (with addenda of place names). Halifax, N.S., 1955. 41p.

3418. Nova Scotian place names. *Journal of education for Nova Scotia* 4th ser. 2:68-71, Dec. 1931; 3:75-77, 85-89, 103-12, 146-51, 172-75, Jan.-Oct. 1932; 5:101-08, 371-73, April-Oct. 1934; 6:87-92, March 1935.

3419. Pacifique, Père. Cap Breton. Société de Géographie de Québec. Bulletin 27:34-50, janv. 1933.
"Includes list of native names (Micmac) with English equivalents."—Griffin.

3420. Post office directory for Nova Scotia, shewing the names of every village, settlement and township in the province. London, H. M. S. O., 1850. 33p.

ONTARIO

3421. Barnard, W. A. Ontario names. *Sylva, your lands and forests review* 12: 26-28, Jan.-Feb. 1956.

3422. Bell, Robert. Meanings of Indian geographical names in the country around Sudbury. Canada. Geological Survey. Annual report v. 5, pt. 1, p. 91F-95F. 1890-91.
Also published separately.

3423. Black, M. J. L. Place names in the vicinity of Fort William, and Fort William streets. Thunder Bay Historical Society. Annual report 16-17:12-25, 80-83. 1926-28.

3424. Brighty, Isabel McComb. A pilgrimage through the historic Niagara district, including a list of place names. St. Catharines, Lincoln Historical Society, 1932. 12p. (Lincoln Historical Society. Publication no. 1)

3425. Campbell, John S. Why this city is called St. Catharines. Named after Catharine Hamilton, wife of Hon. Robert Hamilton—evidence establishing this reviewed—Miss Merritt's contention shown to be baseless. *St. Catharines standard* Dec. 14, 1926.

3426. Canada. Board on Geographical Names. Gazetteer of Canada: Southwestern Ontario. Ottawa, 1952. [123]p.
First volume of the Gazetteer of Canada series.
Later included in the Gazetteer of Canada: Ontario, by Canada. Dept. of Mines and Technical Surveys. Geographical Branch (see no. 3427).

3427. Canada. Dept. of Mines and Technical Surveys. Geographical Branch. Gazetteer of Canada: Ontario. Ottawa, 1962. 614p.
Tenth volume of the Gazetteer of Canada series.
Includes the names in the area covered by the first volume, Southwestern Ontario, by the Board on Geographical Names.

3428. Clark, John S. A study of the word Toronto. Toronto. Ontario Provincial Museum. Annual archaeological report 1899:190-98.

3429. Duff, Louis Blake. Names are pegs to hang history on. Ontario Historical Society. Papers and records 23:223-36. 1926.
Regarding the origin of place-names in Ontario.

3430. —— The romance of our place-names, a series of eight radio addresses, Feb. 20 to April 10, 1934, station CKTB, St. Catharines. Fort Erie, Ont., The Review Co., 1934. 22p.
Indian, French, and English place-names in Ontario.

3431. Eames, Frank. Gananoque, the name and its origin. Gananoque, The Author, 1942. 26p.

3432. Evans, W. Sanford, Statistical Service. Ontario place guide. Winnipeg, 1945. 104p.
To accompany Ontario population maps. 1945.

3433. Gardiner, Herbert Fairbairn. Nothing but names, an inquiry into the origin of the names of the counties and townships of Ontario. Toronto, G. N. Morang and Co., 1899. 561p.
Review: *Canadian magazine* 13:484-85, Sept. 1899.

3434. —— Ontario onomatology and British biography. Ontario Historical Society. Papers and records 6:37-47. 1905.
Names of places remind the author of the history of various British families. Article is largely biographical.

3435. A Gazetteer of the Province of Upper Canada, to which is added, an appendix, describing the principal towns, fortifications and rivers in Lower Canada. New York, Prior and Dunning, 1813. 83p.
Based upon Sir D. W. Smyth, A short topographical description of Upper Canada. London, 1799.

3436. Goulet, Louis. French and Indian place-names in Kent and adjoining counties. Kent Historical Society. Papers 3:38-50. 1917.

3437. Hammond, Mrs. A. Names in Wellington County. *Western Ontario historical notes* 14:24-26, March 1958.

3438. Herrington, W. S. The origin of some of our local names. Lennox and Addington Historical Society. Papers and records 1:29-41. 1909.

3439. Hewitt, John Napoleon Brinton. Iroquois place-names on the north shore of Lake Ontario; *In* Robinson, Percy James. Toronto during the French regime. Toronto, Ryerson Press, 1933. p. 243.

3440. Highway named for Queen. *New York times* May 10, 1939, p. 25, col. 1.
Road between Toronto and Fort Erie to be called Queen Elizabeth's Way.

3441. Hitsman, J. Mackay. They named it Vars. *Ontario history* 49:138, Summer 1957.
Also mentions nearby town named Kars.

3442. James, C. C. The origin of "Napanee." Ontario Historical Society.

Papers and records 6:47-49. 1905.
Early documents show that the original name was Apanee.

3443. Johnson, Henry Smith. Norfolk place names. Simcoe, Ont., Printed for the Norfolk Historical Society by the Pearce Pub. Co., 1934. 15p.

3444. Johnston, Albert J. Lambton County names and places. Sarnia, Lambton County Council, 1925. 55p.

3445. Jones, Arthur Edward. Identification of the Huron village sites of 1615-1650. Ontario. Bureau of Archives. Report 5:xxxii, 1-266. 1908.
The derivation of the Indian names of Huron villages.

3446. Lewis, Ella N. East Elgin place names. St. Thomas, Printed for the Elgin Historical Society by the Sutherland Press, 1935. 25p.
Sketches of pioneer villages in East Elgin, a portion of Elgin County.

3447. McFall, William Alexander. Relations of wars of Europe to the place names of Ontario. n.p., n.d. 7p.

3448. MacLaren, D. H. British naval officers of a century ago. Barrie and its streets—a history of their names. Ontario Historical Society. Papers and records 17:106-12. 1919.
Nearly all the streets of Barrie are named in honor of naval officers of the War of 1812-1814.

3449. Marsh, A. W. Place names of Essex County. Essex Historical Society. Papers 1:58-68. 1913.

3450. Middleton, Jesse Edgar. An historical gazetteer of the counties and districts in the Province of Ontario; *In his* The Province of Ontario, a history, 1615-1927. Toronto, Dominion Pub. Co., 1928. 2:1084-1245.

3451. Moore, William Francis. Indian place names. Wentworth Historical Society. Papers and records 6:17-24. 1915.
"Discusses some twenty-five names of which a majority belong to Brant and Wentworth counties, others like 'Temiskaming' and 'Winnipeg' being of more than local interest. Unfortunately some of the meanings given are not those endorsed by the highest authorities on the subject, but the writer of the paper does not claim infallibility; he only contributes his mite to a much discussed topic which has some highly speculative phases."—*Review of historical publications relating to Canada* 20:191. 1915.

3452. ———— Indian place names in Ontario. Toronto, Macmillan, 1930. 48p.

3453. Myers, Frank A. How Little Current got its name. *Inland seas* 16:119-22, Summer 1960.
Port on northeasterly end of Manitoulin Island.

3454. Names of Niagara Falls, Ontario. *Ontario history* 43:90-91, April 1951.

3455. Ontario. Dept. of Lands and Forests. List of geographical townships in the Province of Ontario, including those designated by letter or number. Toronto, 194?-

Title varies: 19?, List of townships in the Province of Ontario.
Comp. by the Department's Surveys and Engineering Division (earlier called Surveys Branch).
An edition "Revised to May 1949" was published 1949. 23p.

3456. Ottawa may get Finland Ave. *New York times* March 21, 1940, p. 7, col. 4.
Residents petition that Wurtemberg St. be changed to Finland Ave.

3457. Read, E. G. History of the County of Carleton. Women's Historical Society. Transactions 4:5-9. 1911.

3458. Reed, T. A. The historic value of street names. Ontario Historical Society. Papers and records 25:385-87. 1929.
Street names in Toronto.

3459. Riddell, William Renwick. Toronto in cartography. Ontario Historical Society. Papers and records 28:143-45. 1932.
List of maps: p. 144-45.
Traces the appearance of the name Toronto in early maps. Includes also the varied terminology of the Great Lakes.

3460. Robinson, Percy James. The Chevalier de Rocheblave and the Toronto purchase. Royal Society of Canada. Proceedings and transactions 3d ser. v. 31, sec. 2, p. 131-52. 1937.
In connection with the early history of Toronto, the author discusses a theory of the origin of the name Toronto which gains some support from a fresh examination of the terms of the original Toronto purchase.

3461. —— Huron place-names on Lake Erie. Royal Society of Canada. Transactions 3d ser. v. 40, sec. 2, p. 191-207, May 1946.
A study of Rev. Pierre Potier's list, Huron Mss. Ontario Archives 1920. p. 155.

3462. —— Montreal to Niagara in the seventeenth century, a philological excursion. Royal Society of Canada. Proceedings and transactions 3d ser. v. 38, sec. 2, p. 137-53. 1944.

3463. —— Notes on Potier's Huron place-names in the vicinity of Lake Erie, 1745. n.p., n.d. 14p.

3464. —— On the derivation of certain place-names in the Georgian Bay. Royal Canadian Institute. Transactions 10:127-29, May 1915.
Review: *Review of historical publications relating to Canada* 19:208. 1914.

3465. Rouillard, Eugène. Dans l'Ouest et à Ontario; quelques noms géographiques. Société de Géographie de Québec. Bulletin 14:351-55, janv. 1921.

3466. Scadding, Henry. A note on the etymology of Ontario. *Canadian journal of industry* 7:502-08. 1862.

3467. Sinclair, James. The former names of the Thames River. Ontario Historical Society. Papers and records 17:37-39. 1919.

3468. Smith, William Henry. Canada: past, present and future. Being a historical, geographical, geological and statistical account of Canada West. Containing ten county maps and one general map of the province, comp. expressly for the work. Toronto, T. Maclear, 1851. 2v.

3469. ―――― Smith's Canadian gazetteer: comprising statistical and general information respecting all parts of the Upper Province, or Canada West: distance tables; government and district officers and magistrates in each district; list of post offices, with their distances from some of the principal towns; stage and steamboat fares; principal hotels and taverns; rates of toll on the Welland Canal and some of the principal harbours; lists of exports; quantity of crown lands for sale in each township; names and addresses of land agents and forwarders; the leading features of each locality as regards soil, climate, &c., with the average value of land. With a mass of other desirable and useful information for the man of business, traveller, or emigrant. With a map of the Upper Province. Toronto, Pub. for the author by H. & W. Rowsell, 1846. 285p.
Published also 1849. 285p.

3470. Smyth, David William. A short topographical description of His Majesty's province of Upper Canada, in North America. To which is annexed a provincial gazetteer. London, W. Faden, 1799. 164p.
2d ed. rev. by Francis Gore. London, W. Faden, 1813. 123p.
Reprinted: Scadding, Henry. Canadian local history, the first gazetteer of Upper Canada, with annotations. *Canadian journal* n.s. 14:55-72, 208-17, 305-08, 367-87, 513-41, 658-74, Nov. 1873-Dec. 1875.

3471. Sulte, Benjamin. The name of Ottawa. Ottawa Literary and Scientific Society. Transactions 1:21-23. 1897-98.

3472. ―――― Ottawa, ce nom. Société de Géographie de Québec. Bulletin 7:352-65, nov. 1913.

3473. Tait, George. Street and place names and early reminiscences of Bridgebury. Welland County Historical Society. Papers and records 3:104-13. 1927.

3474. Tyrrell, Joseph Burr. Algonquian Indian names of places in northern Canada. Royal Canadian Institute. Transactions 10:213-31, May 1914.
Reprinted separately: Toronto, Univ. Press, 1915.
"During his travels in remote parts of Canada, the writer made a large collection of place names which he presents in four columns. The first lists the Indian name, the second contains the meaning of the names that have been determined, the third includes the names in use on the latest Canadian maps, and the last gives the approximate positions of the places designated."―Price.
Manitoba and District of Patricia, Ontario.
Review: *Review of historical publications relating to Canada* 19:208. 1914.

3475. White, James. Place-names in Georgian Bay (including the North Channel). [Toronto, The Society, 1913]. 81p. (Ontario Historical Society. Papers and records, v. 11)
Names given by Bayfield in the survey of 1819-1822; the local names given by fishermen and others between 1822-1883; and names created by the new survey, 1883-1893.

3476. ―――― Place-names in the Thousand Islands, St. Lawrence River. Pub. by order of Hon. L. P. Brodeur, Minister of Marine and Fisheries of Canada, for the Geographic Board of Canada. Ottawa, Govt. Print. Bureau, 1910. 7p.

Published also in Canada. Geographic Board. Report 9:223-27. 1909-10.
Review: *Review of historical publications relating to Canada* 15:105. 1910.

3477. Williams, David. The origin of the names of the post offices in Simcoe
County. Ontario Historical Society. Papers and records 7:193-236. 1906.
  Review: by James H. Coyne, *Review of historical publications relating to
Canada* 11:129. 1906.

3478. Williams, W. R. Georgian Bay's Grumbling Point. *Inland seas* 7:280,
Winter 1951.
  Grondine Point.

3479. Wintemberg, W. J. Early names of the Grand River, Ontario. Royal Society of Canada. Proceedings and transactions 3d ser. v. 23, sec. 2, p. 125-33.
1929.

3480. ——— Origin of the place and stream names of Waterloo County. Waterloo Historical Society. Report 1927:351-80.

3481. ——— The place and stream names of Oxford County, Ontario. Ontario
Historical Society. Papers and records 22:259-95. 1925.
  List of books and maps consulted: p. 259-61.
  Includes also archaic forms and names no longer in use, with dates of maps on
which these latter are found.

PRINCE EDWARD ISLAND

3482. Bremner, Benjamin. Tales of Abegweit (Prince Edward Island) containing
historical, biographical and humorous sketches and selections, collected, ed. and
written by Benjamin Bremner, with an appendix of place-names in Prince Edward
Island with their origins or meanings. Charlottetown, Irwin Print. Co., 1936. 132p.

3483. Canada. Board on Geographical Names. Gazetteer of Canada: Prince Edward Island. Ottawa, 1960. 19p.
  Eighth volume of the Gazetteer of Canada series.

3484. Canada. Geographic Board. Place-names of Prince Edward Island, with
meanings. Comp. by R. Douglas, Secretary, Geographic Board of Canada. Ottawa,
F. A. Acland, 1925. 55p.

QUEBEC

3485. Arnaud, Charles. List of names of places in the Montagnois language.
Canada. Dept. of Indian Affairs. Annual report 1884, pt. 1, p. 29-31.
  Originally appeared in *Annals of the propagation of the faith* June 1880.

3486. Audet, Francis J. Le Pointe Mondion; origine du nom. Société de Géographie de Québec. Bulletin 18:155-57, mai 1924.

Attempt to establish Joseph Mondion, from mention in historical records, as one for whom place is named.

3487. Baudry, René. D'où viennent les noms "Bras d'Or" et "Labrador"? *Revue d'histoire de l'Amérique française* 6:20-30, juin 1952.

3488. Bedard, Avila. La Commission de Géographie de Québec. Les traductions inopportunes, une motion importante. Société de Géographie de Québec. Bulletin 8:162-64, mai 1914.

3489. Bélanger, René. Nomenclature des noms géographiques indiens de la Côte-Nord. *Saguenayensia* (Chicoutimi) 1:8-9, janv.-fév. 1959.
Indian names, with corresponding French names in some cases, and meaning.

3490. Bell, Robert. Geographical nomenclature—Bell River. Société de Géographie de Québec. Bulletin 2:257-59. 1893-97.
Nomenclature géographique, La Rivière Bell. Traduction par M. Baillairgé, *ibid.* p. 259-61.

3491. Bouchette, Joseph. A topographical description of the Province of Lower Canada, with remarks upon Upper Canada and on the relative connexion of both provinces with the United States of America. London, W. Faden, 1815. 640, lxxxvi p.

3492. ―――― A topographical dictionary of the Province of Lower Canada. London, Longman, Rees, Orme, Brown, Green, and Longman, 1832. 360p.
Published also London, H. Colburn and R. Bentley, 1831.

3493. Canada. Geographic Board. Place-names in Quebec, by James White; *In its* Report 9:153-219. 1909/10.
Includes list of expeditions and explorers in northern Canada (1576-1910).
Review: *Review of historical publications relating to Canada* 16:126. 1912.

3494. ―――― Place-names on Anticosti Island, Que., by Lt.-Col. W. P. Anderson, member Geographic Board of Canada. Ottawa, F. A. Acland, 1922. 15p.
Reprinted from its Report 17:53-65. 1919/21.
Translation: Nomenclature géographique de l'Ile Anticosti. Société de Géographie de Québec. Bulletin 18:297-303, nov. 1924; 19:47-50, 94-99, 174-78, janv.-mai 1925.
Includes both accepted and discarded forms.

3495. ―――― Place-names on Magdalen Islands, Que., comp. by R. Douglas, Secretary, Geographic Board of Canada. Ottawa, F. A. Acland, 1922. 11p.
Reprinted from its Report 17:66-74. 1919/21.
Translation: La nomenclature géographique des Îles Madeleine, Province de Québec. Société de Géographie de Québec. Bulletin 19:228-40, 300-05, oct.-déc. 1925.

3496. Carrière, Gaston. Essai de toponymie oblate canadienne. I. Dans la Province de Québec. *Revue canadienne de géographie* 11:31-45, janv.-mars 1947.
Later included, with some modifications and corrections, in the author's Essai de toponymie oblate canadienne, in *Revue de l'Université d'Ottawa* (see no. 3090).
Lists the places in Quebec which bear names of Oblate Fathers, including date

on which name was proclaimed, bibliographical references, and brief history of the patronymic.

3497. Clarke, John Mason. The heart of Gaspé; sketches in the Gulf of St. Lawrence. New York, Macmillan, 1913. 292p.
The place names: p. 259-89.

3498. Deschamps, Clement E. Municipalités et paroisses dans la Province de Québec. Municipalities and parishes in the Province of Quebec. Québec, Leger Brousseau, 1896. 1295p.
Text in French and English in parallel columns.

3499. Deschênes, E. B. L'apport de Cartier et de Jean Alfonse dans l'onomaststique de la Gaspésie. *Bulletin des recherches historiques* 40:410-30, juil. 1934.

3500. _____ Essai de toponymie gaspésienne. *Bulletin des recherches historiques* 42:148-73, 200-15, mars-avril 1936.

3501. The Eastern townships gazetteer and general business directory; a commercial directory and guide to the eastern townships of Canada, containing also much useful information of a miscellaneous character. St. Johns, Smith & Co., 1867. 133p.

3502. Evans, W. Sanford, Statistical Service. Quebec place guide. Winnipeg, 1946. 130p.
To accompany Quebec population maps. 1946.

3503. Fafard, F. X. Les cantons de la Province de Québec, nomenclature. Québec, 1913. 32p.

3504. Froidevaux, Henri. L'oeuvre de la Commission de Géographie de Québec. Société de Géographie de Québec. Bulletin 11:327-33, nov. 1917.

3505. Ganong, William Francis. The origin of the East-Canadian place-names Gaspé, Blomidon, and Bras d'Or. Royal Society of Canada. Proceedings and transactions 3d ser. v. 22, sec. 2, p. 249-70. 1928.

3506. Gauvreau, Marcelle. La toponymie des Îles de Mingan. Sociétés de Géographie de Québec et de Montréal. Bulletin 2:49-55, avril 1943.

3507. Gravel, Albert. Une page d'histoire locale; les origines du mot Coaticook et l'expédition de Rogers en 1759. *Canada français* 12:187-92, nov. 1924.

3508. Headley, W. Significance of Quebec names. *Canadian bookman* 2:40-41, Jan. 1920.

3509. Huden, John Charles. Historical Champlain maps. *Vermont history* n.s. 27:34-40, 85-87, 191-93, Jan.-July 1959.
Includes identification of names on early maps and modern names that correspond with the map names.

3510. Le Vasseur, N. Le suffixe "ville." Société de Géographie de Québec. Bulletin 13:143-47. 1919.

Discussion of the tendency in Canada, and especially in Quebec, to attach "ville" to even insignificant settlements. Lists those in Quebec.

3511. McAleer, George. A study of the etymology of the Indian place name, Missisquoi. Worcester, Blanchard Press, 1906. 102p.
Bibliography: p. 101-02.
"In his little volume will be found all that is known of the history of the word, with the opinions and discussions of all authorities from the earliest to the most recent,—practically every etymology that has ever been suggested is recorded, and the list of them is an object lesson in the difficulties as well as the 'ease' of etymologizing."—*Review of historical publications relating to Canada* 11:199. 1906.
In the *Review of historical publications relating to Canada* 15:92. 1910, this author is criticized for a further study, The etymology of Missisquoi. Addenda. Worcester, The Author, 1910. 39p., as being careless in his references and etymologies.

3512. Magnan, Hormisdas. Dictionnaire historique et géographique des paroisses, missions et municipalités de la Province de Québec. Arthabaska, L'Imprimerie d'Arthabask, 1925. 738p.

3513. Massicotte, E. Z. Origine des noms de rues et de localités dans la région de Montréal. *Bulletin des recherches historiques* 27:152, mai 1921; 28:49-50, 114-15, 272-73, fév., avril, sept. 1922; 29:52-53, 77-78, 169-70, fév., mars, juin 1923; 30:175-77, 245-46, juin, août 1924; 31:125-26, avril 1925; 33:485, juil. 1927; 34:731-32, déc. 1928.

3514. Morisset, Georges. À propos de nos Plaines. Mais... s', agit-il d' "Abraham" Lincoln? *Revue de l'Université Laval* 12:55-57, sept. 1957.
Plains of Abraham.

3515. Notes sur le nom Québec. *Bulletin des recherches historiques* 19:161-82, juin 1913.
A symposium on what various scholars have said about the origin of the name.
Review: *Review of historical publications relating to Canada* 18:85. 1913.

3516. L'Origine du nom Bic. *Bulletin des recherches historiques* 33:486-89, juil. 1927.
Parish of Bic.

3517. Ouimet, Séraphin. Le nom de Rivière Lairet. *Bulletin des recherches historiques* 62:217-18, oct.-déc. 1956.
In response to a comment *ibid.* 62:117, avril-juin 1956.

3518. Poirier, Pascal. Recherches sur l'origine du mot de Québec. Royal Society of Canada. Proceedings and transactions 3d ser. v. 20, sec. 1, p. 93-98. 1926.

3519. Potvin, Damase. Ménage à faire dans notre toponymie. *Revue de l'Université Laval* 3:309-19, déc. 1948.

3520. Quebec. Bureau of Statistics. Municipal guide. 1922- .
Title varies: 1922-52, List of the municipal corporations of the Province of Quebec.
Title also in French.

3521. Québec. Cadastre Service. Liste des villes, villages, paroisses et cantons cadastrés de la Province de Québec. Comp. par A. J. Duchesnay, Directeur du Service de Cadastre. Québec, 1938. 50 l.
At head of title: Ministère des Terres et Forêts.

3522. Québec. Commission de Géographie. Noms géographiques de la Province de Québec. 3. ed. Québec, Dépt. des Terres et Forêts, 1926. 158p.
1st ed. 1916; 2d ed. 1921.
Published also in English.

3523. Quebec. Dept. of Colonization, Mines and Fisheries. Municipalités, paroisses, cantons, etc. de la Province de Québec de 1896 à 1924, comp. par Odessa Piché. Québec, 1924. 498p.

3524. —— Vastes champs offerts à la colonisation et à l'industrie. La Gaspésie. Québec, 1914. 276p.
Noms géographiques: 258-64.

3525. Quebec. Dept. of Lands and Forests. Les cantons de la Province de Québec. Comp. par le Service des Arpentages du Ministères des Terres et Forêts. Québec, 1936. 42p.
A list of the cantons with the county in which located.

3526. —— Nomenclature des cantons de la Province de Québec, compilations du Service des Arpentages du Département des Terres et Forêts. Québec, 1952. 62p.
Also published 1945, 1950, 1956.
A list of the cantons with location, date proclaimed, etc.

3527. Richardson, Martha E. Montreal street names. *Canadian magazine* 18: 535-37, April 1902.

3528. Robinson, Percy James. Montreal to Niagara in the seventeenth century, a philological excursion. Royal Society of Canada. Proceedings and transactions 3d ser. v. 38, sec. 2, p. 137-53. 1944.

3529. —— The origin of the name Hochelaga. *Canadian historical review* 23:295-96, Sept. 1942.
Traces the derivation of the Indian name for Montreal.

3530. —— Some of Cartier's place-names, 1535-1536. *Canadian historical review* 26:401-05, Dec. 1945.
In the region between Île aux Coudres and Île d'Orléans.

3531. Rouillard, Eugène. À propos de noms sauvages. Société de Géographie de Québec. Bulletin 11:283-85, sept. 1917.

3532. —— L'Abord-à-Plouffe. Société de Géographie de Québec. Bulletin 9:152-54. 1915.

3533. —— Albanel. Société de Géographie de Québec. Bulletin 15:119. 1921.

3534. —— Albert. Société de Géographie de Québec. Bulletin 15:119. 1921.
In honor of Prince Albert (1819-61).

3535. —— Les baies de la Province de Québec. Société de Géographie de Québec. Bulletin 10:231-41. 1916.

3536. —— Betsiamites; quelle est la véritable orthographie de ce nom? Société de Géographie de Québec. Bulletin 13:149-50. 1919.

3537. —— Le canton de Frampton. Société de Géographie de Québec. Bulletin 13:87-89. 1919
Traces name to Mary Frampton, English writer.

3538. —— Le Canton Michaux. Société de Géographie de Québec. Bulletin 9:58. 1915.
Named for famed scientist.

3539. —— Commission de Géographie. Société de Géographie de Québec. Bulletin 13:95. 1919.
Fafard, and River Macamic.

3540. —— Commission de Géographie de Québec: modifications toponymiques —sommaire des traveaux accomplis dans les trois dernières années. Société de Géographie de Québec. Bulletin 10:101-04. 1916.

3541. —— Commission de Géographie, dénominations de cantons, lacs et rivières. Société de Géographie de Québec. Bulletin 11:41-44, janv. 1917.

3542. —— Commission de Géographie, les méchins-lacs de la région de l'Abitibi. Société de Géographie de Québec. Bulletin 11:228-30, juil. 1917.

3543. —— Commission de Géographie. Nouveaux cantons. Société de Géographie de Québec. Bulletin 8:73-75, 166-68, mars, mai 1914; 12:85-87, mars 1918.

3544. —— Commission de Géographie. Nouveaux cantons—Rivière Malbaie, Lacs Squateck. Suppression de dénominations sauvages. Société de Géographie de Québec. Bulletin 8:44-45, janv. 1914; 13:47. 1919.

3545. —— Commission de Géographie. Nouveaux cours d'eau. Société de Géographie de Québec. Bulletin 8:233, juil. 1914.

3546. —— La Commission Géographique. Société de Géographie de Québec. Bulletin 5:217-18, mai 1911; 7:42-43, 103, janv., mars 1913; 8:280-82, sept. 1914; 11:100-02, 166-67, mars-mai 1917; 12:235-36, juil. 1918.

3547. —— Le Comté de Chambly et son fondateur. Société de Géographie de Québec. Bulletin 14:110. 1920.
Biographical sketch of military figure for whom site was named.

3548. —— Création d'une Commission Géographique. Société de Géographie de Québec. Bulletin 6:363-64, nov. 1912.
A Commission for Quebec.

3549. —— De l'orthographie des noms de lieu. Société de Géographie de Québec. Bulletin 5:83-87, mars 1911.
Railroad companies have changed names of places without reason.

3550. ——— Défendons nous! La langue géographique. Société de Géographie de Québec. Bulletin 12:262-63, sept. 1918.

3551. ——— Les deux Lorette. Société de Géographie de Québec. Bulletin 13: 108. 1919.
Two villages in Quebec of the same name, one of which was to be changed to Loretteville.

3552. ——— Deux points géographiques, Pointe-des Monts et Cap-de-Chatte. Société de Géographie de Québec. Bulletin 4:38-43, fév. 1910.

3553. ——— Dictionnaire des rivières et lacs de la Province de Québec. Québec, Département des Terres et Forêts, 1914. 432p.
Also published in Société de Géographie de Québec. Bulletin 7:169-78, 238-48, 303-15, 365-74; 8:18-25, 95-102, 173-80, 220-32, 297-304, 362-71; 9:44-53, 97-104, 166-76, 231-39. 1913-15.

3554. ——— Les Îles de la Province de Québec. Société de Géographie de Québec. Bulletin 10:23-33, 105-15. 1916.

3555. ——— Le Lac Abanel. Société de Géographie de Québec. Bulletin 4:66, fév. 1910.
Restoration of above name to lake known as Petit Lac Mistassini.

3556. ——— Le Lac Chamouchouan. Société de Géographie de Québec. Bulletin 13:111. 1919.

3557. ——— Lac Noir ou Black Lake. Société de Géographie de Québec. Bulletin 15:187. 1921.
Cites desire of Society to see return of French name on maps rather than English.

3558. ——— Le Lac Piakouakamy ou Lake Saint-Jean. Société de Géographie de Québec. Bulletin 13:82-83. 1919.
A reprint, with comment, of history of aboriginal name from records of the explorer Normandin.

3559. ——— Missisquoi, origine et signification de ce nom. Société de Géographie de Québec. Bulletin 4:248-51, oct. 1910.
About the name of a bay of Lake Champlain in Quebec and a river in northern Vermont.

3560. ——— Nomenclature géographique, cours d'eau de l'Abitibi. Société de Géographie de Québec. Bulletin 6:231-34, juil. 1912.

3561. ——— Une nomenclature géographique, les nouveaux noms géographiques de l'Abitibi et du Comté de Pontiac. Société de Géographie de Québec. Bulletin 6:156-64, mai 1912.

3562. ——— Les noms de gares. Société de Géographie de Québec. Bulletin 11:98-99, mars 1917.

3563. ——— Noms de lieux. Cap-de-la-Magdeleine, Rivière, Godbout, Pointe le Heu. Société de Géographie de Québec. Bulletin 11:339-41, nov. 1917.

3564. —— Les noms de villes. Société de Géographie de Québec. Bulletin 11:172, mai 1917.

3565. —— Les noms géographiques dans Québec. *Nouvelle-France* 12:515-20, nov. 1913.

3566. —— Les noms géographiques de la Province de Québec. Société de Géographie de Québec. Bulletin 15:102-07, 166-70, mars, mai 1921.

3567. —— Noms géographiques de la Province de Québec et des Provinces Maritimes empruntés aux langues sauvages; avec carte indiquant les territoires occupés autrefois par les races aborigènes; étymologie, traduction et orthographie. Québec, Marcotte, 1906. 110p. (Publications de la Société du Parler Français au Canada)
Auteurs et ouvrages consultés: p. 5-6.

3568. —— Les noms géographiques de Québec, conference de M. l'Abbé H. Simard. Société de Géographie de Québec. Bulletin 10:74-75. 1916.
Simard deplored the prevalence of aboriginal names on the map of Canada. Rouillard defends their right through history to a place on the map.

3569. —— Noms sauvages: étymologie et traduction. Société de Géographie de Québec. Bulletin 5:410-22, nov. 1911; 6:31-42, janv. 1912.
"A collection of geographical names of the Province of Quebec and the Maritime Provinces, supplementary to the author's 'Noms géographiques' published in 1906."—Griffin.

3570. —— Nouveaux cantons dans la région du Saint-Maurice. Société de Géographie de Québec. Bulletin 6:364-73. 1912.

3571. —— Nouvelles dénominations géographiques. Société de Géographie de Québec. Bulletin 12:94-95, mars 1918.

3572. —— Parcs des îles du Saint-Laurent. Société de Géographie de Québec. Bulletin 15:247. 1921.

3573. —— Quelques noms géographiques. Société de Géographie de Québec. Bulletin 5:382-86, nov. 1911.
Names by the original explorers.

3574. —— Respect aux noms primitifs. Société de Géographie de Québec. Bulletin v. 3, no. 6, p. 30-32, déc. 1909.

3575. —— La Rivière des Géants. Société de Géographie de Québec. Bulletin 13:110-11. 1919.

3576. —— Toponymie de la Côte Nord du Saint-Laurent et du Labrador Canadien. Société de Géographie de Québec. Bulletin 7:208-12, juil. 1913.

3577. —— La traduction des noms de lieux. Société de Géographie de Québec. Bulletin 8:352-53, nov. 1914.

3578. Rousseau, Jacques. Les noms géographiques du Bic. Société de Géographie

de Québec. Bulletin 23:26-36, janv. 1929.
 Parish of Bic.

3579. —— La toponymie de l'Île aux Coudres. Sociétés de Géographie de
Québec et de Montréal. Bulletin 1:89-100, 106-14, 121-27, oct.-déc. 1942; 2:47-
48, mars 1943.

3580. Roy, Carmen. La littérature orale en Gaspésie. Ottawa, 1955 [*i.e.*, 1956].
389p. (Musée National du Canada. Bulletin no. 134. Série anthropologique, no. 36)
 Les noms de lieux dans la tradition (noms géographiques et légendes toponymiques): p. 20-60.

3581. Roy, Pierre Georges. Ce que rappelle le nom Murray Bay. Société de
Géographie de Québec. Bulletin 11:226-27, juil. 1917.

3582. —— Les noms géographiques de la Province de Québec. Lévis, Impr.
par La Cie de Publication le Soleil, 1906. 514p.
 "A compilation in alphabetical order of certain geographical names of the Province of Quebec gathered from French-Canadian authors." Review is critical and
adverse.—*Review of historical publications relating to Canada* 11:112-16. 1907.

3583. Le Trait d'union dans les noms géographiques. Société de Géographie de
Québec. Bulletin 8:87-88, mars 1914.
 Use of hyphen and abbreviation in names with St. or Saint.

3584. Tremblay, Victor. Betsiamites. *Bulletin des recherches historiques*
59:231-33, oct.-déc. 1953.
 References on the first appearance of the name of this river on a map, who gave
it the name, and its meaning, in response to a question *ibid.* 59:178, juil.-sept.
1953.

3585. Vassal, H. List of names of certain places in the Abenakis language. Canada. Dept. of Indian Affairs. Annual report 1884, pt. 1, p. 27-29.
 In vicinity of Pierreville.

3586. Wood, William. The place names of Quebec. *University magazine* (Montreal) 11:220-31, April 1912.
 A popular article treating the names by groups, as language, events and people,
animals, saints, etc.

3587. Wood, William Charles Henry. Place-names of Quebec. 20p.
 Mounted clippings from *The Gazette*, Montreal, Jan. 6-7, 9-13, 1922, in the New
York Public Library.

SASKATCHEWAN

3588. Canada. Board on Geographical Names. Gazetteer of Canada: Saskatchewan. Ottawa, 1957. 92p.
 Fifth volume of the Gazetteer of Canada series.

3589. Gauthier, Alphonse. Le nom de Radville en Saskatchewan. *Bulletin des
recherches historiques* 59:203, oct.-déc. 1953.

3590. Johnson, Gilbert. Place names in Churchbridge municipality. *Saskatchewan history* 6:70-72, Spring 1953.

3591. ——— Place names in Langenburg municipality. *Saskatchewan history* 5:33-34, Winter 1952.

3592. Place names. *Saskatchewan history* 1:23-24, Spring 1948; 1:21-22, Autumn 1948; 2:28-29, Winter 1949; 2:29, Spring 1949; 3:34-35, Winter 1950; 3:111-12, Autumn 1950; 5:33-34, Winter 1952; 6:70-72, Spring 1953; 9:19-20, Winter 1956.
A section of the periodical, compiled variously by Alex R. Cameron, Bruce Peel, Gilbert Johnson, and others. Includes school-district names and names connected with medical history and the fur trade.

3593. Rouillard, Eugène. Le nom de Qu'appelle. Société de Géographie de Québec. Bulletin 4:64, fév. 1910.

3594. ——— Nom géographique. Société de Géographie de Québec. Bulletin 16:52. 1922.
Decision of Canadian Geographic Board to assign the name Bélanger to a river in Saskatchewan.

3595. Tyrrell, Joseph Burr. Report on a part of northern Alberta and portions of adjacent districts of Assiniboia and Saskatchewan. Canada. Geological and Natural History Survey. Annual report 1886, pt. E.
Appendix IV. Cree and Stoney Indian names for places within the area of the accompanying map, p. 172-76.

YUKON

3596. Canada. Board on Geographical Names. Gazetteer of Canada: Northwest Territories and Yukon. Provisional. Ottawa, 1958. 89p.
Seventh volume of the Gazetteer of Canada series.

3597. Kennedy name to a mountain. *Kansas City times* Nov. 21, 1964, p. 2.
Mountain in the Yukon near Alaska to be named Mount Kennedy in memory of President John F. Kennedy.

3598. Rouillard, Eugène. Le Mont Logan. Société de Géographie de Québec. Bulletin 13:246. 1919.
Brief note on mountain named for Sir William E. Logan.

3599. White, James. Place-names—Northern Canada. Canada. Geographic Board. Report 9:231-455. 1910.
Also published separately, 1911. 224p.
A partial report of this study, which deals especially with the names conferred by the explorers in the far north, was published in Royal Society of Canada. Proceedings and transactions 3d ser. v. 4, sec. 4, p. 37-40. 1910.
Review: *Review of historical publications relating to Canada* 16:126. 1912.

AUTHOR INDEX

Numbers listed refer to entries and not to pages.

313

Dawson, George M., 3231, 3259
Dawson, John Frank, 976
Dawson, Robert MacGregor, 3407-08
Dawson, Samuel Edward, 3096
Day, Gordon M., 1978
Deal, N. Harvey, 2865
Dean, James, 2777
DeArmond, R. N., 613
Debenham, Frank, 3376
De Camp, L. Sprague, 610, 2151
De Costa, B. F., 1589, 1947, 2005
De Ford, Miriam Allen, 86, 757
DeHarport, David L., 645
DeKay, James Ellsworth, 2152
De la Hunt, Thomas James, 1209
Delaney, G. F., 3097-98
Delanglez, Jean, 1759-60
Dellenbaugh, Frederick S., 646
Delugach, Al, 1781
Demorest, Rose, 2547
Dempsey, H. A., 3232
Denman, A. H., 2883-85
Denver. Public Library, 977
Denver. Public Library. Western
   History Dept., 978
Denys, Nicolas, 3099
Derrick, Barbara, 2629
Derrickson, Lloyd, 87
Desbois, Paul, 3100
Deschamps, Clement E., 3498
Deschênes, E. B., 3499-3500
Dever, Harry, 1673
Devine, Thomas, 2154
De Voto, Bernard, 89
Dexter, Franklin Bowditch, 1021
Dexter, Ralph W., 1590
Dickoré, Marie, 2405
Dienst, Alex, 2688
Dike, Sheldon H., 2061
Diller, Aubrey, 1344, 2637
Diller, J. S., 758
Dillon, Richard H., 90
Distad, Lucile, 2638
Disturnell, John, 2155
Dobie, James Frank, 91, 2689-90
Dominion Land Surveyors Associa-
   tion, *see* Association of Dominion
   Land Surveyors
Donehoo, George Patterson, 2548-
   49
Donovan, Frank P., Jr., 92, 3101
Dorsey, James Owen, 2496
Doty, J. D., 2987
Doty, Mrs. W. G., 1640

Douglas, Edward Morehouse, 759-60,
   2156-57
Douglas, Lillian, 1472
Douglas, Robert, 3083, 3102-03, 3484,
   3495
Douglas, Verne, 2158
Douglas-Lithgow, Robert Alexander,
   1948
Douglass, C. H. J., 541
Drake, C. M., 761
Drake, Leora Wilson, 2159
Dressler, Albert, 762
Drew, Frank, 1063
Drew, Shelley, 1064
Dubbs, Paul M., 2550
Duckert, Audrey R., 93-94
Dudley, Helen M., 2406
Dudley, Myron Samuel, 1591
Duff, Louis Blake, 3429-30
Dulaney, Carroll, 1574
Dunbar, Gary S., 2865
Dunlap, Arthur Ray, 53, 95-97, 1036-
   40, 2007, 2028
Dunlap, Leslie Whittaker, 542
Dunn, Jacob Piatt, 1210-15, 1761
Dunshee, Kenneth Holcomb, 2160
Durbin, Mildred G., 2407
Dustin, Fred, 1641-42
Dykstra, Lillian, 1643

Eames, Frank, 3431
Eardeley, James W., 2162
Eastman, Elaine Goodale, 99
Eaton, David Wolfe, 1782
Eberhart, Perry, 980
Eberle, William, 100
Eckstorm, Fannie Hardy, 1502-04
Eclectic Society of Little Rock, Ark.,
   684
Edmands, J. Rayner, 1979
Edmonds, W. Everard, 3233
Edwards, Clinton R., 764
Edwards, Elsa Spear, 3031
Edwards, Ralph W., 3234
Edwards, Richard, 1046, 1541, 2365,
   2810
Edwards, Roy, 2691
Edwards, Thomas H., 583
Eells, Myron, 2886
Elliott, Aaron Marshall, 3104-05
Elliott, Katherine, 1783
Elliott, Thomas Coit, 2497-2501
Ellis, Erl H., 102
Ellis, Horace, 1216

Hoffman, M. M., 1273
Hoffmann, Frank A., 1221
Hoge, Thomas A., 177
Hogue, Charles Edward, 1112
Holland, Ann J., 2643
Hollis, C. Carroll, 178
Holloway, O., Willard, 2463
Holman, Frederick V., 2506
Holmer, Nils Magnus, 179, 3119
Holt, Alfred Hubbard, 180
Holtz, Mathilde Edith, 1842
Homburg, Frederick, 181
Hommel, Rudolf, 1604
Honig, Louis O., 1356
Honolulu. Municipal Reference
  Library, 1129
Hoppen, Harry E., 588
Horgan, Paul, 183
Horsford, Eben Norton, 1605
Horwood, Harold, 3342
Hoskin, H. G., 992
Hotchkin, Samuel Fitch, 2565
Hough, Franklin Benjamin, 2195
How, D., 3120
Howe, Samuel Storrs, 1275
Howes, Cecil, 1358-63
Howland, Benjamin B., 2606
Howley, Michael Francis, 3343
Hubbard, Anson M., 1174
Hubbard, Harry D., 816
Hubbard, Lucius Lee, 1509
Hubbell, Allan F., 187
Hubbs, Barbara Burr, 1175
Huden, John Charles, 1952, 2781-84,
  3509
Hudson, Verne R., 2785
Huggins, Dorothy H., 815, 817-25,
  1929
Hughes, Arthur H., 1026
Hughes, Dorothy J., 2389
Huidekoper, A., 2566
Hull, Raymond, 2200
Hume, Edgar Erskine, 2413
Hummel, Ray Orvin, 2828
Hunt, Charles B., 2759
Hunt, Elmer Munson, 1988
Hunt, John Warren, 2992
Hunt, William Ellis, 2414
Hutcheson, Floyd E., 2644
Hutchinson, W. H., 826
Hutton, Tom, 993
Hyde, C. M., 1114
Hyde, Dorsey W., 60
Hyde, John, 188

Idema, Jim, 994
Illinois. Secretary of State, 1176
Indiana. Laws, statutes, etc., 1223
Indiana. State Library. Indiana
  Division, 1224, 1229
Indiana. State Planning Board, 1225
Indiana Board on Geographic Names,
  1226
Indiana Historical Society, 1229
Indiana Historical Society. Library,
  1238
Ingleman, Anna A., 1365
Ingraham, Joseph C., 2204
Inman, Henry, 1366
Iowa, University. School of Journal-
  ism, 1276
Ireland, Norma Olin, 90
Irish, C. W., 1281
Irvine, William Stafford, 1096-97
Irving, Washington, 199, 544
Irwin, Ned, 2664
Isaacs, A. S., 200
Iventosch, Herman, 829

Jack, Walter, 2416
Jacobin, Louis, 616
Jacobs, Jane, 201
Jaeger, Edmund C., 202
James, C. C., 3442
James, George Wharton, 830
James, Leta May, 2645
James, Uriah Pierson, 1763
Jeffords, Gladys Wheeler, 2464
Jenkins, Warren, 2417
Jenkins, William H., 589
Jenks, Albert Ernest, 203
Jenks, William L., 1663
Jennings, Gary, 204
Jensen, Andrew, 205
Johnson, Alexander, 3122
Johnson, Amandus, 206
Johnson, Ava, 1282
Johnson, Bernice Eugenia, 1790
Johnson, E. Gustav, 207
Johnson, George, 3123-25
Johnson, Gerald W., 1551-52
Johnson, Gilbert, 3590-3592
Johnson, Henry Smith, 3443
Johnson, Thomas Cary, 2829
Johnson, William W., 1664
Johnston, Albert J., 3444
Johnston, John, 2418
Johnston, Ross B., 2958
Johnston, Thesba N., 2786

Momsen, Richard, 273
Monaghan, Robert R., 2520
Montana. Historical Society, 1847
Montgomery, Mrs. Frank C., 1383
Montgomery, James R., 2668
Mood, Fulmer, 1616
Moody, Robert E., 2357
Mooney, James, 274, 1051
Moore, Edwin R., 875
Moore, Ely, 1384
Moore, George H., 549
Moore, J. Brewer, 2837
Moore, M. V., 275-77
Moore, William Francis, 3451-52
Moreno, Henry Manuel, 876
Morgan, J. B. F., 2448
Morgan, Lewis Henry, 2239-41
Morgan, Paul, 2716
Morice, A. G., 3286
Morisset, Georges, 3514
Morley, S. G., 877
Morris, Eastin, 2669
Morris, Robert T., 2242
Morse, Jedidiah, 521-23
Morton, John S., 2574
Mott, David C., 1289
Mott, Mrs. Frank K., *see* Mott,
  Gertrude
Mott, Frank Luther, 1290-91
Mott, Gertrude, 878
Moyer, Armond, 278
Moyle, John B., 1723
Mundt, Karl E., 1849, 2649
Munn, W. A., 3348
Murbarger, Nell 880
Murdock, John, 689
Murdock, Samuel, 1292
Murdock, Victor, 1385
Mussey, June Barrows, 279
Myers, C. Clyde, 1386
Myers, Frank A., 3453
Myers, Robert Lee, 1800
Myers, Sylvester, 2967-68

Nason, Elias, 1617
National Geographic Society, 288
Naughton, William A., 290
Nelson, Denys, 3288-89
Nelson, Mildred N., 594
Nelson, William, 2019-20
Nestler, Harold, 291
Neu, Irene, 1896
Neufeld, Jean, 1724
Neuffer, Claude Henry, 2631

Nevada. Constitutional Convention,
  1933
Nevins, Allan, 2342
New Brunswick Historical Society,
  3334
New Hampshire. Secretary of State,
  1993
New Hampshire. State Planning and
  Development Commission, 1994
New Jersey. State Highway Dept.
  Bureau of Planning and Traffic.
  Highway Planning Survey Section,
  2021
New Mexico Folklore Society. Place-
  name Committee, 2084-85
New York (State) Committee on Geo-
  graphic Names, 2261
New York (State) Division of Archives
  and History, 2251
New York Historical Society, 550, 2250
Newton, Charles H., 663
Nichols, Maynard, 293
Nichols, Phebe Jewell, 2999
Nicholson, Meredith, 1236
Nicolar, Joseph, 1503
Noggle, Fred D., 1677
Nomland, Gladys Ayer, 885
Norona, Delf, 2970
Nörrenberg, Constantin, 551
Norris, L., 3291
Norris, Walter B., 1570-71
Norton, Arthur Lauren, 886
Norvell, Claudia W., 2717
Nova Scotia. Dept. of Mines, 3416-17
Noyes, Marion F., 2253
Nye, Wilbur Sturtevant, 2467

O'Brien, Anna, 1801
O'Brien, Frank A., 1675
O'Brien, Michael J., 2254
O'Callaghan, Edmund Bailey, 297-98,
  2257
Och, Joseph Tarcisius, 299
Oculus, *see* Grinnell, Josiah Bushnell
Ogden, Herbert G., 302
Ohio. Dept. of Natural Resources.
  Division of Water, 2431
Ohmert, Audrey Winifred, 1934
Ojibway-Dakota Research Society of
  Minnesota, 1725
Oklahoma City. Public Library, 2468
Oliphant, J. Orin, 2923
Olmsted, Frederick Law, 889
Olson, James C., 303

Skilton, Frank Avery, 2298
Skinner, Alanson Buck, 3004
Skinner, Charles M., 3185
Skinner, Hubert M., 1243
Skinner, L. B., 3186
Sleeper, Myron O., 1963
Sleight, Frederick W., 2098
Smallwood, Joseph Roberts, 3349
Smelser, Marshall, 389
Smith, Agnes Scott, 2299
Smith, Alice E., 3005
Smith, C. Henry, 1686
Smith, Charles Wesley, 2932
Smith, Dorothy Guy, 2300
Smith, Elsdon Coles, 390
Smith, Emerson R., 1673
Smith, Francis E., 2933
Smith, Grace Partridge, 1190-91
Smith, Gusse Thomas, 665-66
Smith, Henry A. M., 2632
Smith, Hermon Dunlap, 1192
Smith, Huron H., 3006
Smith, James L., 2301
Smith, Kenneth G., 1687
Smith, Robinson V., 1997
Smith, Thelma E., 2302
Smith, Victor J., 2731
Smith, William Henry, 3468-69
Smyth, David William, 3470
Snow, Vernon F., 2527
Snowden, Clinton A., 2934
Snyder, Mary P., 2651
Sokol, A. E., 920
Somes, Evelyn, 2732
Sonkin, Robert, 428
Soulas, Jean, 392
South Dakota. Dept. of Finance, 2652
South Dakota. Legislature, 2652
Spafford, Horatio Gates, 2304
Spain. Ejército. Servicio Geográfico, 393
Spears, Raymond Smiley, 2305-06
Speck, Frank Gouldsmith, 1033
Spence, Dorothy Clark, 1448
Sperber, Hans, 1688
Sperry, Omer E., 2733
Spiegelman, Julia, 396
Spieler, Gerhard G., 2593
Spier, Leslie, 2528
Spiro, Robert H., 1747
Spitzer, Leo, 1495
Spofford, Ainsworth Rand, 397
Spofford, Jeremiah, 1620
Spokesfield, Walter Earnest, 2391

Sprague, Marshall, 398
Springer, O., 399
Squires, Monas N., 1824
Standley, Paul Carpenter, 2099, 2111
Stanford, Annabella, 400
Staples, Hamilton Barclay, 401
Starr, Emmet, 2456
State Historical Society of Colorado, *see* Colorado. State Historical Society
Steel, William Gladstone, 405, 2529, 2935
Steger, Gertrude A., 921
Stegner, Wallace, 406-07
Stein, David Allen, 922
Steinwehr, Adolph Wilhelm August Friedrich von, 529
Stennett, William H., 1767
Stephenson, Terry Elmo, 923
Sternberg, Hilgard O'Reilly, 1491
Stevens, Mana Lyman, 2621
Stevens, Ruth Perry, 2308
Stevenson, Andrew, 408, 1417
Stevenson, C. F., 3206
Steward, John Fletcher, 1193
Stewart, D. K., 3300
Stewart, George Rippey, 409-18, 625-26, 819, 924-28, 1128, 1937-38, 2028, 2530, 3187
Stewart, Ora T., 1418
Stewart, Richard D., 1574
Still, James A., 419
Stone, Stuart B., 1964
Storms, J. C., 2309
Story, G. M., 3363
Stovall, Benjamin F., 553
Strathglass, Allan, 3188
Stratton, Margaret Barnes, 1449
Straubenmuller, Gustave, 420
Straus, Nathan, 2310
Straw, H. Thompson, 421
Strecker, John Kern, 2734
Street, O. D., 601
Strickland, Rex W., 2735
Strong, Kate Wheeler, 2313
Strong, Moses M., 3011
Strong, William Duncan, 2936
Strozut, George G., 2531
Stursberg, Peter, 3189
Sugrue, Francis, 2314
Sulte, Benjamin, 3471-72
Summers, George W., 2972
Sutton, George Miksch, 3398
Swaen, A. E. H., 2315

Villiers du Terrage, Marc, *Baron de*, 1493

Virginia. Division of Planning and Economic Development, 2863

Virginia. Division of Water Resources, 2864

Virginia Place Name Society, 2865

Vivian, C. H., 1016

Vizetelly, Frank, 1316

Voegelin, C. F., 223

Vogel, Virgil J., 462, 1196-1200, 1671, 3018

Von Richthofen, E., *see* Richthofen, E. von

Voorhis, Ernest, 1769, 3196

Wagner, Henry Raup, 463-64, 634, 942-44, 3303

Wagner, Leopold, 465

Wagner, Rudolph F., 466

Wahla, Ed J., 1695

Waite, Frederick Clayton, 2449-50

Wakefield, Lucy, 945

Walbran, John T., 3304

Walgamott, Charles Shirley, 1157

Walker, Joseph B., 1970

Walker, Norman M., 1494

Wall, Alexander J., 2347

Wallis, Richard P., 467

Wallrich, William Jones, 1017

Walsh, Martin, 946-47

Walsh, W. H., 468

Walter, Ray A., 2750

Walton, Ivan H., 469, 1696, 3197

Wannamaker, Jim, 948

Ward, Merlin B., 2794

Ward, Townsend, 2596

Ware, Owen, 2634

Warner, Anne, 2351

Warner, Robert C., 672

Waterman, Thomas Talbot, 949-50, 2948-49

Watkins, Arthur Vivian, 470

Watson, Robert, 3305

Weakley, Janet, 1829

Webb, David Knowlton, 2451

Webb, Walter Prescott, 2700

Weber, Frank Thomas Ewing, 1830

Weekley, Larry, 1054

Weidhaas, Walther E., 471

Weise, A. J., 2352

Weisman, Carl M., 2353

Wells, Charles F., 2354

Wells, George Y., 1248

Wells, Harry Laurenz, 951

Welty, Eudora, 472

Welty, Ruth, 1831

Weslager, C. A., 1040, 1042-43, 2033, 2382

West, Robert, 3306

West, Robert C., 473

West Virginia. Constitutional Convention, 2973

West Virginia. University. School of Journalism, 2974

Westervelt, W. D., 1138

Wetmore, Alphonso, 1832

Whalen, George E., 2355

Whaley, Storm, 697

Wheeler, Arthur O., 3239, 3307

Wheeler, E. P., 3020

Wheeler, Everett Pepperrell, 3365

Whipple, Joseph, 1527

Whitbeck, Ray Hughes, 480-82

Whitcher, A. H., 3198

White, Eliot, 483

White, G. D., 3222

White, H. H., 3021

White, James, 3223-24, 3241, 3308-09, 3366, 3400, 3475-76, 3493, 3599

White, Lynn Townsend, 952

White, Marjorie Butler, 2104

White, Mary W., 1412

White, Rose P., 2105-06

White, William (of Canada), 3225

White, William (of Wayne State University), 484

White, William Pierrepont, 2357

Whiting, Joseph Samuel, 953

Whitmore, William Henry, 1625

Whitney, Josiah Dwight, 485

Wickersham, James, 2938, 2950

Wightman, F. A., 3199

Wilburn, Hiram C., 2384

Wilkins, Ernest Hatch, 487, 3200-01

Wilkinson, Herbert James, 1079

Willcockson, Mrs. Edwin, 1317

Williams, David, 3477

Williams, David Alan, 2865

Williams, J. W., 2752

Williams, John D., 2358

Williams, John Fletcher, 1734

Williams, Mabel Berta, 3228, 3242-43, 3253

Williams, Mary Ann Barnes, 2394-99

Williams, Ora, 1318

Williams, Samuel C., 2676

Williams, W. R., 3478

Williamson, Andrew W., 1735
Williamson, Lela, 2753
Willis, Roystein E., 2754
Willis, William, 1528
Willson, Beckles, 556
Willson, Roscoe G., 673
Wilson, E. W., 2385
Wilson, Herbert M., 488
Wilson, P. W., 489
Wilson, Raymond R., 2478
Winship, A. E., 1626
Wintemberg, W. J., 3202-03, 3479-81
Wisconsin. State Historical Society, 3022
Wishart, Helen Collier, 955
Witherell, B. P. H., 3023
Witter, Janet Waldrow, 2537
Wolfe, Theodore F., 2035-37
Wolfenden, Madge, 3310
Wolle, Muriel Vincent Sibell, 490-91, 1860
Wood, Beatrice Dawson, 956
Wood, Edwin Orin, 1699
Wood, William, 3586
Wood, William Charles Henry, 3587
Woodbridge, Hensley C., 1461
Woodbury, Jack E., 3024
Woods, Betty, *see* Woods, Dora Elizabeth Ahern
Woods, Dora Elizabeth Ahern, 2110

Woods, Robert E., 1462
Woods, William S., 1495
Woolf, Henry Bosley, 2834
Wooton, Elmer Ottis, 2111
Worcester, Joseph Emerson, 536
Wordie, J. M., 3401
Wraight, A. J., 492
Wrenn, C. L., 493
Wright, C. E., 1071
Wright, Esther Clark, 1579
Wright, Harry Andrew, 1627-28
Wright, John, 3402
Wright, John Kirtland, 494
Wright, Muriel H., 1770, 2479-82
Wright, Walter W., 1529
Wrigley, Sarah A., 1215
Wurzlow, Helen Emmelin, 1496
Wyatt, Roscoe D., 957-58
Wyllie, John Cook, 2865

Yost, Fielding H., 1700-01
Young, Della I., 2483, 2755
Young, Robert W., 2112
Yount, W. H., 497

Zabriskie, George A., 557
Zelinsky, Wilbur, 498-99
Zeusler, F. A., 635
Zimmer, Gertrude Minnie, 1834
Zumberge, James H., 1736
Zwart, Elizabeth Clarkson, 1319

SUBJECT INDEX

Numbers listed refer to entries and not to pages.

Mesa Verde National Park, Colo., 967, 1014
Metamora, Mich., 1686
Metheglin Creek, Tex., 2688
Mexia, Tex., 2750
Michigan Territory, 1751
Michigander, nickname, 1666-67, 1672, 1679, 1688
Middle East names in the U.S., 98
Middle West, U.S., 236, 1766
Mikado, Mich., 1676
Military posts, 10, 346, 639, 641-42, 664
Miller Co., Mo., 1821
Mills, Maryland, 1557
Milwaukee, Wis., 2979
Mineral Point, Wis., 3008
Mines, 56, 103, 273, 324, 655, 657; California, 762; Colorado, 965, 980, 1002; Montana, 1860; Nevada, 1919-20, 1924; Oklahoma, 2461
Mining camps, how named, 490-91
Minnesota: vegetation names in, 271
Miracle miles, shopping centers, 268, 703
Miramichi River, N.B., 3329
Missionary names, 23
Missions, 649; California, 716; Florida, 1058, 1065; New Mexico, 2062; Quebec, 3512
Missisquoi, Vt., 2787
Missisquoi Bay, Que., 3559
Missisquoi River, Vt., 2790
Mississippi, 1765; name, 1743
Mississippi River, 1768, 1770
Missoula Co., Mont., 1850
Missouri, 1765; name, 1797, 1822, 1825, 1833
Missouri River, 462
Missouri Territory, 1749
Mo., Missouri's abbreviation, 1824
Mobridge: Mont., 1849; S.D., 2649
Mocho Mountain, Calif., 786
Mohave, Ariz., 148
Mojave, Calif., 148
Moniteau, Pa., 2538
Monomack, N.H., 1970
Monkton Mills, Md., 1579
Monmouth Co., N.J., 2025
Monroe Co.: Ala., 572; N.Y., 2186, 2247
Montana: name, 1853
Montana Territory, 1856

Montell, Tex., 2744
Montgomery Co., Ala., 560
Montgomery Peak, Calif., 868
Montmorenci, S.C., 2634
Montreal, Que., 3529
Moorish names, 2044
Moretown, Vt., 2794
Mormon names, 205, 652, 893, 2756
Morton Co., N.D., 2397
Mt. Gretna, Pa., 2572
Mount Rainier National Park, Wash., 2916, 2944
Mount Revelstoke National Park, Alta., 3228, 3253, 3306
Mountain passes, California, 759
Mountains, 84, 161, 233, 286, 457, 514; Alaska, 611, 614, 621, 632; Alberta, 3239; Arizona, 639; Arkansas, 685; British Columbia, 3254, 3263, 3290, 3302, 3306; California, 760, 769-70, 776, 782-83, 841, 871, 884, 894; Canada, 3079, 3084, 3102; Colorado, 982, 991, 998, 1011; Maine, 1502; Montana, 1844; Nevada, 1924; New Hampshire, 1996; New Mexico, 2043, 2098; New York, 2157; North Carolina, 2371, 2385; Oklahoma, 2482; Oregon, 2529; Pennsylvania, 2592; Texas, 2719; Virginia, 2802, 2840, 2865; Washington, 2887-88, 2905, 2935; Wyoming, 3046
Mountrail Co., N.D., 2399
Mugu Laguna, Calif., 822
Mugu Point, Calif., 822
Mulhall, Okla., 2466
Mullet Island, Calif., 828
Murray Bay, Que., 3581
Muscatine, Iowa, 1304
Muskingum, Ohio, 2414
Myths, Indian, in Northwest names, 233

Nacogdoches Co., Tex., 2725
Namesake towns, 40
Napanee, Ont., 3442
Natchez, Miss., 1744
Natchez Trace, 327
Natchitoches Parish, La., 1465
National parks, 406, 1005
Nationalism, shown in names, 218
Natrona Co., Wyo., 3049
Navahú Pueblo, N.M., 2073, 2076
Navel, in place-names, 2064
Navy, place-names honoring: British, 3448; U.S., 65, 1303, 1647

Neenah, Wis., 2976
Nemaha Co., Kan., 1406
Nevada: name, 1933, 1940-41
New Brunswick, Can., 3152
New England: name, 1954
New England names, 2169, 2422
New France, 3131, 3170
New London, Conn., 1019
New Mexico, 126
New Orleans, La., 1476, 1495
New York City, 2137, 2158, 2284;
　Borough of Queens, 2280
New York State, 394
New York State. Board of Geographic
　Names, 2129, 2252
Newfoundland, 3078, 3109, 3148
Newport News, Va., 2811, 2838-39
Newton, Ohio, 2405
Niagara Falls: N.Y., 2242; Ont., 3454
Nicasio, Calif., 821
Nicknames, 5, 32, 254-55, 258, 260-
　62, 294-95, 337, 376, 381-82, 386,
　388, 465, 484
Nicknames, cities, 1909; Florida,
　1057; New Mexico, 2079; New
　York, 2272; Ohio, 2409; Penn-
　sylvania, 2544, 2574
Nodaway Co., Mo., 1819
Norfolk Co., Ont., 3443
Norse names, 226, 1593
Northmen names, 226
Northwest, The, 233, 432, 463; Old,
　1752
Northwest Territories, 3113
Norumbega, New Eng., 1944, 1947,
　1949
Norwalk, Conn., 1028
Norway, Me., 1529
Norwegian names, 164
Nova Scotia, 3078, 3152
Nova Scotia names, 1579
Novato, Calif., 821
Nueces Co., Tex., 2737

Oahu, Hawaii, 1115, 1123
Oak Hill, Ala., 561
Oakland: Calif., 85; Kan., 85
Obelisk, Pa., 2575
Oblate Fathers, places named for,
　3496
Ocean Co., N.J., 2025
Ocracoke, N.C., 2363
Ocracoke Island, N.C., 2382
Odebolt, Iowa, 1261

Ohio: name, 1756, 2407, 2419
Ohio River, 1761, 2427
Ohio Valley, 118
Oil fields, how named, 185; North
　Dakota, 2386; Texas, 2730
Okanagan names, 3245, 3265, 3269,
　3271, 3291, 3293, 3299, 3301
Okanogan, Wash., 2897
O'Keefe, B.C., 3257
Oklahoma: name, 2479, 2481
Old Forge, N.Y., 2197
Old Spanish trail, 150
Olivella River, N.M., 2071
Oliver Co., N.D., 2397
Olmsted Island, Md., 1550
Omaha, Neb., 1884, 1899, 1905
O'Mahoney Lake, Utah, 2766, 3061
Onalaska, 173
Onomastics, 4, 6, 96, 113, 186, 238,
　331-32, 355, 460, 494
Onondaga Co., N.Y., 2138
Ontario: name, 3466
Ontario Co., N.Y., 2234
Orange Co., Calif., 923
Oregon: name, 2490, 2494, 2497-2502,
　2525-27, 2530, 2533
Organ Pipe Cactus National Monument,
　Ariz., 658
Ormsby Co., Nev., 1936
Osawatomie, Kan., 1384
Osceola, Ill., 1187
Osoyoos, B.C., 2897
Otoe Co., Neb., 1891
Ottawa, Ont., 3471-72
Ottawa Co.: Kan., 1377, 1409; Mich.,
　1669
Ottawa River, Can., 3089, 3203
Ottumwa, Iowa, 1293
Overland Park, Kan., 1412
Owen, Mount, Wyo., 3047
Owingsville, Ky., 1425
Oxford Co., Ont., 3481
Ozark, origin of name, 1820
Ozark Mountains, 497

Pabineau, N.B., 3330
Pacific Northwest, 223
Paducah, Ky., 1450
Pagan Creek, Va., 2822
Palmetto State, nickname for South
　Carolina, 2629
Palo Alto, Calif., 874
Palouse, 1154; Wash., 2942
Pancho Villa State Park, N.M., 2107

Pudding, Calif., 751
Pueblos, N.M., 2062, 2077
Puente, Calif., 824
Puget Sound, Wash., 2875
Puowaina, Honolulu, 1112
Purgatoire River, Colo., 1000
Purton, Va., 2796
Putes Creek, Calif., 870
Put-in-Bay, Ohio, 2444
Puyallup, Wash., 2900

Qu'appelle, Sask., 3593
Quebec, 3113; name, 3515, 3518
Quebec. Commission de Géographie,
    3504, 3540, 3546, 3548
Queen Elizabeth Islands, N.W.T., 3391
Queen Elizabeth's Way, Ont., 3440
Queens Borough, *see* New York City.
    Borough of Queens
Quesesosi, Calif., 719, 825
Quivira, Calif., mythical city, 464

Radville, Sask., 3589
Rafinesque, Mount, N.Y., 2130
Railroad names, 1918
Railroad presidents, place-names
    honoring, 92, 3101
Railroaders, place-names honoring,
    247, 408, 1330
Rainier, Mount, Wash., 2874, 2877,
    2879, 2882-85, 2889, 2907-08,
    2920-21, 2924, 2934, 2938-39,
    2943, 2946, 2950
Randolph Co.: Ala., 588; Mo., 1789
Rapidan River, Va., 2795
Rawhide Buttes, Wyo., 3053
Rawlins, Wyo., 3037
Real estate developments, 131, 2238
Red Rock, Lake, Iowa, 1315
Religious names, 441, 471, 2059, 2091
Rensselaer Co., N.Y., 2129
Renville Co., N.D., 2399
Revolutionary War names, New York,
    2169
Rhode Island: name, 2597, 2608, 2613
Richardson Co., Neb., 1887
Richmond Town, R.I., 2603
Rio del Espíritu Santo, Miss., 1760
Rio Grande, 183
Rio Jesus Maria, Calif., 713
Ripton, Vt., 2771
Rivers, 3, 46, 52, 56-57, 143, 145-46,
    161, 182, 213, 215, 227, 233, 249,
    277, 432, 1755, 1764

Alabama, 564, 582, 593, 600
Arizona, 639
California, 871, 926, 956
Canada, 3079, 3139, 3155
Georgia, 1081, 1084, 1101
Hawaii, 1135
Indiana, 1202, 1223, 1232, 1235
Iowa, 1305
Kansas, 1329, 1344, 1352, 1355,
    1375-76, 1379, 1398, 1411
Kentucky, 1435
Maine, 1507, 1512
Maryland, 1547, 1560
Michigan, 1670, 1694
Missouri, 1782
Montana, 1844
Nebraska, 1862, 1878, 1881, 1894
Nevada, 1924
New Brunswick, 3328, 3332
New England, 1946, 1953
New Mexico, 2074
New York, 2138, 2319-20
Nova Scotia, 3409
Ohio, 2418, 2431, 2439-40
Oklahoma, 2482
Oregon, 2504
Pennsylvania, 2571, 2579
Quebec, 3553
Schoharie Co., N.Y., 2269
Sierra Co., Calif., 918
South Carolina, 2627
Texas, 2680, 2699, 2711, 2714, 2719,
    2734
Virginia, 2802, 2863-65
Washington, 2887
West Virginia, 2968
Wisconsin, 2978, 3017
Wyoming, 3034, 3041-42
Rivière, Que., 3563
Roach ponds, Me., 1504
Roads: Georgia, 1094; New York, 2204
Roanoke, Va., 2852
Robert S. Kerr Reservoir, Okla., 2477
Robidoux Creek, Kan., 1324
Robson, Mount, B.C., 3268, 3284
Rockport, Neb., 1865
Rocky Mountain National Park, Colo.,
    1013
Rocky Mountains, 321, 3241, 3308
Rondout, N.Y., 2193
Roosevelt Co., N.M., 2105
Rose Teed Lake, Alaska, 620
Royale, Isle, Mich., 1641
Russell Co., Ala., 577